# THE SHAFT TOMBS OF WADI BAIRIYA

Volume I

Preliminary report on the clearance work on the
WB1 site

by

the joint-venture mission

of the

New Kingdom Research Foundation

with the

Ministry of Antiquities

Piers Litherland

NEW KINGDOM RESEARCH FOUNDATION

# The Shaft Tombs of Wadi Bairiya

Volume 1

First published 2018

Published by the New Kingdom Research Foundation
in association with Genius Loci Publications.

Piers Litherland © 2018
Piers Litherland has asserted his moral rights.

All rights reserved. No part of this publication
may be reproduced, stored in a retrieval system or
used by any means, without prior written
permission from the publisher.

ISBN: 978-0-9930973-1-7

British Library Cataloguing in Publication Data

A CIP record for this book is available from the British Library.

The author and publisher cannot accept responsibility or
liability for information contained herein, this being in some
cases difficult to verify and subject to change.

Layout and cover design by Kate Buckle

Printed and bound in England by Short Run Press, Exeter

For Jenny -
personification
of dedication.

# Acknowledgements

The mission would like to thank the Supreme Council of Antiquities (SCA) of the Ministry of Antiquities for permission to work on these sites.

We would like to thank His Excellency Dr Khaled El-Enany, His Excellency Dr Mamdouh el-Damaty; the Permanent Committee of the SCA; Dr Mohamed Ismail; Mr Hany Abu El-Azm; Mr Abdul Hakim Karar, Mr Sultan Eid, Dr Mohamed Abdul Aziz, Dr Mustapha Waziri, Mr Talat Abdul Aziz, Mr Mohamed Yahya, Mr Ahmed Nazir and Mr Abel El-Hagag Taya Hassanein.

We would like to thank our inspectors Mr Abdul Ghany, Mr Hussein Ahmed Hussein, Mr Taha Hussein, Mr Sayed Ali Sayed, Mr Mohamed Ali El-Naggar and Mr Mohamed Shams El-Deen. I would also like to thank the following: our reis, Mohamed Ghalan, and all our workmen; Sheikh Abu El Ez M. Ibrahim; El-Tayeb Mahmoud Ibrahim Amar, our driver and general factotum. Thank you also to the people of Egypt for making the foreign members of the mission so welcome.

We would like to acknowledge the invaluable help of: The McDonald Institute, Cyprian Broodbank, Kate Spence, Hratch Papazian and Corinne Duhig; the staff of AERA and in particular Sayed Sallah and Mohamed Saied; Ray Johnson and the staff of Chicago House; Frédéric Colin and Cassandre Hartenstein; Susanne Bickel and her team; Fredrik Hagen, Lise Manniche, Angus Graham, Marc Gabolde, Richard Redding, Betsy Bryan, David Aston, Salima Ikram and Megan Spitzer, Jacobus van Dijk, Hourig Sourouzian and Dina Faltings.

It was Betsy Bryan who first suggested a connection between the WB1 ladies and Amenhotep III on the basis of her examination of the canopic fragments in the Egyptian Museum in Cairo in 1984. The provenance of those objects was then unknown. In view of the difficulty in finding those fragments again, Betsy Bryan's photographs, kindly made available to us, have been invaluable. Frédéric Colin and Cassandre Hartenstein could not have been more helpful with the material in the Strasbourg University collection and in particular with the matching of the Menkheperre fragment with the 3-D print of the jar it came from. Jacobus van Dijk alerted me to the article about the stela of Nebamun which led to Dina Faltings of Heidelburg University confirming its findspot several hundred metres from the WB1 tombs. I am most grateful to them all.

As far as the text is concerned, particular chapters are the result of contributions from specialists in the subjects they cover. Chapters Three and Four rely heavily on records created by Rabee Eissa and Hanan Mahmoud. Chapter Seven is based closely on the reports prepared by Sherif M. Abdelmoniem, our senior ceramicist, and Chapter Eight is similarly based on the reports prepared by Ahmed Gabr, our osteologist, with analysis and evaluation by Corinne Duhig. Chapter Twelve is based on a report prepared by Salima Ikram with input from Megan Spitzer. None of the balance of this preliminary volume would have been possible without contributions from all members of the NKRF team. However, I am particularly grateful to Alexis Pantos for his excellent photographs and work on the fires in the tombs, to Aude Gräzer Ohara for her systematic work on the canopic jar texts; to Rosa Vane for her exceptional skill dealing with the three-dimensional jig-saws which the stone vessels presented; and to Mohamed Abd El-Baset and his team of surveyors.

For their help with this publication I would like to thank Charles Arnold, Kate Buckle and Nigel McGilchrist. Geoffrey Martin, Judith Bunbury and Aude Gräzer Ohara were extremely generous with their time looking at the drafts.

Without Geoffrey Martin and Mohsen Kamel this mission would never have taken place.

It would be remiss not to acknowledge the excellent products of Akubra Hats Pty Ltd and of Samantha Jolly of Jolly Good Sticks.

I will always be grateful to Johnny Stow, Dick Marshall and David Birt. A big thank you to my wife and our three children for not rolling their eyes too often.

**Piers Litherland**
Lucca, October, 2018

# Members of the mission 2014-2018

Geoffrey Martin and Piers Litherland - *Directors of the Mission and Field Directors*
Mohsen Kamel - *Archaeological Director*
Judith Bunbury - *Geologist and Deputy Mission Director*

Ali El-Asfar - *Head of the Ministry of Antiquities team 2014-2015*
Mahmoud Afifi - *Head of the Ministry of Antiquities team 2015-2017*
Fathi Yassen - *Head of the Ministry of Antiquities team 2017-2018*

Ahmed Ezz - *Archaeologist 2014-2015*
Abd El-Nasser Mohamed - *Archaeologist 2014-2015*
Mostafa El-Saghier - *Archaeologist 2015-2016*
Mohamed Saliem - *Archaeologist 2015-2016*
Hanu Abu El-Azm - *Archaeologist 2016-2017*
Mahmoud Mossa - *Archaeologist 2016-2018*
Ahmed Hassan - *Archaeologist 2016-2018*
Ramadan Ahmed - *Archaeologist 2017-2018*

Rabee Eissa Mohamed - *Archaeologist*
Hanan Mahmoud - *Archaeologist*
Aude Gräzer Ohara - *Archaeologist and Epigrapher*
Mohamed Abd El-Baset - *Chief Surveyor*
Andreas Dorn - *Hieraticist*
Sherif M. Abdelmoniem - *Ceramicist*
Nermeen Aba Yazeed - *Ceramicist*
Rosa Vane - *Translator and Conservator*
Alexis Pantos - *Photographer and Archaeologist*
Ahmed Mohamed Gabr - *Osteologist*
Graham Smith - *Geologist*
Ahmed Hassan - *Surveyor*
Amr Zakaria - *Surveyor*
Sophie Hunter - *Conservator*
Stephen Goddard - *Photographer*
Amal Eweida - *Photographer*
Yaser Mahmoud Hussein Abu Zaid - *Draughtsman*
Soha Kamel - *Archivist*
Lamia el-Hadidi - *Conservator*
Freya Sandarangani - *Archaeologist*
Rebekah Miracle - *GIS specialist*

## Directors of the New Kingdom Research Foundation
Piers Litherland, Geoffrey Martin, Mohsen Kamel, Nigel McGilchrist, Judith Bunbury

# Contents

| | |
|---|---:|
| Introduction | 1 |
| **Chapter One**<br>**The setting and history of the site** | 5 |
| **Chapter Two**<br>**Description of the WB1 site and its initial condition** | 8 |
| **Chapter Three**<br>**Clearance of the Shaft Tombs** | 17 |
| **Chapter Four**<br>**Architecture** | 69 |
| **Chapter Five**<br>**Canopic jars** | 115 |
| **Chapter Six**<br>**Canopic jar heads, stone vessel lids, other stone vessels and objects** | 130 |
| **Chapter Seven**<br>**Ceramics** | 140 |
| **Chapter Eight**<br>**Human Remains** (Corinne Duhig contributed the analysis and evaluation of the human remains) | 149 |
| **Chapter Nine**<br>**Faience** | 169 |
| **Chapter Ten**<br>**Glass** | 176 |
| **Chapter Eleven**<br>**Wood: including dockets, duck spoons, furniture, coffins, shabtis** | 190 |
| **Chapter Twelve**<br>**Other finds** | 226 |
| **Chapter Thirteen**<br>**Animal Bones** (Salima Ikram contributed the analysis and evaluation of the animal bones) | 250 |
| **Chapter Fourteen**<br>**Investigation and clearance of the spoil-heaps** | 256 |
| **Chapter Fifteen**<br>**Investigation and clearance of the huts and wells** | 279 |
| **Chapter Sixteen**<br>**Wadi El-Agaala and Wadi Bairiya** | 292 |
| **Chapter Seventeen**<br>**Landscape and climate** | 367 |
| **Chapter Eighteen**<br>**Conclusions** | 398 |
| Appendices | |
| **Appendix One** | 407 |
| **Appendix Two** | 408 |
| **Appendix Three** | 409 |
| Sources of Illustrations | 412 |
| Select Bibliography | 413 |
| Index | 420 |
| Biographies | 425 |

# INTRODUCTION

*Figure 1. An overview of the West Bank at Luxor. The green dots show the locations of burials of XVIIIth dynasty family members (Map data: Google, DigitalGlobe).*

To those visiting its ancient sites today the city of Luxor appears to be merely the latest urban imprint on a landscape which has remained structurally unchanged since the early dynastic period. The Theban massif provides one desert margin to the west, the flatter desert another margin to the east. Within these bounds the Nile follows its apparently timeless course, providing water to the narrow riparian strip which is, and during the pharaonic period always was, habitable Egypt.

On the East Bank the modern city still takes its measure from Karnak in the north and Luxor Temple in the south. On the West Bank the centre of the cluster of temples which crowd the foot of the cliffs appears to be El-Qurn, the eastern peak of the Theban mountain. Tourist buses travel a route along the base of the mountain from Ramesses III's memorial temple at Medinet Habu in the south-west to Carter's House just to the north-east of Dra Abu el-Naga. Between these two points are all the major archaeological sites, and all the tourist destinations, of note *(Figure 1)*.

Even studies concentrating on Amenhotep III contain maps which show nothing southwest of Malqata[1]. Yet this view of the West Bank is very much a creation of the recent tourist age. Sites dating to the reign of Amenhotep III have been known for many years to exist well to the west of Malqata. The northern end of the enigmatic "cleared strip" of desert associated with Amenhotep III is 7.25 km to the west of Malqata. Between these lie the sites of Kola el-Hamra, Kom el-Abd, Deir el-Shelwit and Kom el-Samak.

Our recent work in the wadis to the west of the Theban massif has provided a reminder that in the XVIIIth dynasty burial activity on the West Bank extended much further west into what is now desert than is usually appreciated[2].

The WB1 site in the Wadi Bairiya which is the subject of this preliminary study extends evidence of this royal burial activity still further north and west into what is today an inhospitably dry landscape. The WB1 site, which contains the burials of a great wife, a lesser wife, a son and a daughter of Amenhotep III together with at least thirteen 'Ornaments of the King', is remarkable in being completely exposed. Unlike the cliff and shaft tombs of the Western Wadis, the site is not hidden away. A first thought is that it sought security in a remote, unfrequented site on an extreme margin of the landscape of the time.

However, some of the more surprising evidence to emerge from the clearance of these shaft tombs has forced a reconsideration of many of the assumptions which condition modern thinking about this landscape. There are roads which cross the WB1 site and surround it. These connect the site with Malqata and, probably, with Kom el-Abd. The XVIIIth dynasty surface of the WB1 site, which sits on a plateau 15-20 metres above the wadi floor, was saturated by water, showing signs both of water erosion and of plant life just under the surface. This water can only have arrived in the form of rain.

It is generally assumed that the rainfall bands in the Holocene moved steadily south and saw a progressive drying out of the grasslands which covered what is now the high desert in Egypt. This is, indeed, what took place over a very long period of time. However, within that period there were marked fluctuations in the speed and direction of that southward progress. Rainfall in the Theban hills today is catastrophic when it arrives in the form of storms every twelve years or so. However, it now appears that there were recurrent periods in which Egypt was much, much wetter than it is today. One of those periods was the early New Kingdom and specifically the XVIIIth dynasty. It is almost certain that the area to the north and west of Malqata was not desert - in the sense that we use this word - in that period *(Figure 1)*.

Work by Hillier, Graham, Bunbury and others has challenged the view that the Nile has followed a timeless course. It appears to have been restlessly changing course during the

---

1. e.g. Kozloff, A. (2012) *"Amenhotep III: Egypt's Radiant Pharaoh"*, Cambridge University Press, Cambridge page xvi Map 4, and Kozloff, A. and Bryan, B. (1992) *"Egypt's Dazzling Sun: Amenhotep III and His World"*, Cleveland Museum of Art, Cleveland page xxiii Map 2.
2. Litherland, P. (2014) *"The Western Wadis of the Theban Necropolis"*, New Kingdom Research Foundation, London..
3. Hillier, J., Bunbury, J. and Graham, A.(2007) *"Monuments on a migrating Nile"*, Journal of Archaeological Science, 34 (7), pp. 1011 - 1015; and Toonen, W., Graham, A., Pennington, B., Hunter, M., Strutt, K., Barker, D., Masson-Berghof, A., Emery, V. (2017) *"Holocene fluvial history of the Nile's west bank at ancient Thebes, Luxor, Egypt, and its relation with cultural dynamics and basin-wide hydroclimatic variability"*, Geoarchaeology, 2017; 00:1–18. https://doi.org/10.1002/gea.21631

pharaonic period. As they observe, the first maps of Luxor, made during Napoleon's Description de l'Égypte, and subsequently by John Gardner Wilkinson, show Karnak and Luxor Temples on raised mounds. These early maps support the findings by Hillier and others which suggest these temples were once on islands. Angus Graham's team's work on the West Bank is also revealing evidence of a very different Nile divided into several streams.[4].

A corroborative picture has emerged from our work of a greener, wetter landscape in which today's isolated desert sites were once connected and part of an extensive plan which included, at its centre, the vast (1.0km in width by 2.4km) body of water at Birket Habu constructed by Amenhotep III. Well-preserved to the north-east of Birket Habu is the palace and city of Amenhotep III. Further east still is the immense spread of Amenhotep III's memorial temple at Kom el-Hettan.

The floodplain of Wadi Bairiya has obliterated much of what may have existed immediately to the north-west of the spoil-heaps of Birket Habu and the only structures which have survived here are all on higher ground.

However, if all the known sites of Amenhotep III are included, a major shift westwards in the centre of activity emerges. The shape of the Birket Habu lake, with the arms of the "T" turning both east and west, suggests that the planned landscape was intended to extend not just to the north-east, where the record is weighted by surviving monuments protected from the wash of the Wadi Bairiya, but to the south-west as well. The central axis provided by the Birket Habu body of water runs straight towards the WB1 site (*Figure 1*).

The roads we have identified running around and across the WB1 site connect it to both Malqata and the area round Kom el-Abd. When Barry Kemp excavated Kom el-Abd in 1974[5] he suggested that the site may have been used for chariots. One of the roads we have found which leads from the WB1 site towards Kom el-Abd, is a prepared road, 3.5m to 4m wide, of a type also found at Akhetaten[6] with an even, hard surface ideal for chariots. This road also penetrates the great Wadi el-Agaala to the north-east of the WB1 site where images of gazelles, hares, wild bulls and lions have been found on the wadi walls.

The second type of road we have identified seems to have been a major caravan-style route (composed of many single strands all moving in the same direction) cutting across the Qena bend. This route was heavily-used and is littered with ceramic fragments in huge quantities (one site has sherds a metre deep in places scattered over an area 60m by 50m). These ceramic fragments are principally of two types: early New Kingdom and Roman. There is very little material from periods between these two dates.

The dramatic decline in rainfall at the end of the XVIIIth dynasty supported by the Greenland ice core data (Chapter Seventeen) for global weather, difficult to date

---

4. Graham, A., Strutt, K., Hunter, M., Pennington, B., Toonen, W., Barker, D. (2014) "*Theban Harbours and Waterscapes Survey, 2014*", JEA 100 pp. 41-53.
5. Kemp, B., (1977) "*A Building of Amenophis III at Kom el-Abd*", Journal of Egyptian Archaeology, Volume 6 pp. 71-82.
6. Kemp B., (2012) "*The City of Akhetaten and Nefertiti: Amarna and its people*", Thames & Hudson, London, and Stevens A., (2012) "*Akhenaten's Workers: The Amarna Stone Village Survey 2005-2009*", Egypt Exploration Society, London Volumes I (pp. 69-80) & II (pp. 199-200).

precisely, but possibly contemporary with the move to Akhetaten raises the further possibility that abandonment of the huge investment made by Amenhotep III in this region of the West Bank at Luxor, was influenced by climate change. The Nile inundation was the chief driver of agricultural production. It seems sensible that higher rainfall at the latitude of Thebes would have been accompanied by higher rainfall in Uganda and in the Ethiopian highlands which feed the Nile inundations. Weather patterns are complex and it is possible that what was causing higher rainfall in the Theban area was an isolated meteorological phenomenon. However, the Tempest Stela[7], for all that it may have been propogandist in intent, suggests an extraordinarily high inundation right at the start of the XVIIIth dynasty.

Whether or not the weather was a contributing factor to the stresses of the late XVIIIth dynasty, the clearance of the WB1 shafts has nevertheless invited a broad re-assessment of the landscape of Amenhotep III and of the activities which took place there.

The identification of these architecturally unique shaft tombs as the burials of a great wife, a wife, a son and a sister or daughter of Amenhotep III is remarkable enough. The hitherto successful and almost certainly deliberate erasure from history of these people and the other members of the court of Amenhotep III buried in the tombs, can only add interest to the site. These people are unknown other than in material derived from the WB1 site. The destruction of their names was complete and successful until that material began to re-surface in the early twentieth century. Who attacked these burials in pharaonic times and why this was done remains a mystery.

The many artefacts found on the WB1 site and the information gathered from the archaeological and geological surveys will necessitate a number of specialist catalogue fascicles. These will include volumes on the stone vessels and a catalogue volume of the other objects. We are also planning a separate volume once more work has been done on the climate and landscape issues we have identified.

The present volume will provide an overview of the location, architecture and development of the tombs, the principal objects and some tentative landscape conclusions. It is a preliminary report because new evidence is emerging all the time. Future findings may cast doubt on the tentative conclusions presented here. They are presented in good faith on the basis of our current understanding of the site and in the hope that they will contribute eventually to a better understanding of this period of Egyptian history.

Piers Litherland

**Lucca**
**October, 2018**

---

7. Sethe, K. (1927) "*Urkunden der 18. Dynastie*", Volume I. Hinrichs, Leipzig pp. 14-24.

# CHAPTER ONE
# THE SETTING AND HISTORY OF THE SITE

*Figure 2. The location of the WB1 shaft tombs.*

The Wadi Bairiya (WB1) shaft tombs are situated in the modern desert to the west of the main Theban massif on the West Bank at Luxor in Upper Egypt. They lie on the western side of the Wadi Bairiya, separated from the Theban hills by the cutting of that wadi. All the other XVIIIth dynasty burials in the western region are hidden in wadis which descend from the main Theban mountain. The WB1 shaft tombs are cut into rising ground at the point where the wadi broadens out into a floodplain.

To the modern eye they appear extremely isolated. They are roughly six kilometres into the present desert from the edge of the cultivation and seven kilometres by motor vehicle from Malqata to the south-east. They are ten kilometres from the modern west bank of the Nile. As the crow flies they are five kilometres due west of the Valley of the Kings, 2.82 kilometres north-west of the nearest known shaft tomb in Wadi D (the tomb of the Three Foreign Wives of Thutmose III) and 2.28 kilometres from the location which Howard Carter suspected contained shaft tombs in Wadi F *(Figure 1)*.

The rock into which the WB1 shaft tombs are cut is of poor quality: layers of hard limestone divided by rough, vertically-fractured marl in between. The harder layers have resisted erosion and so stand proud of the wadi floor which is made up of fine, soft, white debris striated by the floodwater collected in the vast bowls of the Wadi Bairiya and Wadi el-Agaala and disgorged through their narrow exits.

The main drainage from the Wadi Bairiya, the Wadi el-Agaala and the smaller wadis to the west emerges through these narrow channels to pour onto the broad and flat expanse of arid floodplain. When rain falls on the high desert to the north-west of these two great wadis, as happens every decade or so in modern times, the water eventually finds its way down a gulley which terminates just to the north-west of the remains of Birket Habu. In ancient times it would probably have helped feed this great man-made body of water. Prior to the creation of the Birket Habu lake these water flows would have ensured that this area was marshy wetland. Two other drainage channels lie between the north-west corner of Birket Habu and the XVIIIth dynasty site of Kom el-Abd to the west.

The part water has played in shaping this landscape over longer geological and prehistoric periods is all too evident in this modern landscape. What is less clear is the part water played in shaping the history of the region and, in particular, the history of the XVIIIth dynasty. Most of the monuments which survive within 10km to the west of the Theban Massif date to the late XVIIIth dynasty and to the Roman occupation of Egypt. There is a dearth of material from between these two dates. Several of these sites (Kola el-Hamra and the WB1 site most notably) are deep in the desert, well beyond the edges of the modern cultivation. There is little obvious sign of water in these places today.

The modern setting is, therefore, remote and dry. The shaft tombs are isolated from the other monuments on the West Bank not only by being further into the desert but by being on the other side of a divide separating them from the main Theban massif. They are unusual too in being on completely open ground. The fifteen to twenty metres of elevation from the wadi floor if anything makes them, and especially the spoil-heaps thrown up round them, visible from all sides. Given the trouble which was taken to conceal the burials of royal women in the Western Wadis nearby, it is puzzling that these tombs should be so exposed..

## The history of the site

There are only two written records relating to the WB1 site. The first consists in the two scant paragraphs which Howard Carter devotes to them in his article covering his tour of the Western Wadis following the discovery of the Tomb of the Three Foreign Wives of Thutmose III and the cliff-tomb prepared for Hatshepsut in 1916[1]. As they are the only independent reference to the site, they are worth quoting in full:

---

1. Carter, H. (1917) *"A Tomb Prepared for Queen Hatshepsuit and Other Recent Discoveries at Thebes"*, Journal of Egytian Archaeology, Volume 4 pp. 107-118.

*"Still further north-west, at a distance of about two kilometres is the great Wady Sikkat el Agala (Pl. XIX, top left corner). It is by far the largest valley of the entire site, larger indeed than the valley of the Tombs of the Kings on the eastern side of the mountain, even when this is understood to include the third and larger arm which extends beyond Wadyein. This great valley runs almost due east from the plain of Akhabat el Bayrieh, and its first arm extends to the ridge of the plateau not far from the head of the Wady el Gharby, where it abuts upon immense cliffs. The second arm branches off towards the north about one kilometre from the entrance, and forms the main bed of the valley. This principal branch continues in a northerly direction for many kilometres and has many lateral valleys. Opposite the entrance and a few hundred metres out in the plain is a small rising piece of ground where there are five open pit-tombs, which have been plundered in both ancient and modern times.*

*They appear to have been royal, for a fragment of an alabaster Canopic jar (burnt) bears the beginning of the word for king, a part of the human-headed lid is of the finest workmanship, and from pot-sherds around the mouths of these pits - of the finest hard grey earthenware - one would claim them to be of the period of Amenophis III. Higher up on the rising ground are many stone huts of the type adapted to workmen. A large, wide road crosses the plain below these remains and, at a sharp bend, enters the valley on the east; here it divides into two for a short distance, and further on possibly ends in a loop; or else it may form a loop and then proceed further. It is from this road that the valley derives its name, and the question arises, to what does it lead? The natives say that there are tombs here, but in the course of my very cursory inspection I found no trace of any. In the eastern part I noted the sign and beside it ; there are also many marks upon stones in the bed of the valley, and these alone would make careful investigation desirable. The remoteness of the valley, however, makes the question of water for the workmen one of some difficulty."*

It is important that Carter noted only that the tombs were probably royal and, judging from the pottery sherds, probably of the period of Amenhotep III.

The second published reference to this site is in the report on our archaeological survey of the Western Wadis in 2013. Following Carter's circuit of the wadis[2] further east (Wadis A, B, C, D, E, F and G) we came to this site at the end of our survey. The condition of the tombs then, and of the surface, is described in our report on those wadis. We had only a few hours on the site. The importance of the more immediate evidence for us then was that it might confirm that the burials of the royal family of the XVIIIth dynasty had indeed spread steadily west and north from the main Theban Massif.

It was clear early on that Carter had been right about the dating of the site. The ceramic evidence pointed to an XVIIIth dynasty date but the question remained open as to just who was buried here and, indeed, why such an exposed and apparently remote site had been chosen.

It was clear from our cursory examination of the tomb which was easiest to access (Shaft Four) that these were tombs of unique architectural complexity with multiple chambers on different levels. We therefore applied for permission to re-clear them. The Ministry of Antiquities duly granted us permission to re-clear the WB1 site and to conduct an archaeological survey of the surrounding Wadi el-Agaala and Wadi Bairiya. Work started under the auspices of a joint-venture between, on the one hand, the Cambridge Expedition to the Valley of the Kings and the New Kingdom Research Foundation and, on the other, the Ministry of Antiquities, in October, 2014.

---

2. Litherland P. (2014) op. cit. Chapter Ten.

# CHAPTER TWO
# DESCRIPTION OF THE WB1 SITE AND ITS INITIAL CONDITION

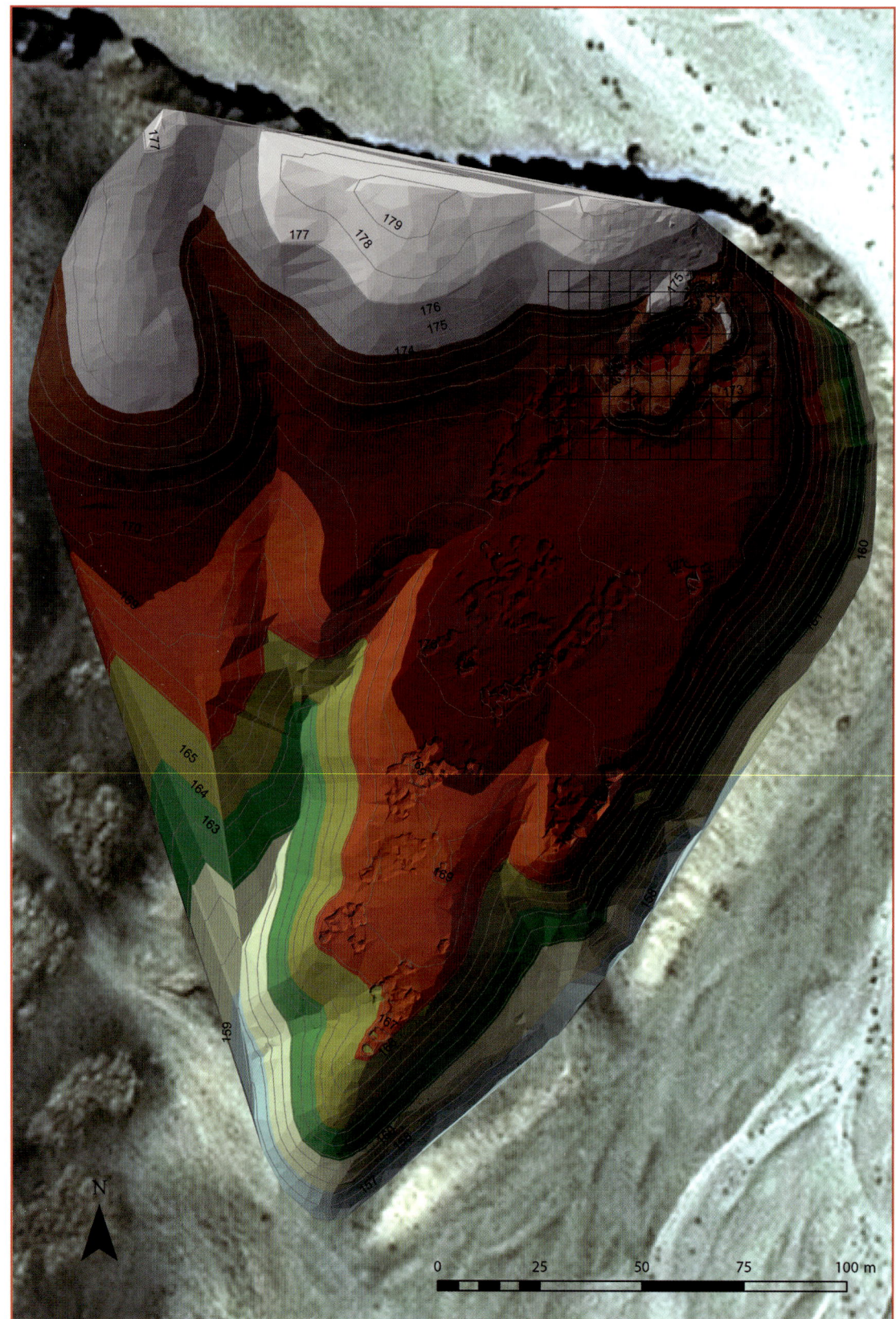

*Figure 3. The WB1 site with contours added.*
*(Due to the angle of the satellite photograph there is some distortion.)*

The WB1 site occupies the north-eastern corner of a tongue of rising ground to the west of the mouth of the Wadi Bairiya. Along its northern margin runs a line of cliffs twenty metres high. From the northern cliff-edge the ground slopes gradually downwards towards the south and there are two small valleys which would probably have been the principal access routes to the burial site in ancient times. To the west the ground continues to rise. A saddle divides this higher ground from the high point of the site still further west which is crowned with workmen's huts. Near this high point the ground narrows into an isthmus before broadening out northwards into a wider plateau which runs north-west rising eventually to the high desert. To the south of the site the ground continues to fall away *(Figure 5)*.

*Figure 4. An unmarked satellite photograph of the WB1 site before work started. The shafts are clearly visible in the top right-hand corner of the elevated ground, so too is the Farchout Road crossing the site from top left to bottom right. Less easy to pick out are the remaining sections of the prepared road which cross the plain to the north of the cliffs and then cross the site heading west and south-west.*

Along the eastern margin of the site there are more workmen's huts. The western margin too is marked with huts so that they surround the entire tongue of higher ground. Running alongside them, in places obscured by modern vehicle tracks, are ancient roads, the largest of which crosses the site diagonally and continues south-east to Malqata and north-west to the high desert and Farchout. This road consists of a series of separate narrow paths moving side-by-side in the same direction. It is marked, where it crosses the floodplain, by low piles of stones just visible enough for someone on foot to pick out the route ahead. To the west of this road (the northern part of which has been used by a heavy caterpillar-tracked vehicle) are three apparent "wells", currently all dry. The exact nature of these wells remains unclear, but they undoubtedly acted as a water source of some sort, and possibly provided water storage, for those involved in the construction of the WB1 tombs.

*Figure 5. The WB1 site looking south-west over the lower flood plain of the Wadi Bairiya. The white tents are just to the left of the shaft tombs.*

Running round the tongue of rising ground is a different type of road. This type is between three and a half metres and four metres wide and prepared by clearing to the sides all the large rocks and stones. What is left is a firm, flat road-bed covered in fine gravel. This type of road runs down the western margin of the Wadi Bairiya floodplain towards Kom el-Abd but is lost in the sand quarries 3km to the north of that site and 3.4km south of WB1. It is not visible on the eastern side, but a small part of the road arcs across from the WB1 site to the mouth of the Wadi el-Agaala. It is visible there in two short stretches and then re-appears in the centre of that great wadi on higher ground to the sides of a great natural amphitheatre. Carter records that he thought the road might have formed a loop in this amphitheatre which gave the wadi its name[1].

These roads are of great importance in connecting the WB1 site with other monuments in this area of modern desert. They suggest a level of activity in ancient times which these regions do not see today. They raise questions about just what this activity consisted of and why there was activity then which has not continued into modern times.

---

1. Carter, H. (1917) op. cit. quoted above in full.

The shaft tombs are located in the north-eastern corner of the site some twenty-five metres south of the cliffs at a point where the slope from the cliff-tops eases and levels out. When found they were surrounded by an oval of spoil-heaps forty metres by forty-five metres in extent, higher in the south and west than in the north and east. Before clearance began five partially-filled shafts and one wholly-filled shaft were visible. The openings form a Y-shape, the V of the Y opening to the east, the stem running from east to west *(Figure 6)*.

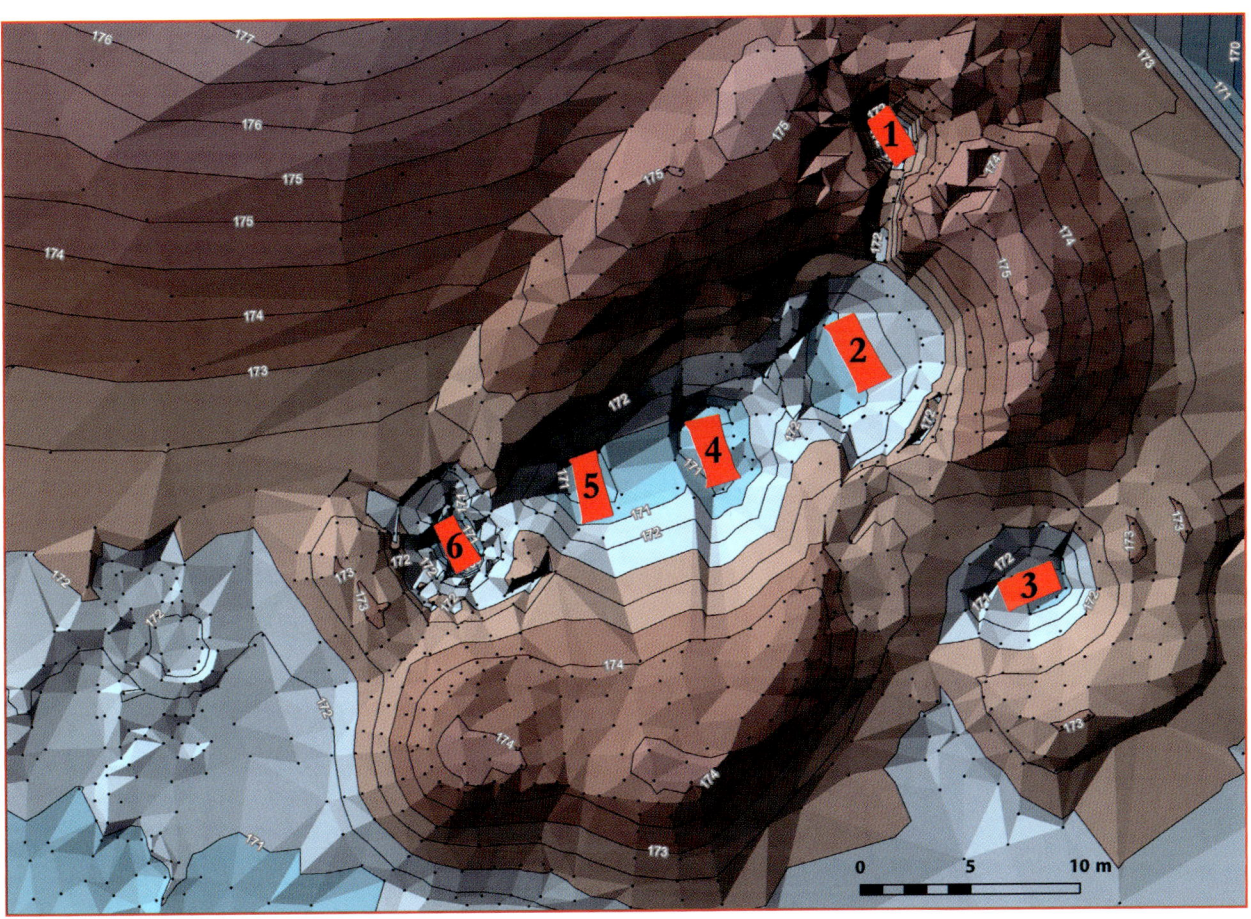

*Figure 6. The shaft tombs and contours as found. Shaft Seven was hidden under the spoil-heaps south of Shafts Four and Five.*

The shafts are numbered north to south and then east to west (*Figure 6*). The spoil-heaps were surrounded by many shallow pits excavated to a depth of no more than seventy-five centimetres. Judging by the way in which stones have been sorted into piles in these pits, they were used to extract the fine red soil which lies just under the hard surface of flinty debris.

Some of these pits appear to be ancient and the soil was most likely used for plastering the walls of the tombs. Other pits are hardly eroded at all and are probably modern. Whether the mud extracted in modern times is used for plastering or ceramics is not known.

# The condition of the site when found

*Figure 7. The shafts and the spoil-heaps before work started looking south down the Wadi Bairiya flood-plain.*

Although remote, the site had been visited regularly. When we first identified the location, the surface, as in Carter's day, was littered with pottery sherds. These were mostly fine Marl-D amphora sherds which are found in such quantity at Malqata *(Figure 8)*. Also visible were tiny fragments of faience and glass, pieces of shaped limestone and small green hardstone fragments *(Figures 9 and 10)*.

The margins of the shafts had in every case been eroded and soil from the spoil-heaps had fallen, been washed or been blown back into the tombs. Shafts One, Five and Six were almost completely choked with debris and were inaccessible. At the bottom of Shaft Two an entrance to a chamber to the south was visible. The bottom of Shaft Three was entirely blocked, but a drystone wall had been built across the narrow axis of the tomb creating a step some five metres below the surface. Shaft Four was the least encumbered of the shafts with crawling access visible to chambers off the southern and northern ends. Scratched on the plaster of the southern chamber was an Arabic graffito dated 2012.

*Figure 8. Marl-D ware and beer jar sherds on the surface of the the WB1 site when first found.*

*Figure 9. A faience fragment and Marl-D amphora sherd on the surface of the site when first found.*

*Figure 10. A small fragment of a stone vessel lying on the surface of the WB1 site when found.*

*Figure 11. The shafts and spoil-heaps before work commenced from the west.*

It was clear that the debris inside the accessible chambers had been moved about relatively recently. It was just possible to see through from the chambers of Shaft Four into the chambers of Shaft Two. Initially this raised the possibility that the substructure of the tombs was designed as a single architectural unit.

The architecture was clearly complex. There are shaft tombs in the Valley of the Queens which have multiple chambers. Two have more than one chamber off both narrow ends of the shaft (QV63 and QV69[2]). However, no other shaft tombs of the XVIIIth dynasty have multiple chambers off both ends of the shafts and chambers on different levels. In their architectural complexity alone these shaft tombs have proved to be unique.

During the course of the clearance of these shafts we were to find evidence of almost continual visitation from a fairly thorough initial destructive event, robbery or clearance through the Third Intermediate Period, Roman and Coptic times to the early twentieth century and present day.

*Figure 12. Looking west along the line of Shafts Two (with the ladder inserted), Four, Five and Six.*

---

2. Thomas, E. (1966) "*The Royal Necropoleis of Thebes*", Privately printed, Princeton Figure 17, p. 191 and Leblanc, C. (1989) "*Architecture et évolution chronologique des tombes de la Vallée des Reines*", BIFAO 89, Le Caire pp. 227–47.

**Some of the questions which arose before clearance began were as follows:**

- How many shafts were there in total and were these part of a larger burial ground?

- Were these separate tombs connected by robbers' holes or were they components in a single piece of architecture intentionally connected underground?

- Why were two of the shafts made so large (1.5m by 3m$^3$)?

- Why were the tombs not better hidden and was there always visible surface debris around the shaft tops?

- Why was this remote site chosen?

- Why are the tombs detached from the main Theban massif?

- Who were the people buried here?

*Figure 13. Looking east along the line of shafts. the cut through the spoil-heaps was made by water pouring from Shaft One into Shaft Two.*

---

3. cf WV24 1.63m by 2.7m; KV40 2m by 2.24m; KV56 1.6m by 2.42m; KV58 1.49m by 1.98m. Only the multi-chambered KV27 shaft tomb has similarly large dimensions being 1.48m by 3.2m.

# CHAPTER THREE
## CLEARANCE OF THE SHAFT TOMBS

Clearance work began on 12th October, 2014, with collection of surface material from what was numbered Feature 1001. A large amount of material was collected in and around the mouth of the shafts, from all parts of the spoil-heaps and from the area immediately surrounding the outer slopes of the spoil-heaps.

*Figure 14. Ceramic fragments on the surface of the WB1 site.*

This material consists of ceramic fragments (*Figure 14*) of which twenty crates were collected in the first week. These were of three broad types of pottery:

a) New Kingdom sherds of beer jars and Marl-D amphorae of a date after Amenhotep II and typical of the reign of Amenhotep III;

b) late Roman amphorae;

c) modern water storage jars common from the XIXth century onwards..

Of the remainder of finds, over 20% collected loosely from the surface consisted of limestone canopic jar fragments. Many fragments of faience tiles, wooden pieces and lithics were also found with smaller quantities of glass fragments, hardstone (serpentine) fragments and pieces of human and animal bone.

An important point arising from these surface discoveries, confirmed by our subsequent work inside the shafts, and particularly in the lower chambers of Shaft Five, is that context was almost useless as a guide to the original positioning of objects. The quantities of material found just under the recently-created surface of the spoil-heaps and mixed in with all levels of the shafts, plus the raking angles of the infill in the shafts, all suggest that the objects in the tomb chambers were removed at some stage from their original burial positions to the surface.

*Figure 15. Wooden objects from various features cut into small pieces.*

Quite where the material was broken-up remains unclear. Some of the destruction may have taken place in the tomb chambers, as there are signs of burning in several chambers, most notably in Shaft Four.

Subsequent examination of the fragments has confirmed that a great deal of effort went into breaking up the material from these burials. The gilded wooden material was burned to retrieve the gold but many pieces of furniture were cut into pieces no more than five centimetres long (*Figure 15*). The stone vessels and their lids were all smashed in a manner which suggests something more than accidental damage or robbery. This broken material then gradually slid back into the tombs, along with varying amounts of the original shaft fill, wind-blown sand and dust and material washed in by occasional but, over a chronic period of three thousand years, cumulatively destructive rainstorms.

Some of the upper chambers in the shafts remained empty, notably Chamber Ba in Shaft Four. Chamber Ba in Shaft Two was partially filled in modern times by robbers who used it to hold debris removed from Chamber B. Other than at the entrance from the shaft where debris had slumped into Chamber A and Chamber B, the lower chambers in Shaft Five, apparently untouched since ancient times, were almost empty. The southern suite of rooms (Chambers B, Ba and Bb), contained nothing except a scattering of human remains, sherds and wooden fragments which lay beneath debris fallen from the ceiling (*Figure 57*). Chamber A was similarly empty but for a group of storage jars (the only ones found more or less intact) and some termite-damaged wooden fragments.

Some of the material removed from the tombs slid down the outer sides of the spoil-heaps and, no doubt, the better remaining pieces were removed by robbers ancient and modern[1].

---

1. A canopic jar base was found being used as an oil lamp in a Coptic settlement in the Wadi Bairiya (WB2) just a kilometre north of WB1. Coque, R. et al (1972) "*Graffiti de la Montagne Thebaine I,3 Complements aux secteurs A et C, Frange du Sahara Thebain*", CEDAE, Le Caire plate ccxxxvii.

Before considering the objects, which will be dealt with in detail in forthcoming specialist fascicles, the architecture and development of the tombs will be considered shaft by shaft in the order in which they were cleared.

The shafts were cleared in a sequence dictated by their accessibility as follows:

- first, Shaft Two, already accessible via a narrow path through the spoil-heaps to the south-west;

- second, Shaft Six, at the western extreme of the line of shafts;

- third, Shaft One, at the north-eastern edge;

- fourth, Shaft Three, at the south-eastern edge; then

- fifth, Shaft Five, between Shaft Six and Shaft Four..

These were all cleared in the first half of the first season between October and December, 2014. In the second half of the first season, between March and May, 2015, we cleared

- sixth, Shaft Four.

It was not until the spoil-heaps had been largely cleared in the second season, between September and December, 2015, that we uncovered and cleared

- finally, Shaft Seven.

What is presented here is a chronological account of the clearance work and of the principal evidence which emerged during that process. When we began work the architecture of the tombs was known only from a very brief visit in March, 2014[2] when only one of the shafts was accessible. Although we knew from that visit that these shaft tombs were unusual in design it was only as the tombs were cleared that the full complexity of their architecture became apparent.

*Figure 16. Initial clearance work round the top of Shaft Two. Looking east.*

---

2. See Litherland, P. (2014) op. cit. p. 82.

# CLEARANCE OF SHAFT TWO

*Figure 17. Preliminary clearance work to stabilise the badly-eroded top of Shaft Two. The cut to the right of centre in the upper part of the photograph was created by water pouring through from Shaft One into Shaft Two where it caused chronic damage. The reddish layer visible to the right of the bottom of the cut and encircling the tomb shaft is the Abdul Ghany layer just below the XVIIIth dynasty surface level.*

*Figure 18. Platform established at the top of Shaft Two to accommodate the winch. Shafts Four, Five and Six can be seen to the left. Abdul Ghany is the figure on the right.*

---

3. This is a layer of uniform fine brown desert marl which lies just beneath the XVIIIth dynasty surface. It was first noted by, and therefore named after, our first inspector, Abdul Ghany.

Preparatory work on the surface to stabilise the shaft tops was necessary before work began on clearing the shafts. The surface layer into which the shafts were excavated consists of a pebbly conglomerate which varies in cohesion. This layer, which is roughly 2m to 2.5m deep, had eroded badly making the tops of the shafts appear everted. Rain

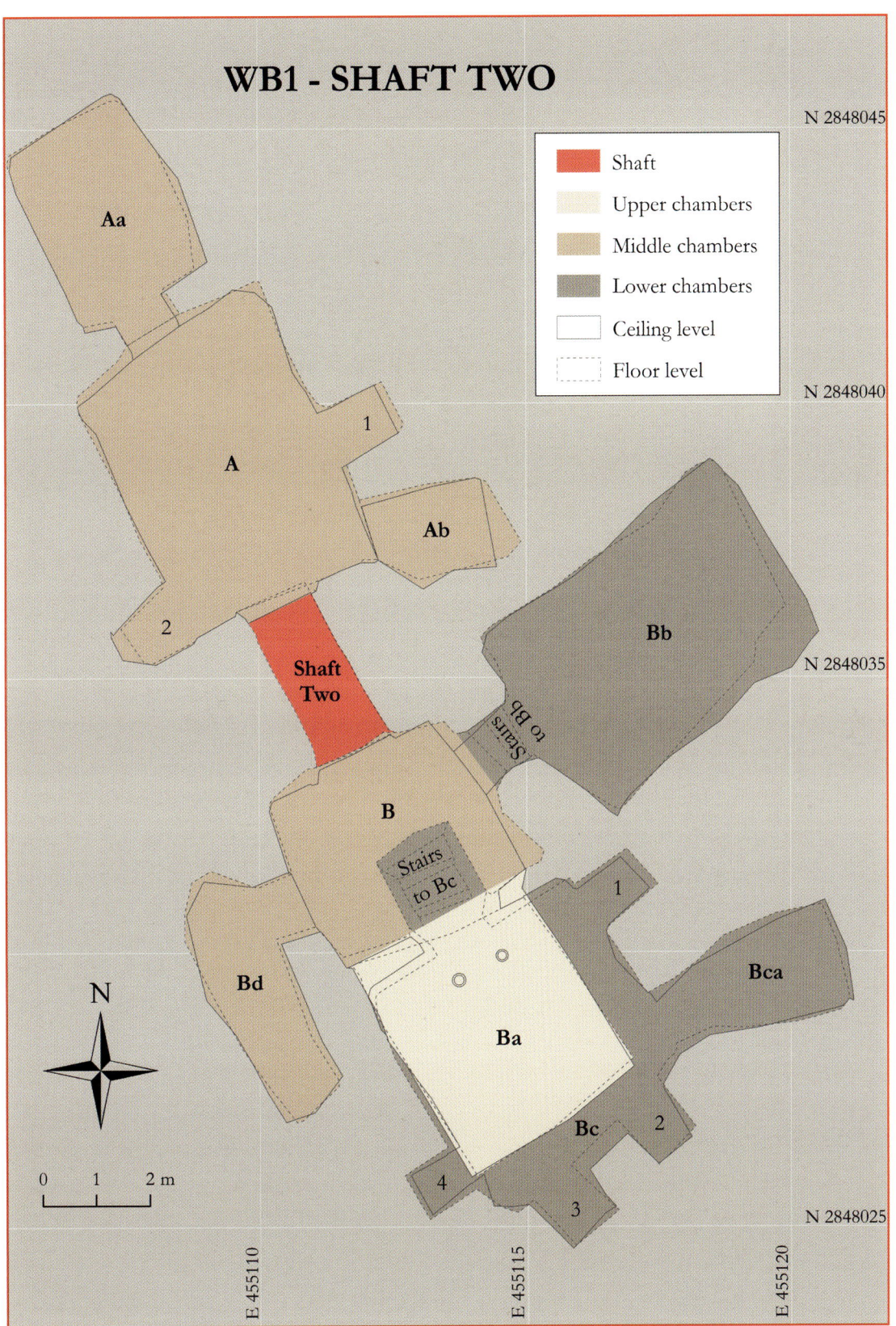

*Figure 19. Final plan of Shaft Two. Chamber Ba is above the level of Chamber B. Steps lead down from Chamber B into Chamber Bb Chamber Bc. The final metre of Chamber Bb may have been created by a collapse in the eastern wall. The material there was extremely loose.*

and human activity had rendered this layer friable, and so the area round the shaft top had to be levelled to create a safe and stable platform for steel H-beams and wooden supports to be erected to bear the weight of the winch and the barrows for removing the excavated material to the sieves.

Once this work was complete clearance inside the shaft began. The shaft measured 1.5m E-W by 3m N-S. The fill in the lower part of the shaft was composed almost entirely of material washed in from the spoil-heaps above. Mixed in with this were larger fragments from the conglomerate layer and large stones which were originally part of the door blockings. Work then moved to clearance of the tomb chambers in the following sequence:

on the southern side of the shaft

- Chamber B;

- Chamber Ba;

- Chamber Bc and Bca;

- Chamber Bb;

- Chamber Bd; then

on the nothern side of the shaft

- Chamber A;

- Chamber Aa; and finally

- Chamber Ab.

Clearance work was carried out in difficult circumstances with the heat in the chambers some 5°C higher than the surface temperature which was over 50°C at times early in the season. Visibility and air quality were poor. Despite powerful lighting the dust caused constant problems particularly with photography attempted while work was in progress. The ventilation system which brought fresh air down the seven-metre shaft tended to disturb and circulate the dust and often had to be turned-off for this reason.

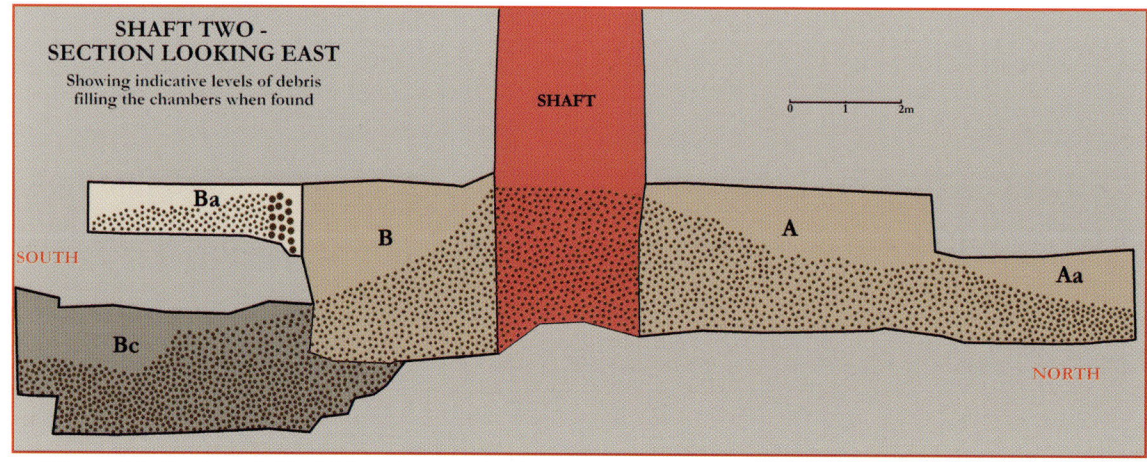

*Figure 20. Section of Shaft Two showing the distribution of the fill confirmatory of its having fallen back down the shafts and spread progressively downwards and outwards.*

---

4. All chambers were given letters proceeding from north to south and clockwise. Niches were numbered clockwise.

The chambers of Shaft Two were filled with debris the composition of which was for the most part homogeneous, being a mixture of fine desert marl, stone chips and larger boulders and rock fragments. The bottom of the shaft was filled to just below the top of the doorways giving north onto Chamber A and south onto Chamber B. At the entrance to Chamber B the fill sloped down angling towards the top of the door into Chamber Bc. Chamber Ba was partially filled with rubble held in place by a rough retaining wall of larger stones. This material had probably been removed from Chamber B by robbers who had constructed the retaining wall across the opening. This and the fact that the far end of Chamber Ba was still empty suggests that the whole of Chamber Ba was empty until those recent robbers appeared. This in turn supports our later conclusion that at some stage all the shaft tombs at WB1 were cleared and left empty. They then re-filled with debris which entered the tombs from the spoil-heaps above. This process, driven by wind, rainstorms and movement of people on the surface would have seen the lower chambers gradually filled up and the higher chambers left empty (*Figure 20*). The fill was then churned by robbers in ancient and modern times searching in the debris for objects to remove.

*Figure 21. Shaft Two Chamber A (looking north) when found. The fill has been moved about by modern robbers but still slopes down from the entrance at the shaft towards the north and Chamber Aa. Note the curvature of the ceiling formed by the upper layer of hard rock. The dark staining on the ceiling to the right was caused by bats.*

## Shaft Two - Southern Chambers
### Chamber B

Chamber B measured 3.8m E-W, by 3.4m N-S with a ceiling 3.16m high. The fill in this chamber was a mixture of limestone fragments of various sizes and fine desert marl and sand. There was no clear stratification in the material, especially in the upper levels of the fill which was loose and showed obvious signs of having been disturbed. Mixed in with this loose admixture were pottery sherds of various types in large numbers, fragments of faience, scattered pieces of broken canopic jars, broken pieces of alabaster[5] vessels, small

---

5. In this publication 'alabaster' is a translation of the Egyptian word *šs*.

*Figure 22. Shaft Two Chamber B looking south after initial clearance of the surface debris. The retaining wall of larger stones built by modern robbers across the entrance to Chamber Ba is clearly visible. The buried entrance to Chamber Bc is just visible straight ahead and the entrance to Bd to the right. The scale is 120cms.*

fragments of wood, animal and human bones and pieces of linen. One of these pieces of linen proved to be a belt (*Figure 23*) possibly dating to the Coptic period and perhaps indicative of a period of re-use of these chambers as dwellings.

Chamber B produced relatively few objects, and this was perhaps not surprising as it was one of the chambers more accessible to robbers who would have had the opportunity to sift through the debris repeatedly. Pottery sherds proved to be the dominant category of objects but, these aside, limestone fragments of canopic jars, worked alabaster fragments and ceramic tools were the next most plentiful. Single examples of faience, glass and bone were found here with two fragments of linen and two lots of wooden fragments. Included in the wood finds were the first examples of tubular wooden objects, spirally-

*Figure 23. A belt found early in the clearance of Chamber B in Shaft Two.*

engraved and generally of ebony (*Figure 24*). We were to find these in large numbers in all the shafts and their function remains uncertain. They may be wig-spirals from coffins or statuettes.

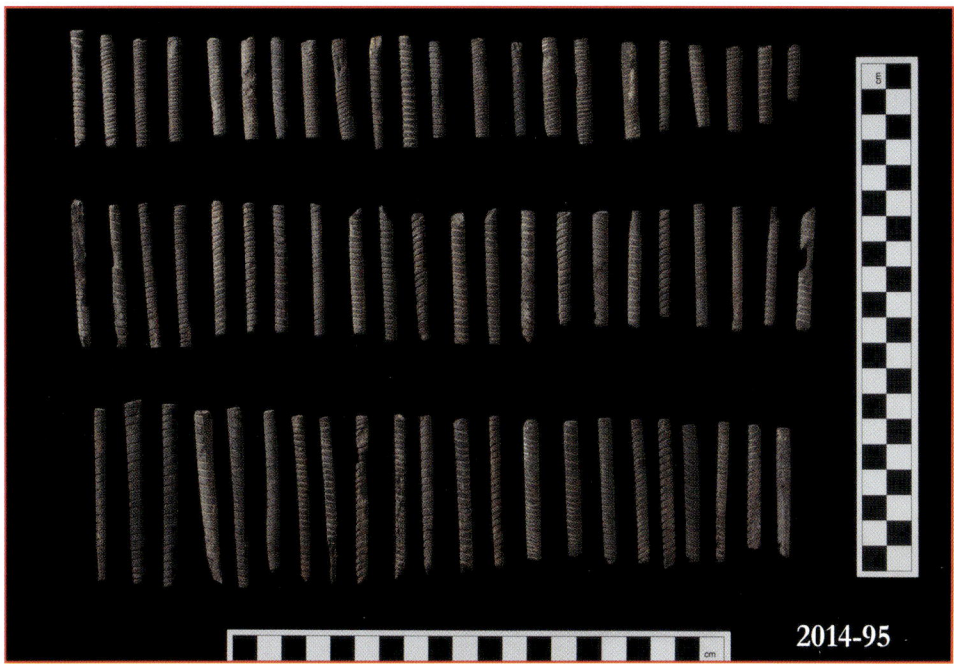

*Figure 24. Spirally-engraved wooden objects which may be wig-spirals from coffins.*

## Chamber Ba

The fill of the Chamber Ba shelf was similar to that of Chamber B, although there were more fragments of wood. These accounted for 20% of the other finds (excluding sherds) from this chamber. Amongst the limestone pieces were several inscribed fragments and a complete, human-headed canopic jar lid (SV106).

*Figure 25. The canopic head from Chamber Ba (SV106).*

The walls of this shelf were plastered and the floor seems also to have had mud plaster applied to it to even out the irregularities. The precise function of this chamber, or shelf, remains unclear but later examination of the floor, which also forms the ceiling of Chamber Bc below, shows that this layer was left unusually thick. It is also fractured (as is the ceiling) and the subsequent use of large stones to support the ceiling of Bc (*Figure 26*) at the entrance suggests that fears about the stability of this floor/ceiling led to the abandonment of plans to complete this chamber.

## Chambers Bc and Bca

Chamber Bc (4.20m N-S by 4.55m E-W by 2.30m high on the west to 2.60m high on the south), is to the south of B and lies underneath Ba. It is accessed by steps. In the chamber there are five openings or niches: two on the east, one of which has been enlarged into a separate chamber (Bca), two on the southern side and two on the western side. Niches 1, 2 and 3, although badly eroded can be seen to have stood some 90cms above the floor level of the chamber. The entrance to Chamber Bca is similarly elevated. Niche 4, by contrast, runs from just below the ceiling of the chamber to the floor.

*Figure 26. Work in Chamber Bc underway after the steps had been cleared and the first debris removed from the chamber. The photograph shows clearly that the southern wall of Chamber B is built of blocks created from the hard layer forming the door lintel.*

*Figure 27. Chamber Bca while clearance of Chamber Bc was under way. The dust made clearer photographs very difficult.*

Chamber Bc was almost completely filled with debris with, at the most, crawling space in certain parts. The debris was notably finer than that higher up, suggesting it had settled after being washed in.

These areas produced a similar range of other finds (excluding sherds) with wooden fragments and canopic jar pieces in the majority. Two human-headed canopic jar lids (SV102 and SV103) came from this chamber, but very little faience, glass or linen. Four human bones were found here, two of them from Chamber Bca.

*Figure 28. SV102 (left) and SV103 (right) from Chamber Bc in Shaft Two.*

It should be noted that Bca looks as though it was originally a niche of similar dimensions to the other niches in what we have assumed is a burial chamber. A line of plaster 1.1m into Bca from the wall of Bc is visible on the rock. It is very difficult to tell if this marks a final end to the plastering or whether it is just the way the plaster has eroded and fallen away. The suggestion remains, however, that this niche was enlarged at a date subsequent to the preparation of the original design of the chamber. A child's bone found in here may be evidence that this niche was enlarged to accommodate its burial. However the bone could be intrusive.

*Figure 29. The entrance to Chamber Bb at the time that clearance work was starting in this chamber.*

## Chamber Bb

Work moved on to Chamber Bb which, like Bc, has steps leading down to a large chamber to the east of Chamber B. The dimensions of this chamber are 4.05m N-S by 5.7m E-W and 1.95m high at the southern end, falling to 1.7m high in the north-eastern corner. However, it is possible that the real E-W dimension of the chamber is 4.25m, giving the chamber a squarer shape more in keeping with the dimensions of burial Chamber Bc (4.20m N-S by 4.55m E-W) but with a ceiling lower than the height of that chamber (2.30m to 2.60m). There are several reasons for believing this to be the case.

First, the plastering of the walls stops at a point 4.25m from the entrance wall. Second, there is a plaster line across the ceiling at the same point. The rock beyond this point is of a very poor quality and the debris found at this eastern end of the chamber, together with the paucity of finds in this location, was consistent with the idea of a collapse in the eastern wall at some point subsequent to the original clearance of the tombs.

This possible burial chamber has no niches. By far the largest number of objects discovered here were limestone canopic jar fragments. Many of these were inscribed. Some were incised with fake hieroglyphs, probably added by robbers trying to augment the value of the pieces. There was very little ceramic material, faience or alabaster in this location. Three bones were the only human remains.

*Figure 30. Discovery of the SV104 canopic jar head in Chamber Bb.*

*Figure 31. SV104 found in Chamber Bb of Shaft Two.*

## Chamber Bd

This small chamber off Chamber B was the last of the southern suite of chambers to be cleared. It measured 4.65m E-W by 1.35m N-S, with a sloping ceiling 1.8m at its highest. There was no marked difference in the fill of this chamber to that of Chamber B, but the debris contained a large quantity of white-painted storage jar sherds. The predominance of these, and relative lack of other finds, inclines us to designate this a storeroom. Later evidence from Shaft Five (Chamber A) suggests that storage jars were

*Figure 32. The entrance to Chamber Bd off Chamber B.*

*Figure 33. The rubble-filled interior of Chamber Bd*

not always removed from the chambers, being of little value. However, they would not have survived intact in situ when debris fell into the shafts. There were only eight other numbered finds in this chamber: two human bones, two jar dockets, two wooden objects, one piece of faience and a single canopic jar fragment.

It was through the middle of the western side of this chamber that an irregular opening had been made through to Shaft Four, most likely by later intruders. It opens into Niche 2 of Chamber B in that tomb. The opening is 95cms from the floor of Chamber Bd, and is 80cms high by 65cms wide, just large enough to crawl through.

## Shaft Two - Northern Chambers

Following the clearance of the southern suite of chambers work moved to the northern part of the tomb where there were only two chambers and a niche to be cleared. As shown in Figure 34, again these were filled with debris, although it was possible to stand just inside the entrance of Chamber A. It is not surprising that the northern rooms in all the shafts were less filled than the southern rooms. The slope of the terrain above ground would naturally have meant more flooding into the southern chambers. In the case of Shaft Two the cutting through from Shaft One would have seen water flowing from north to south, bringing debris with it back into the tomb chambers.

## Chamber A

This chamber measures 5.62m (N-S) by 3.6m (E-W) and 2.73m in height. It opens directly off the shaft. The debris here was again a mixture of small limestone fragments, larger limestone blocks (many from the original door blockings situated just inside the chamber entrance) and desert marl and rocks washed in from above.

In this debris there were quantities of pottery sherds - mainly white-painted storage jar fragments. Amongst these were jar dockets with hieratic inscriptions. There were several wooden fragments inscribed in hieratic, along with large numbers of canopic jar fragments, many inscribed. Among the wooden objects was part of a fan inscribed with the text: "Ornament of the King, the King's Wife Henut". This discovery provided the first confirmation of two things: one that we were dealing with royal tombs; and, second, that some of the names involved, at the very highest level of the XVIIIth dynasty royal family, were not well-known.

*Figure 34. Chamber A looking north towards Chamber Aa while clearance work was in progress. Clearly visible in this photograph is the hard white plaster filling of the ceiling cracks.*

*Figure 35. Fragment of a fan found in Chamber A of Shaft Two, naming the Ornament of the King, the King's Wife Henut.*

*Figure 36. The base of an Anubis or Imy-wt fetish (inset is a view of the top).*

Over 40% of the finds from this chamber (excluding pottery sherds) were canopic jar and alabaster vessel fragments. A quarter were wooden pieces. In addition to the

*Figure 37. Three Canopic jars from Shaft Two bearing the names (left to right) Sati, Tawosret and By.*

fan fragment these included a hand covered in black varnish, probably from a statue. Another notable find from this chamber was a limestone object in the shape of a truncated cone with a hole drilled through the middle (*Figure 36*). This is the base for an Anubis fetish similar to those of alabaster found in KV62 (Objects 194 and 202 in the Handlist[6]) and also represented in private tombs such as the tomb of Senedjem at Deir el-Medina.

The canopic jar fragments found here provided us with the names of three more individuals in addition to the King's Wife Henut. These were Sati (SV5), Tawosret (SV6) and By (SV38), all of whom appear to have had the title 𓐍𓂝𓏏 generally translated as "Ornament of the King".

## Chamber Aa

This chamber opens directly to the north of Chamber A. The entrance (1.1m wide by 1.6m high) is situated roughly in the middle of the north wall of Chamber A and gives onto a smaller chamber 3.62m (N-S) by 2.87m (E-W) and 1.6m in height.

This chamber contained debris of the same nature as Chamber A. Again the objects found here, other than ceramic sherds, consisted overwhelmingly of canopic jar fragments.

## Chamber Ab

Chamber Ab is a small chamber off the south-eastern corner of Chamber A. An opening 1.10m wide by 1.45m high gives onto a space of the same height and 1.80m (N-S) by 2.25m (E-W). It was filled with light grey limestone fragments mixed with desert marl containing a few pottery sherds, animal and human bones and faience fragments. It would appear most likely that this was a storage chamber as it is scarcely large enough to contain any form of burial.

---

6. Murray, H. and Nuttall, M. (1963) "*A Handlist to Howard Carter's Catalogue of Objects in Tut'ankhamun's Tomb*", Griffith Insitute, OUP, Oxford p. 8.

## CLEARANCE OF SHAFT SIX

Shaft Six was cleared next as it stands at the western extreme of the central line of shafts and could be accessed easily. To the north of Shaft Six a depression had been cut into a layer of soft brown marl by water running down the slope to the north and streaming down the northern edge of the spoil-heaps into this shaft. The shaft (1.05m E-W by 2.25m N-S) proved to be a commencement only 4.25m deep.

*Figure 38. Shaft Six when found looking south-east.*

The shaft was entirely filled with clear layers of distinctive water-borne brown marl mixed with slip-glazed Marl-D sherds. These sherds also appeared in great numbers in and around the top of the shaft on the surface and embedded in the marl layer either side of the water-worn depression to the north of the shaft.

It was clear that over a lengthy period the once empty shaft had been filled by successive episodes of flooding. Layers of fine mud from the surface had been washed in repeatedly with fragments of Marl-D amphorae once scattered on the surface.

As the shaft was cleared it was noted that the mud layers a metre and more below the surface were still damp, despite the total absence of moisture on the surface. This factor was of interest in connection with evidence found later in the northern chambers of Shaft Five.

*Figure 39. Shaft Six when cleared.*

## CLEARANCE OF SHAFT ONE

Shaft One (1.15m E-W and 2.3m N-S) proved to be another commencement. The bottom of the shaft (1.4m deep overall) was filled with fine water-borne debris which contained pottery sherds but very little else. It seems to have acted as a reservoir for water which had over the centuries eroded a trench through the spoil-heaps into Shaft Two. Water falling on the high ground of the slope above Shafts One and Two would therefore have found its way into Shaft Two. This accounts for the very poor state of preservation of the walls and niches in Chamber Bc of Shaft Two in particular.

*Figure 40. Shaft One when found.*

*Figure 41. Shaft One when cleared.*

# CLEARANCE OF SHAFT THREE

*Figure 42. The top of Shaft Three before clearance work began.*

*Figure 43. The shaft of Shaft Three looking due east, showing the dry-stone wall built N-S across the shaft.*

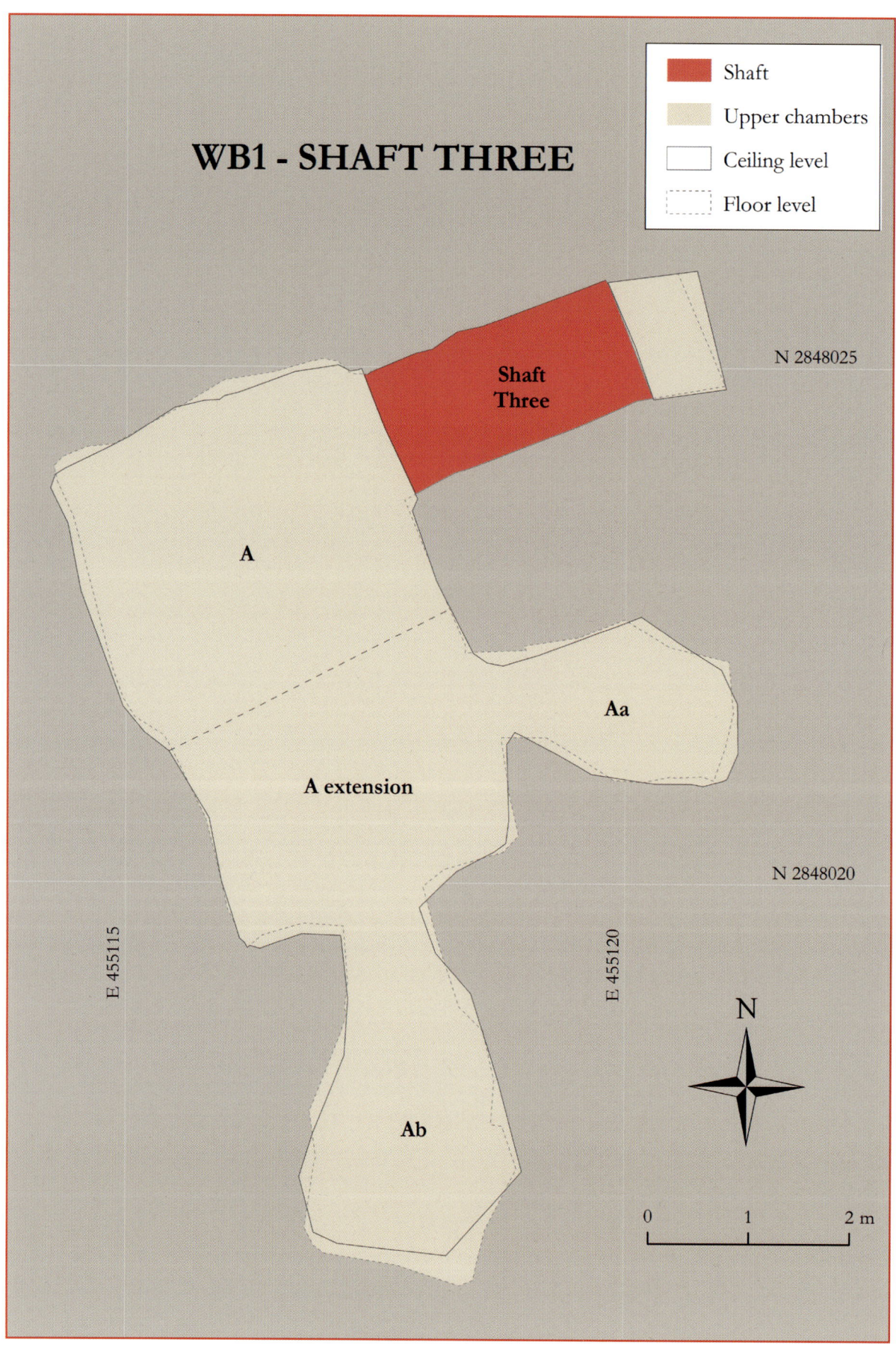

*Figure 44. Plan of Shaft Three.*

*Figure 45. Shaft Three: waiting for the installation of the winch.*

Work on the clearance of Shaft Three began on 8th November, 2014. This shaft was excavated into a flat piece of ground some twenty-five metres south of the northern slope of the site. The shaft measured 2.62m E-W and 1.4m N-S and was the only one of the visible shafts to be oriented along an E-W axis. The shaft was less full of debris than the main row of shafts (Two, Four, Five and Six ) running from east to west. This was at least in part because water falling down the northern slope would have flowed west before reaching the Shaft Three shaft top.

Visible at the bottom of the shaft was a drystone wall built across the shaft at about the halfway point and running from north to south. Whoever sunk this shaft was aware, as we were later to discover, that there were chambers only to the west of the shaft. The wall was built to stop debris cluttering the entrance to Chamber A and so it must have been built after debris had accumulated in the bottom of the shaft. When this might have been is less easy to establish.

Shaft Three proved to have only three chambers all on the same level. However, Chamber A (3.4m E-W by 5.8m N-S and with a ceiling 1.7m high) showed signs of having been created in two stages. A possible change in the plasterwork suggests that it was enlarged to the south in a phase which may also have included the construction of Chamber Aa (1.95m E-W by 1.6m N-S and 90cms high) and Chamber Ab (2.05m E-W by 2.9m N-S and 95cms to 1.45m high). Neither of these subsidiary chambers is complete, both having very low ceilings, their floors being roughly 70cms higher than the floor of Chamber A. The outlines of the doorways to these chambers have been completed in both cases.

*Figure 46. The entrance to Chamber A off the shaft in Shaft Three.*

*Figure 47. The strange 'niche' at the eastern end of Shaft Three where the rock has been cut away above and below the hard layer of limestone.*

*Figure 48. Another view of the shaft in Shaft Three showing the difference in heights between the floor of Chamber A and the shaft.*

At the eastern end of the shaft there is a niche of a curious nature which may represent the start of excavation for an additional chamber at this end of the shaft. The ancient masons have cut through a very hard layer of stone and had begun to create a door to the east, at the same time deepening the shaft. The hard layer has been left standing proud of cavities above and below (*Figure 47*). The eastern edge of Shaft Three is just ten metres from the edge of the plateau. This provides enough room for only a small chamber to be created without the risk of collapse. What exactly was envisaged is unclear. The signs that the shaft was being deepened endorse the view that work on this tomb was abandoned prematurely (*Figure 48*). The floor level of the shaft is below that of Chamber A which is unusual.

The finds in Shaft Three consisted of a similar admixture of fragments to Shaft Two: canopic jar fragments, wooden pieces, one alabaster fragment and four very badly charred bones. There was a much higher number of glass and faience fragments. These were fairly evenly distributed through the three chambers, supporting the idea that they had washed in from above. The presence of more glass and faience points to activity on the surface connected with the dismantling of these burials. We were later to find very large numbers of small finds on top of, and in between, the spoil-heaps above Shaft Three and in the area just to the south of Shafts Two and Four.

# CLEARANCE OF SHAFT FIVE

*Figure 49. Shaft Five (looking north-east) was completely blocked with debris when found. Its location was marked by a large depression rather than a visible shaft.*

*Figure 50. Preparation work to stabilise the top of Shaft Five. A channel cut into the top layer of desert marl can be seen in the far left-hand corner of the shaft between the workman in red and the workman holding the bucket. Water and debris coming down the line of the spoil-heap behind filled both Shaft Five and Shaft Six to its left.*

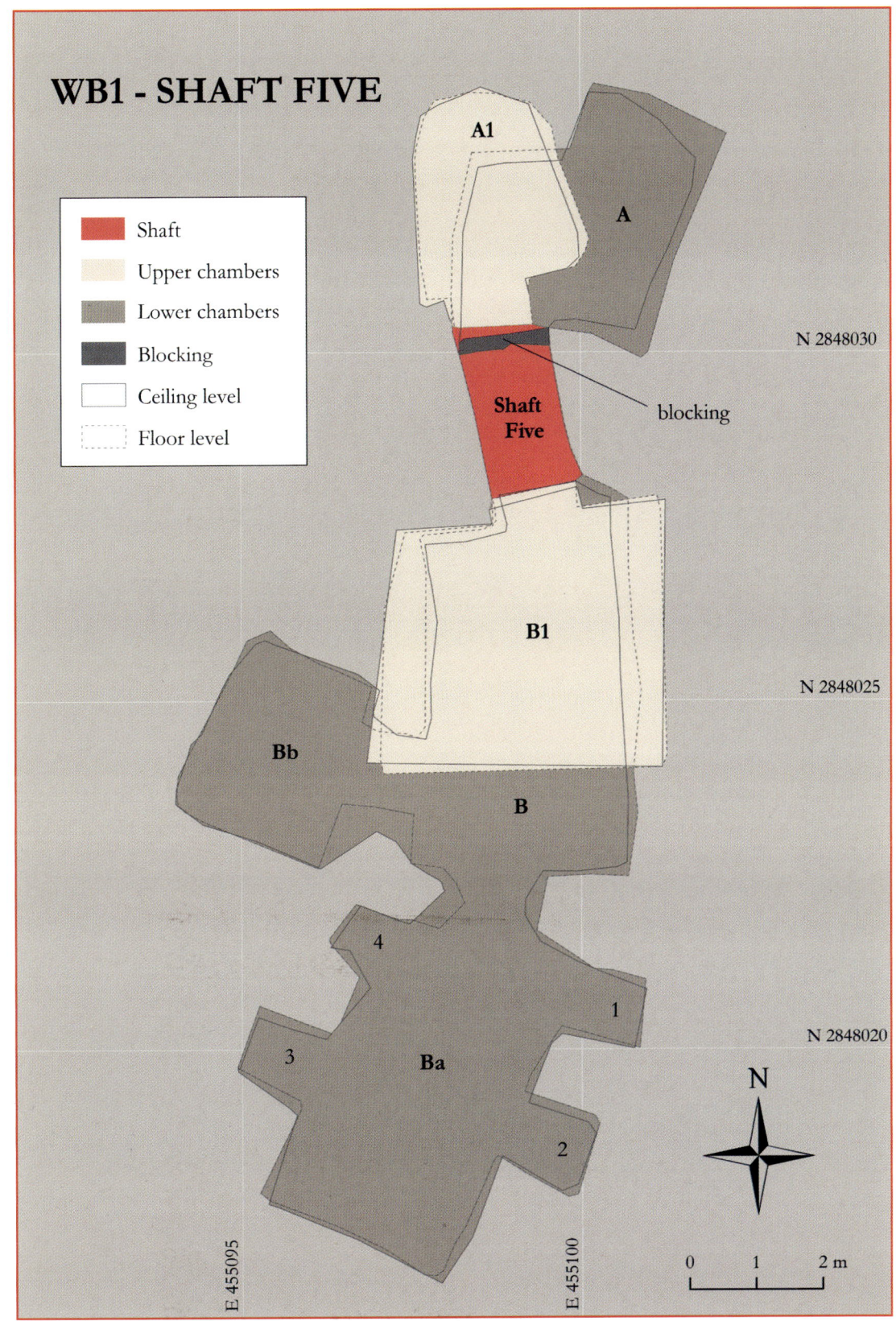

*Figure 51. Plan of Shaft Five.*

Work on the Shaft Five shaft began with preparations to level the area around the shaft top on 8th November. The shaft opening measured 1.3m in width (E-W) by 2.8m in length (N-S); smaller than Shaft Two but similar in size to Shaft Three. The shaft was completely blocked with debris when found. All that was visible was a depression in the ground between Shaft Four and Shaft Six.

By the 11th November the top of doors on the southern and northern ends of the shaft were visible, suggesting a similar design to Shafts Two and what was then visible of Shaft Four.

*Figure 52. Uncovering the southern door in Shaft Five leading to Chamber B1.*

## Upper chambers of Shaft Five

### Chamber B1

To the south of the shaft an opening 1.2m wide but only 1.1m high gave onto Chamber B1. This proved to be an extensive, squarish room (3.75m N-S and 4.25m E-W) but with a very low ceiling, only 90cms in height. The walls had been plastered with mud and were coated with a light yellow (perhaps once white) secondary layer.

*Figure 53. Chamber B1 looking north post-clearance. Traces of plaster are clearly visible.*

The fill again sloped from the north, suggesting it had fallen down the shafts and had progressively filled the chambers from the entrance. The fill contained just four objects, two pottery scrapers, a fragment of faience and a fragment of wood.

## Chamber A1

The opening off the northern end of the shaft is 1.25m wide by 1m high and leads to a second chamber with a low-ceiling (1m high). This chamber is 3.1m N-S and 2.3m E-W and clearly unfinished. Notwithstanding its unfinished state, the walls had been plastered. Again the finds in here were very small in number: four pottery implements and a single fragment of faience.

*Figure 54. Chamber A1 looking south towards the shaft and B1 beyond. Despite the obviously unfinished nature of the floor the walls still bear signs of plaster.*

At this stage there was a degree of disappointment and puzzlement about the truncated form of what looked like the entire tomb. However, it was soon noticed that the plastering of the shaft walls seemed to penetrate the established floor level. Investigation of the floor soon showed that the compacted floor, although hard, was not the original bottom of the shaft. The shaft continued down a further two and a half metres, making it the deepest of the shafts at 8.7m. The plastering of the shaft (*Figure 55*) suggests that that the shafts were originally not filled with rubble (the introduction of which would surely have damaged the plaster) but left open between burials. Had the shafts been filled with, emptied of, and then re-filled with rubble repeatedly the plaster would not have survived.

## Lower Chambers of Shaft Five

The fill here contained a much higher concentration of pottery sherds than the upper fill, most of them coming from wheel-made white-painted storage jars. At the bottom of the shaft there were four further chambers.

## Chamber B

Chamber B, to the south, is entered through a door off the shaft which is 1.45m wide by 1.65m high. The chamber is long and low, being 5.7m N-S and 3.1m E-W with a ceiling 1.6m in height. It became clear from the relative lack of debris in this chamber that it had been sealed since ancient times. A small amount of debris had spilled into the chamber from the shaft, but most of the debris inside was in the form of small limestone fragments which had fallen from the rough and friable ceiling *(Figure 57)*.

*Figure 55. The entrance to Chamber Bb with B1 above.*

Strewn across the floor of this and the neighbouring chambers were human remains. These were all reduced to bones, no soft tissue surviving, but unlike the fragments recovered from the other shafts, the bones were in relatively good condition, and had not been burned or broken by trampling. The absence of any weathering suggested they had lain undisturbed within the chambers of Shaft Five since the original intrusive activity.

*Figure 56. The eastern wall of Chamber B post-clearance looking north-east.*

## Chambers Ba and Bb

*Figure 57. The southern end of Chamber Ba as found. Most of the debris in this room has fallen from the ceiling. The disarticulated human remains lay under these rocks, but on the surface of a very thin layer of otherwise fine desert marl.*

A similar state prevailed in Chambers Ba and Bb. Ba is a niched chamber directly south of Chamber B. There are two niches to the east and two to the west. The chamber is 5.05m N-S and 2.9m E-W but its ceiling is only 1.2m high. Chamber Bb is situated off the south-western corner of Chamber B. It is 3m N-S and 2.3m E-W with a ceiling only 1.15m high. It would appear to be a store-room.

The objects in this southern suite of rooms were notable not only for the very large number of human bones but also for the complete absence of canopic equipment. Amongst the objects were numbers of glass coffin inlays in the form of glass eyebrows and hieroglyphs. These appear to have fallen from the objects to which they were originally attached, possibly when they were removed from the tomb.

*Figure 58. The door from Chamber B through to Ba beyond post-clearance.*

The state of these chambers supports the view that the objects and some of the mummies in all these shaft tombs were removed to the surface and, in the case of the furniture and coffins, there broken up and burned. The complete absence of canopic jars in the Shaft Five chambers supports the suggestion that these were removed and smashed on the surface. It is only in those shafts which have lain open for centuries and into which fragments have fallen from the surface that large numbers of pieces of canopic jar and other broken fragments have been found.

It subsequently transpired that this notion was complicated by the finds in Shaft Four and the condition of its walls, then later still by the finds on the surface.

## Chamber A

Chamber A, to the north, is an irregularly-shaped chamber reached through an entrance off the shaft 1.35m wide and only 1.4m high. The room is L-shaped and on the western side is 2.45, N-S and 3.3m E-W at its widest point. On the eastern side the chamber measures 3.5m N-S and 2.10m E-W. The height of the chamber varies between 1.4 and 1.5m.

Chamber A retained part of its original blocking with seal impressions in the mud coating. Regrettably, these seal impressions have so far evaded elucidation. The mud in which they were impressed was mixed with straw which has fallen out leaving a surface which is impossible to read, despite consolidation work. Just inside this blocking to the east of the small entrance lay a number of almost intact storage jars, relatively small in size and containing what appeared to be embalming refuse. One bore the inscription "The Little One brought from Perunefer".

*Figure 59. The surviving blocking to Chamber A.*

At the north-western point the chamber collides with Chamber A of Shaft Four, a small hole becoming apparent in our clearance work. Chisel marks are visible here which suggest that this part of the chamber was in the process of being enlarged when work stopped. The proximity of Chamber A in Shaft Four may explain this stoppage.

*Figure 60. Chamber A during clearance looking south towards the shaft. The blocking is covered in debris on the right.*

*Figure 61. Chamber A looking west post-clearance.*

*Figure 62. The small stone head, possibly from an unsual shabti figure, found in Chamber B of Shaft Five.*

The condition of the storage jars in this chamber was very poor. They were almost intact but the fabric of the jars had suffered from being wet over an extended period and had lost integrity. The effects of water damage were apparent also in the salt crystals growing out of the poor quality, fractured limestone in this chamber and in this chamber and Chambers B and Ba. The source of the water seeping into these chambers was Shaft Six which acted over the years as a natural reservoir for water flowing down the line of the spoil-heaps to the north. Having filled Shaft Six, the water then leaked into the Shaft Five chambers through fissures in the rock.

One enigmatic object found in Chamber B of Shaft Five was a carved stone head (*Figure 62*) which was so crude that it was immediately thought to be a modern fake. However, the other evidence before us in this shaft strongly suggested that these chambers had not been entered since ancient times. The faking of objects would appear to be a relatively modern exercise responding to an appetite for the acquisition of antiquities.

The first half of the season ended at this point and it was not until our return at the beginning of April, 2015, that we completed the clearance of the shaft tombs (Shaft Four) and began to turn our attention to the clearance of the spoil-heaps and the surface debris littering the site.

# CLEARANCE OF SHAFT FOUR

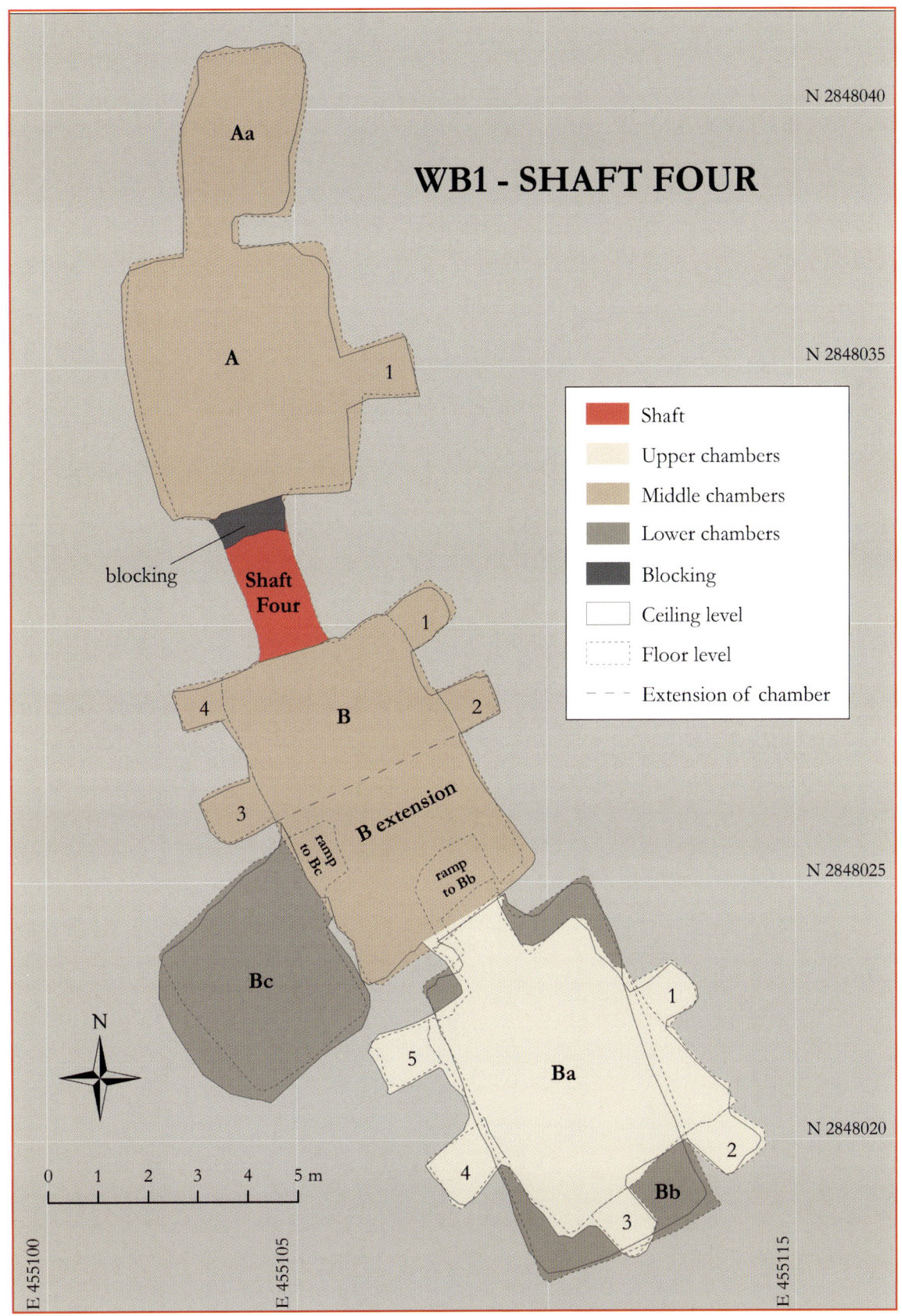

*Figure 63. Plan of Shaft Four.*

## Shaft Four - Northern Chambers

Work in Shaft Four began on 5th April, 2015. As the top of the shaft was cleared and prepared for the winch to be positioned an exquisite glass inlay of a finger or thumb, just 2cms in length, was found in the debris round the shaft mouth *(Figure 64)*.

The shaft was 1.45m to 1.5m E-W and 3m N-S. Following very much the same pattern as Shaft Two, debris had flowed down into Shaft Four and filled the two chambers immediately to the north and south of the shaft and the lower chambers leading off both Chamber A and Chamber B. In the southern suite of chambers both Chamber Bb and Bc were completely choked with debris. The fill in Chamber B had been moved about and a small amount had been pushed up and into the doorway of the otherwise completely empty Chamber Ba. The south-western margin of Chamber B had collapsed

*Figure 64. The small inlay digit found on the surface at the mouth of Shaft Four.*

into Chamber Bc. The ceiling of Chamber Bc was also later revealed to have collapsed with half-metre cubes of fallen rock lying on the top of the debris.

In the northern group of chambers the debris was less deep but filled the bottom metre and a half of the chamber, concealing the opening to Niche A1 and leaving just the top few centimetres of the door into Chamber Aa visible..

**Chamber B**

Clearance of the shaft and Chamber B itself soon began to reveal small objects of a more specific nature than those discovered in the other shafts. The quantity of finds was larger overall. Much of it was mixed in with a dark grey marl. This was darkened by charcoal which, being light, is easily moved by water and wind and, being fragile, crushes easily into very small fragments. The initial conclusion here was that much of the material found in this tomb relates to the location on the spoil-heaps where the dismantling and burning of objects cleared from the tombs in ancient times took place. This seems to have been located in an area between and to the south of Shafts Two and Four, and north-west of Shaft Three *(see Figure 66)*. However, subsequent examination of the plaster in Chamber B (and elsewhere in Shaft Four) suggests that there were large fires in the tomb chambers.

*Figure 65. Chamber B looking north towards the shaft, showing the level to which the chamber was filled with debris washed in from above.*

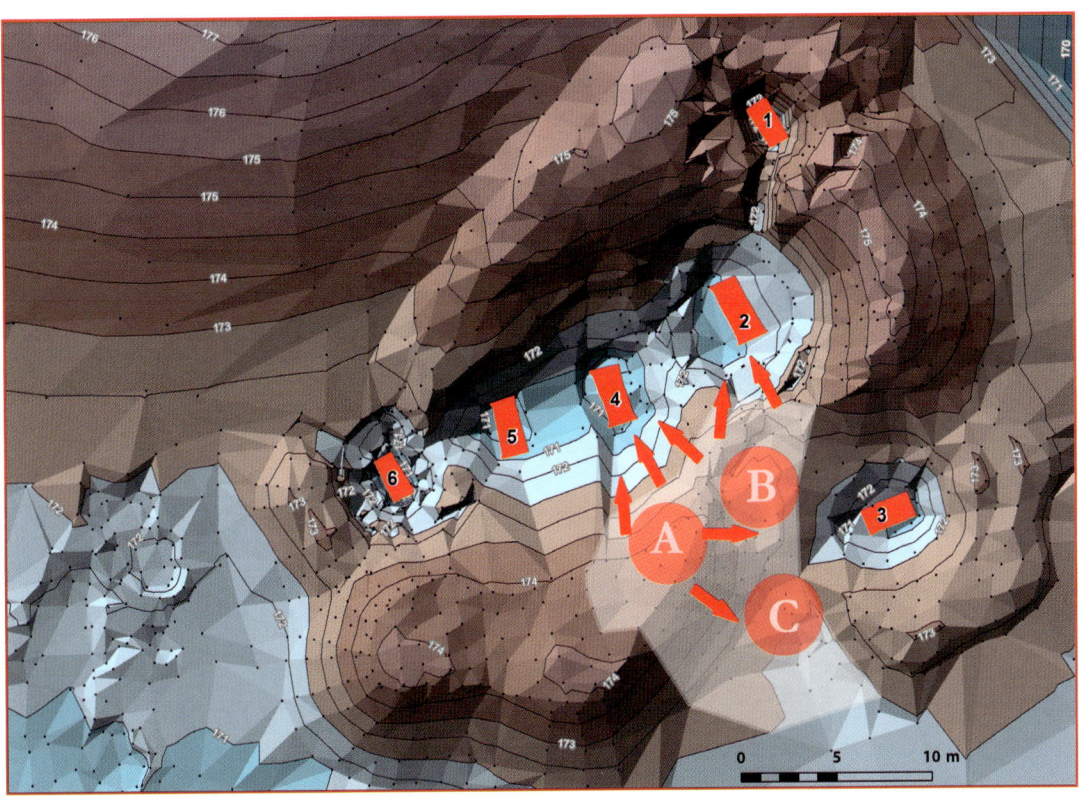

*Figure 66. From finds discovered in Shafts Two and Four and later, during surface clearance around areas B and C, and scattered throughout the white-shaded area, it appears as though much of the dismantling and destruction activity took place on top of the spoil-heaps in area A. Similar activity may also have taken place on top of the spoil-heaps to the east of Shaft Two.*

A glass chevron inlay (2015-45) from a coffin (similar to a red one found in Shaft Two, Chamber Bc) was an early find in the shaft fill (*Figure 67*), and whilst unremarkable in itself, close observation reveals that it was once inserted into some form of gilded matrix, most likely wooden. The only known wooden structures with *rishi*-work glass inlays on them are two coffins, one in KV55 and the other in KV62. This chevron suggests there were once coffins of a similar standard in these tombs.

*Figure 67. Glass rishi-work chevron from a coffin. There are traces of gilding, particularly down the right-hand edge.*

The fill of Chamber B contained a range of material similar to that found in Shaft Two - predominantly ceramic sherds, limestone canopic jar fragments, fragments of wood, faience fragments from furniture, ceramic dockets and bones, both human and animal. There was a greater number of alabaster fragments from vessels of various sorts, some inscribed and some clearly from canopic jars. There were large numbers of glass inlays from coffins in the form of eyebrows, eye-liners and many eye components of white stone. There were also more serpentine vessel fragments. These appeared initially to be of two colours, green and black. However, subsequent work restoring these vessels was

*Figure 68. Serpentine vessel (SV 202) in the process of being re-assembled. Contiguous pieces from the same vessel are of quite different colours, showing that they were first broken, then scattered, after which some fragments were exposed to fire.*

to demonstrate that the black pieces had been turned black by burning and had once been green *(Figure 68)*.

This burning had taken place subsequent to their being broken as contiguous pieces from the same vessel are of quite different colours. This is consistent with the evidence of the canopic jars, many of which have component pieces of different colours and textures. Pieces of the same vessel were recovered from different shafts and different locations above ground.

Chamber B also contained an unusual number of seals. There were six seals or seal fragments found in this fill. One, of hard grey mud, showed only the impression of the string and linen into which it had been pressed. One, also grey, showed in two halves, the name and title "King of Upper and Lower Egypt, Nebmaatre". The remaining four, all badly burned, were parts of the jackal and nine captives necropolis seal.

Amongst the glass inlays were a badly burned face of red glass (*Figure 69*) and two "n" water-sign inlays of great delicacy. The other glass fragments were principally from inlaid mummy masks similar to those in KV46, the tomb of Yuya and Tuyu *(Figure 70)*.

*Figure 69. Badly burned glass coffin inlay.*

*Figure 70. A selection of glass inlays from various features. They are mostly inlays from coffins and mummy masks but include some fragments of glass bottles.*

Amongst the many glass fragments found in Shaft Four there were many which were burned beyond recognition. Some of the use of fire when the tombs were cleared almost certainly relates to the recovery of gold. We know from the Abbott and Amherst Papyri[1] that tomb robbers set fire to mummies to get at the gold amulets concealed in the wrappings. Gold melts at 1064°C. Glass fragments we recovered have bubbled, showing that they had boiled (*Figure 71*). Glass melts at between 1400°C and 1600°C. This suggests that the fires were well oxygenated. We thought initially that this favoured their location on the surface rather than in the tomb chambers. More recent study of the walls and floors of Chambers B, Ba and Bc in particular suggests that there were very fierce fires in these chambers.

Amongst the surface debris in Chamber B were parts of a cigarette box dating to the

*Figure 71. Fragments of glass inlays which have bubbled in the exceptional heat.*

1950s, adding further evidence of the very long period during which these tombs have been picked over by robbers.

## Chamber Ba

Chamber Ba was the chamber in the tomb which contained the least debris. The little there was had been pushed up out of Chamber B, and possibly Chambers Bb and Bc by robbers looking to tunnel through the debris to the lower chambers.

---

1. Peet, E. (1925) "*Fresh Light on the Tomb Robberies of the Twentieth Dynasty at Thebes*", Journal of Egyptian Archaeology, Volume 11, 1/2 pp. 37-55.

*Figure 72. The entrance to Chamber Ba looking south from Chamber B. Robbers have pushed debris out of Chamber B up into the empty Chamber Ba in order to get access to Chamber Bb (the entrance to which is concealed in the lower centre of the photograph) and to Chamber Bc off to the right.*

*Figure 73. Chamber Ba as found. Apart from debris pushed up into the chamber from below it was clear to floor level.*

## Chamber Bb

By contrast, Chamber Bb was almost completely blocked with debris, with a crawling space cleared through the uppermost layers.

*Figure 74. The entrance to Chamber Bb when first cleared.*

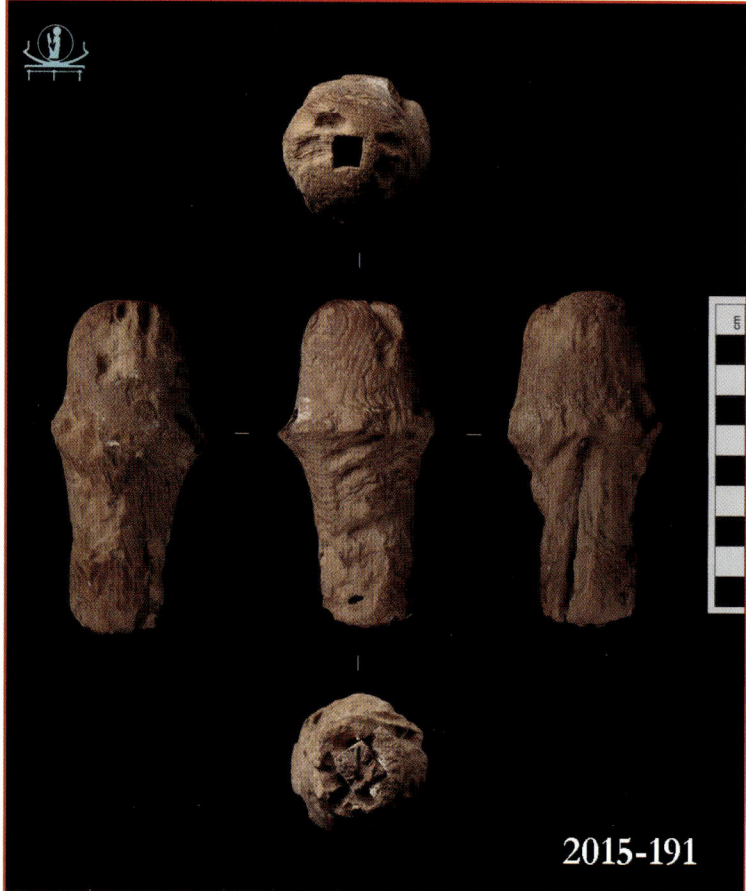

*Figure 75. A composite photograph of the head of the pole of an Anubis fetish.*

It was immediately apparent that the very hard limestone layer which runs through Chamber B, and which had been used as the floor of Ba, was of a convenient thickness to form the ceiling of Chamber Bb. A steep ramp descending from B into Bb may once have been in the form of steps. If they existed they have been eroded by flooding.

Objects in Chamber Bb were dominated by large numbers of wooden fragments and further pieces of limestone canopic jars. The wooden pieces included the knob from the top of an Anubis fetish pole (*Figure 75*) and among the limestone pieces was the base of the same object. There were also ebony wig fragments and glass inlays from coffins, kohl tube sticks, wooden shabti fragments (badly burned), furniture knobs and combs made of bone. Only one human bone was found in this chamber. Six alabaster fragments were recovered from here, five of them inscribed.

Amongst the more intriguing objects found in Bb were the major parts of four small limestone canopic jars and fragments of a canopic jar head (*Figure 76*). Other parts of this assemblage were found in the shaft fill of Shaft Four. One fragment of a jar was recovered from Chamber Bd in Shaft Two.

These small vessels match a piece of limestone canopic jar in the University of Strasbourg Collection originally purchased in 1903 by W. Spiegelberg and bought at the same time as Legrain obtained his purchases for the Cairo Museum. This piece (IES1396) fits perfectly into one of the jars (SV65) and identifies them as having been made for "the King's Son, Menkheperre". A plastic replica of the jar was sent to Strasbourg to confirm this *(Figure 77)*.

*Figure 76. The four reconstructed canopic jars found in Chamber Bb of Shaft Four and Chamber Bd in Shaft Two. The University of Strasbourg fragment 1396 has been digitally added to SV65 (second from the right).*

## Chamber Bc

Once Chamber B was cleared sufficiently for the entrance to Bc to be seen clearly it became apparent that it too, like Bb, had once had a steep ramp or steps cut down into it. There is no trace of the steps today but this may be due to water ingress and to the poor quality of the rock at this level. Whilst the rock layer which forms the floor of

*Figure 77. The Strasbourg fragment fitted into a 3-D print of SV65, thus confirming its provenance (photograph by kind permission of the University of Strasbourg).*

*Figure 78. The state of Chamber Bc when clearance had just started. The perilous state of the ceiling is clearly visible.*

Chamber Ba (and ceiling of Chamber Bb) was relatively stable and had none of the fissures visible in the same layer in Shaft Two, the ceiling of Bc had collaped in places and the dividing wall between the south-west corner of Chamber B and Bc had also fallen in. On top of the fill in the chamber were several large pieces, fifty centimetres cubed, which had fallen from the ceiling. The danger of working in this location proved beneficial for us as it meant that this chamber had not been fully emptied of its inscribed pieces. We were to find some of the most important objects recovered during the mission from under this debris. Foremost among these was an alabaster fragment from a canopic jar (*Figure 79*) bearing the name of Nebetnehet in a cartouche. She is known from only two other objects: the lower portion of a shabti in the British Museum[2] and an alabaster canopic jar fragment in the Petrie Collection at University College London[3] naming her as "the Great Wife of the King, his beloved, Nebetnehet". Another piece recovered here was a small vase or jar with the inscription "The King's True Son, his beloved" (*Figure 80*).

The chamber measured 3m E-W by 3.6m N-S with a ceiling 1.6m high. The last objects were not removed from Chamber Bc until the ceiling had been stabilised. Work moved on to the northern suite of chambers while this was being done.

---

2. British Museum reference: YCA51080/EA54845.
3. UC15808.

*Figure 79. An alabaster fragment of a canopic jar naming a royal woman called Nebetnehet known from a matching piece in University College London to be a Great Wife of the King.*

*Figure 80. Small alabaster vessel found in Chamber Bb with the inscription "The King's True Son, his beloved".*

*Figure 81. The bottom of Shaft Four looking north into Chamber A.*

## Shaft Four - Southern Chambers

### Chamber A

The bottom half of the door sealing from the shaft into Chamber A remained in place and beyond this opened onto a large chamber 4.2m E-W by 5.2m N-S with a ceiling 2.6m in height. The sides of the bottom of the shaft had been plastered. This plaster survived to a height of about a metre.

*Figure 82. Looking north into Chamber A at the time clearance began.*

The room was blocked with debris to a height which concealed completely the entrance the niche A1 on the eastern side and covered most of the door into Chamber Aa to the north.

*Figure 83. Looking south from Chamber A to the shaft and partially intact blocking. Figure 81 shows the other side of this blocking.*

*Figure 84. A very nearly complete canopic jar inscription naming the King's Ornament Mutnofret, found in Chamber A. It retains not only the inlaid colour but also the black marks made by the scribe outlining the text before it was cut into the vessel surface.*

## Niche A1

The niche in the eastern wall of Chamber A measures 1.2m by 1m and 1.15m deep. On the left hand side there is a robber's hole through into Niche A2 of Chamber A in Shaft two. This is 1.08m high and 48cms wide.

*Figure 85. Chamber A post-clearance with large stones from the original blocking lying in the chamber and Chamber Aa beyond.*

## Chamber Aa

Chamber Aa is an asymmetrical chamber which veers distinctly to the right (east). The entrance is cut low in the middle of the northern wall of Chamber A but the western wall of Chamber Aa runs north straight from the left-hand (western) door jamb. The eastern wall is 1.3m from the door. The chamber is 1.57m high, 3.2m N-S by 2.45m E-W.

*Figure 86. The entrance to Chamber Aa. Large stones from the blocking had been pushed into this chamber by intruders.*

It was largely filled with the same rubble fill as Chamber A but, interestingly there were very few finds discovered here. There were no canopic jar fragments and only a single fragment of an alabaster vessel, two pieces of linen, a ceramic sherd tool, some faience fragments and one wooden fragment.

## CLEARANCE OF SHAFT SHAFT SEVEN

Found under the spoil-heaps and measuring 1.25m N-S by 2.75m E-W it was initially hoped this might be the shaft of an additional tomb. There were always doubts about its depth as the opening lies directly over Niche Ba1 of Shaft Five. It turned out to be a mere 1.1m deep. The edges show signs of having been sealed at one time with a gypsum and aggregate mix, similar to that which sealed the other shafts (*Figure 89*).

This suggests there was something inside it which needed preservation and protection. What this might have been is open to question. The situation of the shaft and its shallow depth suggest a foundation deposit rather than a burial. If there was a burial here it was of a perfunctory nature. Against the idea of this being a foundation deposit is the fact that no cultural material of any sort was found in it. Foundation deposit material was of no value to those who cleared the tombs. As this shaft had lain undisturbed under the spoil-heaps since ancient times it is difficult to understand what might have happened to the remains of such a deposit. However, we have found some small dishes which are characteristic of such a deposit. A further possibility it that it was an embalming cache. Mud-sealing material (2015-619) very similar to that found in the embalming cache of Tutankhamun (KV54) was found in the WB1 spoil-heaps (*see Figure 382 below*).

Shaft Seven was filled entirely with secondary debris, its orignal contents having been completely removed.

*Figure 87. Shaft Seven as found during the clearance of the spoil-heap debris.*

*Figure 88. Shaft Seven when emptied looking south. The mounds on the southern side may be the spoil from its original creation.*

*Figure 89. Traces of the gypsum and aggregate sealing on the eastern end of Shaft Seven.*

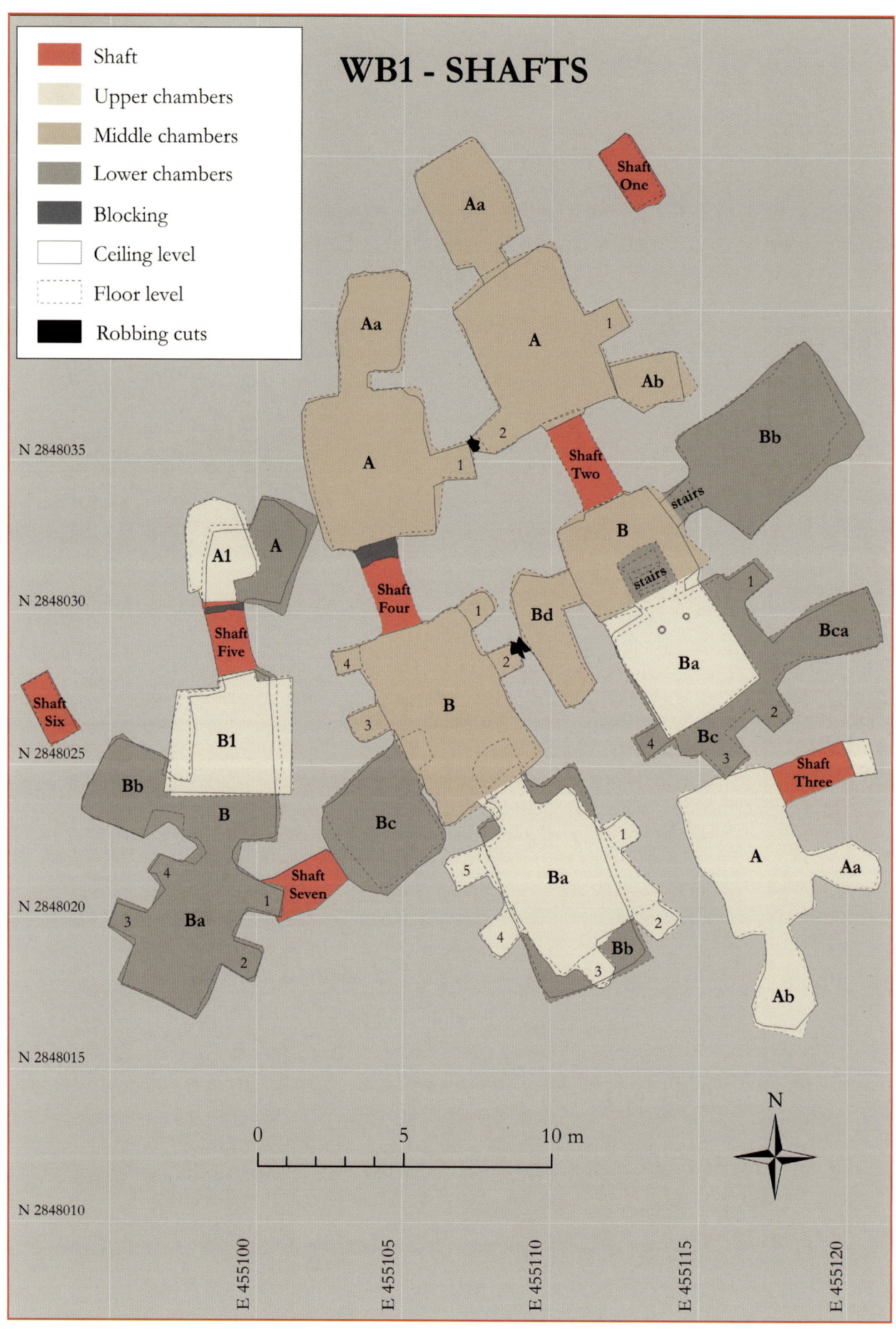

*Figure 90. A plan of all the shafts showing the location of Shaft Seven above Niche Ba1 in Shaft Five.*

# CHAPTER FOUR
## ARCHITECTURE

The architecture of the WB1 shaft tombs is exceptional in several respects. The tombs are single structures but, unlike the tombs which exist in larger burial grounds, they form a single closely-grouped unit. The tombs appear to have been enlarged more than once and the rooms re-arranged. The three more complex tombs have chambers off both the narrow ends of the shaft and the two larger tombs have chambers on three different levels within the southern suites. There are no other known tombs which share these complexities.

From the enlargement and re-design of the tombs it is clear that the burials were re-opened and the burials inside them moved and added to. The human remains suggest these were family tombs. Questions have arisen previously about whether or not multiple burials contained groups of people who all died at the same time, or whether they were re-opened and added to. The differing styles of grave goods in the WB1 shaft tombs, the differing ages of those buried there and the architectural changes all point, in the case of this burial ground, to the same tombs being re-used for family burials and to individuals being added to the tombs as they died.

The tombs are as close together as it is possible to be. The distance between the adjacent chambers of neighbouring tombs underground is mostly within 2m. Shaft Five is at an angle which places its northern Chamber A within just twenty centimetres of Chamber A in Shaft Four. Its southern chambers bend away sharply and the south-eastern corner of Shaft Four's Chamber Ba is some twenty-two metres from the south-western corner of Shaft Four's Bb.

When we first explored the tombs we wondered if they were not part of a single structure. Quickly it became apparent that the connections between the tombs were made by robbers not by the original architects or builders.

In the Valley of the Queens there are several shaft tombs which have multiple chambers and four which have chambers off the shaft in different directions (QV4, QV62, QV63, QV69) (see *Figure 91*). However, there are no other shaft tombs of the XVIIIth dynasty which have:

- chambers off both ends of the shaft (Shafts Two, Four and Five);
- multiple chambers off both ends of the shafts (Shafts Two, Four and Five);
- chambers on multiple levels - three in the case of Shafts Two and Four and two in the case of Shaft Five.

These tombs are, therefore, uniquely complex. They are also the first non-kingly tombs to include steps. Later XIXth dynasty tombs created for royal wives, such as the tomb of Nefertari, share this feature and it is tempting to make comparisons between their multi-chambered tombs and the WB1 shaft tombs. However much the plans may resemble one another it is very clear that the XIXth dynasty monuments were created for one

---

1. This distance was so great and the angle at which these southern chambers in Shaft Five veer away from their neighbour so dramatic that we were convinced that there must be another structure below the surface which Shaft Five was trying to avoid.
2. Thomas, E., (1966) op. cit. and Leblanc, C. (1989) "*Architecture et évolution chronologique des tombes de la Vallée des Reines*", BIFAO 89 pp. 227-247
3. Schmidt, H. and Willeitner, J. (1994) "*Nefertari: Gemahlin Ramses II*", Verlag Philipp von Zabern, Mainz am Rhein. pp. 106-7.

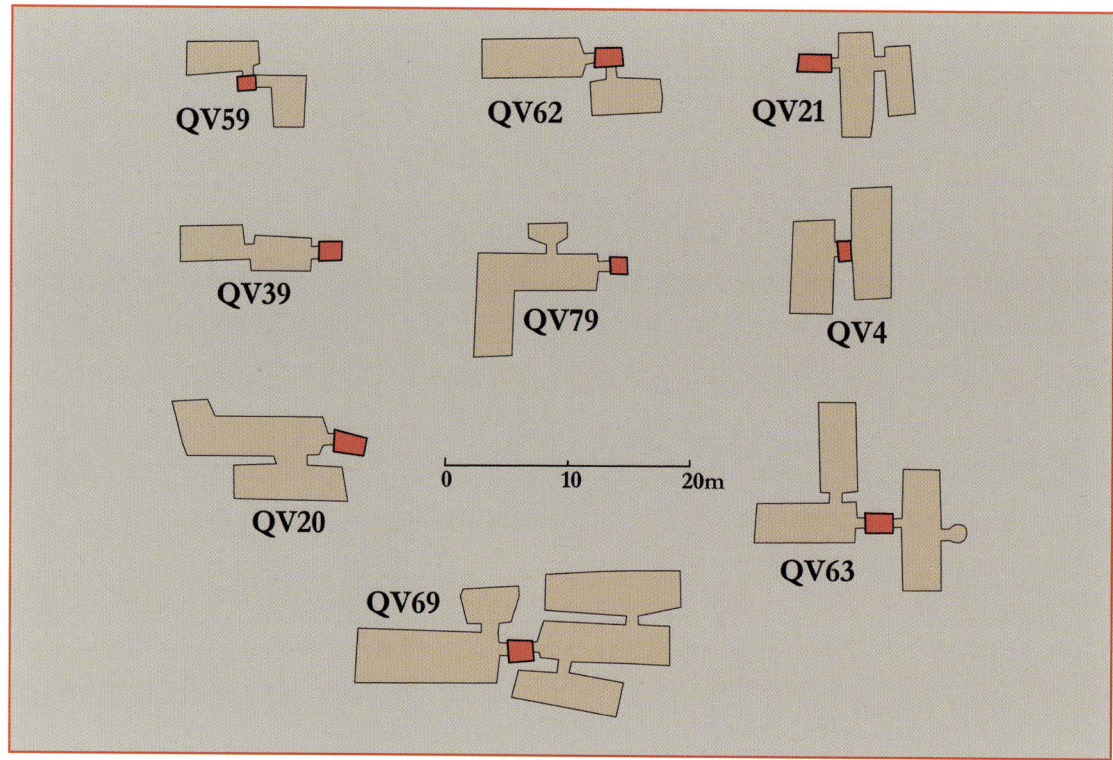

*Figure 91. The early tombs in the "Valley of the Queens" which have multiple chambers off different faces of the shafts (adapted from Leblanc, C. (1989) op. cit.)*

person. All the evidence we have collected from the WB1 shaft tombs suggests that their size and complexity is due to their having been enlarged in several construction phases to cater for more than one individual. Since evidence from the human remains points to these people having all been closely related they can fairly be described as family tombs.

Another difference between the WB1 tombs and the later XIXth dynasty tombs for members of the royal family is decoration. We have found extensive traces of mud plaster and, in the case of Shaft Four, finer gypsum plaster. In the case of Shaft Four's Chambers B and Ba the white plaster has turned black. There has been some debate about this black colour. Close examination reveals a very fine coating which in places is present with definite straight lines suggesting paint. However, it now seems clear that this blackening is the result of the burning of furniture coated with unguents which have evaporated in the heat.

Elsewhere in the WB1 shaft tombs the mud plaster is painted white. There is no surviving trace of any wall painting or other decoration.

The rock into which the WB1 shaft tombs were cut is of very poor quality. The opportunities offered by this rock and by the more stable layers in particular will have dictated much of the final architectural design.

The limestone of the Valley of the Kings, where the masons will have done much of their work, flakes fairly consistently once fractured with pounders. The vast numbers of thin flakes with percussion marks from chisels which can be found all over the Valley of the Kings are testament to a methodical process of first cracking the rock to open up fissures and then using a chisel to loosen and separate the flakes. Work there took

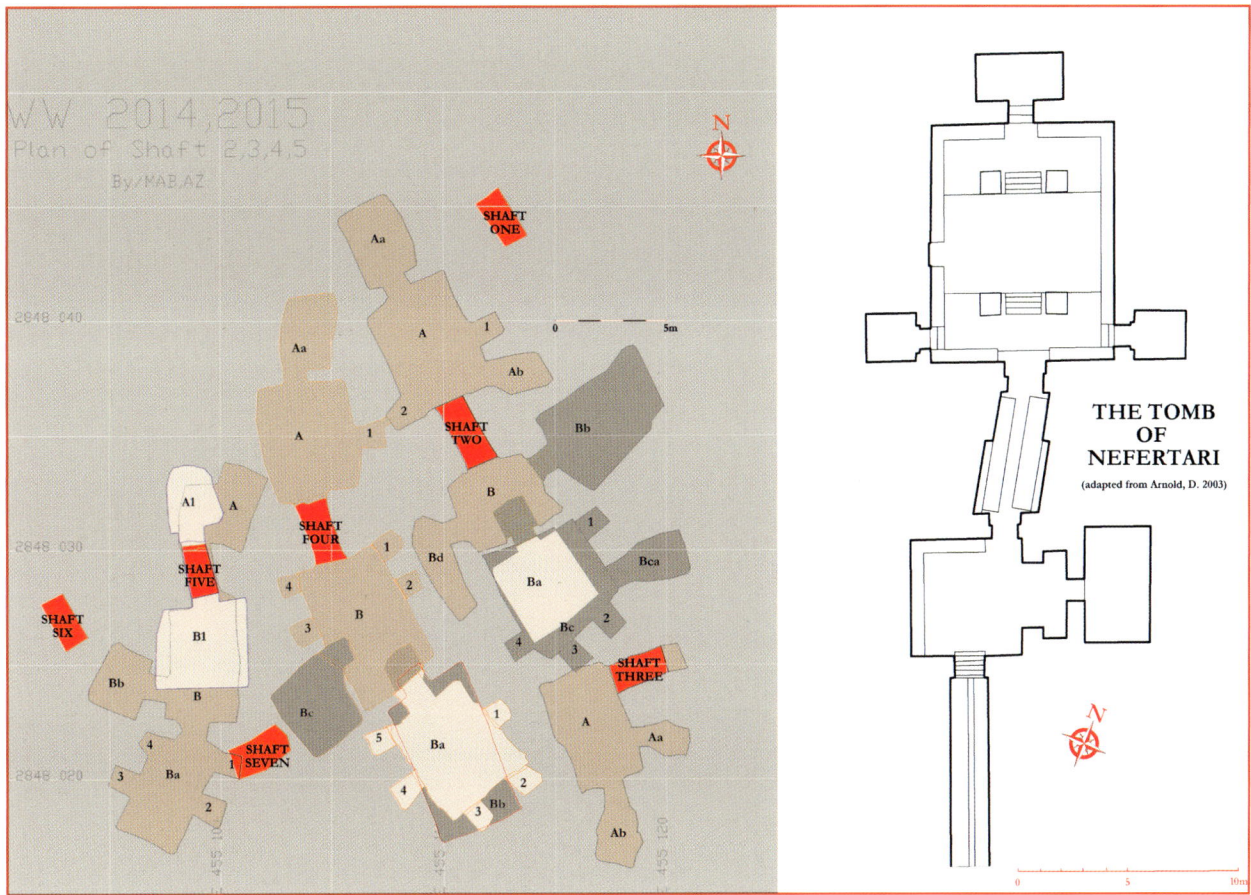

*Figure 92. The WB1 shaft tombs, left, compared with the tomb of Nefertari very roughly to the same scale (Source: Arnold, D. Encyclopaedia of Egyptian Architecture p. 161).*

place from top to bottom and usually with two gangs working side by-side, one on the left, one on the right[4]. Flakes were loaded into baskets which were then emptied outside the tomb mouths. The debris in the Valley of the Kings is uniform in nature because the limestone occurs in beds which in places are in excess of 50m thick. The limestone layers are for the most part of a fairly similar consistency, although occasional bands of schist and rows of flints complicate the subterranean matrix.

The rock on the WB1 site could not be more different. A glance at the cliffs (*Figure 93*) which form the north perimeter of the site shows the very clear stratigraphy which the ancient masons had to penetrate. Whilst the harder layers offer opportunities for the creation of floors and ceilings, they are neither uniformly horizontal nor uniform in thickness. This may account for some of the marked differences in ceiling heights in the various WB1 tombs.

At the top of the strata is a layer of conglomerate consisting of rounded pebbles held together by a matrix of light brown rock which varies in consistency. This layer erodes easily as can be seen at the shaft mouths where the edges of the shafts have long been lost, worn down by water ingress and material falling back into the shafts. Beneath this conglomerate layer is a layer of relatively thick rock of variable quality which sits above

---

4. Hornung, E. (1982) "*Tal der Könige*", Artemis Verlag, Zurich and Munich, Chapter Three.

a more stable limestone band. It is this band which is visible at the bottom of the shafts and results in the best-defined sections of the shafts. Its bottom forms the ceilings of the larger chambers in Shaft Two and Shaft Four.

Beneath that layer is a layer of friable stone fairly easily chipped out in hand-sized blocks. It is this layer which has produced most of the chambers. However, the larger chambers have in some cases had to cut through harder layers in order to achieve horizontal floors since the hard layers themselves undulate, in places narrowing the available space dramatically as will be seen in the case of Chamber A in Shaft Four.

*Figure 93. The cliffs forming the northern perimeter of the WB1 site. The conglomerate layer is visible at the top, resting on the first of a series of limestone layers interspersed with more friable layers.*

## THE ARCHITECTURAL DEVELOPMENT PHASES OF SHAFT THREE

The simplest of the tombs is Shaft Three. Situated on flat ground it is the tomb least liable to flooding from the northern slopes which affected the other tombs.

Shaft Three resembles the standard shaft tomb of the XVIIIth dynasty as found in the Valley of the Kings (cf KV48[5]). It has a shaft 7.95m deep and which is 1.4m wide and

---

5. Weeks, K. ed. (2005) "*Atlas of the Valley of the Kings: Study Edition*", American University in Cairo Press, Cairo p. 116.

2.62m long. Off the western end of the shaft (which is the only shaft apart from Shaft Seven oriented longitudinally east-west) there is a single chamber which shows signs of having been enlarged in at least one additional phase. The current size of the chamber is 3.4m E-W by 5.8m N-S. The ceiling height is 1.7m. It would appear that the tomb originally consisted in a single chamber 3.4m E-W and 3.3m approximately N-S.

The principle evidence for this enlargement is the preservation in the line of the western wall of Chamber A of a change in angle. This now presents itself as a vertical ridge (*Figures 95 and 96*) marking the point at which the wall would have turned east along the dotted line E-E demarcating Phase One in Figure 95. There is no marked change in the plastering, however (*Figure 96*). The plastering of this tomb preserves evidence of blackening by fire (*Figure 97*). The few human remains retrieved from this shaft were badly burned.

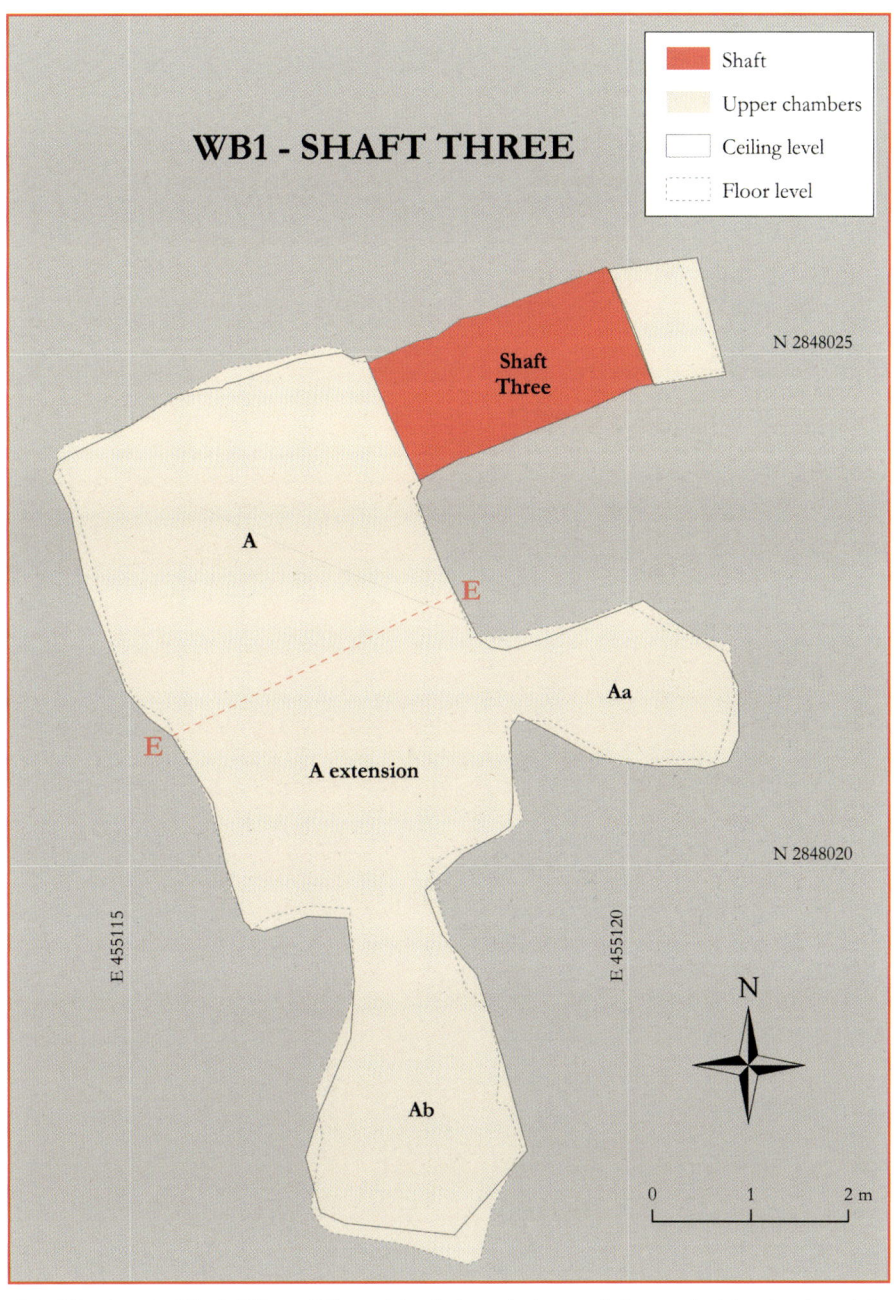

*Figure 94. Phasing in Shaft Three. The original size of the tomb is marked by the dotted line E-E.*

*Figure 95. Chamber A in Shaft Three. On the left the protrusion from the line of the wall marks the point at which the orginal southern wall of the chamber ran from east to west.*

*Figure 96. Looking south from the first phase of Chamber A into the extended area and the two storerooms. In the case of Ab, straight ahead, it is clear that a full-length door was envisaged giving onto a chamber with the same height as Chamber A.*

*Figure 97. Blackening apparent on the walls in Chamber A.*

*Figure 98. The shaft of Shaft Three looking east. It looks as though there may have been plans either to add rooms at a lower level or to lower the floor of Chamber A.*

It is less clear whether Chambers Aa and Ab were part of phases separate to Phase Two. The doorway into Chamber Ab (*see Figure 96*) is the full height of Chamber A and this suggests that a chamber and not a niche was intended. This room has all the appearance of an incomplete second chamber. Chamber Aa is less worked by contrast but here too there is a suggestion from the way the stone is being removed from top to bottom that a full chamber and not just a niche was envisaged. That these chambers were not completed is notable in the light of the other incomplete tombs on the WB1 site and incomplete work in the shaft of Shaft Three.

In the shaft of Shaft Three (*see Figure 98*) it looks as though there may have been plans to add rooms off the eastern end of the shaft and indeed possibly to deepen the shaft. The undermining of the hard layer at the eastern end of the shaft may simply have been the working method chosen by the masons to remove these hard layers. Once isolated from above and below large blocks could be broken off as has been done in Shafts Two and Four. Why this work-in-progress was abandoned is unclear. It is clear that, despite being the simplest tomb in design terms, Shaft Three was also incomplete.

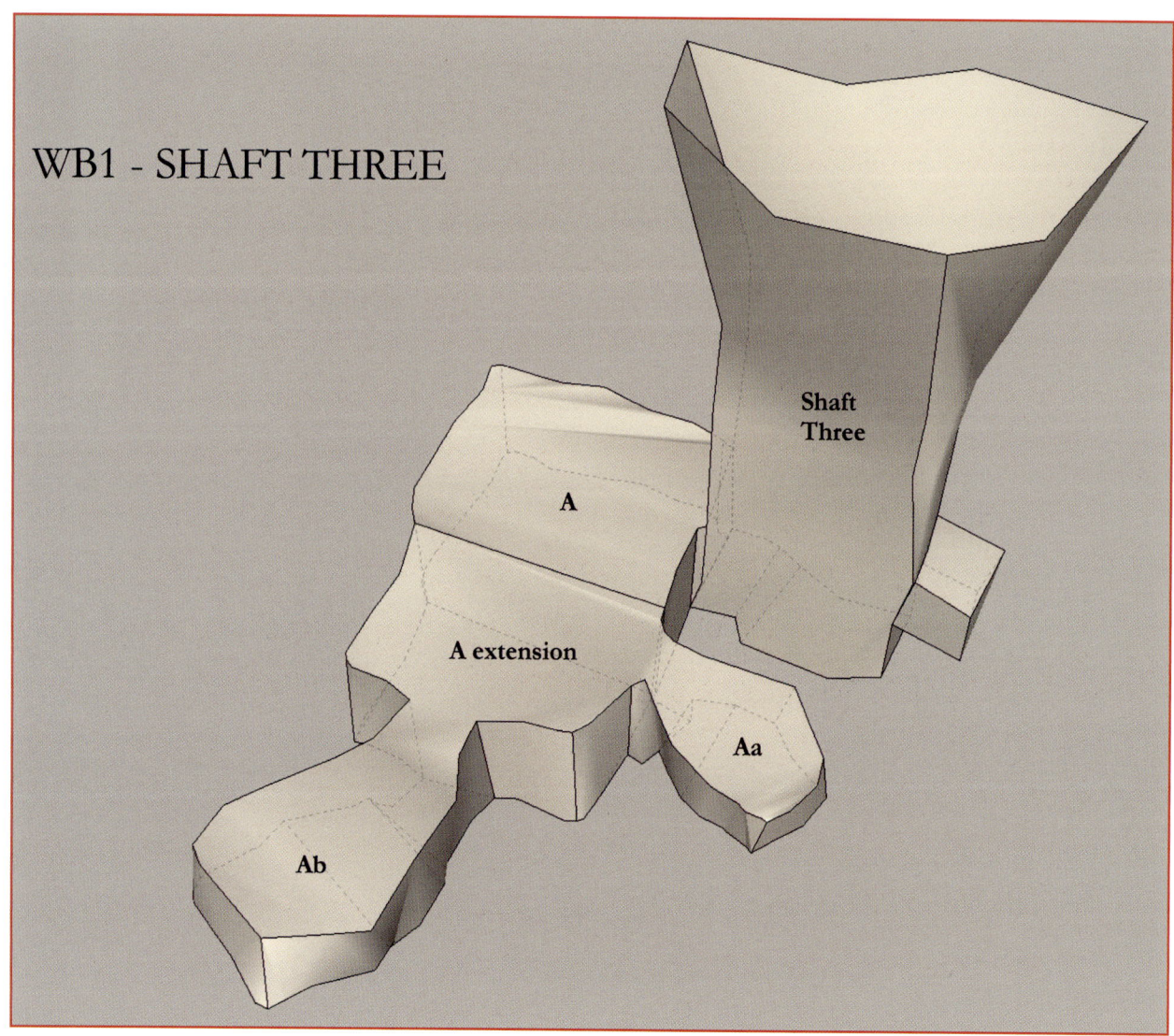

*Figure 99. A three-dimensional view of Shaft Three looking north.*

# THE ARCHITECTURAL DEVELOPMENT PHASES OF SHAFT TWO

Shaft Two is very much more complex than Shaft Three. It is situated at the eastern end of a row of four shaft openings extending to the west and oriented longitudinally approximately north-south. It is the most complex of the tombs with a total of nine chambers on three levels (*Figure 113*).

## The southern chambers

It looks as though Shaft Two may also have begun with a single chamber. Chamber B retains traces of its possible original dimensions: 3.8m E-W by 3.4m N-S. There are other signs too in the height of the shaft at the central point (*Figure 100*). The bottom of

*Figure 100. The original depth of Shaft Two is visible here in the centre of the shaft. This may relate both to an original floor higher and original ceiling lower than at present in Chamber B (on the far side of the shaft in this photograph).*

the shaft in Shaft Two shows the original depth of the shaft as it may have related to the single chamber B).

Chamber B could have had a number of niches, now converted into doors, or lost in the enlargement of the chamber. It is particularly difficult to see where these might have been since the ceiling has been raised and the floor lowered. The south-eastern corner of this chamber has what looks like the beginning of a low door or the remains of a niche in the eastern wall (*Figure 101*). The overall chamber is now an impressive near-cube of an antechamber 3.16m E-W, 3.8m N-S and 3.16m high.

At some stage this putative niched chamber, Chamber B, was moved forward and downwards with access via steps. Chamber Bc is therefore part of a later phase but where it fits into the sequence is less clear.

Chamber Ba, above Chamber Bc, was possibly intended to be the original location of Chamber Ba. In Shaft Four, B was moved up, not down, and the same layer which forms the ceiling of Chamber Bc in Shaft Two (and Chamber Bb in Shaft Four) was clearly intended to form the floor of Chamber Ba in Shaft Two (*Figures 101 and 102*). However, this layer in Shaft Two is fractured. A deep structurally dangerous crack runs from the middle of what is now the door to Chamber Bc southwards (*Figure 102*). This vertical fissure cuts right through the layer of rock and the matrix which has been partially cut away above. It is also visible in repairs which have been made to the ceiling of this incomplete chamber.

In Shaft Four's Chamber Ba this matrix has been completely cut away, leaving a thinner, hard layer which forms the floor of Chamber Ba and the ceiling of Chamber Bb. This layer appears uniform. The success of this architectural use of this layer in Shaft Four may mean that Chamber Ba in Shaft Four pre-dates the failed experiment with Ba in Shaft Two.

*Figure 101. The eastern side of Chamber B in Shaft Two showing the cavity just above the scale which is either the remains of a former niche or the beginning of an abandoned door.*

*Figure 102. Looking south in Chamber B of Shaft Two. The hard layer which forms the ceiling of Chamber Bc with the obvious vertical fracture and the repairs to the ceiling of Chamber Ba visible above.*

The sides of the doorway into Chamber Bc in Shaft Two have been built up using blocks cut from the layer above - a good example of materials to hand being put to practical use in shoring up the potentially unstable ceiling of Bc.

Chamber Bc contains four niches. Three of these (1, 2 and 3) are raised off the ground whilst a fourth reaches the floor, looking as though a door to a new chamber may have been contemplated at this point. A fifth niche, also raised off the ground has been enlarged into a small chamber in which, as noted above (p. 28), some children's bones were found. Chamber Bc is similar in overall design to Chamber Ba in Shaft Four but just as Chamber B in Shaft Four is longer than Chamber B in Shaft Two, so too Chamber Bc in Shaft Two is of similar, squarer dimensions to Chamber B in the same tomb. What this says about the relative importance of the occupants of these chambers is unclear. It is tempting to consider larger chambers the burials of more important individuals. Whether the niched chambers are burial-chambers is by no means certain and the utter confusion of the objects in the intrusive debris is no help in clarifying their function.

The niches are all badly eroded by water and only patchy traces of plastering survive. This plastering is of brown mud painted with a white lime-wash which has in places turned yellow.

The creation of Chamber Bb may result from the failure of Chamber Ba overhead to be developed into a larger and higher chamber. Chamber Bb is a large room, approached by steps leading off Chamber B. There is reason to believe that it was originally roughly 4m N-S by 4m E-W., the current E-W measurement of 5.7m being the result of a collapse

*Figure 103. The same view looking south in Chamber B of Shaft Four showing the successful use of the same layer as shown in Figure 102.*

*Figure 104. Chamber Bc looking north towards Chamber B and the shaft beyond.*

*Figure 105. Chamber Bc looking south with the Bc4 niche reaching to the floor on the right, the Bc2 and Bc3 niches straight ahead and the entrance to Chamber Bca, above floor level, to the left.*

*Figure 106. The eastern end of Chamber Bb looking east. The scale is laid across the point which may mark the original extent of the chamber, the area beyond it possibly having been eroded by water ingress.*

in the eastern wall. There is a line of plaster down the northern and southern sides of this chamber, and a mark across the ceiling which would support this view. The rock at the eastern end is extremely friable and we found a larger than usual amount of debris at this end suggesting that the enlargment of this room may have been the result of the eastern wall collapsing following the ingress of floodwater. Cracks in the ceiling have been extensively repaired with hard, grey plaster *(Figure 107)*.

The walls of Chamber B showed the remains of mud plaster in varying states of preservation. In places it was possible to see that this had been painted with a white limewash, in other places, and particularly at the levels where water had flowed into the chamber, there was no extant plaster at all. Changes in the type of plaster provided the first suggestions of multiple phases in the development of the tombs which became clearer once the chambers were completely cleared. However, the cutting through the spoil-heaps above Shaft Two from Shaft One demonstrates how much water flowed into Shaft Two. This water would have been highly destructive and so definitive judgements about the condition of the plaster are not possible.

*Figure 107. Chamber Bb looking west towards Chamber B with the entrance to Bd visible beyond. The poor quality of the rock is clearly visible especially on the right.*

A tentative conclusion about this southern suite of rooms would see Chamber B as an antechamber and Chamber Bc as the principal burial chamber containing perhaps the additional burial of a child or several children in Bca. Chamber Bb is probably a burial chamber for an important but, lacking niches, less senior individual than the occupant of Chamber Bc. The ultimate function of Ba remains obscure but it may have contained storage jars, as Bd certainly did. Equally it is just high enough to accommodate smaller coffins but not sarcophagi.

Chamber Bd is an irregular, narrow room with a pronounced slope in the ceiling from north to south. The southern door-jamb is built up of blocks of the same type as those which form the northern wall of Chamber Bc. Chamber Bd measures 4.65m N-S by only 1.35m E-W. The ceiling is 1.8m at it highest point just inside the door to Chamber B but only 1m high at the southern end. Opposite the door from Chamber B in the western wall of Bd there is a small, irregular robber's hole some 40cms wide by 50cms high at a height of 80cms above the chamber floor. This connects to Niche B2 in Shaft Four.

*Figure 108. Chamber Bd looking south. The robber's hole through to Shaft Four's B2 niche is on the upper right. This small chamber contained large quantities of white-painted storage jar sherds.*

## The northern chambers

The northern suite of rooms in Shaft Two consists of three chambers and two niches. Chamber A is another large chamber created with great effort by cutting through a hard layer of limestone in order to give it additional height. Whether, as in the case of Chamber B, this was because it was originally smaller and was extended is a moot point. Here again cracks in the ceiling have been repaired with very hard, grey plaster or cement *(Figure 109)*.

*Figure 109. Chamber A in Shaft Two looking north to Chamber Aa. Visible as a line on the side walls descending in height is the hard layer of limestone the masons have cut through arduously to raise the ceiling height. To the right is Niche A1.*

*Figure 110. The east wall of Chamber A showing Niche A1 and storeroom Ab (to the right). Clearly visible here is descending layer of hard limestone sloping from right to left. This is somewhat exaggerated by the raking lines of staining on the wall showing the angle at which wet debris entered the tomb in various flooding episodes.es.*

*Figure 111. The interior of Chamber Aa in Shaft Two looking north.*

*Figure 112. The interior of Chamber Aa looking south towards the shaft. Thick mud plaster survives on the walls of the chamber with faint traces of white paint.*

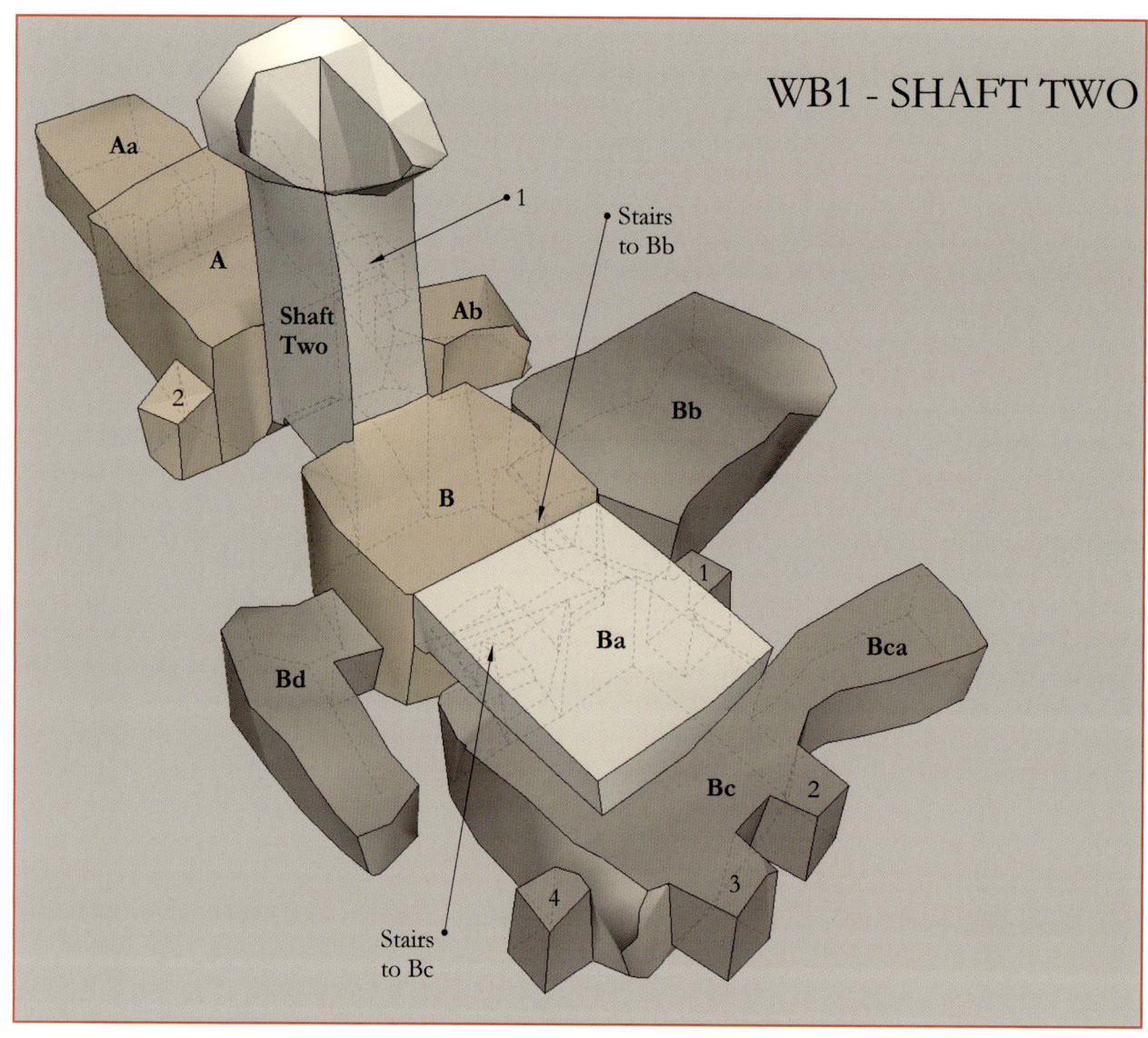

*Figure 113. A three-dimensional view of Shaft Two looking north.*

## THE ARCHITECTURAL DEVELOPMENT PHASES OF SHAFT FIVE

Shaft Five presents very different architecture to Shaft Two. In Shaft Two (and later in Shaft Four) we see a full development of northern and southern suites of rooms with several possible burial chambers in the southern suite of rooms and at least one to the north. We see chambers on three different levels.

In the case of Shaft Five there are chambers to north and south but the chambers on different levels are separated, and do not share the same entrance from the shaft. This is so evidently the case that the lower suite of rooms in Shaft Five was never re-opened by modern robbers who believed, as we did initially, that Chambers A1 and B1 were the only constituent parts of the tomb.

The shaft in Shaft Five is slightly smaller (1.3m by 2.8m) than that of its neighbours to the east. The plastering of the shaft is particularly well-preserved. The other WB1 tomb shafts were plastered but less of the plaster survives. The fact that the shafts were plastered suggests that the shafts were left open between burials. Had the shafts been filled with rubble each time a new burial was added the plasterwork would have been

*Figure 114. The shaft of Shaft Five looking north. Above is the clearly unfinished Chamber A1 (0.8m in height). Below, with much of the plaster intact on the walls of the shaft and with part of the original blocking still in place, the entrance to Chamber A (1.5m in height).*

damaged repeatedly by the insertion and removal of the rubble fill. There are no signs of repairs to damaged plaster.

It is possible that Shaft Five represents an intermediate stage in the development of more complex tombs like Shafts Two and Four. The upper chambers of Shaft Five are at the same height as the ceilings of Chambers A and B in both Shafts Two and Four. The lower chambers of Shaft Five are at a similar level to the floors of Chambers A and B in Shafts Two and Four.

*Figure 115. Looking south in the shaft of Shaft Five. The entrance to Chamber B (1.6m in height) is straight ahead and above it is the entrance to Chamber B1 (0.9m in height).*

However, there are difficulties with this solution. The first is the fact that the bottom of the shafts in both Shaft Two and Shaft Four seems to preserve an earlier floor level relating to the original state of their respective Chambers B. The second is that for there to be two levels of rooms both sets of rooms would have very low ceilings. In the case of Shaft Five the low ceilings are the result of incomplete work, certainly in the case of A1 and B1.

Interestingly the space between the hard layers of limestone also narrows as the site progresses west. It may well be that the rock forced low ceilings on the workmen, especially if they were working to a deadline.

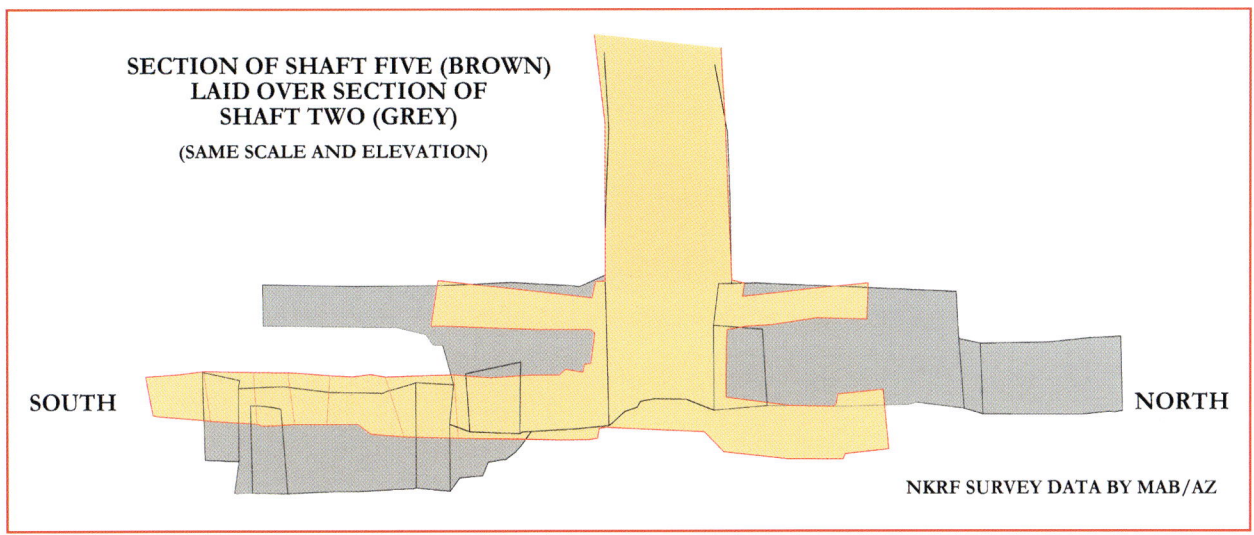

*Figure 116. Section looking east of Shaft Two laid over a similar section of Shaft Five to the same scale.*

## The lower southern chambers

It is possible that Shaft Five also started life as a shaft with a single chamber at the bottom but there is no evidence in the plastering or architecture to support this. Chamber B in Shaft Five is now 5.7m N-S, 3.1m E-W and 1.6m in height. Chamber Bb opens off Chamber B to the west and measures 3m N-S, 2.3m E-W and 1.15m in height. It is possible that Chamber Bb and Ba are additions as their ceiling heights are notably lower.

Chamber Ba is 5.05m N-S, 3.1m E-W and 1.2m in height. We believe this to have been a burial chamber but why it should have had a ceiling so much lower than the niched chambers in Shafts Two and Four is a puzzle. Perhaps this is additional evidence of haste in the completion of a particular burial.

*Figure 117. Chamber B looking south towards Chamber Ba.*

*Figure 118. Chamber Ba looking south. The uneven state of the floor may indicate that it is unfinished.*

## The upper southern chamber

It is difficult not to be struck by the similarity between Shaft Five's Chamber B1 and Shaft Two's Chamber Ba. They are of similar breadth and width and, more strikingly of similar heights. Both rooms are incomplete although they show some precision in their lateral dimensions. B1 is 3.75m N-S, 4.45m E-W and 0.9-1.2m in height (cf Chamber Ba in Shaft Two: 4.25m N-S, 3.6m E-W and 1.1m in height). The walls were plastered.

*Figure 119. Chamber B1 looking south.*

*Figure 120. Chamber A1 looking north. The floor was clearly still incomplete when work was stopped.*

## The northern lower chamber

Chamber A seems to have been left incomplete. To the north-east an extension was in the process of being excavated (and there are clear chisel marks on the wall) but may have been abandoned when it came too close to Shaft Four's Chamber A (within 20cms). The chamber is therefore L-shaped. At its longest N-S its eastern side is 3.5m.

*Figure 121. Chamber A looking north. The abandoned extension veers right (east) towards Chamber A in Shaft Four with which it collides.*

The shorter western wall is 2.45m N-S. The southern wall, broken by the entrance to the shaft, is 3.3m E-W. The shorter, northern wall is 2.1m E-W. Patches of mud-plaster in here are particularly well-preserved and were coated with a white lime-wash.

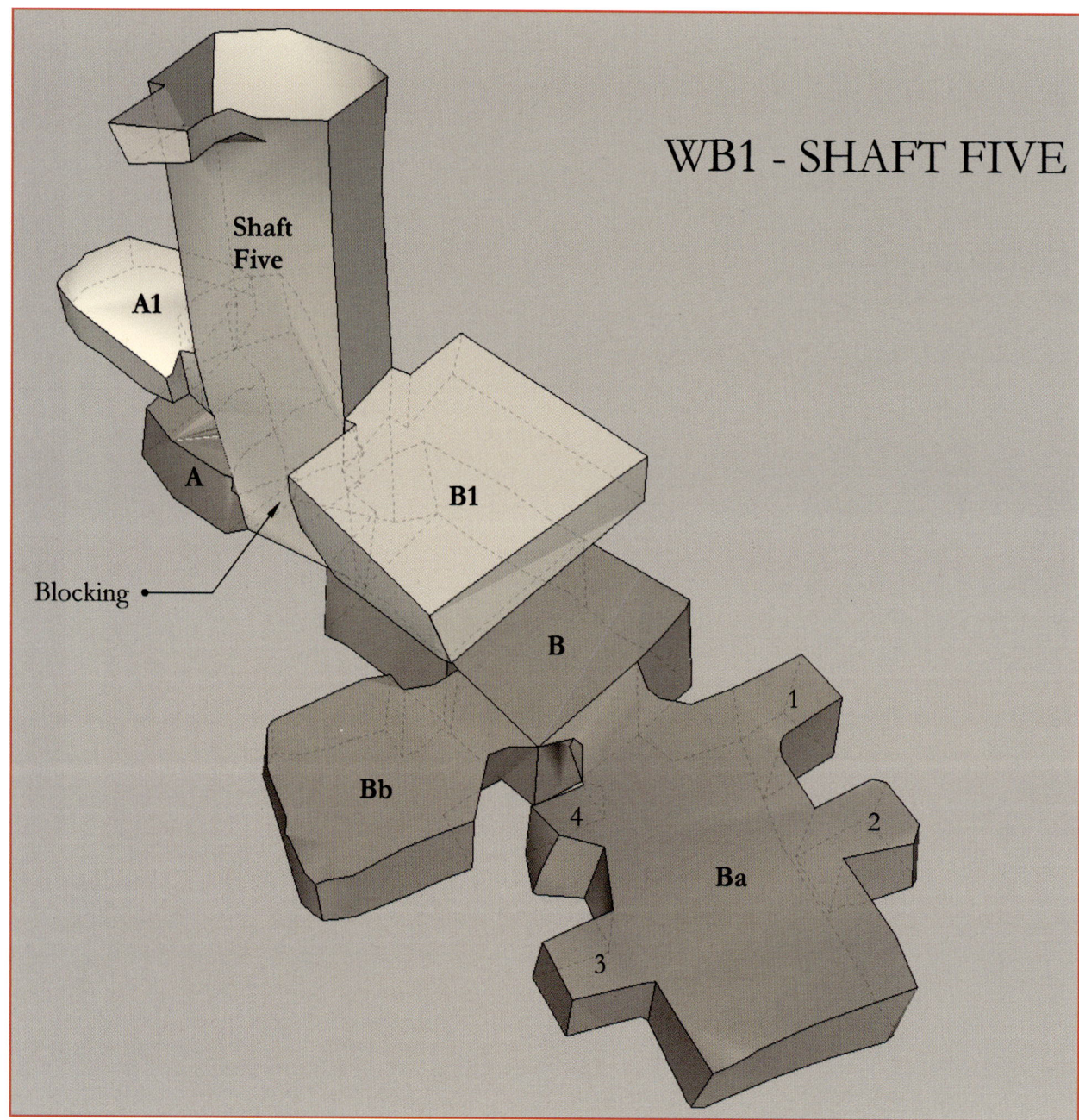

*Figure 122. A three-dimensional view of Shaft Five looking north.*

## The upper northern chamber

Chamber A1 *(Figure 120)*, to the north of the shaft, is very different to B1. Like B1 it has a low ceiling but there is clear evidence here in its irregular form and in the worked floor that it was in the process of being constructed when it was abandoned. It measures 3.1m at its widest N-S and 2.3m E-W with a ceiling 0.8-1.0m. The walls are plastered.

# THE ARCHITECTURAL DEVELOPMENT PHASES OF SHAFT FOUR

Shaft Four has fewer chambers than Shaft Two but the dimensions of the major rooms, their niching and the high standard of plastering all suggest that this was the highest status tomb on the site. The chambers appear more regular but this may be because of the better plastering (gypsum in the case of the northern part of Chamber B) and because more of this plaster has resisted water damage which has badly affected the mud plaster in other shafts.

Shaft Four was protected from water damage by the spoil-heaps to the north of the shaft. These diverted water running down the slope to the north to the east into Shafts One and Two and to the west into Shafts Six and Five. Shafts Two and Five therefore took in the greatest share of any local flooding to the benefit of Shaft Four.

*Figure 123. Niche B4 in Shaft Four looking west. At the bottom of the niche the white gypsum plaster is clearly visible covering the floor of the niche. The blackening stops short of the floor of the niche in both the centre and the left of the photograph.*

## The southern chambers

As with Shaft Two, it seems possible that Chamber B started life as the only chamber at the bottom of a slightly shallower shaft. An initial chamber reaching just south of niches B2 and B3 would have produced a chamber very similar in E-W (4m) and N-S (3.2m) dimensions to the first stage we envisage for Chamber B in Shaft Two (3.8 E-W by 3.4m N-S). There is a change in the type of plastering at this point. Black colour lies over a thick layer of white gypsum plaster which extends just beyond an E-W line from Niche B2 to Niche B3. Beyond that line Chamber B and Chamber Ba the black colour is on top of brown mud plaster.

Four niches survive in Chamber B, all between 80cms high, 1m wide and 1m deep. They are all approximately 70cms above floor level. The subsequent extension of Chamber B created its present length (N-S) of 6.5m with a ceiling height of 2.46m. This extension would have had to be prior to the creation of Ba, Bb and Bc. In what order they were established is not clear but it seems logical that Chamber Ba was completed before Bb. Accessing Ba would have been difficult once the ramp or stairs down to Bb were cut (the door into Ba currently 'floats' over 80cms above the floor of Chamber B immediately above the stairs or ramp down into Bb. Chamber B and Ba both contain niches, there being five in Chamber Ba.

There has been debate about whether or not these chambers were painted black, burned black by fire or have turned black due to a chemical reaction in the rock. Attribution to fire would be the more comfortable explanation because fire is often set in tombs and there is abundant evidence of burned objects on the WB1 site.

*Figure 124. Fragments of gypsum plaster from Chamber B in Shaft 4 showing the thickness of the plaster and the use of potsherds to fill in the larger irregularities.*

*Figure 125. An enlargement of a section cut through a fragment of the Chamber B gypsum plaster showing that the black colour has a definite thickness.*

However, fire tends not to leave the very clearly delineated lines visible in *Figure 123* above. The explanation that the white areas below were covered with debris is plausible but the divisions show no signs of fuzziness or blurring. They are definite. Close examination of Niche 1 in Chamber B has shown that the very clear white line here was caused by a pile of white gypsum plaster placed on top of the pre-existing plaster floor of the niche. This pile of plaster was presumably being used to continue plastering the room when it was left in place. Subsequent changes in the tomb caused this pile of plaster to dry out and become friable so that it lost it integrity.

The change in composition in the plaster is an additional factor supportive of there having been a fire in this chamber. A careful re-cleaning of the tomb floors and walls has revealed signs of burning in three of the southern suite of chambers in Shaft Four: Chambers B, Ba and Bb. The walls and ceiling of Chamber Bc are too badly damaged for any conclusions to be reached about that chamber. The coating on the ceilings of Chambers B, Ba and Bb penetrates cracks in the rock which paint would not have done. It is a thick, resinous coating of the sort which might derive from the burning of resinous woods covered with bitumen. In the floor of Chamber Ba we have found broken but once gilded glass coffin fragments set in hard resin. These look as though they are the remnants of a coffin (of a child) burned *in situ*.

On balance, therefore, it seems more likely that these chambers were blackened by a fire of a sort which was not repeated in the northern chambers (A, Aa).

It is curious that fire would only have been used in three out of a possible twenty-four chambers. This raises the possibility that the people buried here were particularly targeted for elimination. The small coffin suggests the presence here of the son of

*Figure 126. Shaft Four Chamber B looking south.*

the king, Menkheperre (a jar belonging to him was found nearby in Chamber Bc). The superior state of the architecture and plastering in these rooms points also to the Great Wife of the King, Nebetnehet, whose named alabaster jar fragments were also found in Chamber Bc.

The suggestion that these two were the special target of the opprobrium which resulted in these burials, and their names, being so comprehensively destroyed may be supported by further investigation of the human remains. The majority of the bones which have survived are not burned but a minority are. If these relate to particular individuals this would support the idea of those individuals being targetted for destruction.

Having been extended to the south, the original form of Chamber B was effectively raised and pushed further into the rock in the form of Chamber Ba. This is the best preserved of all the chambers in the tomb complex. The black colouring in here lies on top of brown mud plaster rather than gypsum plaster. In places the rock itself is blackened. There are five niches between 60cms and 85cms above the floor. They are asymmetrically arranged. Ba1 is in the middle of the eastern lateral wall. Ba2 and Ba3 are unevenly spaced in the southern wall. Ba4 is in the middle of the western lateral wall opposite Ba1. Ba5 is in the corner to the west of the door.

Chamber Bb is accessed via a ramp which may once have been in the form of steps. No trace of these steps survives. The chamber uses the natural layer which forms the floor of Chamber Ba as its ceiling. This layer undulates but for most of its length the chamber is 2.15m in height.

*Figure 127. Chamber B west side with the entrance to the lower chamber of Bc to the left of the central niche (B3).*

*Figure 128. The east side of Chamber B showing the robber's hole through Niche B2 to Chamber Bd in Shaft Two.*

Bb is 3.9m wide (E-W) and 7.3m long (N-S) at it longest making it the largest chamber in the tomb complex.

The western margin of the entrance has collapsed. It does not look as though this happened in ancient times. When we cleared this area there was no sign of the gap having been filled with built blocks. The wall which is visible along the eastern margin of Chamber Bc (the south-western corner of Chamber B see *Figure 133*) was built by us to stabilise the margin of Chamber Bc.

*Figure 129. Chamber B looking north towards the shaft and the partially intact blocking of Chamber A.*

*Figure 130. Chamber Ba looking south.*

Chamber Bc is currently 3m (E-W) by 3.6m (N-S) with a ceiling height of approximately 1.6m. This ceiling height is difficult to measure precisely as the whole of the ceiling area is fractured into loose blocks 50cms by 50cms in size and currently supported by props. The chamber is accessed by what is now a ramp off Chamber B which may once have been in the form of steps.

*Figure 131. Chamber Ba looking north towards Chamber B and the shaft beyond.*

*Figure 132. Chamber Bb looking south.*

*Figure 133. Chamber Bb looking north towards Chamber B and the shaft beyond. The entry slope bears no surviving traces of steps.*

*Figure 134. The interior of Chamber Bc looking south-west. The extremely fracturing of the ceiling is visible above the central prop.*

*Figure 135. Chamber A in Shaft Four. In the bottom left hand corner can be seen the hole going through into Shaft Five's Chamber A.*

## The northern chambers

The nothern suite of chambers in Shaft Four is altogether simpler than the southern suite, consisting of just two chambers and a niche.

Chamber A opens straight off the northern end of the shaft and is 4.2m (E-W) by 5.2m (N-S) with a ceiling 2.6m high. This compares with Chamber A in Shaft Two which is 3.6m (E-W) by 5.62m (N-S) with a ceiling height of 2.73m.

Chamber A was once plastered with brown mud and gypsum plaster and bears traces of white paint. The lateral walls bear the marks of successive flooding events in the form of brown stains. These show where wet material has been washed into the chamber. In order to create a consistent height for this chamber the hard rock layer which elsewhere has been used to created floors and ceilings has been cut through. Using it as a ceiling would have resulted in Chamber A at the northern end being less than a metre high.

The shape and orientation of Chamber Aa (1.57m high by 2.45m E-W and 3.2m NS) are singular. The chamber entrance is located in the middle of the northern wall of Chamber A but the western wall of Aa is merely a continuation of the doorway, the lateral dimension of the chamber being all to the east (*Figure 138*). The chamber bends markedly to the east giving the plan of the northern rooms of Shaft Four a distinct curve.

Figure 136. The eastern wall of Chamber A in Shaft Four showing both the water-staining and the cutting through of the sloping hard layer. Just visible through Niche A1 is the robber's hole through into Shaft Two's Niche A2.

Figure 137. The western wall of Chamber A in Shaft Four showing the raking line of water ingress which marked the high point of the debris filling the chamber. In the bottom left can be seen the small hole which breaks into in Shaft Five Chamber A

*Figure 138. Chamber Aa looking north. The level reached by debris washed into the chamber is clearly visible.*

*Figure 139. Chamber Aa looking south into Chamber A. Note the asymmetrical positioning of the door in the southern wall.*

Roughly in the middle of the eastern wall of Chamber A is a niche 1.2m high and 1.2m E-W and 1.15m N-S. In the north-eastern corner a hole has been cut through to niche A2 in Shaft Two. This opening is 85cms high by 50cms wide and does not form part of the original design. Quite when this opening was created it is impossible to say but it would have greatly facilitated the work of ancient robbers or those involved in destroying the burials. The existence of robbers' holes in both the rooms north of and south of the shafts may indicate that the shafts were filled with rubble when the holes were created.

*Figure 140. Niche A1 looking east through the robber's hole into Niche A2 in Shaft Two.*

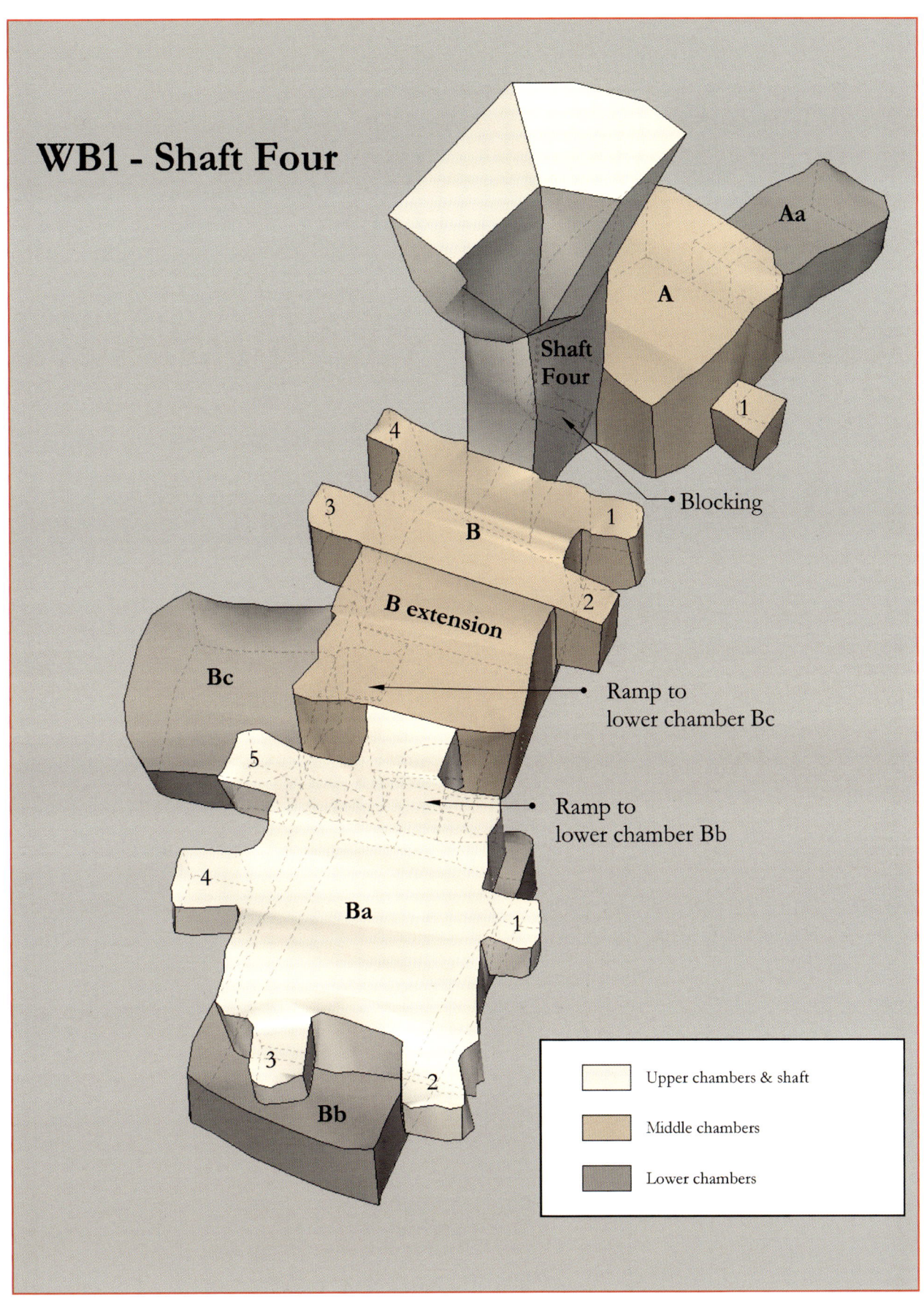

*Figure 141. A three-dimensional view of Shaft Four looking north.*

## GRAVE GOODS

Amenhotep III's Great Wife Tiye was provided with a shrine for her burial and the dismantled panels were found in KV55[6]. Their size may explain why the corridor of KV55 was at some stage enlarged. The large dimensions of both the shafts and some of the chambers in the WB1 tombs has been remarked on. Later coverage of the faience fragments will suggest a possible connection with shrine panels. It is sufficient at this juncture to observe that shrine panels of the size of the KV55 panels made for Tiye (the long sides 3.51 wide by 2.25m high and the short sides 2.28 wide by 2.25m high according to Martha Bell[7]) could have been manoeuvered into Shaft Four or Shaft Two.

Panels of that size would have stood in only two chambers if Shaft Four: Chamber A, with 35cms clearance overhead and Chamber B with 20cms clearance overhead. They could not have stood in Shaft Four's Chamber Ba or Bc.

In Shaft Two panels of that size could have stood in Chamber A with 40cms of clearance overhead, in Chamber B with more than 90cms overhead clearance and in Chamber Bc with 35cms clearance overhead. They could only have been put into Chamber Bc before the entrance was built up with stones.

Sarcophagi of wood or stone could easily have been introduced via the larger shafts and accommodated in their respective chambers.

## THE LESSER SHAFTS

### Shaft One

Shaft One is the northernmost of the shafts and is situated at the eastern extreme of the site only 18 metres from the cliffs to the north and 3 metres from the now eroded slope to the east. Its long sides are oriented slightly to the west of north in the same general direction as Shafts Two, Four, Five and Six.

Shaft One is oddly placed. It can only ever have been intended to be a small tomb given both the shaft dimensions and its proximity to the edge of the plateau, especially to the east. It is also so situated that any water running off the slope behind is bound to pour into this shaft. Over the years this is exactly what has happened. So much water has flowed into and out of this commencement that it has cut a channel through the later debris piles and the surface underneath and so made passage for water to flow into Shaft Two. Excess water has also flowed eastwards down the slope to the wadi floor below cutting a visible channel down this side of the site.

---

6. Reeves, C. (1990) "*Valley of the Kings: The Decline of a Royal Necropolis*", Studies in Egyptology, Kegan Paul International, London pp. 42-49.
7. Bell, M. (1990) "*An Armchair Excavation of KV55*", JARCE XXVII pp. 89-137.

*Figure 142. Shaft One looking south with the cut through to Shaft Two at the top right of the photograph.*

The shaft is only 1.4m deep and 1.15m E-W and 2.3m N-S. Only Shaft Six has smaller E-W and N-S dimensions. The walls are cut with precision and this suggests that a proper funerary monument was intended, not as we have considered, a basin or reservoir designed to catch floodwater and divert it from the tombs below. The floor of the shaft is rough and much damaged by water.

It remains possible that this was an embalming cache. For comparison, Tutankhamun's embalming cache measures 1.4m deep by 1.25m E-W and 1.9m N-S.[8]

*Figure 143. Shaft One looking north with the cut through to Shaft Two at the bottom left of the photograph.*

8. Winlock, H. (2010) *"Tutankhamun's Funeral"*, The Metropolitan Museum of Art, New York. p. 24.

## Shaft Six

Shaft Six is situated west of Shaft Five and forms the westernmost extreme of the line of shafts aligned roughly east-west. Shaft Six is the smallest of the shafts in terms of its E-W (1.05m) and N-S (2.25m) dimensions but it is considerably deeper than Shaft One at 4.25m.

When found Shaft Six was filled from bottom to top with fine, reddish desert mud typical of the Abdul Ghany layer[9] which lies just under the XVIIIth dynasty surface. This was the layer which was collected for use in plastering the interior of the other shafts. Mixed in with this mud were fragments of Marl-D offering jars of various types. The northern edge of the shaft was badly eroded and the surface of the slope immediately to the north was also eroded into a channel 50cms deep in places. This was created by water which had run down the northern edge of the spoil-heaps from the north and east.

*Figure 144. Shaft Six looking north.*

---

9. As noted in Chapter Three, Clearance of Shaft Two (*Figure 17 above*), this is a layer of uniform fine brown desert marl which lies just beneath the XVIIIth dynasty surface. It was first noted by, and therefore named after, our first inspector, Abdul Ghany.

*Figure 145. Shaft Six showing its position at the western end of the northern spoil-heaps and the direction of water flows down the slopes to the north and along the edge of the spoil-heaps into the shaft.*

This flow of water in ancient times had swept into the tomb Marl-D amphorae fragments resting on the surface in a series of progressive floods. This is further evidence that at some stage the tombs were completely emptied and, indeed that Shaft Six was at some stage empty. It only filled up after it had been cleared and it was then filled entirely with surface debris mixed in with abandoned and broken offering ware.

Surprisingly, given the summer temperatures and the almost complete absence of anything other than intermittent rainstorms in the last five hundred years, from a depth of roughly a metre down this mud fill was still damp when uncovered. The contents of Shaft Five's Chamber A were badly affected by damp and it looks as though moisture from Shaft Six's repeated floodings seeped through eastwards underground into the northern chambers of Shaft Five. The white-painted storage jars in Shaft Five's Chamber A were extremely friable and were covered in salt crystals leeched out by the moisture. The walls were also covered in salts in both the northern and southern chambers.

The precision of the cutting in Shaft Six again indicates that it was intended as a funerary monument and not for any other purpose. We were to discover later that it had been sealed in ancient times. This suggests usage which required protection and this in turn raises two possibilities:

- that this was a perfunctory and hurried burial in an unfinished shaft; or
- that this was an embalming cache.

*Figure 146. The bottom of Shaft Six looking north.*

*Figure 147. Bottom of Shaft Six looking south.*

Against it being an embalming cache is its depth which seems excessive for the material contained for example in KV54, Tutankhamun's embalming cache in the Valley of the Kings. KV54 is only 1.4m deep at its deepest, the same depth as Shaft One as noted above.

## Shaft Seven

Shaft Seven only came to light during clearance of the main, southern spoil-heap. For some time we had been puzzled by the dramatic movement in the axis of Shaft Four and of Shaft Five. Shaft Two has a more or less straight axis centred on its shaft. Shaft Four's northern rooms bend markedly eastwards and Chamber Aa is asymmetrically biassed to the east. Shaft Four's southern suite of rooms also bend from west to east.

Even more marked is the way that Shaft Five's southern rooms bend to the west in

*Figure 148. Shaft Seven looking west.*

contrast to Chamber A to the north of the shaft which bends east. (Figure 149).

We were therefore intrigued by the possibility that there might be further tombs concealed under the spoil-heaps. These would be of great interest since the spoil-heaps were created during the clearance of the tombs and anything underneath those spoil-heaps (theoretically) would have lain undisturbed since those clearances took place.

When Shaft Seven appeared it looked at first as though we might have discovered just such a tomb. Its east-west orientation suggested a connection with Shaft Three. However, from the start the position of this shaft indicated that it would not be as deep as other shafts since it lies directly over Shaft Five's Niche Ba1.

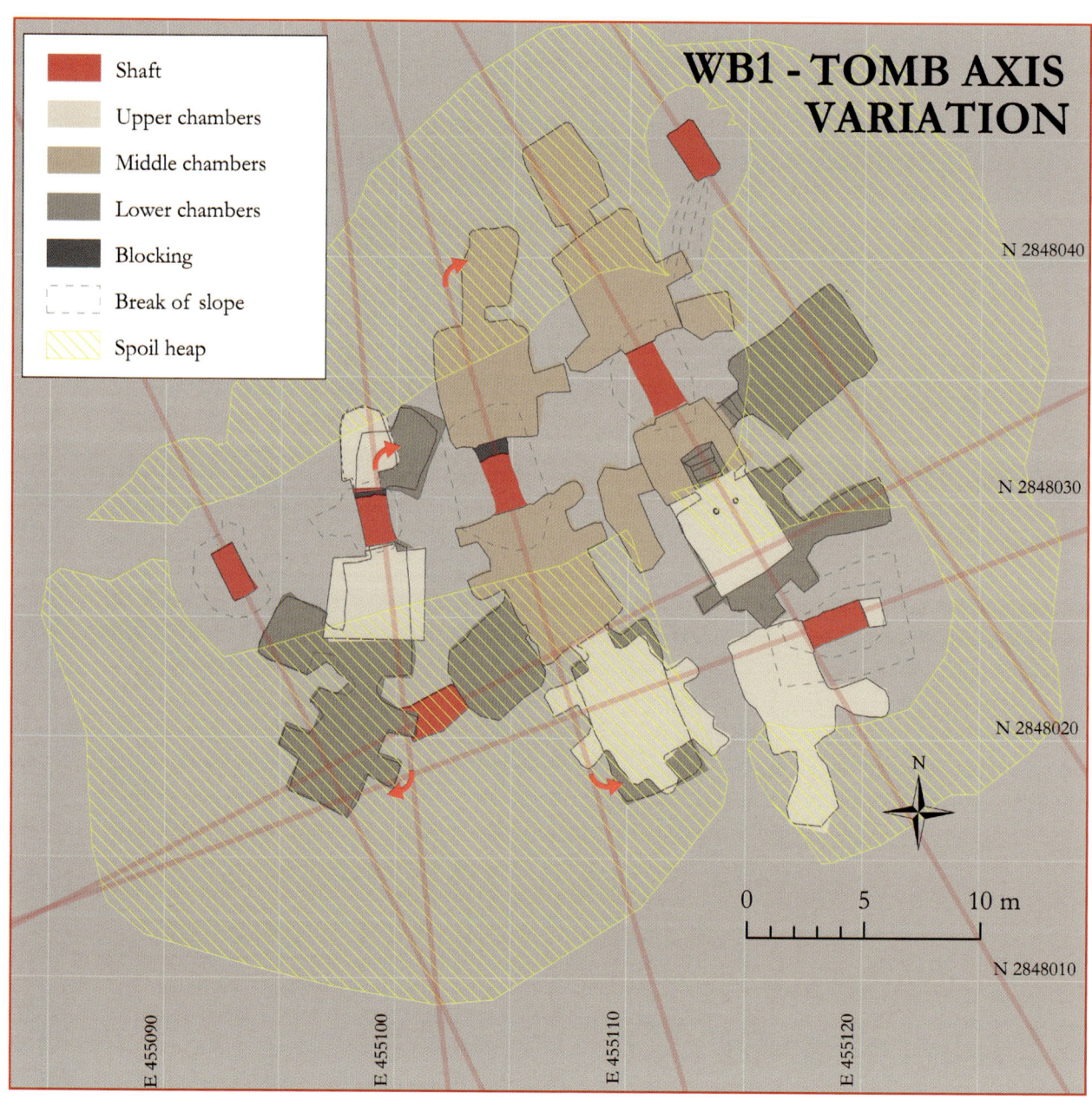

*Figure 149. A site plan showing the axis of each shaft. The arrows show the deviation from the central line in Shafts Four and Five.*

*Figure 150. Shaft Seven looking east.*

Once clearance began in earnest it was clear that this was either another commencement, an embalming cache or, just conceivably, a foundation deposit. Around the edges of the shallow shaft, which is dug into the very poor upper marl layer of the site, there are traces of greyish-white cement, or concrete, composed of a mixture of gypsum and fine white stone chippings. Taken together with later discoveries round the edges of the tomb shafts, this suggests that this shallow pit was used for some purpose important enough for the contents, whatever they were, to have been sealed.

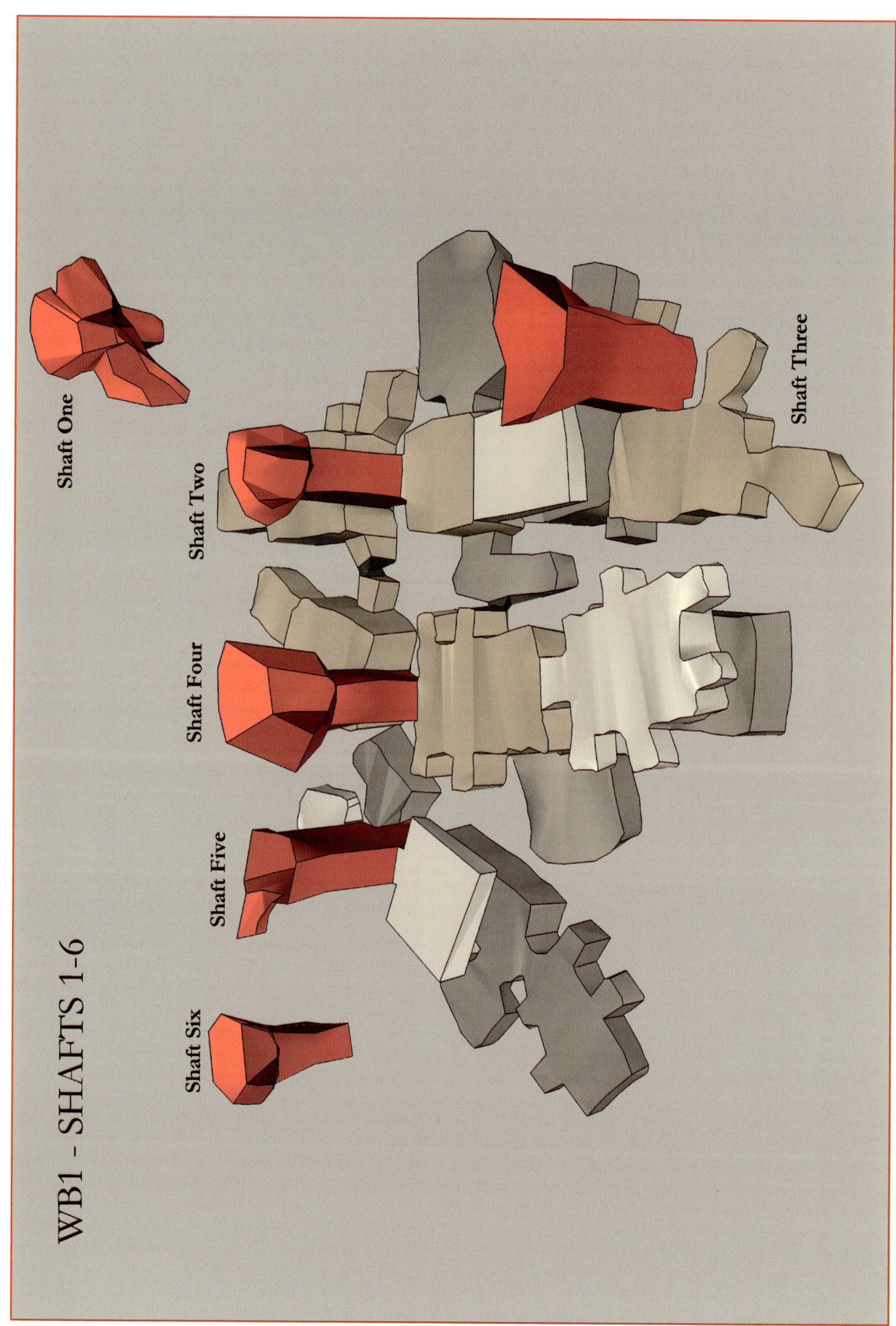

*Figure 151. A three-dimensional view of Shafts One to Six.*

# THE OBJECTS

*This review of the objects will provide an overview of the main finds from all shafts. These will be presented by object category rather than shaft by shaft since, as already described, the evidence suggests the contents of the tombs were removed from their various chambers at some stage. Some fragments bear signs of burning which took place after they were broken. If the major fires were in the shafts some breaking of the canopic jars may have taken place inside the tombs. However, in time many fragments found their way to the surface. Subsequently some fell back into the shafts amongst other debris washed and blown back. Others fell or rolled down the outer surfaces of the spoil-heaps.*

*When the re-assembling of the canopic jars was undertaken it was apparent that in some cases parts of the same object were found in different shafts, or scattered widely on the surface. The context in which the objects were found therefore tells us very little about their original positioning. The specialist volumes will provide details of the original locations of these objects.*

## CHAPTER FIVE
## CANOPIC JARS

Notwithstanding this caveat about context, if a jar is defined by the majority of its constituent pieces (ignoring small fragments found elsewhere), the percentages of the total of jars coming from the various shafts with chambers was as follows:

| | |
|---|---|
| **Shaft Two** | **59%** |
| **Shaft Three** | **8%** |
| **Shaft Four** | **32%** |
| **Shaft Five** | **None** |
| **Surface** | **1%** |

The fact that Shaft Five, the lower levels of which were untouched since antiquity, contained no canopic fragments is supportive of these objects having been removed for breaking on the surface. The location of that activity on the surface of the spoil-heaps to the south of Shafts Two and Four is supported by the high percentages of jars retrieved from those two shafts.

If we set aside for the moment the two and a half tons of ceramic sherds recovered from the site, by far the most numerous objects were from the category of stone vessels. Within the latter category the canopic jars were the largest contributors to our early understanding of the site. To date a minimum of eighty canopic jars have been identified, making them the largest single collection of these jars ever recovered in Egypt.

Carter mentioned canopic jar lids of the finest workmanship[1] were found on the site and there must, indeed, have been many wonderful pieces carried away from the area. Thirty-eight fragments (possibly more which were subsequently joined) were taken from this site sometime before 1903 when they were purchased in Luxor by Georges Legrain, acting for the Egyptian Museum in Cairo. Lord Amherst and W. Spiegelberg purchased others. When Lord Amherst's collection was dispersed in early 1922 some of his collection was

---
1. Carter, H. (1917) op. cit. p. 112.

*Figure 152. The canopic jars re-assembled during the first season.*

*Figure 153. Canopic jars re-assembled during the second season.*

acquired by the Petrie Museum at University College London[2]. The Egyptian Collection in Strasbourg University acquired pieces from Spiegelburg. Some fragments found their way into private hands. A single shabti fragment from this site is in the British Museum.

It was not until the first names appeared on the canopic fragments in Shaft Two that a connection could be made with these museum pieces. Subsequently these reference pieces were invaluable in contributing to the history of the WB1 tombs.

We have identified 253 stone vessels from our clearance work at WB1 to date. This number is subject to change as some of the fragments currently identified as coming from separate vessels may in time prove to be from other vessels already identified. Of the stone vessels the 80 re-assembled canopic jars are in the same range as the number of people whose remains we have found on the site: twenty-three adults. There are

2. Raisman, V. and Martin, G. (1984) "*Canopic Equipment in the Petrie Collection*", Aris & Phillips, Warminster pp. 13 & 14.

names which are included in the Cairo Museum material unaccounted for on the WB1 site. One additional name, Tuka, is not found on the Cairo canopic fragments.

One additional canopic jar base was found near the site by Christiane Desroches-Noblecourt in a rock-cut Coptic chapel in the Wadi Bairiya which we have designated WB2[3]. This vessel is no longer on the WB2 site. The material in the Egyptian Museum in Cairo provides at least another five vessels. There is therefore a minimum total number of 86 canopic jars from the WB1 site so far.

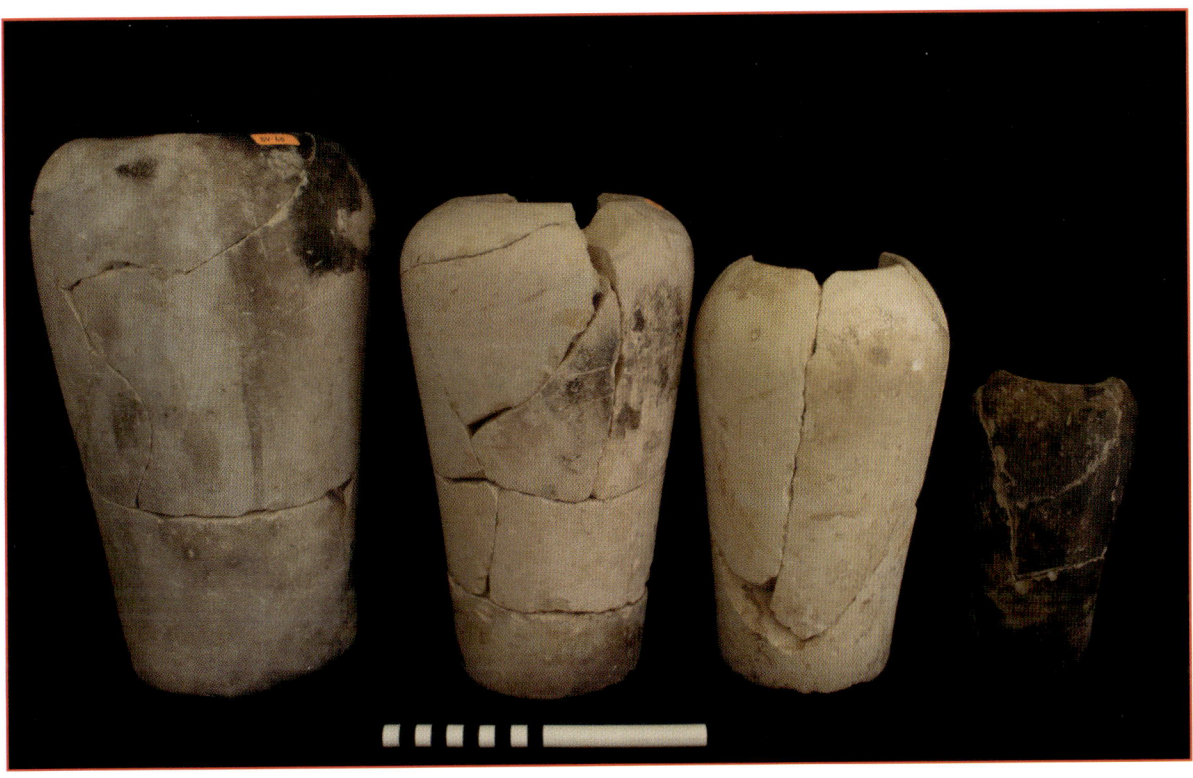

*Figure 154. The variation in the sizes of canopic jars (all these from the second season).*

The jars vary in size from 38 cms high to only 20 cms in the case of the jars attributed by us to Menkheperre (see *Figure 154*).

### The names and inscriptions

The first evidence of the occupants of the tomb was the appearance of the title "Ornament of the King" on an inscribed fragment. Shortly after this the first names became apparent and Geoffrey Martin was quickly able to match these to the names listed by Porter & Moss[4] under "Tombs of Princesses, temp. Amenophis III. Position unknown."

Included in the Porter & Moss list were the following: Queen Henut, Queen Nebtnuhet, Prince Menkhperre, Princess Ti'a, royal concubines Sitti, Tuy, Tausret, Hatti, Hezti, Mut..., Tentnet, Hatshepsut, By, Pa-ih, Kafi and a man called Nebamun all listed by

---

3. Coque, R. et al (1972) "*Graffiti de la Montagne Thebaine I,3 Compléments aux secteurs A et C, Frange du Sahara Thebain*", CEDAE, Le Caire. This was brought to my attention by Marc Gabolde.
4. Porter, B. and Moss, R. (1964) "*Topographical Bibliography of Ancient Egyptian Hieroglyphic Texts, Reliefs and Paintings I, Part 2: Royal Tombs and Cemeteries*", Oxford University Press, Oxford. pp. 769 & 770.

Legrain in his article in the Annales du Service of 1903. Porter & Moss also refer to material in the Petrie Collection at University College London and in the collection of the University of Strasbourg[6].

A piece bearing the name Kafi and giving her the title "Ornament of the King" was sold at Christie's on 25th October, 2012[7]. This Christie's piece matches in style at least one jar fragment (SV59) found on the WB1 site.

The information noted above confirmed that we had discovered the original source of this material, formerly believed to have come from the Valley of the Queens. During the excavation seasons described above we discovered canopic jar fragments or other limestone and fan fragments (Henut) belonging to the majority of the individuals named in Legrain's 1903 article. In some cases names have been recovered only on ceramic dockets and often without titles.

From stone vessel inscriptions we recovered the following names:

1. **Nebetnehet** - Great Wife of the King - Alabaster jar fragments SV142 and SV158. She is also known from Legrain 2 and 3 in the Egyptian Museum in Cairo and UC15808 in the Petrie Museum at University College London.

2. **Henut** - Ornament of the King and Wife of the King - Limestone oil jar SV175[8]. She is known also from Legrain 1 in the Egyptian Museum in Cairo and wooden fan 2014-186 at WB1.

3. **Menkheperre** - Son of the King - Limestone canopic jar SV65. The name on the fragment from this jar (IES1396) has been matched by means of a replica to SV65 (*see Figures 76 and 77*). He is known also from jar docket 25 from the WB1 site and from Legrain 6 and 7 in the Egyptian Museum in Cairo.

4. **Tiaa** - Daughter of the King - Limestone canopic jar SV3. She is known also from UC15809 in the Petrie Museum at University College London.

5. **Sati** - Ornament of the King - Limestone canopic jars SV5. SV177 and SV226 bear her distinctive "nickname" but not her name. She is known also from Legrain 26 in the Egyptian Museum in Cairo.

6. **Tuy** - no title visible - Limestone canopic fragments SV149 and 161. She is also known from Legrain 14-16 where she has the title Ornament of the King.

7. **Takhat A** - no title visible - Limestone canopic jar SV58.

---

5. Legrain, G. (1903) "*Fragments de Canopes*", ASAE Vol 4, Le Caire pp. 138-149.
6. They also refer to material, later found to be unconnected with the WB1 site, in the Aberdeen Anthropological Museum in Scotland and in the Metropolitan Museum of Art in New York, United States of America.
7. Lot 41, Sale 7207, 25th October, 2012, Christie's South Kensington, London. "An Egyptian Limestone Canopic Jar Fragment. New Kingdom, Circa 1550-1069 B.C."
8. Henut's name alone appears in a cartouche on SV175.

8. **Takhat B** - no title visible - Limestone canopic jars SV72 and SV75. She may be the same Takhat known from Legrain 27-28 where she has the title Ornament of the King.

9. **Tawosret A** - Ornament of the King - Limestone canopic jar SV6.

10. **Tawosret B** - Limestone canopic jar fragment SV129. She is also known from Legrain 20-22 in the Egyptian Museum in Cairo where she has the title Ornament of the King[9].

11. **By** - Ornament of the King - Limestone canopic jar SV38. She is also known from Legrain 33, 34 and 35 in the Egyptian Museum in Cairo.

12. **Kafy** - Ornament of the King[10] - Limestone canopic jar SV56 and SV59. She is also known from Legrain 37 in the Egyptian Museum in Cairo.

13. **Tuka** - Ornament of the King - Limestone canopic jar SV16, alabaster dish SV109 (another part of SV109 is in the Strasbourg Museum collection IES1397).

14. **Mutnofret** - Ornament of the King - Limestone canopic jar SV46. This name may be the same as Legrain 30 in the Egyptian Museum in Cairo. The name Mutnofret also appears on jar dockets 4, 20, 22 and 113 from WB1.

15. **Iuy** - no title visible - Limestone canopic jar head SV105. Her name is written in hieratic on top of this head. Her name also appears on jar docket 7 from WB1. She is also known from the usurped Legrain 29 in the Egyptian Museum in Cairo where she has the title Ornament of the King.

16. **Hedjti** - no title visible - Limestone canopic jar SV71. She is also known from Legrain 29 in the Egyptian Museum in Cairo usurped by Iuy.

17. **Itesresu** - Ornament of the King – Alabaster jar SV118. Canopic jar SV28 (which matches the canopic jar fragment in the Strasbourg Museum collection IES1395) bears the title Ornament of the King but only a single element of the name. However, SV28 matches Legrain 10 and 11 on the Egyptian Museum in Cairo which were made for Sati but usurped by Itesresu.

From ceramic dockets the following additional names were recovered:

18. **Tentiunet** (Jar dockets 3, 71).

19. **Henuy** (Jar docket 60).

20. **Mutuy** (Jar docket 94).

21. **Henuttaneb** (Jar docket 5, 18).

22. **Surer** (Jar docket 16).

---

9. The name Tawosret appears also on jar dockets 15, 44, 46, 105 and 111 from WB1 but it is not possible to know to which of the two women with this name these refer.
10. The title is absent from the SV59 fragment but present on the Christie's fragment.

Further tentative identifications include:

23. **Nebamun** - possibly Limestone canopic jar fragment SV40 (known also from Legrain 38 in the Egyptian Museum in Cairo).

24. **Hat.....** - Ornament of the King - Limestone canopic jar SV33 (possibly also from Legrain 23-25 and 32 in the Egyptian Museum in Cairo)..

25. **Hat.....** - Ornament of the King - Limestone canopic jar SV124 (possibly also from Legrain 23-25 and 32 in the Egyptian Museum in Cairo).

26. **Mut.....** Limestone canopic jar fragment SV239 (possibly also from Legrain 30 in the Egyptian Museum in Cairo).

From these canopic jar fragments we therefore discovered the owners of these tombs. The architecture of the tombs and the human remains supported the view that these tombs were the tombs of a family or related group of individuals who were attached to departments, houses or estates at the heart of the court of Amenhotep III.

## Inscriptions, titles, houses and epithets

The inscriptions on the jars are unusual. The basic formulae, which usually appear in four columns of text, of Imsety and Isis protecting the liver, Hapy and Nephthys protecting the lungs, Duamutef and Neith protecting the stomach and Qebesenuef and Serket protecting the intestines are standard for canopic equipment of the XVIIIth dynasty[11]. Texts are sometimes retrograde. The style of glyphs varies from crude, narrow signs with the texts cut at an angle off the vertical, to beautifully-cut broad signs once filled with blue paste (*Figure 155*).

*Figure 155. Examples of styles of inscripton. Bottom centre shows the blue colouring and black scribal outlines.*

---

11. Budge, E. (1893) "*The Mummy: Chapters on Egyptian Funerary Archaeology*", Cambridge University Press, Cambridge pp. 240-245. .

Only occasional traces of this filling survive but in the case of SV46 not only is the filling still in place but the traces of the scribal text to be followed by the engraver are visible[12].

Only two male names have been recovered by us in the WB1 shaft tombs: Menkheperre and Surer. Nebamun may be the owner of SV40 but this is far from certain[13]. Menkheperre was the son of the King and there can be little doubt from the style of his badly-damaged canopic jar lid SV108 (*Figure 170*) that he was the son of Amenhotep III. Surer is known from jar docket 16 which describes him as "the little one"[14]. Nebamun lacks a title but has an epithet, surname or nickname, "The Troop Commander" (see below page 124).

*Figure 156. Small limestone vessel naming Henut.*

---

12. SV46 is a good example of how difficult context is in these shaft tombs. The main parts of the upper body of the jar were found in the shaft fill of Shaft Four. The text was found in the Chamber A of Shaft Four. Parts of the base, which was in several fragments, were found in Shaft Two Chamber B and parts in Shaft Two Chamber Bc.
13. Nebamun is known only from the Legrain purchases (Cairo 38) in the Egyptian Museum in Cairo but see below p. 117.
14. Translated by Marc Gabolde.

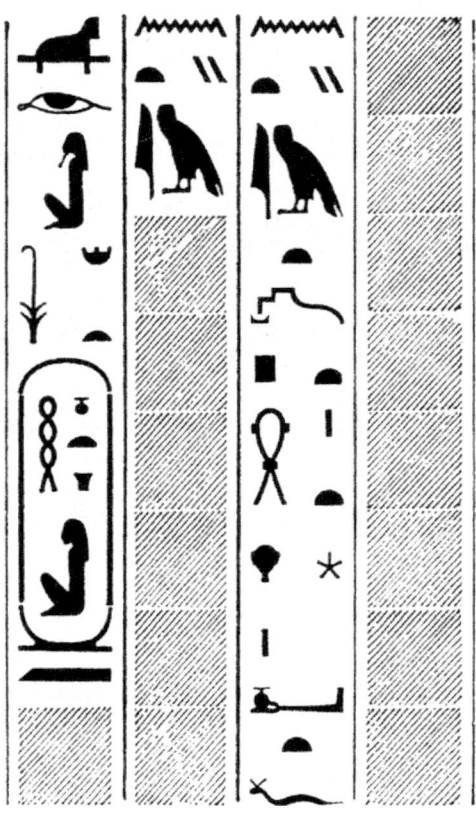

*Figure 157. Legrain copy of the alabaster canopic jar fragment naming "the King's Wife Henut".*

Nebetnehet is described as a Great Wife of the King. Her full titles taken from SV142 and the similar fragment in the Petrie Museum (UC15808) are: "the hereditary princess, great of favour, possessor of grace, sweet of love, the Great Wife of the King whom he loves Nebetnehet". Henut is described on the wooden fan fragment 2014-186 as "Ornament of the King" and then inside her cartouche is the name "the King's Wife Henut" (*Figure 35*). On another stone vessel (SV175) only her name appears within the cartouche (*Figure 156*).

In the Egyptian Museum in Cairo the alabaster fragment Legrain purchased describes Henut as "the King's Wife Henut" (*Figure 157*).

The remaining women whose names survive are either King's Ornaments or, where their names appear only on dockets, have no titles.

In most cases, in addition to their names and titles and the standard canopic formulae, these jars bear additional information of two sorts. The first indicates attachment to a house or estate within the court. The houses are all connected with institutions described by people, thus: "the House of the Bodyguard of Pharaoh, l.p.h." or "the House of the Heirs of the King" ,"the House of the Wife of the King", "the House of the Dazzling Aten". It would be consistent to regard the reference to "the House of the Dazzling

Aten" as referring to the house of a person, namely Amenhotep III who thus was the Dazzling Aten.

It is impossible to discern whether the "the Wife of the King" referred to is Tiye, Nebetnehet or even Henut. Tiye is the Great Wife of Amenhotep III who is most frequently mentioned on monuments of his reign. It is tempting to regard this reference to "the House of the Wife of the King" as referring to her. However, this is by no means self-evident. There are now known to have been four Great Wives of Amenhotep III: Tiye, his two daughters Sitamun and Iset, and now, in addition, Nebetnehet. Curiously, there are no known references to Nebetnehet other than on material from the WB1 site.

References to these "houses" are known elsewhere and most pertinently from the work in tomb KV40 in the Valley of the Kings being conducted by the University of Basel[15]. However, additional information added to the WB1 canopic jars, often in horizontal bands of text added below the standard vertical texts, is unique to WB1. This information comes in the form of surnames, nicknames or simply epithets of a very particular nature.

These epithets have been commented on before[16] but translations of the epithets vary and so a firm grasp of their meaning remains elusive. Previous versions include (as translated by Georges Legrain originally and since by Marc Gabolde):

The King's Ornament Sati, known as the One who beats with rage/beats with the rage of the Aten the Great.

The King's Ornament Takhat, known as the One who dances..........

The King's Ornament Tawosret, known as the One who spends many nights of pleasure in the city of the Aten the Great.

The King's Ornament Hati, known as the Companion of the One who has appeared in the Domain of the Dazzling Aten.

The King's Ornament Tuy of the House of the Dazzling Aten known as She who is the kitten of her mother.

The implications of these unique epithets remain unclear. Translations we are preparing vary markedly from those above. The meaning of the title "Ornament of the King (or King's Ornament)" is also not fully understood. It was retained, for instance, by Ay's wife Tey when Ay became king. Some have translated it as "concubine". It seems strange to us that a king's wife would want to retain a title indicative of the favour of a previous king. This title may indeed have meant something entirely different. We can only be sure that the title was a source of some pride[17] and that it connected the women who bore it with the court.

---

15. I am grateful to Professor Susanne Bickel and her team for making it possible to compare material.
16. Millet, N. (1988) "*Some Canopic Fragments of the Reign of Amenhotep III*", GM 104 pp. 91-93.
17. Nebamun's daughter, "Segrettawi", for instance, is shown in his TT90 tomb with this title and the headdress and accoutrements which accompany it. Davies, N. (1923) "*Two Officials of Tuthmosis IV*", EES, London Plate XXII.

## Nebamun, the Troop Commander

As mentioned above, amongst the canopic jars purchased by Legrain and now in the Egyptian Museum in Cairo is a jar inscribed for Nebamun, the Troop Commander. (Legrain 38).

In 1923 Norman de Garis Davies published Theban Tomb 90 which belonged to a Nebamun who held several titles, including those translated by Sir Alan Gardiner as "Captain of Police" and "bearer of the standard of the royal ship Maryĕ-Amūn". The tomb is located just below the summit of Sheikh Abd el-Qurna. The decoration and finishing of the tomb are not of very high quality and the inscriptions have deteriorated since Robert Hay first recorded them as Tomb 22 in his numbering system.

The Nebamun of TT90 had two wives, Tiye and Sensenebtu, and at least seven daughters and seven sons. Amongst his daughters shown in the tomb were Segerettawy (who held the title "Ornament of the King"), Tawosret, Mutnofret and Iwy.

There are, therefore, several possible connections with the WB1 material:

- the TT90 Nebamun's name and title (the title "*p3-ḥry-pd.t*" appears in Plate XXXIII[21]) connect him to the Legrain canopic jar inscription 38;
- a daughter of the TT90 Nebamun holds the title "King's Ornament" placing this family close to the court;
- the TT90 Nebamun has three other daughters with names found on WB1 canopic jars: Mutnofret, Tawosret and Iwy.

Amongst the TT90 Nebamun's other titles, given to him on his retirement, is the title "Commander of Military Police on the West of Thebes". This title was apparently given to him in a transitional period from the end of the reign of Thutmose IV into the beginning of the reign of Amenhotep III. Apart from the mention of retirement in TT90, the Nebamun of that tomb is shown with at least two grandchildren.[22]

In November, 1980, a University of Heidelberg mission found fragments of a stela of Nebamun "standard bearer of the bark Beloved-of-Amun" and "Chief of the Western Desert Police". These fragments were found "near one of the many stone circles, lying 1-2km apart, that were built along a road extending from near Deir el-Shelouit westward some 15km into the desert". This appears to be the prepared road which leads ultimately to the WB1 site. Dr Dina Faltings, who found the stela, has confirmed the find-spot as within nine hundred metres of the WB1 shaft tombs[24].

If, as now seems probable, the two Nebamuns are the same, it is not clear why his tomb TT90 would have been abandoned and why he would have been buried in a cemetery

---

18. Davies, N. (1923) op. cit. pp. 19-38.
19. Gardiner, A. and Weigall, A. (1913) "*A Topographical Catalogue of the Private Tombs of Thebes*", Bernard Quaritch, London. Pl. III.
20. Hay British Museum Add. MSS 29853A, 125 et al.
21. Davies, N. (1923) op. cit..
22. Davies, N. (1923) op. cit. pp. 23 & 29.
23. Eid, Y. (1984) "*A newly discovered Stela of Neb-Amon, Chief of the Western Desert Police*", ASAE 70. pp. 19-20.
24. Personal correspondence with Dr Faltings.

otherwise associated with royal women and children. If his burial was made at WB1 then the period of usage of these tombs would seem to cover almost the whole of the reign of Amenhotep III. The Nebamun of TT90 is mentioned in his Sheikh Abd el-Qurna tomb as being of retirement age and is pictured with two grandchildren. He is unlikely, therefore, to have survived long into Amenhotep III's reign. The surviving head SV108 (*Figure 170*) identified by us as belonging to the King's Son Menkheperre belongs stylistically to the latter part of Amenhotep III's reign. These two pieces of evidence would therefore endorse the view that these tombs were used over an extended period of time and were enlarged and re-opened during that period.

## The condition of the jars

All the canopic jars on the WB1 site have been broken. Robbery might account for considerable accidental damage but the re-assembly of these jars by our mission has been made from over 1,500 fragments. Every jar has been broken into a minimum of four pieces and many have been smashed into small fragments (*see Figure 158*).

Care appears to have been taken to remove completely the inscribed parts of the jar. Some of the jars bear chisel marks inside (*Figure 159*) and in most cases it is clear that the first breaks were made using a sharp instrument, most likely a chisel, placed at the top edge of the jar and used to create vertical cracks down the height of the jars. It is well-known from surviving records at Deir el-Medina that chisels were carefully-controlled state property. Casual robbers would hardly have gone to the trouble of first stealing these tools and then using them laboriously to break large stone vessels into numbers of fragments in excess of those needed to render the objects unusable

The difficulty of reconstructing the jars was made greater since not only were they

 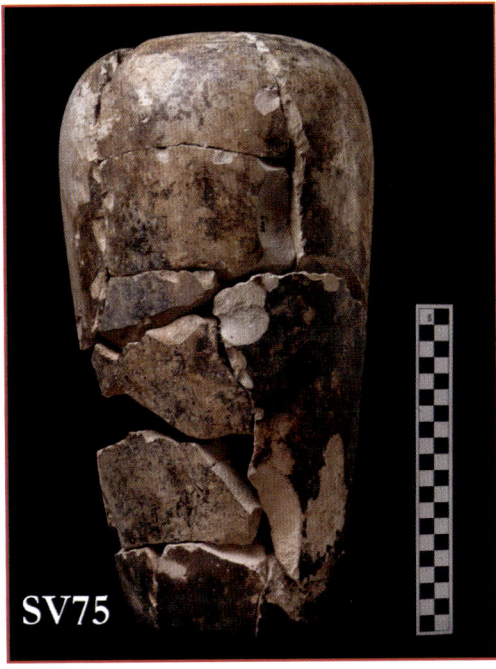

*Figure 158. Two examples of canopic jars showing the extent to which they have been deliberately broken. Note also the variation in colour of adjacent fragments.*

*Figure 159. Chisel marks on the inside of SV11.*

*Figure 160. SV3 (left) names the King's Daughter Tiaa and SV5 (right) names The King's Ornament Sati.*

*Figure 161. SV6 (left) names The King's Ornament Tawosret. SV16 (right) is more difficult to interpret but appears to name The King's Ornament Tuka.*

*Figure 162. SV38 (left) names The King's Ornament By. SV58 (right) names The King's Ornament Takhat.*

broken into many fragments but the limestone of which they were made varied widely in colour. Initially we thought there were different limestones involved, one grey (see SV38 and SV58, *Figure 162*), one slightly pink. However, it became clear during the reconstruction of the vessels that colour was no guide to which pieces belonged to which vessel. The discoloration was the result of fire damage. This had, in some cases blackened the outside of pieces but in others had changed their colour entirely. It is evident that this damage by fire took place after the vessels were broken into pieces as adjacent pieces from the same jar can be of quite different colours, as in the case of SV7 (*Figure 163*). Fire damage and melted unguents also found their way over the edges of fragments in a way which would have been impossible had the jars still been intact.

As will be seen later from the review of the wooden, glass and faience fragments and

*Figure 163. SV7 showing the different colours of adjacent pieces.*

the condition of the human remains, this fragmentation is a consistent feature of all the objects. Apart from four canopic heads no object from the tombs under discussion has survived intact. In the case of the wooden fragments many have cut marks on both side of pieces less than 5cms in length. Many of the skull and long bone fragments have similarly been reduced to coin-sized fragments. Much of the wood and many of the bones have been burned. One of the canopic jars was made of the finest alabaster cut from the same quarry and same seam as that used to make the canopic jars of Yuya, father-in-law of Amenhotep III, whose burials was found, along with that of his wife, Tuyu, in KV46[25]. These valuable vessels have been smashed rather than stolen for re-use.

The inescapable conclusion from the condition of these jars is that these burials were

---

25. Davis, T. (1907) *"The Tomb of Iouiya and Touiyou"*, Constable, London.

*Figure 164. SV111. The surviving profile of a jar made of identical material to that from which the canopic jars of Yuya (KV46) were manufactured.*

*Figure 165. One of the canopic jars of Yuya found in KV46 and now in the Egyptian Museum in Cairo. It is made from stone almost identical to that used to manufacture SV111.*

*deliberately* destroyed. The names of these important individuals were to remain unknown until the discovery of the canopic jar fragments by robbers early in the twentieth century and their subsequent acquisition by museums and collectors. Their original burials were only identified by our mission over a hundred years later.

Why these burials should have been deliberately destroyed is a question we cannot answer. Nor can we establish who was responsible for this very effective damnatio *memoriae*.

# CHAPTER SIX
# CANOPIC JAR HEADS, STONE VESSEL LIDS, OTHER STONE VESSELS AND OBJECTS

## Canopic heads

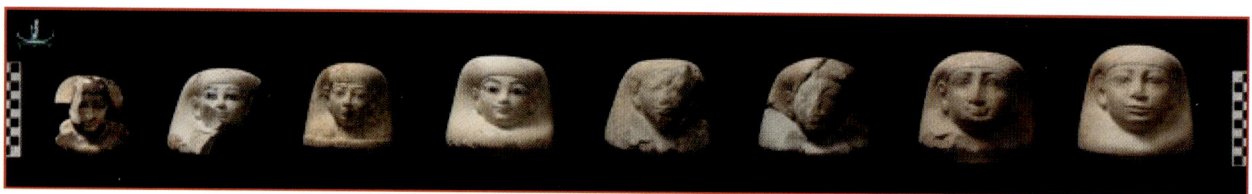

*Figure 166. The better preserved canopic heads.*

The picture of destruction outlined above is shared by the human-headed canopic jar lids. Four of these have survived almost intact (SV102, SV104, SV105, SV106) but most are badly broken. In some cases the faces have been laboriously hacked away (SV85) (*Figure 167*) or, in the case of the alabaster heads, split (SV159 and SV160) (*Figures 168 and 169*).

*Figure 167. A reconstructed limestone canopic jar stopper (SV85) with the face deliberately hacked away.*

Those heads which survived more or less intact were all discovered by us low down in the shafts where, presumably, they had rolled early in the process of destruction. The heads vary in style from broad-featured faces characteristic of the reign of Thutmose IV to the sharper, almond-eyed features typical of the latter part of the reign of

*Figure 168. Alabaster canopic jar stopper fragment SV159.*

*Figure 169. Reconstructed alabaster canopic jar stopper fragments SV160.*

Amenhotep III. A few of the heads retain black paint marking the eyes and eyebrows, but in most cases any decoration has been washed or weathered off. Only two partial faces from alabaster heads survive, both broken and one browned by fire damage (SV159). Other pieces of alabaster heads survive but these too are damaged by fire and broken into many fragments. Fire damage renders the alabaster extremely friable and virtually impossible to reconstruct.

Close inspection of SV105, one of the more complete heads, has revealed that it has the name "Iwy" written acoss the top in hieratic (*Figure 639*). The small, reconstructed SV108 head is the only one which fits the Menkheperre jars identified from the SV65 component fragment in Strasbourg. These are the only two heads we have been able to associate with specific names.

*Figure 170. The badly damaged limestone canopic lid of Menkheperre (SV108).*

## Lids

A surprising quantity of flat, and mostly circular stone-vessel lids survive. These are also all broken. However, apart from the alabaster and serpentine vessel fragments, there are no vessels or vessel fragments to which these flat lids would have belonged. They were, presumably, removed from the site for re-use. A possible explanation for this is that the deliberate destruction was aimed only at objects bearing names or at those essential to survival in the Afterlife.

*Figure 171. An example of part of a circular flat limestone lid (SV190) assembled from fragments discoloured in different ways after the lid was smashed.*

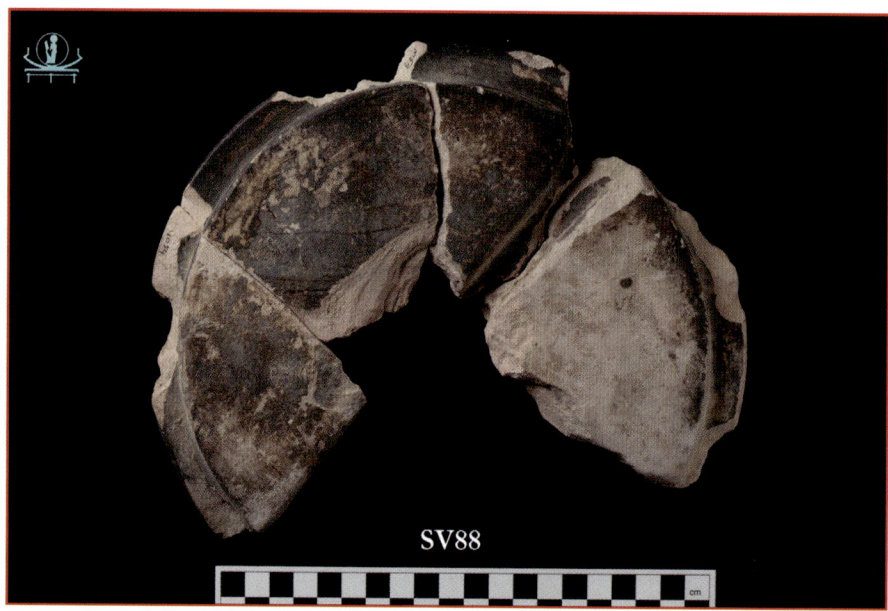

*Figure 172. This circular limestone lid (SV88) is divided on the underside into three sections.*

Amongst these flat lids there is one (SV88, *Figure 172*) which is divided down the underside. It would clearly have sat on a vessel divided into three compartments. Another lid (SV184) is oval rather than round (*Figure 173*) and a recently added fragment suggests it took the form of a cartouche. The tomb of Tutankhamun contains a wood and ivory cartouche-shaped box and lid[1].

---

1. Object 269 "Casket of cartouche form" found in the Treasury. See Murray, H. and Nuttall, M. 1963 "*A Handlist to Howard Carter's Catalogue of Objects in Tut'ankhamun's Tomb*", Griffith Institute, Oxford p. 11.

*Figure 173. SV184. The only limestone lid recovered which is not circular in shape.*

## Serpentine

*Figure 174. SV202. Serpentine dish fragment with a central divider. The photograph shows the discolouration of the stone (right) by fire.*

Serpentine fragments were evident on the surface of the site from the first day of our investigations. As pieces were collected it looked at first as though there were two different types of serpentine, black and green. However, as in the case of the canopic jars, the blackening is the result of fire damage. The temperatures involved have not just coated the outsides with soot but have changed the colour of the stone completely. This is very obvious from re-assembled fragments. Fragments of the same vessel joined side-by-side can be of entirely different colours (*Figure 174*).

## Alabaster

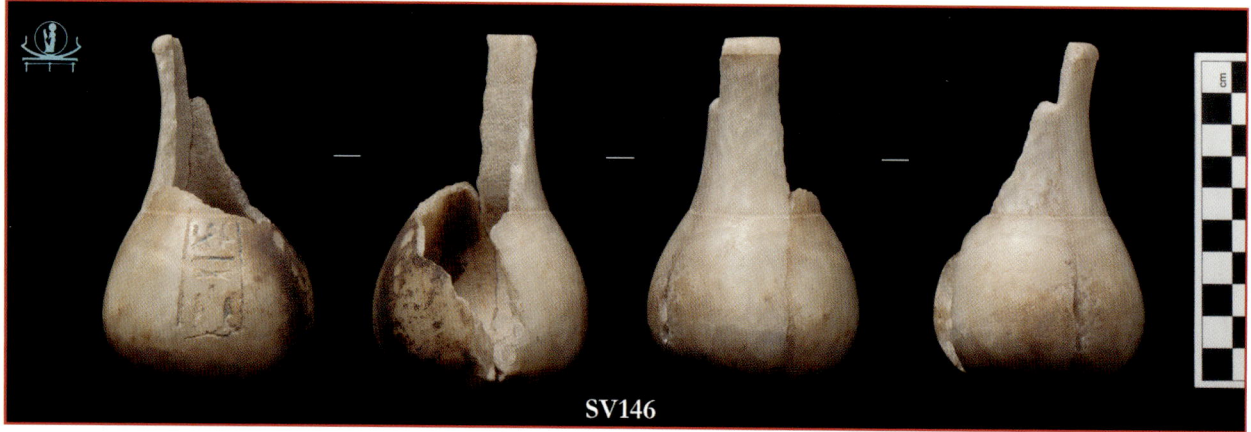

*Figure 175. A small alabaster jar (SV146) inscribed with the text "the King's True Son, his beloved".*

Amongst the other vessel fragments recovered were a variety of alabaster vessels. Most of a small vase inscribed with the text "the King's True Son, his beloved" (SV146, *Figure 175*) came from under the collapsed ceiling in Shaft Four Chamber Bc.

*Figure 176. A small fragment (SV154) of an alabaster jar naming an "Ornament of the King".*

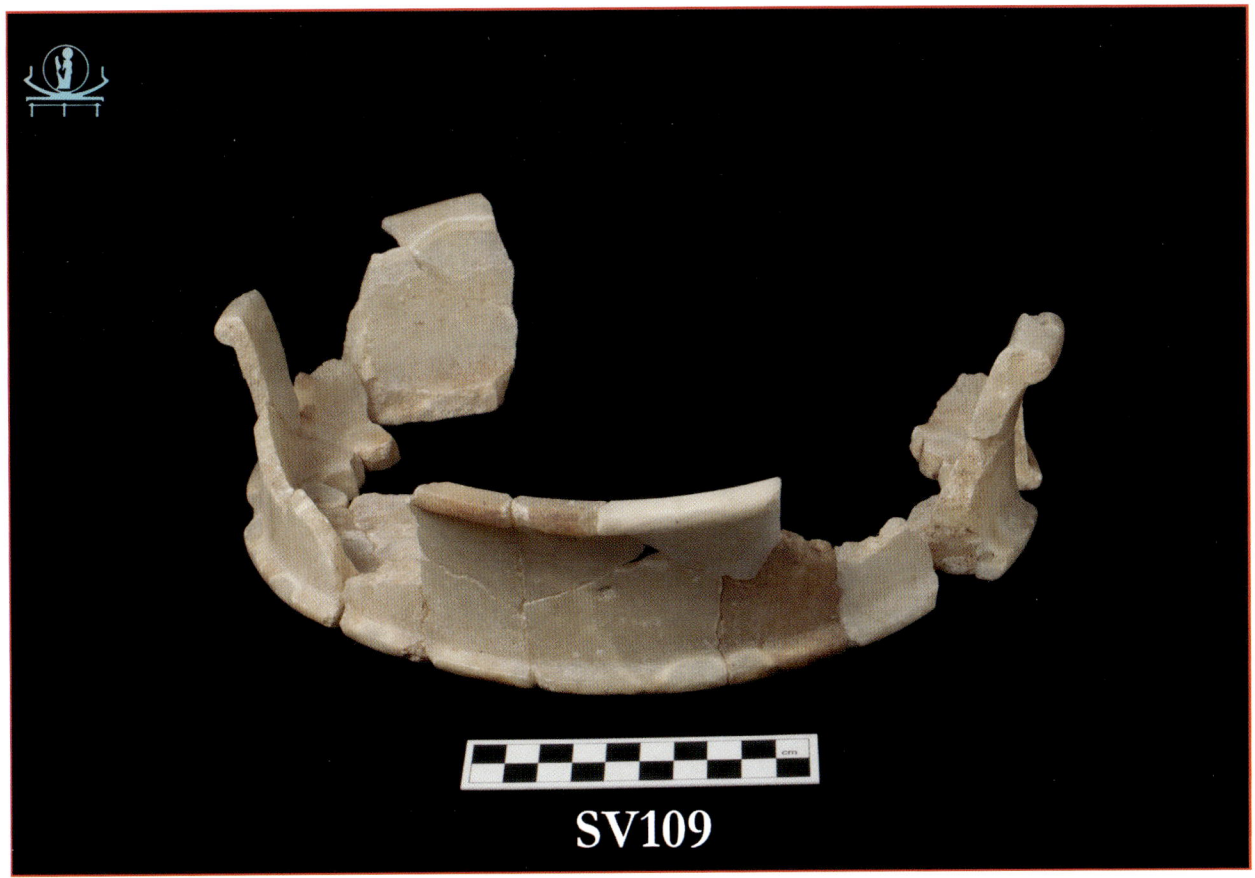

*Figure 177. SV109. Re-assembled fragments of a convex-bottomed alabaster dish part of which is in the Strasbourg collection.*

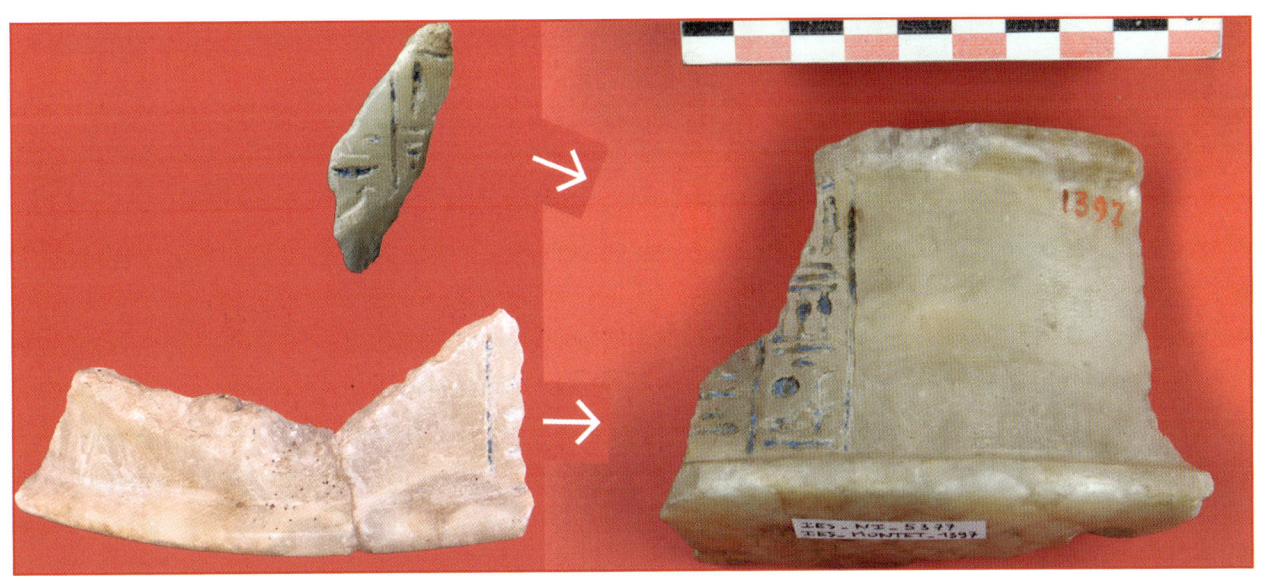

*Figure 178. Additional pieces of SV109 (left) inserted into a photograph of another fragment (IES1397) of the same vessel in the Strasbourg collection.*

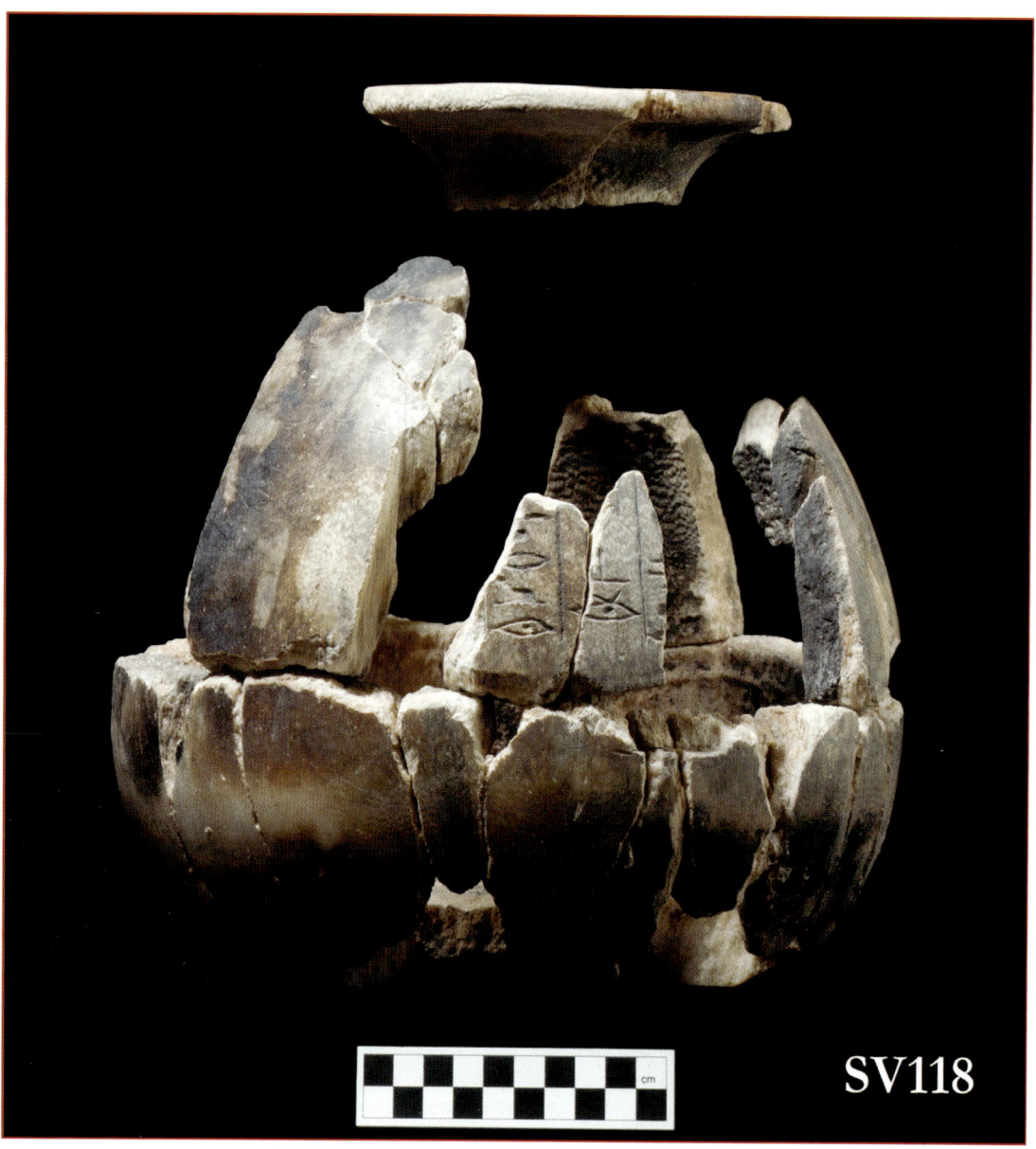

*Figure 179. Large inscribed alabaster jar SV118 shown with the separated neck in place. The name of the owner is Itesresu.*

### Other stone objects

Amongst the other notable stone objects found either in the shafts or on, or beside, the spoil-heaps were a scattering of lithics, two bases of Anubis fetishes, the bottom of a single shabti and a curiously crude head from Shaft Five which might be from an unusual shabti.

A number of worked flints were discovered around the mouth of Shaft Two, sitting immediately on top of the XVIIIth dynasty level. As will be seen, we were to find more of these when the spoil-heaps were cleared. These flint tools would appear to have been being used by the builders of the tombs. Some are undoubtedly Neolithic implements being re-used.

*Figure 180. Anubis fetish bases.*

Large fragments of what appeared to be solid limestone flower-pots were found in Shaft Four. These proved to be the first examples of Anubis fetish bases found since the discovery of complete examples in the tomb of Tutankhamun (KV62 see *Figure 181*). Examples of these are regularly portrayed in tombs and temples but physical examples are otherwise unknown.

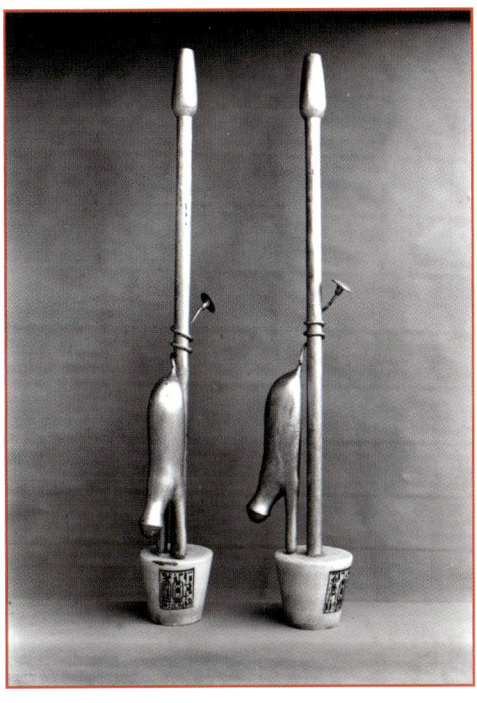

*Figure 181. The pair of Anubis fetishes from the tomb of Tutankhamun (KV62).*

*Figure 182. The Nebetnehet shabti fragment in the British Museum? (no scale provided).*

Two of these, of different sizes (*Figure 180*) were recovered and could be re-assembled. The partial remains of a third suggests that there were originally at least two pairs of these. The examples found in KV62 were of alabaster. All three of those on the WB1 site were of limestone. We were later to find wooden objects which were parts of the upper parts of these fetishes.

*Figure 183. Composite photograph of an alabaster shabti fragment recovered from Shaft Four Chamber Bb.*

Surprisingly few small objects were recovered during the re-clearance work presumably because the most portable objects were long ago carried off by robbers. The presence of the bottom of a single shabti of Nebetnehet in the British Museum is evidence of how such objects have found their way from the Wadi Bairiya to a wide number of destinations. There may yet be objects from these tombs in collections of which we are unaware.

---

1. Photograph taken by the British Museum and reproduced with permission. The museum website gives the size as follows: height 4.14cms; width 2.53cms; depth 3.04cms.

Our clearance work recovered only two stone shabti: one, a single alabaster fragment (2015-180, *Figure 183*) of the foot of a small but beautifully-made shabti with a blue-painted horizontal text; two, the blackened foot of a hardstone shabti (2016-154, *Figure 184*) with the bottom of three columns of vertical text. In neither case is there any trace of the name of the owner.

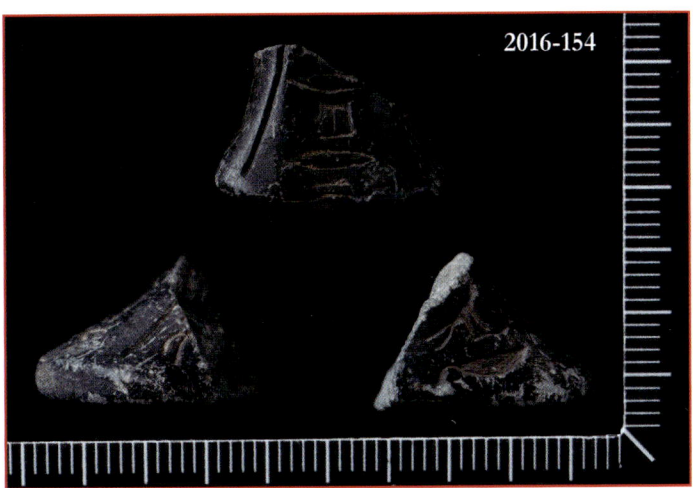

*Figure 184. The foot of a hardstone shabti (2016-154) from Shaft Four blackened by fire.*

From Shaft Five came an enigmatic head which could possibly be from a shabti. It is crudely carved and the head-dress is unusual. This piece was found in amongst the rubble which had fallen from the ceiling in Chamber B of Shaft Five, a chamber which we believe had been undisturbed since ancient times. It is highly unlikely, therefore, to be intrusive. Its style and the crudeness of the carving are puzzling.

*Figure 185. Carved limestone head from Shaft Five Chamber B. (See Figure 63 for other views and scale.)*

# CHAPTER SEVEN
# CERAMICS

Very large quantities of ceramic material were recovered from the WB1 site, in total more than two metric tons. This quantity is consistent with a large number of high status burials. As described above, the surface of the site when found was littered with ceramic fragments. However the majority of the ceramic finds were recovered from the fill of the shafts. As with the other finds, a specialist volume will deal with the ceramics in detail and only an overview of the main material will be provided here.

*Figure 186. Marl-D amphora sherds on the surface between Shafts Five and Six.*

*Figure 187. Sherds laid out for analysis in the first season.*

The ceramic material from WB1 consisted overwhelmingly of small sherds. The only exception was the pottery from Chambers A and Bb in Shaft Five. The other material had all been disturbed and re-deposited. Some of the pots reconstructed contained sherds from four or five different features. In addition, many of the features contained material from mixed periods.

*Figure 188. Squat jar temp. Thutmose III.*

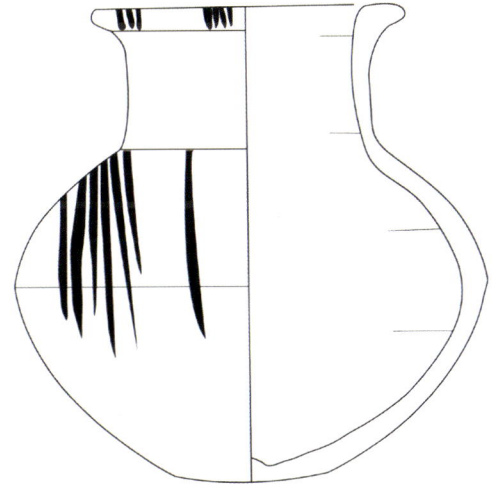

*Figure 189. Squat jar temp. Thutmose III profile.*

The ceramic material indicates four principal phases on the site:

1. Early XVIIIth dynasty

A squat jar with a flat rim, cylindrical neck, round shoulders and flat base (Figures 188 and 189). It bears black decoration on a brown background. All the parallels for this type of pot date to the early XVIIIth dynasty. This pot may have been an heirloom piece[1].

---

1. Aston, D. personal communication with Sherif M. Abdelmoniem.

*Figures 190 (left) and 191 (right). White-painted storage jars.*

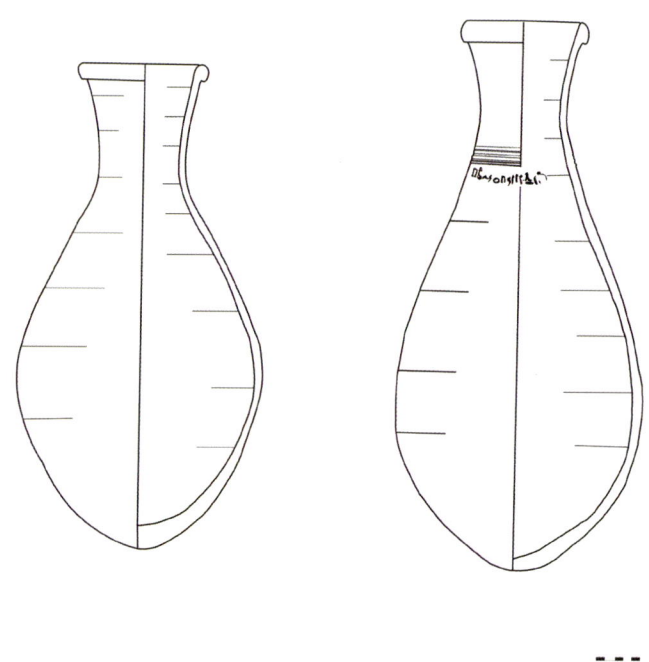

*Figures 192 (left) and 193 (right). White-painted storage jar profiles.*

## 2. Late XVIIIth dynasty (Amenhotep III – Amenhotep IV/Akhenaten)

This phase consists in many large storage jars, Marl-D amphorae, bowls and jars. It represents 90% of the whole body of ceramic material.

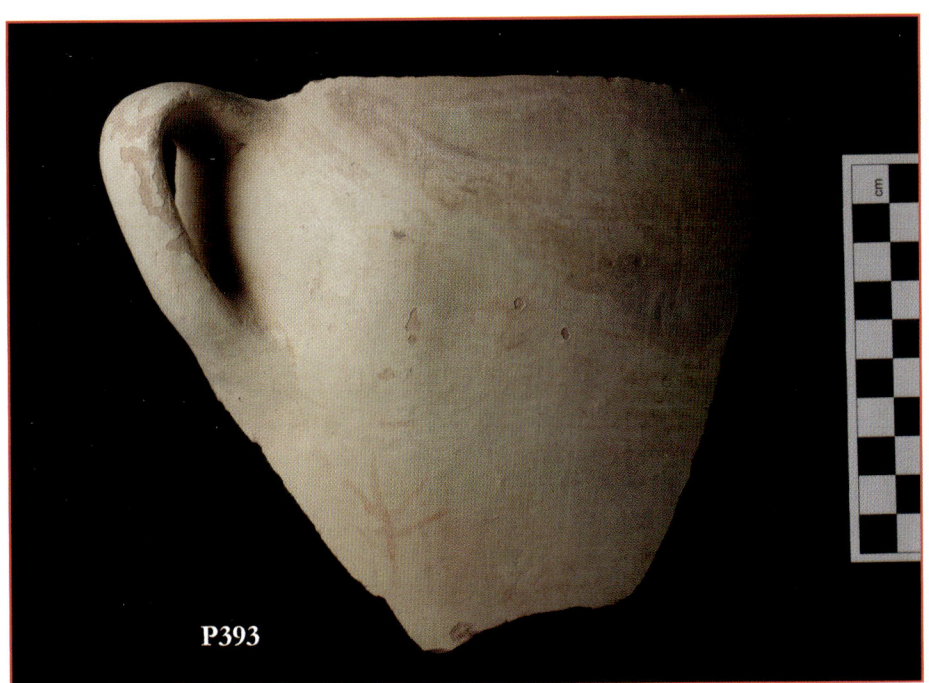

*Figure 194. The upper part of a Marl-D amphora typical of the reign of Amenhotep III.*

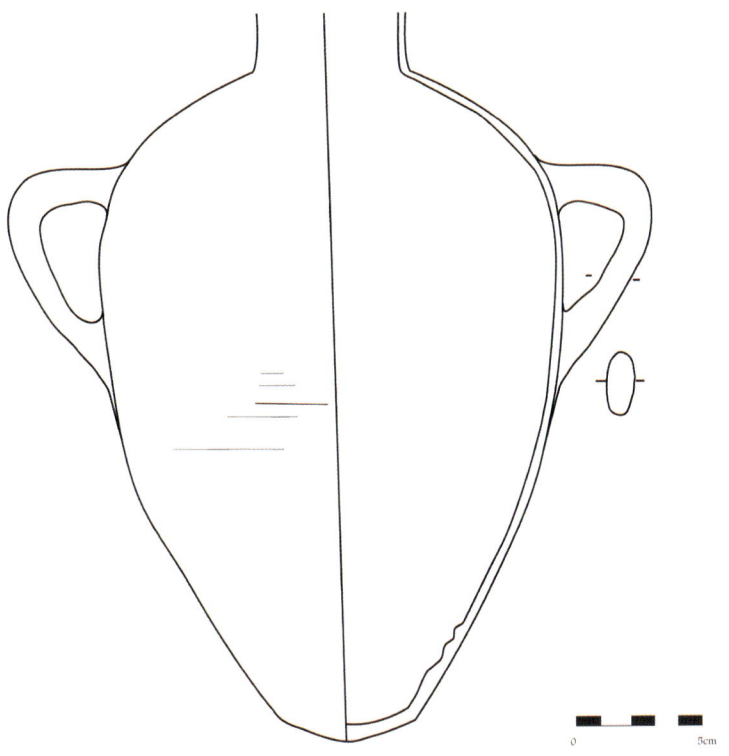

*Figure 195. The profile of a Marl-D amphora typical of the reign of Amenhotep III.*

3. Third Intermediate Period

Sherds from this phase were recovered mainly from the spoil-heaps although several sherds were found in Shafts Two and Four. This material represents around 2% of the whole body of ceramic material.

*Figure 196. Third Intermediate Period (XXIst dynasty) ovoid jar.*

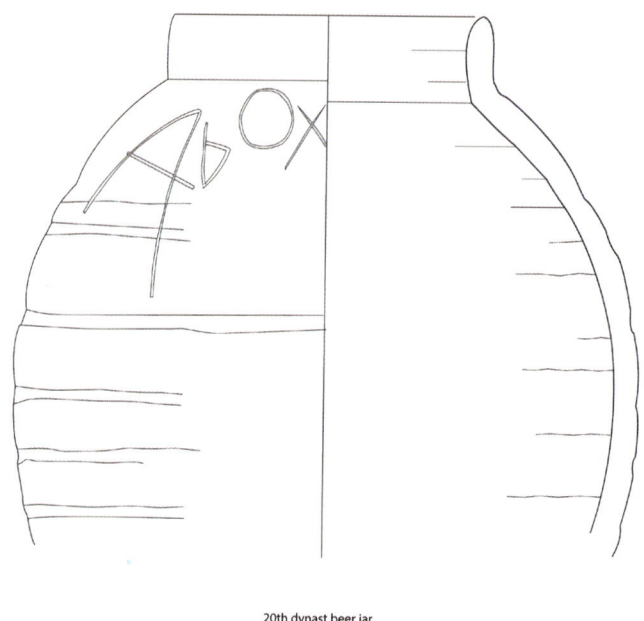

20th dynast beer jar

*Figure 197. Third Intermediate Period (XXIst dynasty) ovoid jar showing pot-marks.*

4. Byzantine sherds

Many sherds from Late Roman 7 amphorae were recovered. These accounted for roughly 8% of the whole body of ceramic material. The sherds came mainly from the surface but were also found in quantity in Shaft Four. This raises the possibility that Shaft Four was partially cleared and used as a hermitage in the Coptic period. The Wadi Bairiya contains at least nine Coptic sites.

From the surviving rims the following totals have been calculated:

| | |
|---|---|
| White-washed storage jars | 166 |
| Marl-D amphorae | 159 |
| Open forms (bowls) | 18 |
| Closed forms (jars) | 41 |
| Stands | 5 |

The weights recovered from the various shafts can be summarised as follows:

| | | |
|---|---|---|
| Shaft Two | 773.00kg | 38% |
| Shaft Three | 119.55kg | 6% |
| Shaft Four | 695.00kg | 34% |
| Shaft Five | 279.50kg | 14% |
| Shaft Six | 106.75kg | 5% |
| Spoil-heaps | 47.00kg | 2% |
| Surface | 21.50kg | 1% |

These quantities and the very mixed nature of the ceramic material in each shaft support the view that much of this material was removed from the shafts and taken to the tops of the spoil-heaps from where it fell back into the shafts. However, the large quantity of white-washed storage jar fragments found in the lower fill in Shaft Two Chamber Bd and the largely complete white-washed storage jars found in Shaft Five Chambers A and Bb suggest not everything was removed.

The white-washed storage jars from the WB1 site are consistently of a narrow, slender form. They are wheel-made and although their shape is different to the broader, more open-mouthed jars found with some contemporary material[2], we remain confident of their Amenhotep III date[3]. Comparisons with storage jars portrayed on *talatat* dating to the reign of AmenhotepIV/Akhenaten confirm that such jars were being used into that reign, often alongside vessels of different profiles used for different purposes.

Vessels recovered from burials at Soleb, and dating to the reign of Amenhotep III, are the same size and have identical profiles[4]. The Soleb examples are decorated, however.

## Other types of note

### Foundation deposit material

Only four sherds, all of XVIIIth dynasty date, were found which may relate to foundation deposits. These might explain the function of Shaft Seven. The material was found widely scattered and no other material peculiar to foundation deposits, such as named plaques and model tools, was recovered.

---

2. In particular see the jars found by the University of Basel in KV40: https://aegyptologie.philhist.unibas.ch/fileadmin/user_upload/aegyptologie/Forschung/Projekte/King_s_Valley/Report_2014-2015.pdf
3. I am grateful to David Aston who inspected the ceramics on site and was of the same opinion.
4. Schiff Giorgini, M. (1971) "*Soleb II. Les Nécropoles*", Sansoni, Firenze. p. 125 Figs 180 & 181.

*Figure 198. Possible foundation deposit material.*

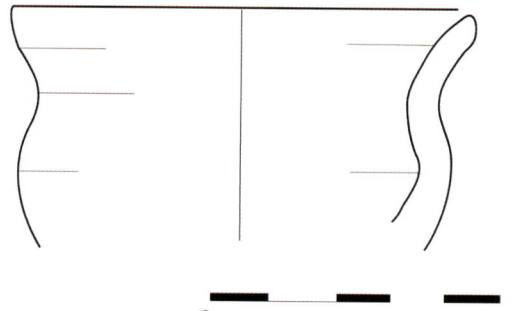

*Figure 199. Possible foundation deposit material profile.*

## Red-slipped storage jars

Two examples of this type of New Kingdom vessel came from the spoil-heaps.

*Figure 200. Red-slipped storage jar.*

## Beer jars

These represent 7.2% of the total quantity of ceramics. The largest number of beer jar sherds was recovered from Shaft Two (54%), followed by Shaft Four (24%). Shaft Three accounted for 7% of these sherds, Shaft Five 3% and the spoil-heaps 12%. These were all compatible with an XVIIIth dynasty date.

*Figure 201. Hathor face.*

## Hathor vessel

A single example of a Hathor vessel was found in Shaft Two Chamber A. The shape of the vessel is not known as only the Hathor face has survived. Similar XVIIIth dynasty fragments have been found at Gurob and Malqata[5].

## Polychrome vessels

Two examples of polychrome vessels were recovered from the spoil-heaps.

One of these jars is similar to a type found in large quantities at Malqata with examples dating from the reign of Thutmose IV through to Akhenaten. The second example is probably earlier and of a type found from the reign of Thutmose IV.

*Figure 202. Polychrome vessel.*

---

5. There examples in the Manchester Museum: www.egyptmanchester.wordpress.com/tag/blue-painted-pottery/.

*Figure 203. Polychrome vessel.*

## Tools

Many sherds were found with worn edges indicative of use as tools. In most cases it is not possible to be sure when these were used. They could have been used when the tombs were being created. Equally, they could have been used at any time when the fill of the tombs was being excavated by robbers. Some tools (*Figure 204*) show signs of plaster covering the working edges and so must relate to the original construction of the tombs.

*Figure 204. Sherd used for plastering.*

# CHAPTER EIGHT
# HUMAN REMAINS

(Corinne Duhig contributed the analysis and evaluation of the human remains)

The human remains recovered from the surface, spoil-heaps and shafts on the WB1 site were in poor condition. Many other tombs which have been extensively robbed still contain mummified human remains, the bodies being of very little interest once stripped. In the case of the WB1 shafts two toes retained some attached soft tissue but otherwise the other human remains had all been reduced to bone. These bones were all disarticulated and there were no identifiable bodies.

The bones recovered from Shaft Five, Chambers B, Ba and Bb were the most complete but even here the bones were scattered across the chamber floors. The bones recovered elsewhere were broken and in many cases recovered in very small fragments. Many of the recovered jaw bones were without teeth. We had expected to recover these during our clearance work but by the time initial excavation was completed few teeth had been recovered.

Damage to the bones appears to have been caused by many factors: fire, weathering, crushing from rock and debris movement and intrusive human activity.

The bones were collected feature by feature and examined for age, sex, pathological lesions and non-metric traits. All important diagnostic bones were numbered.

The methods used were those of White, T. & Folkens, P. (2005) and Bass, W. (1987)[1] as well as Ortner, D. & Putschar, W. (1985) and Scheuer, L. & Black, S. (2000)[2].

## SHAFT TWO

All the bones from this shaft were fragmented, burnt, weathered and discoloured. Long bones and skulls were the most fragmented.

The MNI of fourteen from this shaft was determined from the two right innominates (both lacking the pubic bone) and twelve fragments of right ilia. Additionally, there were ten right femora and eight left femora. It should be borne in mind that the looting of these shafts might well have led to portions of the same individual being re-deposited in different shafts, so that the overall MNI (a closer representation of how many individuals were originally deposited) will not be a simple addition of the number from each shaft — see the Conclusions section.

Skull fragments were reconstructed to form four incomplete skulls for four individuals.

### Sex and age

Sex could be determined by the conformation of the sciatic notch and pre-auricular areas of the innominates/ilia, and on the skulls, the form of the mastoid process, mandibular mental eminence and supra-orbital margins.

---

1. White, T. & Folkens, P. (2005) "*The Human Bone Manual*", Academic Press/Elsevier Publishing, Burlington, San Diego, London and Bass, W. (1987) "*Human Osteology: a laboratory and field manual*", Missouri Archaeological Society, U.S.A..
2. Ortner, D. & Putschar, W. (1985) "*Identification of pathological conditions in human skeletal remains*", Smithsonian Institution Press, Washington; and Scheuer, L. & Black, S. (2000) "*Developmental Juvenile Osteology*", Elsevier Publishing, San Diego and London.

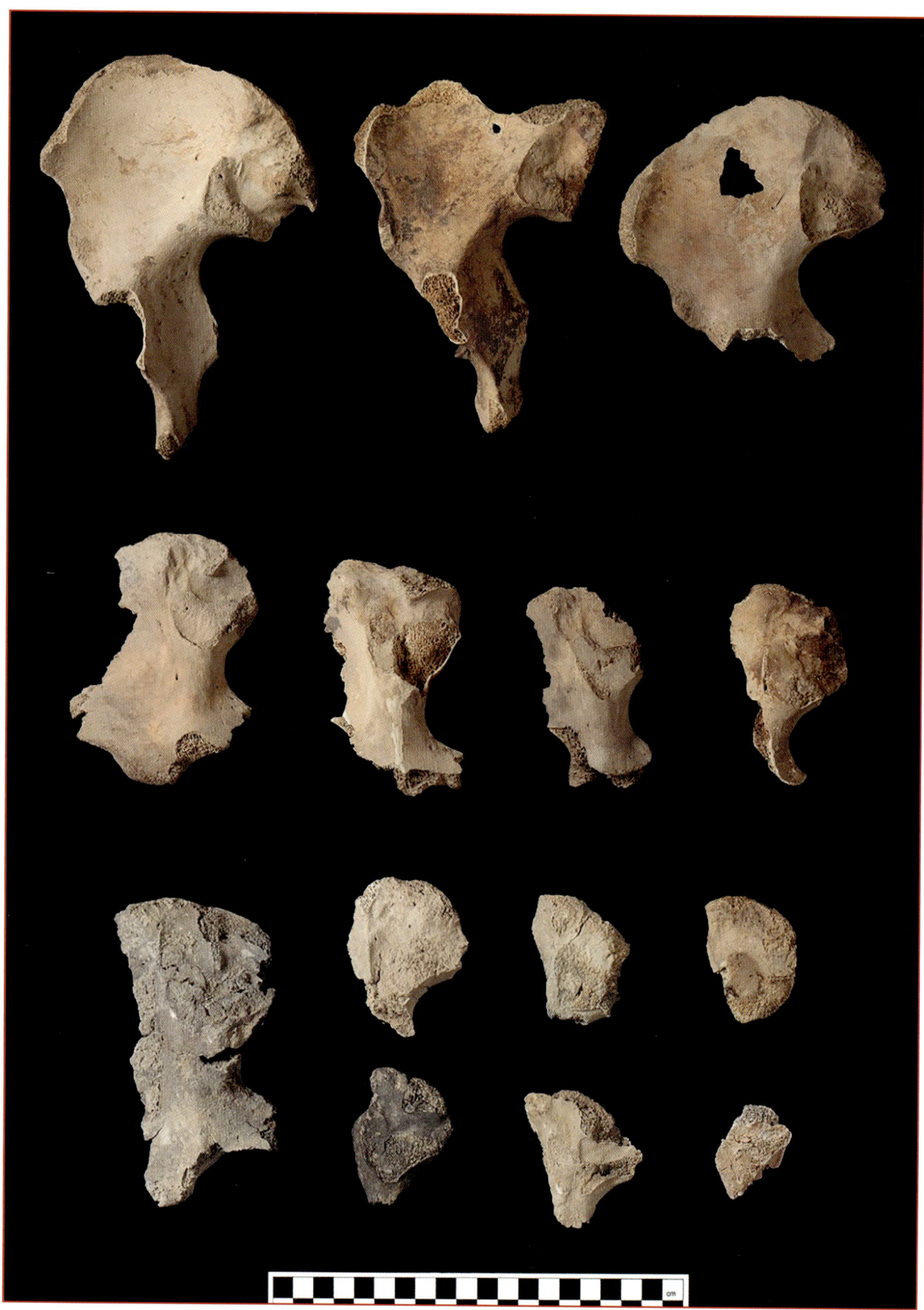

Figure 205. Innominates/ilia from Shaft Two.

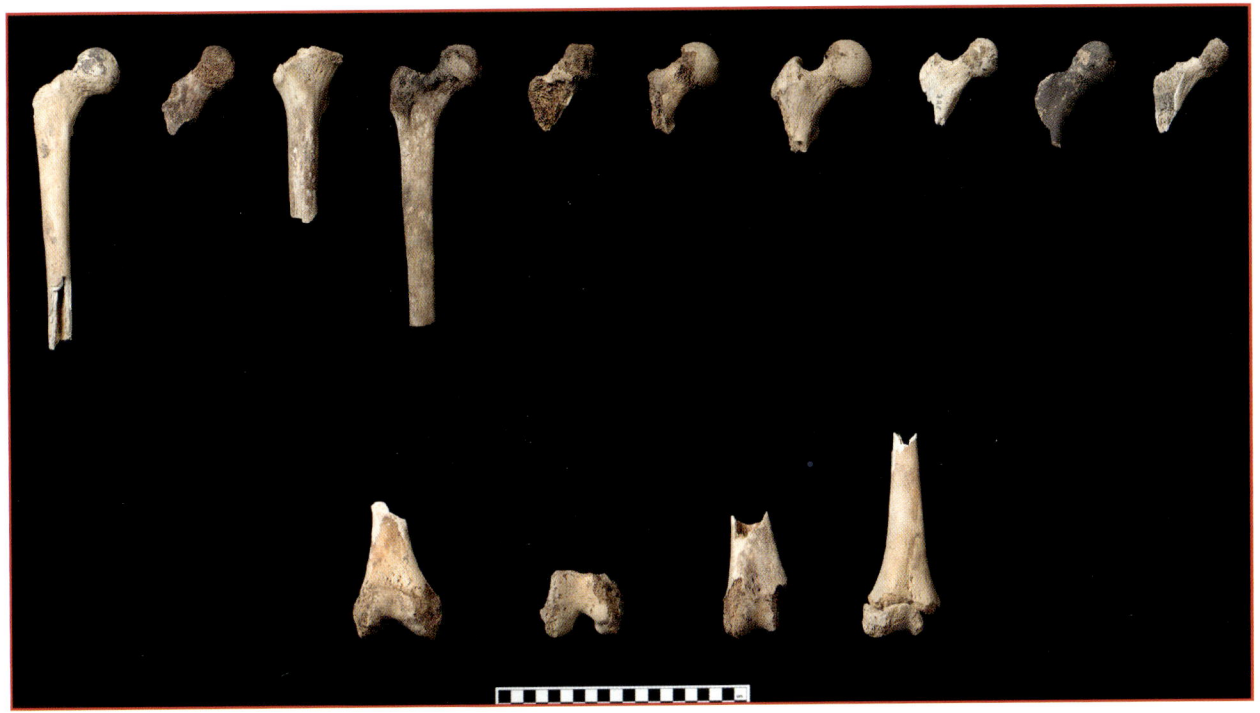

*Figure 206. Right femora from Shaft Two.*

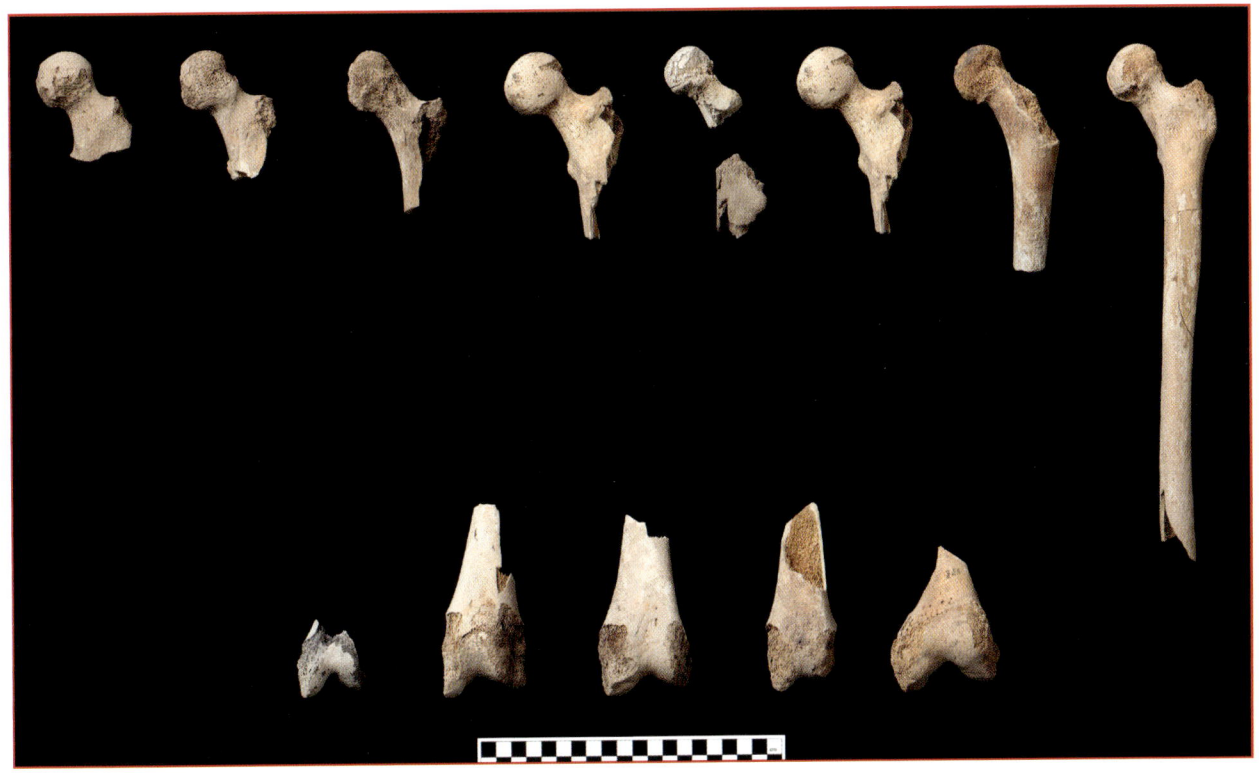

*Figure 207. Left femora from Shaft Two.*

Using the right innominates/ilia, the sex-age distribution is:

| Specimen | Bone | Sex | Age |
| --- | --- | --- | --- |
| 1 | R innominate | F | 35–39 |
| 2 | R innominate | F | Adult |
| 3 | R ilium fragment | F | Adult |
| 4 | R ilium fragment | F | Adult |
| 5 | R ilium fragment | F [if not fully adult, sex not attributable] | N/D |
| 6 | R ilium fragment | F [if not fully adult, sex not attributable] | N/D |
| 7 | R ilium fragment | ?F | 18–20 |
| 8 | R ilium fragment | ?F | 18–20 |
| 9 | R ilium fragment | ?F [if not fully adult, sex not attributable] | N/D |
| 10 | R ilium fragment | N/D | 25–29 |
| 11 | R ilium fragment | N/D | N/D |
| 12 | R ilium fragment | N/D | N/D |
| 13 | R ilium fragment | N/D | N/D |
| 14 | R ilium fragment | N/D | N/D |

Two skulls are female, one probably female, and one male in form. The male skull does not necessarily add to the number of individuals, because it might be associated with one of the ilia Nos. 10–14. Epiphyseal (growth-plate) closure in the post-cranial bones also indicated two individuals of 18-22 years old at death, possibly the same as the two possible-females, Nos. 7 and 8..

### Pathology

The skull fragments showed evidence of *cribra orbitalia*[3] in two adult left orbits (*Figure 208*). The occipital and right parietals in two of the reconstructed skulls display *cribra crani*[4]. The left first maxillary molar from Feature 1009 shows evidence of dental caries. The skull numbered 227 has evidence of possible *meningitis*[5] (*Figure 209 and 210*).

---

3. This pitting and sieve-like bone growth within the eye orbit is a sign of iron deficiency anaemia due to inadequate iron in the diet, inaccessible dietary iron or iron loss/malabsorption due to intestinal parasites. It can indicate malaria, which can cause iron deficiency by inhibiting iron absorption and/or suppressing the production of red-blood cells, but there are complex interactions between the effects of the malaria parasites and other parasites, and existing iron deficiency actually inhibits malaria infection. Spottiswoode *et al.* (2014); Waldron, T. (2009) "*Palaeopathology*", Cambridge University Press, Cambridge. pp. 136-7.
4. Similar pitting and porosity in the bones of the skull vault, with the same aetiology although slower to appear and to heal — *cribra orbitalia* is described as the 'sentinel lesion'.
5. Meningitis is inflammation of the meninges, membranes which encase the brain within the skull. It sometimes leaves characteristic markings, raised and 'worm like' on the inner bone surface of the skull, although in the past people rarely survived meningitis long enough for the bone changes to manifest. E.g. Ortner, D., (2003) "*Identification of pathological conditions in human skeletal remains*", Academic Press/Elsevier Science, New York p. 93.

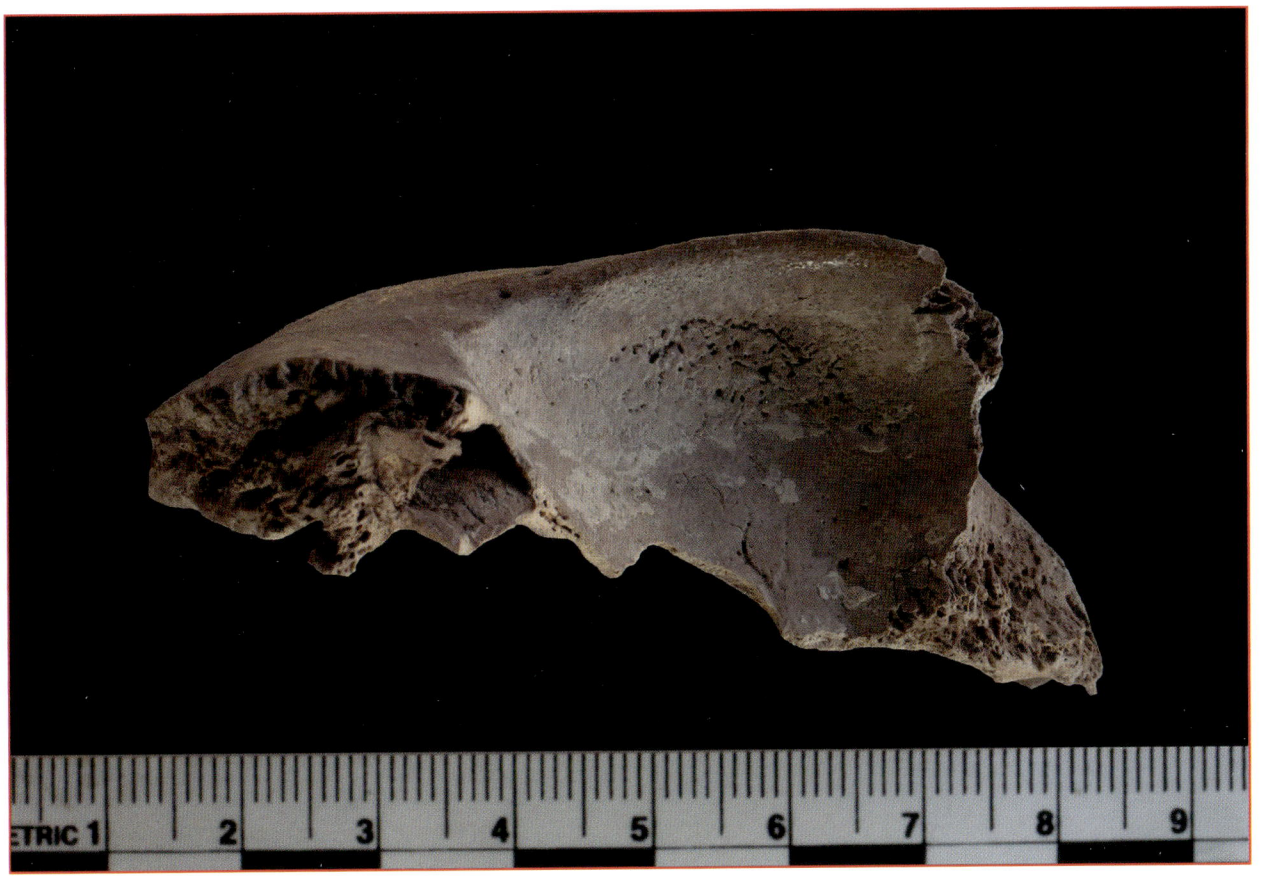

*Figure 208. Cribra orbitalia from Shaft Two.*

*Figure 209. Skull 227 from Shaft Two.*

*Figure 210. Evidence of meningitis in Skull 227 from Shaft Two (detail: the internal surface of the skull vault).*

**Non-metric traits**[6]

Four left humeri have septal apertures of the coronoid fossa (*Figure 211*) which can suggest a genetic relationship. However, it is impossible to evaluate this without DNA testing. Many royal mummies share this trait and it has also been observed in very many non-royals. Its occurrence varies widely across populations but appears to have a direct relation to the gracility of the population (because the coronoid fossa is thinner the more delicate the bone is, and it can thus perforate more easily); ancient Egyptians, tending to have gracile skeletons, are more likely to manifest the trait.

The reconstructed parietal fragments show evidence of parietal foramen in three skulls. This trait is, however, frequent in most populations, with a prevalence from 37% to nearly 80% (Hauser & De Stefano 1989: 81) , so it is unlikely to be informative at this site.

One right lateral incisor has an accessory tubercule and very slight shovelling (Figure 213). These traits have a heritable element and might indicate relatedness were there any other individuals found with them — although not the case here.

---

6. Hauser, G. & de Stefano, G. (1989) "*Epigenetic Variants of the Human Skull*", E. Schweizerbart'sche Verlagsbuchhandlung (Nägele u. Obermiller), Stuttgart, Germany. Saunders, S. & Rainey, D. (2007) "*Nonmetric Trait Variation in the Skeleton: Abnormalities, Anomalies, and Atavisms*" in eds Katzenberg, M. and S. R. Saunders, S. (2007) "*Biological Anthropology of the Human Skeleton*", doi:10.1002/9780470245842.ch17.

7. Ahmes-Nefertari, Meryetamun, Thutmose I, Thutmose III, Yuya, Amenhotep III, Tiye, CG61075, Tutankhamun, Seti I, Ramesses II, Ramesses VI. Harris, J. & Wente, E. (1990) "*An X-Ray Atlas of the Royal Mummies*", University of Chicago Press, Chicago and Hawass, Z. & Saleem, S., (2016) "*Scanning the Pharaohs*", American University in Cairo Press, Cairo.

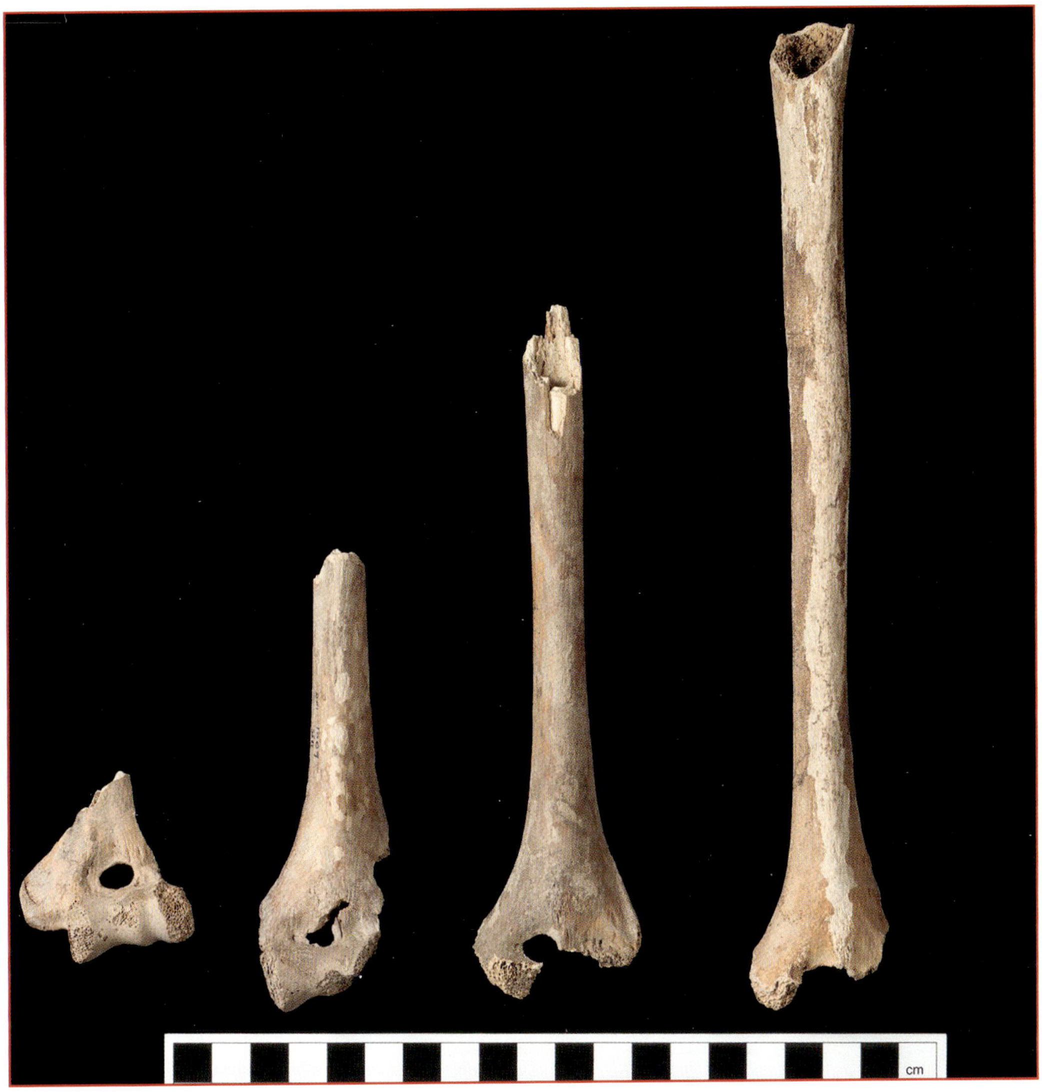

*Figure 211. Septal apertures of the coronoid fossa in humerus bones from Shaft Two.*

*Figure 212. Accessory tubercle in a right lateral incisor from Shaft Two.*

## SHAFT THREE

Shaft Three contained a disappointing quantity of human remains consistent with its slightly more distant location (10m as opposed to 5m in the case of Shaft Two and Four) from the principal site at which the dismantling of the burials seems to have taken place (to the south of Shafts Two and Four). The shaft contained a mixture of badly burnt skull, pelvis, vertebra, rib, clavicle, foot and long bone fragments. There are no duplications so the resulting MNI is one adult individual of unknown sex.

There were no traces of any pathological or non-metric traits.

## SHAFT FOUR

The features which contained human remains in this shaft were 1004, 1053, 1054, 1055 and 1056. Only a few fragmented and burnt human bones were recovered, from various areas of the body. These are tabulated below for age and sex and then the MNI is calculated.

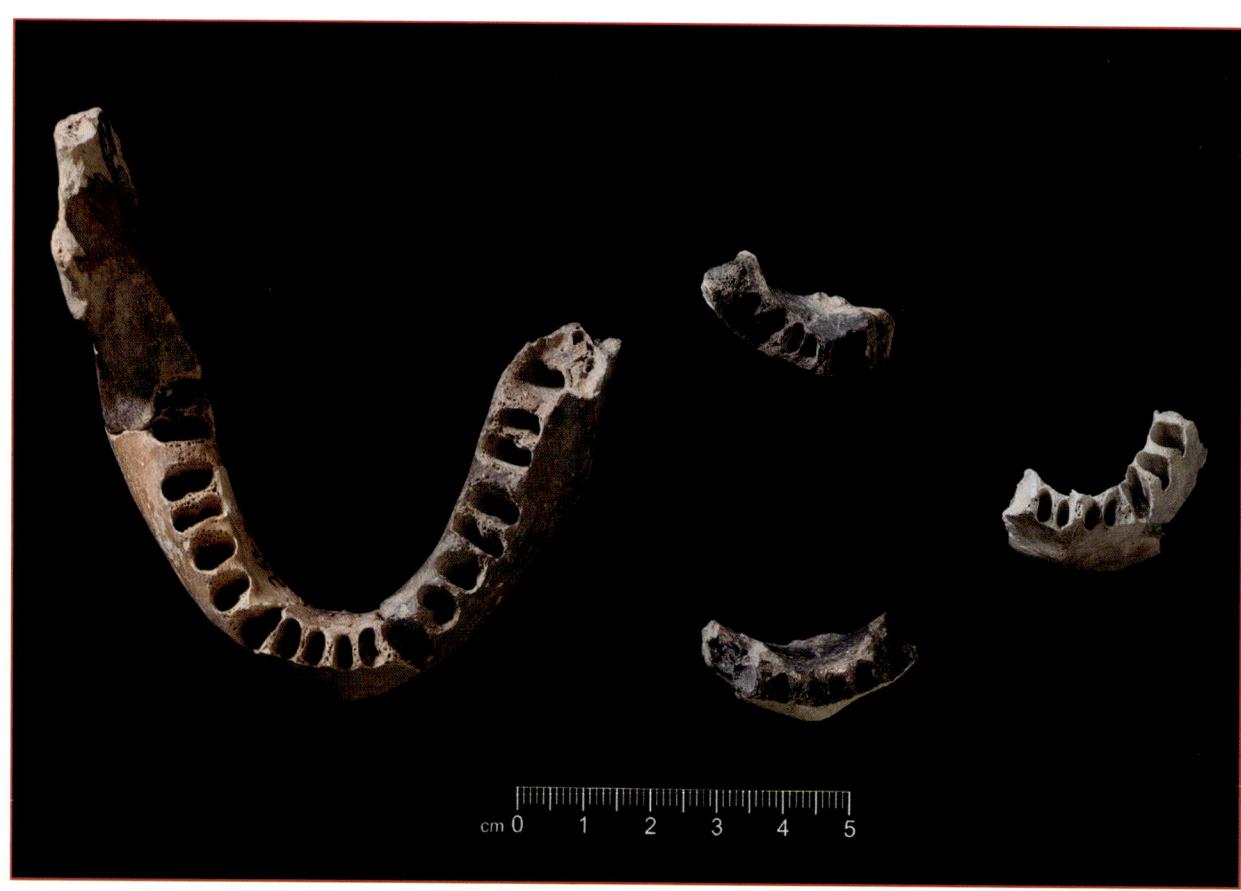

*Figure 213. Mandible fragments from Shaft Four.*

| Specimen | Bone | Sex | Age |
|---|---|---|---|
| 1 | mandible | F | N/D |
| 2 | mandible | ?F | N/D |
| 3 | mandible | N/D | N/D |
| 4 | mandible | N/D | N/D |
| 5 | L distal femoral epiphysis | N/A | ??12 years |
| 6 | R distal femoral epiphysis | N/A | ??12 years |
| 7 | R proximal humeral epiphysis | N/A | ??12 years |
| 8 | vertebral body 'unfused' | N/A | 1–6 years |
| 9 | proximal epiphysis of hand phalanx | N/A | 1–6 years |
| 10 | ilium fragment | F | Adult |
| 11 | R humerus with septal aperture | | |
| 12 | R humerus with septal aperture | | |

The number of individuals can be calculated as:

| Individual | Bone(s) | Sex | Age |
|---|---|---|---|
| 1 | mandible and ilium | F | Adult |
| 2 | mandible | ?F | Adult |
| 3 | mandible | N/D | Adult |
| 4 | mandible | N/D | Adult |
| 5 | (a) proximal humerus and (b) distal femur | N/A | child or adolescent of 12+ |
| 6 | (a) vertebra and (b) phalanx | N/A | 1–6 years |

Therefore, six individuals at least are represented, and potentially seven or eight depending on the relative ages of 5(a) and 5(b) and 6(a) and 6(b).

## Pathology and non-metric traits

No pathological changes were present. Two right humeri have septal apertures, one is a small pinhole and the other is a true perforation. One right parietal fragment has a parietal foramen.

## Shaft Five

The bones in Shaft Five were in a better state of preservation than those in Shafts Two, Three and Four. The reason for this is clear: the bones had lain undisturbed since antiquity with the majority of the human remains recovered from the lower part of Shaft Five, a part of the tomb which was undetected by modern robbers.

All the bones in this shaft were disarticulated, but there were few traces of discolouring or burning.

## Minimum Number of Individuals

The femora were the most plentiful elements, and these were used to produce an MNI, totalling 14 individuals. Tabulation of the ages and sexes of the pelvic bones and skulls increases this number slightly to 16. It must be borne in mind that age and sex determination are uncertain when working with completely disarticulated bones, and further work including additional measurements will be required to clarify the numbers and ages.

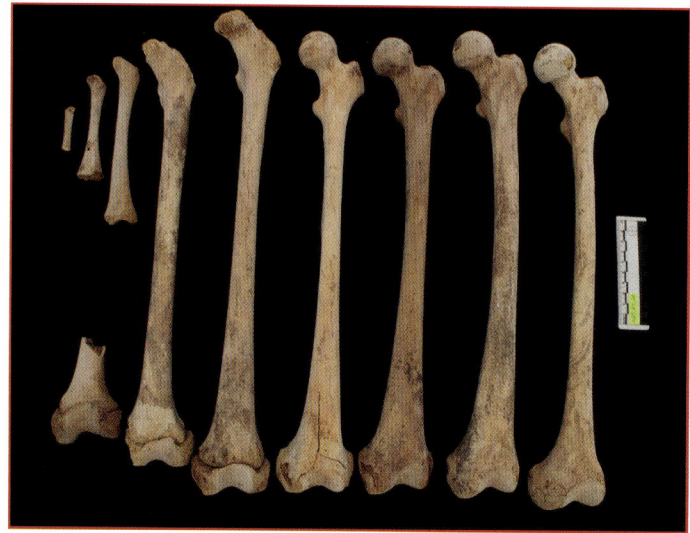

*Figure 214. Left femora from Shaft Five.*

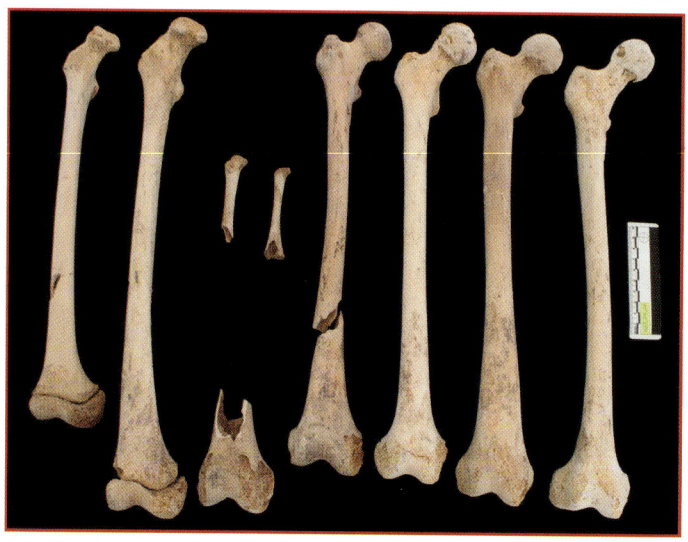

*Figure 215. Right femora from Shaft Five.*

## FEMORA COMPOSITE FOR MNIs

| Bone | side | segment | age | measurements / comments / non-metric | ID | MNIs |
|---|---|---|---|---|---|---|
| Femur | L | shaft | ?1.5 m | see bone 8 in 1025 (?same ind. of 1.5 m) | 126 | 1: 1.5 m |
| Femur | R | C | 1.5 m | | 8 | |
| Femur | L | C | 6-12 m | without epiphysis GL: about 107mm | 14 | 1: 6–12 m |
| Femur | R | P⅓, M⅓ | infant | | 10 | |
| Femur | L | C | 18 m | missing epiphysis | 1 | 1: 18 m |
| Femur | L | D⅓, DE | 9–12 | DE is open & loose. Belongs to 102 | 54 | 1: 9 y |
| Femur | R | shaft glued | 9 y | Maresh | 102 | |
| Femur | L | C. [PE found as separate piece] | 12–15 | DE loose and open | 106 | 3 from L: 12–15 |
| Femur | L | C | 12–15 | miss PE. DE is open & loose | 53 | |
| Femur | L | PE, P⅓, M⅓ | 12–15 | DE is open & loose. Miss the head | B13 | |
| Femur | L | great troch. E. | 12–15 | [?part of #B13] | B2 | |
| Femur | R | DE | 12–15 | age approximately | B9 | |
| Femur | R | great trochanter | 12–15 | age approximately | B11 | |
| Femur | R | missing DE | 12–15 | open epiphysis | 18 | |
| Femur | L | C | 15: 20 | marked by E line. (Allen Fossa) prob pair | 19 | 2: ?15–20 y |
| Femur | R | C | 15: 20 | marked by E line. (Allen Fossa) prob pair | 17 | |
| Femur | R | DE | 15:20 | bigger and developed more than above | B10 | |
| Femur | R | great trochanter | 15:20 | bigger and developed more than above | B12 | |
| Femur | R | C | 17:20 | DE closing 90% (McKern) (Allen Fossa) | 103 | 1 : 17–20 y |
| Femur | L | C | >20 | (Allen Fossa) perhaps pair with #51 | 20 | 4 from R: adult |
| Femur | L | C | adult | glued (Allen fossa small) | 52 | |
| Femur | L | C | adult | | 105 | |
| Femur | R | C | adult | Allen fossa [perhaps pair with #20] | 51 | |
| Femur | R | C | over 20 | | 104 | |
| Femur | R | D⅓ | adult | match with #B5? | B6 | |
| Femur | R | PE | adult | match with #B6 or #B14? | B5 | |
| Femur | R | DE | adult | match with #B5? | B14 | |
| | | | | | | TOTAL 14 |

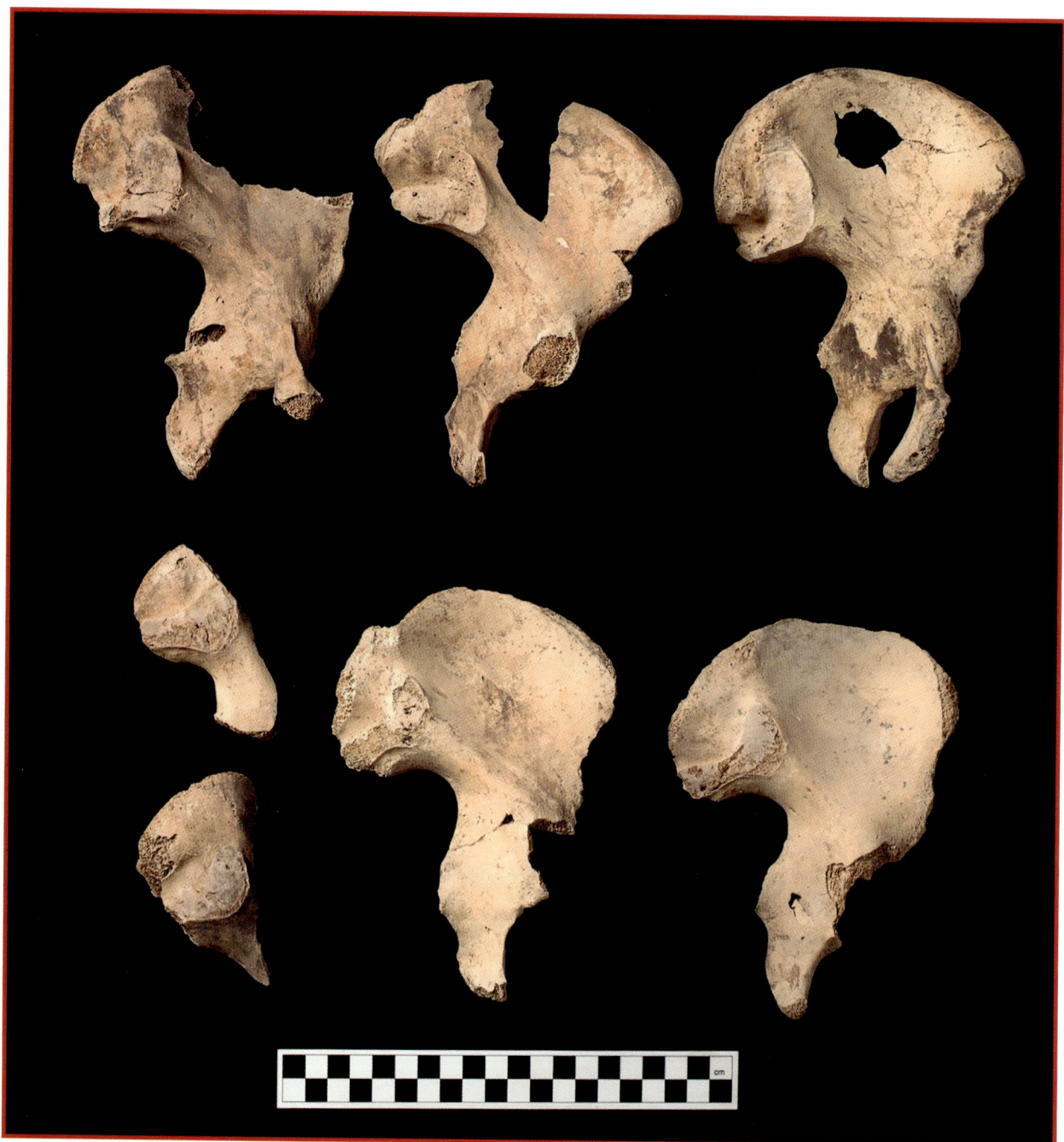

*Figure 216. Left innominates/ilium fragments from Shaft Five.*

There are six right and six left innominate bones that are late teenage or adult. These do not conveniently pair up. Pairing them as far as is feasible produces one ?female of 40–49 years, one female of 20–25 years, one ?female of the same age range, and one 'sex not determinable' of the same age range again. This conveniently, perhaps deceptively, matches the MNI of four adults that is given by the femora.

In addition there are three individuals aged 15–20 years represented by innominates, one of whom shows a lesion which is commonly — though not absolutely exclusively— indicative of late-stage pregnancy[8]. This individual, therefore, is skeletally immature and would normally be classified as 'sex not determinable', but she can be listed as female because she was almost certainly a mother.

Remains of the skulls, plus all the evidence from the other bones found, support the predominance of females amongst the adults, but there are two mandibles/mandible fragments that appear ?male and an occipital bone that appears male. It is hoped that additional measurements of some bones can clarify whether there were in fact any adult males present.

## Sex and age

The ages are given in the table above: one individual of 1.5 months, one of 6–12 months, one about 18 months, one 9 years, three 12–15 years, two possibly 15–20 years or possibly adult, one 17–20 years and four adults.

Sex cannot be determined for immature skeletons, because the skeletal changes caused by puberty are still developing.

For the adults, using only features of the the skull and pelvis to determine the sex, just one individual — represented by a mandibular fragment — might be male, while all others that can be determined are female or possibly female. One almost complete pelvis is that of a woman of 40–49 years, and two female innominate bones are of the age 20–24 years (they might well form a pair, hence representing one young woman only) while another possible-female innominate is again around 20–24 years.

## Pathology

The frontal bone fragments from the skulls of four individuals (two adults and two immatures) showed evidence of *cribra orbitalia* (*Figures 217 and 218*). As explained above, this disorder indicates a systemic iron deficiency from one or more of a variety of causes. It is more commonly found in immature individuals, because their bone responds more rapidly to the need for increased red-blood-cell production, and it tends to heal in later life. *Figures 217 and 218* below show the healing form in one of the adult skulls and the still-active form in one of the the immature skulls.

A fourth lumbar vertebra showed evidence of spondylolysis (*Figures 219 and 220*). The arch of the vertebra has broken, for which the cause is usually a combination of weakness at the junction of the arch and the body of the vertebra, and a shearing stress

---

8. A very marked pre-auricular sulcus of 'groove of pregnancy' form, caused when the ligaments holding the pelvis tightly together soften due to the effects of late pregnancy hormones.

on the lower back which breaks through the line of weakness. In modern times various sports are implicated, commonly canoeing, where the lower back is stressed while the legs are fully extended, although it is not difficult to imagine other activities in ancient times.

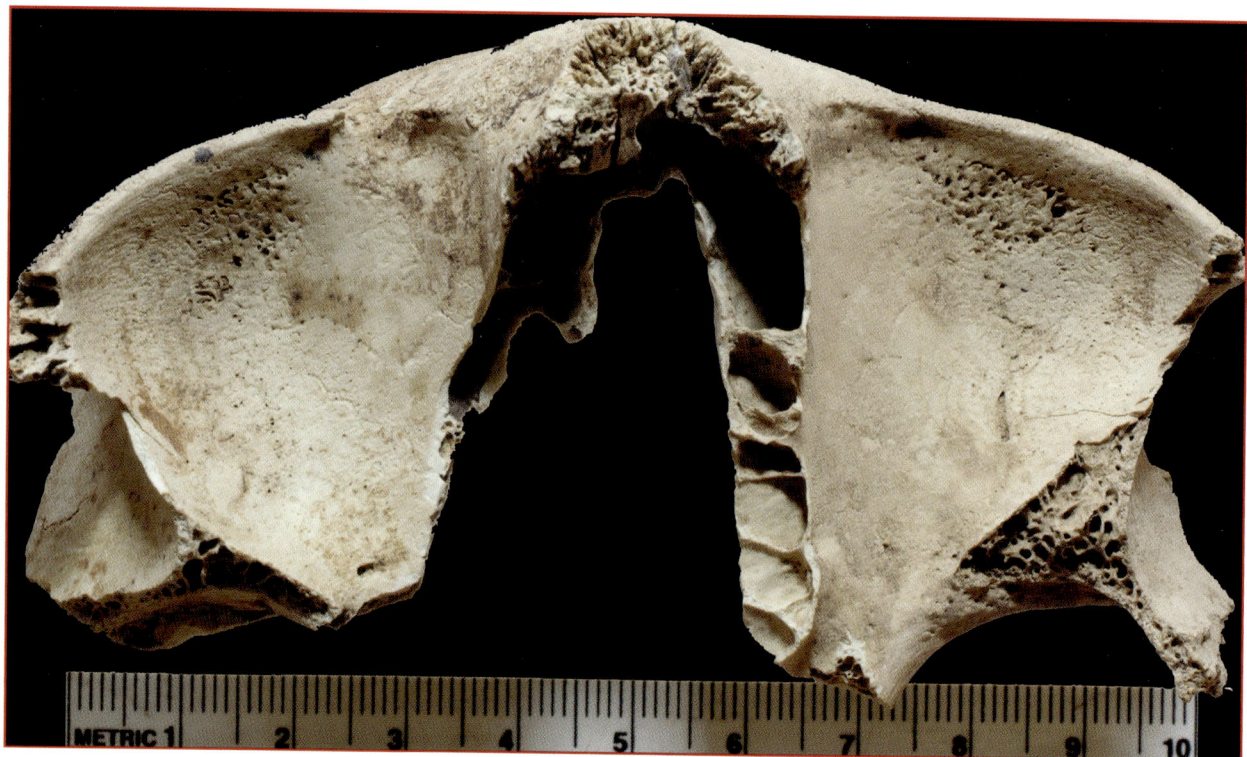

*Figure 217. Adult frontal bone from Shaft Five Chamber Ba showing signs of cribra orbitalia.*

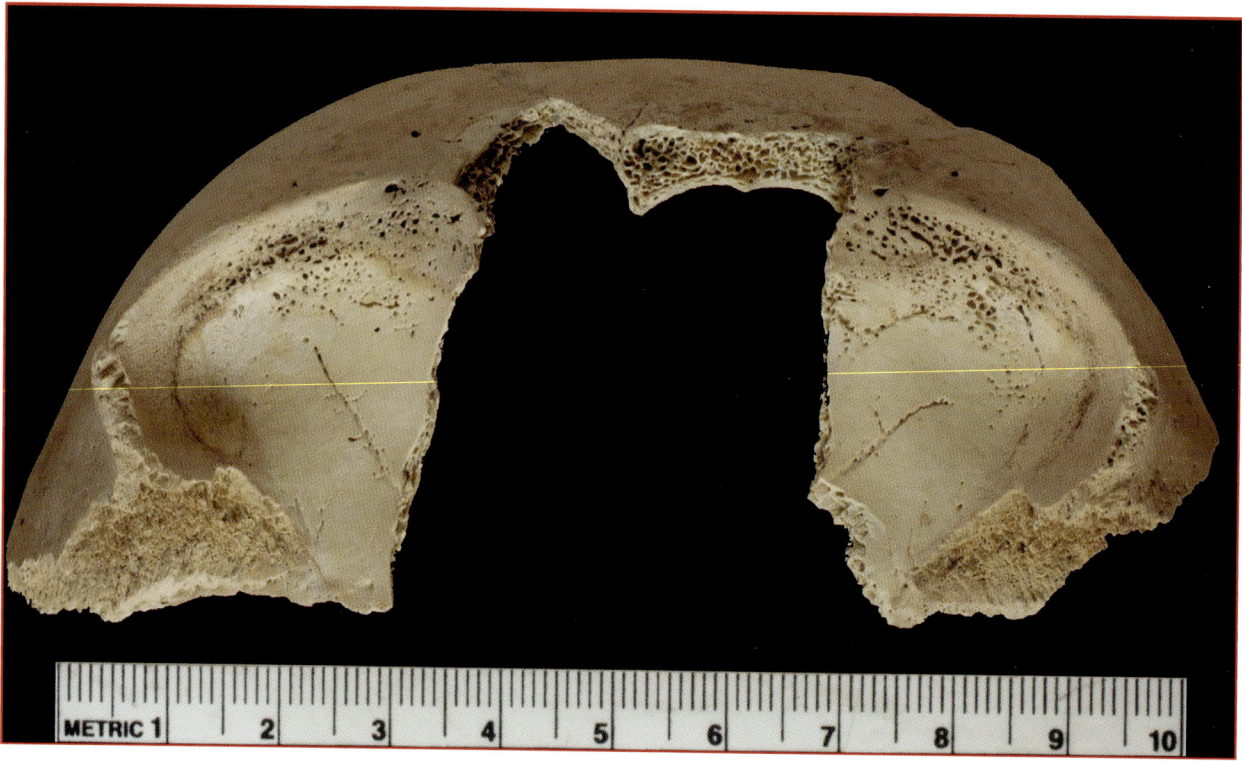

*Figure 218. Juvenile frontal bone from Shaft Five Chamber B showing signs of cribra orbitalia.*

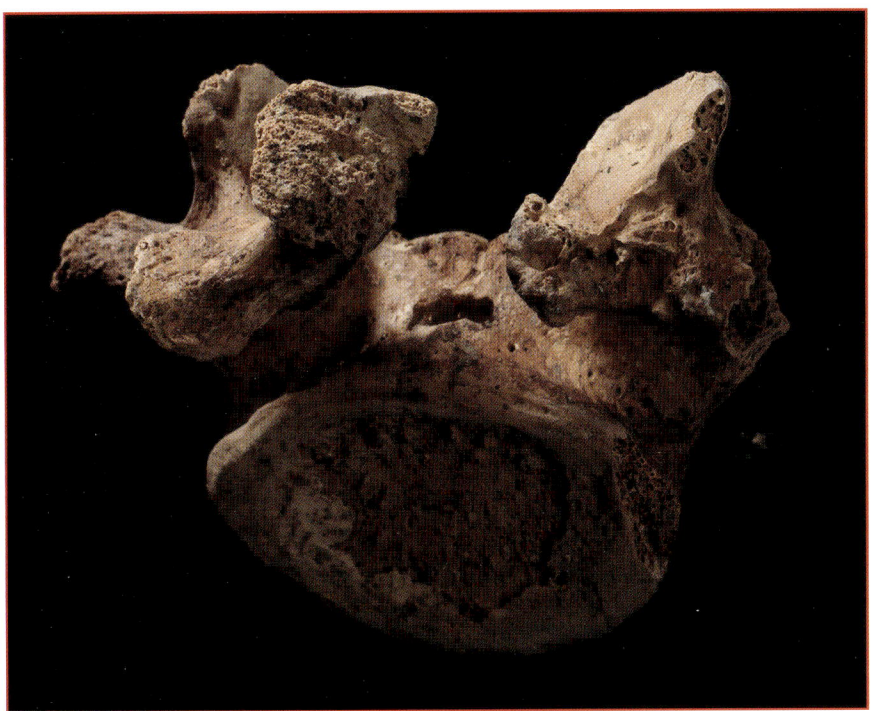

*Figure 219. Fourth lumbar vertebra from Shaft Five Chamber Bb showing evidence of spondylolysis. The edges of the break have disorganised bone, showing that there was some movement of the broken-off fragment.*

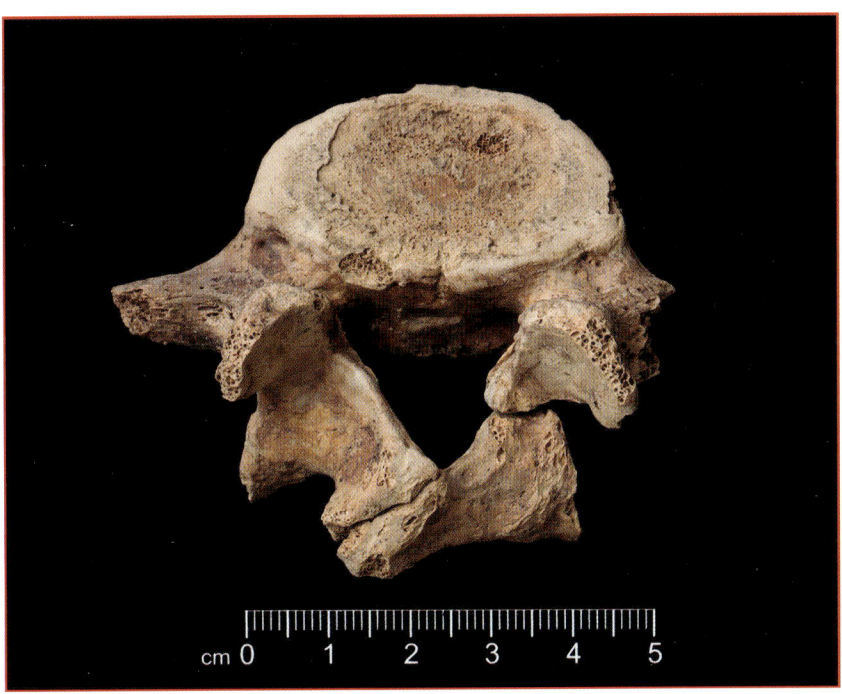

*Figure 220. The same fourth lumbar vertebra as in Figure 15 re-united with the fragment broken off due to the stress fracture. The fragment was found a year later than the vertebra.*

A right mandibular molar 2 showed evidence of dental caries. This is relatively uncommon in ancient Egypt, except in the very old, because the diet lacked refined carbohydrates; loss of tooth enamel due to extreme wear, consequent infection of the pulp and resultant abscesses and recession of the bony gums because of tooth movement were all common, and are largely absent in the remains from WB1 only because there are so many young individuals.

### Non-metric traits

Five individuals displayed septal apertures of the coronoid fossa, as discussed above, and three individuals had supra-orbital notches in the frontal bones.

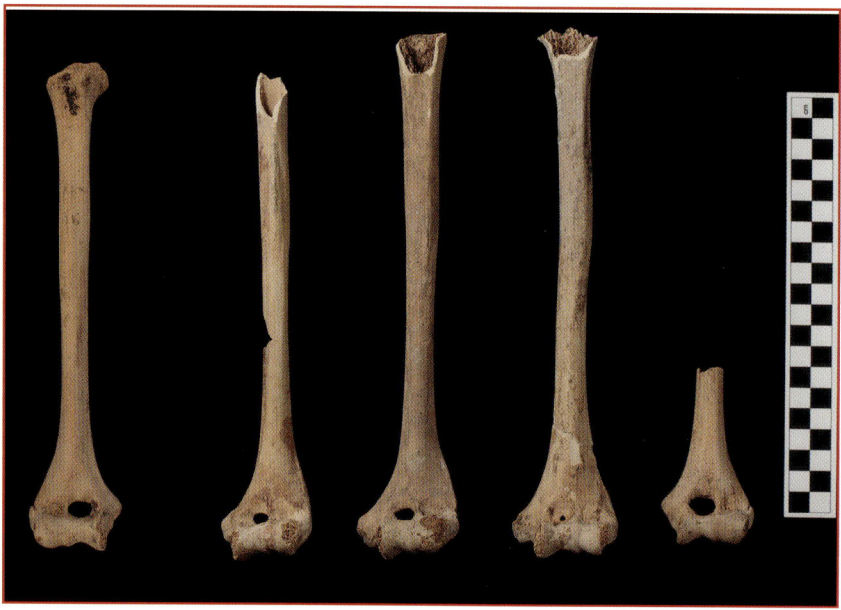

*Figure 221. Humerus bones from Shaft Five showing septal apertures of the coronoid fossa.*

We were able to reconstruct a skull from different fragments from feature 1026 (Skull 123 from Chamber Bb: *Figures 222 and 223*). This probable female had a right lateral incisor with 'shovelling', which describes the effect of the edges of the tooth crown being turned-in or thickened to produce a shovel-shaped profile. This trait is more often found in Mongoloid than Caucasoid skulls[9]. Shovelling can be so extreme as to produce a tube, as in this case (*Figure 224*) when it is called an invaginate tooth — although the genetic cause of invagination is likely to be different to common shovelling.

The skull also showed antemortem loss of both right and left middle incisors, with healed and thinned bone where the two sockets had been. This tooth loss might have been caused by dental caries resulting from the shovel/invaginate shape of the teeth but three reasons are against this explanation: there was no sign of caries in the single surviving lateral incisor; such extreme shovelling or invagination tends to be on the lateral, not the central incisors, and the amount of healing shows that the teeth had been lost at the same time and some years previously, so probably in the mid-teenage years. If dental caries were not the culprit, the cause is most likely to be trauma, and this could be accidental (either fallling directly on to the face or being struck) or deliberate avulsion: a practice associated with many ancient and modern cultures, connected with a *rite de passage* for children or teenagers. It was, however, not practiced in ancient Egypt and the skull form of this individual does not suggest ancestry from outside the Nile valley.

---

9. Mongoloid skull characteristics are found in populations from central to east Asia and in native Americans; Caucasoid skull characteristics are found in populations from Europe, western Asia and north Africa, including ancient Egyptians. There are no absolutes, however, and any individual will be a mixture of traits, so this example of shovelling (if, indeed, it is not a strictly invaginate tooth with its probable different genetic cause) does not imply that Skull 123 is that of a person from outside the Nile valley.

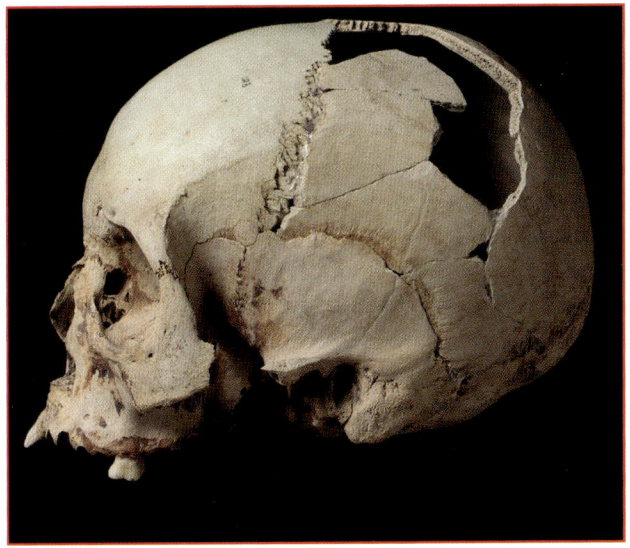

*Figure 222. Skull 123 from Shaft Five Chamber Bb (lateral view).*

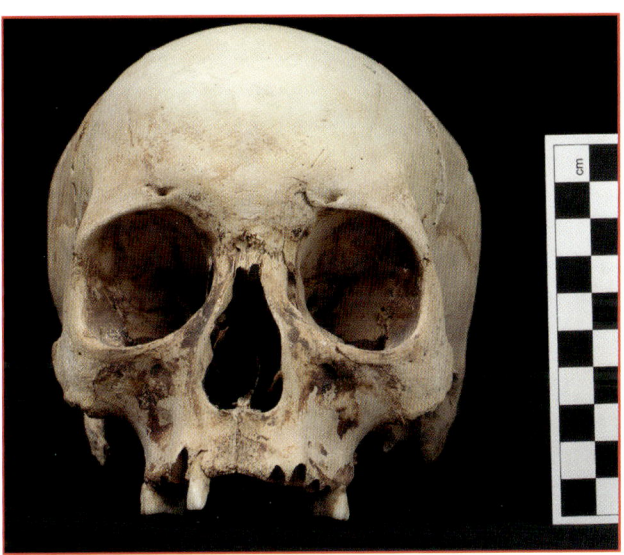

*Figure 223. Skull 123 from Shaft Five Chamber Bb (frontal view).*

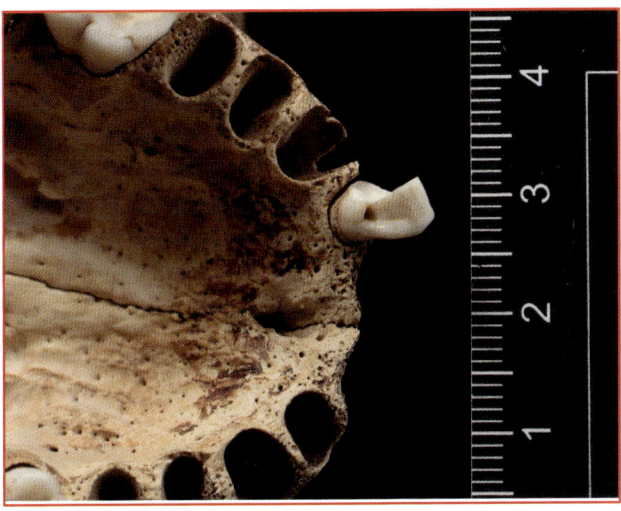

*Figure 224. Detail of skull 123 from Shaft Five Chamber Bb showing the shovel-shaped/invaginated right lateral incisor and the ante-mortem loss of both left and right medial incisors.*

**Stature**

Initial stature estimates[10] are giving heights from approximately 151.2 to 157.4 cm (4' 11 1/2" to 5' 2"). In the next field season, measurements will be taken of all relevant femora with sex determination, and statures calculated.

## CONCLUSIONS

With the exception of the material in Shaft Five, what is striking is the extremely poor condition of these human remains. The Shaft Five material seems to have been left in the southern suite of chambers or to have fallen back in there very early in the overall history of the shafts. The material which found its way back into Shafts Two, Three and Four was distinguished by being for the most part burned and highly fragmented. Some of the fragments would have been damaged by weathering over long periods of exposure but the number of burned fragments retrieved from the shaft fill tells a different story: *Figure 226* shows skull fragments and *Figure 227* long bone fragments from Shaft Four which have been reduced to pieces less than 2cms in extent.

As indicated, the main process of dismantling the burials seems to have taken place above and to the south of Shafts Two and Four on top of the spoil-heaps. The human remains from the main burials which occupied these grander tombs seem to have suffered the worst damage and thus to have been the principal focus of destruction.

As the material from Shafts Two, Three and Four is likely to be commingled, a composite MNI/sex/age table was prepared for these three shafts. Taking conservative estimates (eg, assuming that, unless there are reasons to separate them, left and right bones pair, each skull will match with at least one innominate, and so on) gives a minimum of sixteen individuals:

- 1–6 years
- 12+ years
- ?female of 18–20 years x 2
- female of 35–39 years
- female adult x 3
- sex not determined 25–29 years
- sex not determined immature or adult x 6
- male

Assuming that the Shaft Five bones were within the chambers of their own burial shaft (despite their having been disturbed *in situ* anciently), the minimum number is sixteen, as discussed in the relevant section:

- 1.5 months
- 6–12 months
- 18 months
- 9 years

---

10. Raxter M. et al. (2008) "*Stature estimation in ancient Egyptians: A new technique based on anatomical reconstruction of stature*", American Journal of Physical Anthropology, 136(2), pp.147-55.

- 12–15 x 3
- 15–20 years x 3 (one female and parous)
- 17–20 years
- female 20–25 years
- ?female 20–25 years
- ?female 40–49 years
- sex not determined 20–25 years
- male

So far as can be determined at this stage, only one person was in middle age at death; all the others were in young adulthood down to infancy or childhood. Comparison with a large number of large ancient Egyptian cemeteries (excavated in the late 19th and early 20th century) shows that a mortality profile with such young ages is unusual[11], with few children in the cemeteries and many individuals living to advance age. On the other hand, the skeletal remains from the non-elite cemeteries of Amarna, dating to the reign of Akenaten, show very high mortality rates for the younger individuals[12], and perhaps this is a more realistic representation of mortality in late XVIII dynasty Egypt, which we can see paralleled in our sample. Clearly, elite status was no protection from ills and early death.

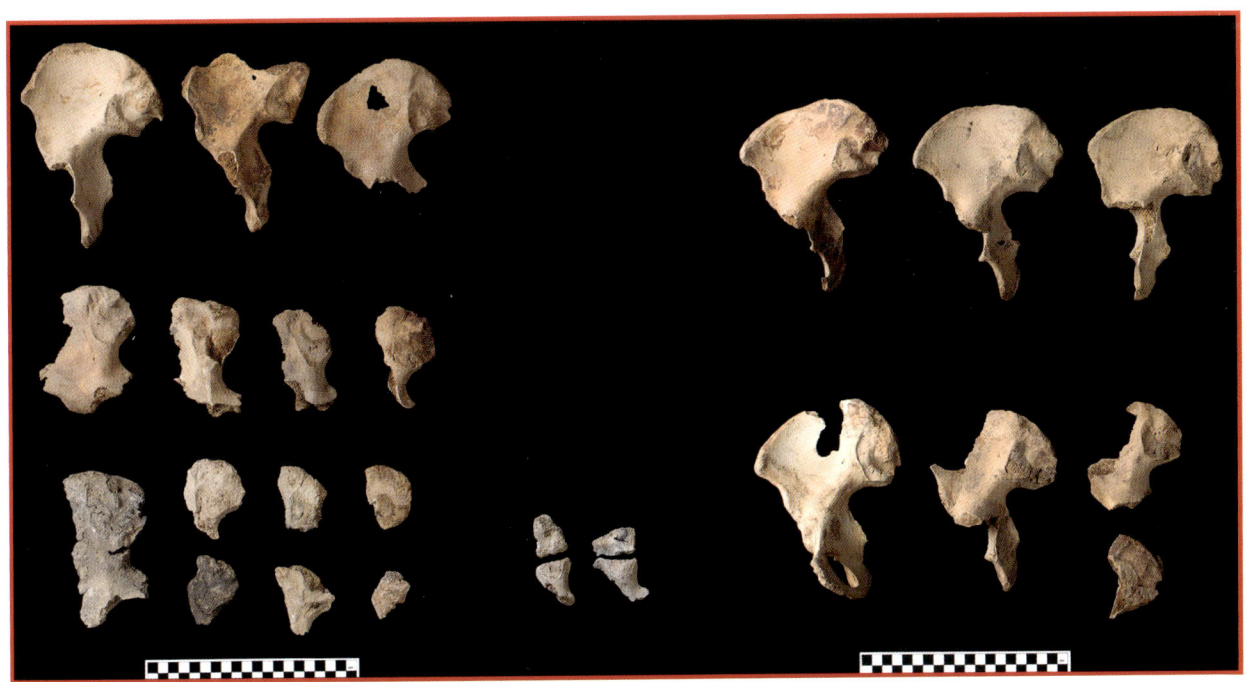

*Figure 225. All the innominates and innominate fragments recovered from the WB1 shaft tombs.*

---

11. Duhig, C., (2000) "*They are eating people here! Skeletal indicators of stress in the Egyptian First Intermediate Period*", Unpublished PhD thesis, University of Cambridge. Note the space between the comma and "Unpublished".
12. e.g. Dabbs, G. & Davis, H. (2013) http://www.amarnaproject.com/documents/pdf/STC-2013-bioarchaeology.pdf

Many instances of disease and trauma have been found, as well as non-metric traits: cribra orbitalia and porotic hyperostosis, dental caries, incisor loss of unknown cause, lumbar-vertebra spondylolysis, possible meningitis, septal apertures of the humeri, dental shovelling and accessory tubercle, extreme dental shovelling/invaginate tooth, parietal foramina, and supraorbital notches; the very severe dental disease common in ancient Egypt is, however, missing, due to the youth of the individuals in this assemblage.

In addition, there is skeletal evidence for one very young woman having had a pregnancy: we do not know if it was the cause of her death, but it reminds us of the hazards of childbearing and childbirth that were common in the ancient world.

The injury to the lumbar vertebra is interesting in that the canopic jars identify one of the women buried here as a dancer. Such an injury would be consistent with the sort of vigorous dancing represented on the famous 'back-flip' ostracon in the Egyptian Museum in Turin[13].

*Figure 226. Skull fragments from Shaft Four as found.*

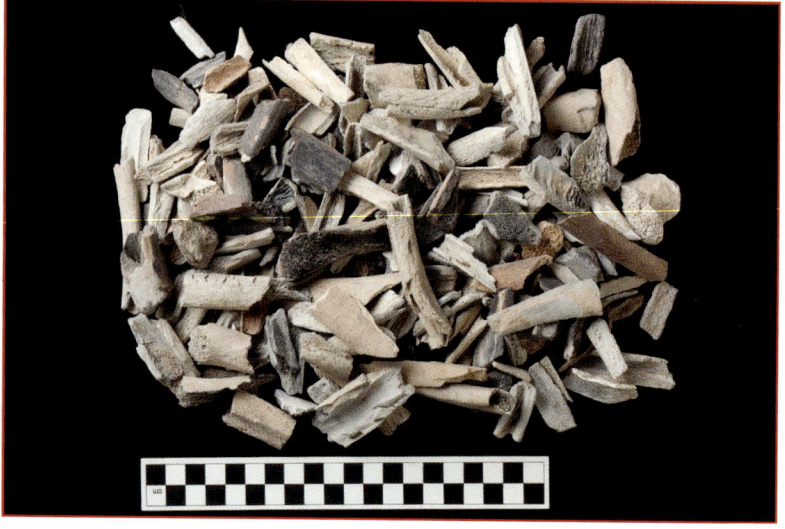

*Figure 227. Long bone fragments from Shaft Four as found.*

---

13. "Vassilika, E. (2009) *"Masterpieces of the Museo Egizio in Turin"*, Fondazione Museo delle Antichita Egizie di Torino, Scala, Firenze p. 96 Inv. no. C 7052."

# CHAPTER NINE
# FAIENCE

*Figure 228. A small faience chip as found on the surface on our first visit to the site.*

Thanks to its bright colour, the scattering of faience on the site was noticeable even in tiny pieces when we first arrived. A very great quantity of fragments was recovered from the shafts. The vast majority of these were broken tiles from furniture. Many of these were badly burned and the colours varied accordingly.

*Figure 229. A selection of faience fragments showing the variation in both colour and shape.*

The weights of faience fragments recovered were as follows:

| | | |
|---|---|---|
| Shaft Two | 1.09kg | 7% |
| Shaft Three | 0.16kg | 1% |
| Shaft Four | 13.82kg | 88% |
| Shaft Five | 0.16kg | 1% |
| Surface | 0.50kg | 3% |
| **Total** | **15.71kg** | |

As can be seen Shaft Four was overwhelmingly the largest source. The surface total consisted of many very small pieces.

The fragments were mostly of no discernible shape. However, there were a few exceptions to this and they took four forms:

- extremely rare moulded faience objects forming necklace components (two in total);
- beads (one);
- hair-rings (one fragment)
- shaped faience tiles identifiable as coming from individual furniture designs.

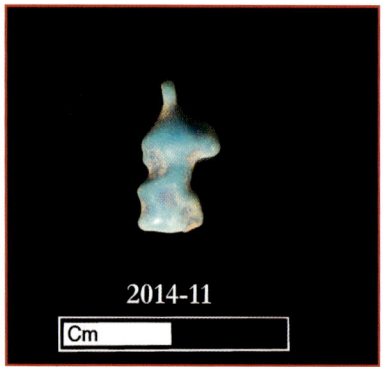

*Figure 230. A dancing Bes component from a necklace.*

*Figure 231. A wadjet eye necklace component.*

Of the two moulded faience objects one was a dancing "Bes" component from a necklace (*Figure 230*) with a pierced loop. The other was a *wadjet* eye component pierced laterally and presumably from a necklace (*Figure 231*).

*Figure 232. Composite tripartite image of a single very small faience bead.*

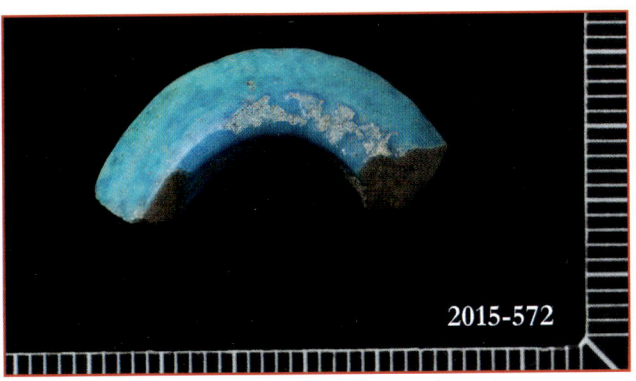

Figure 233. Part of a faience hair-ring recovered from the spoil-heaps.

Figure 234. Detail of a shaped piece with traces of gilding along the edge.

The few beads recovered were extremely small, mostly cyclindrical and of glass. One spherical faience bead was recovered from the surface with traces of its original stringing still inside it (*Figure 232*).

The shaped tiles can be identified as coming mostly from furniture bearing the same decorative designs as occurred on furniture in tomb KV46, the tomb of Yuya and Tuyu, the parents-in-law of Amenhotep III (*Figure 238*)[1]. However, the shaped tiles found on the WB1 site are much larger than those from KV46 (the inlays of the WB1 *ankh* loops are approximately 7cms high versus 3cms high in respect of the KV46 box).

A large number of tiles retain gilding along the edges, demonstrating that they were contained in a gilded matrix. Some small fragments have survived which confirm that this was a wooden matrix, splinters of wood being retained in the plaster to which the faience tiles originally adhered (*Figure 235*).

Figure 235. A composite photograph of two small faience fragments retaining the plaster and wood into which they were set.

1. Killen, G. (2017) "*Ancient Egyptian Furniture Volume II - Boxes, Chests and Footstools*", Oxbow Books, Oxford. pp 63-66.

Surviving shaped tile fragments appear to confirm a *was* sceptre, *ankh* and *djed* pillar design (*Figures 236 and 237*).

*Figure 236. Shaped pieces including the interior of an ankh loop (left).*

*Figure 237. Shaped faience pieces forming the djed-ankh-was design.*

*Figure 238. The djed-ankh-was design on a casket from KV46, the tomb of Yuya and Tuyu.*

---

2. Adapted from Hawass, Z. (2009) "*The Lost Tombs of Thebes*". Thames & Hudson. London p. 248.

Some tiles are shaped into *rishi*-work patterns and may therefore have come from outer coffins (*Figures 239 and 240*). The tear-drop shape is from the bottom of a *was*-sceptre, however.

*Figure 239. Shaped rishi-work chevrons and other inlays the majority most likely from coffins.*

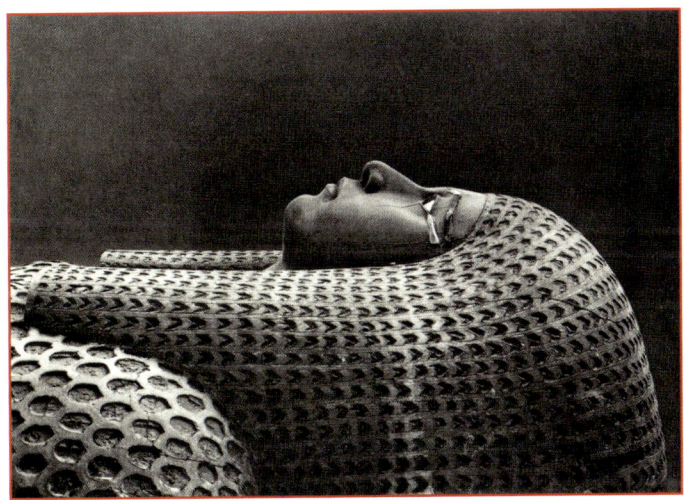

*Figure 240. The early XVIIIth dynasty outer coffin of Meryetamun which shows the emplacements which were probably once filled with faience inlays like those in Figure 239 above* [3].

The reign of Amenhotep III is renowned for the quality and exceptional workmanship of its faience. The sphinx of Amenhotep III in the Metropolitan Museum of Art[4] is a deep "Amarna blue", the very colour of the tiles from WB1 which have not been damaged by fire. The word for faience was *tjehen* (*thn*) which also means "dazzling", the same word used to describe the "Dazzling Aten".

The masterpieces[5] of faience workmanship of Amenhotep III's reign seem to indicate a great affection for this material. It should be no surprise then that tiles from furniture similar to that given to Yuya and Tuya, Amenhotep III's parents-in-law, should be found in the tombs of his wives.

---

3. Winlock, H. (1932) "*The tomb of Queen Meryet-Amun at Thebes*", Metropolitan Museum of Art, New York.
4. Friedman, F. ed. (1998) "*Gifts of the Nile: Ancient Egyptian Faience*", Thames & Hudson, London p. 78 Amenhotep III as Sphinx in the Metropolitan Museum, New York.
5. e.g. Friedmann, F. ed. (1998) op. cit.. p. 8 Cosmetic Jar of Amenhotep III & Tiye in the Louvre; p. 80 Amenhotep III Bookplate of Amenhotep III in the Louvre; p. 90 Vessel fragment with Gazelles in the Metropolitan Museum of Art, New York; p. 83 Round Wig in the British Museum, London.

*Figure 241. A further range of faience fragments with the most severely fire-damaged at the bottom.*

Such fragments as have survived have done so because they were broken when the furniture they decorated was dismantled and burned. The very small number of amulets and jewellery components speaks loudly of the removal of all anonymous items and the subsequent picking clean of this site by many generations of robbers.

The size of the WB1 fragments suggests either very large versions of the type of furniture found in KV46 (*Figure 238*) or the possibility of shrine panels. The shrine panel remains recovered from tomb KV55, made for Tiye by her son Akhenaten, bear no trace of faience inlays. However, the outer shrine of Tutankhamun (Shrine I) is decorated with a repeating pattern of two gilded *djed* pillars and two gilded *tyet* amulets against a blue faience background[6]. Both Chambers A and B in Shaft Four would have accommodated shrine panels of the estimated size of the KV55 panels.

---

6. Piankoff, A. (1955) "*The Shrines of Tut-Ankh-Amon*", Bollingen Foundation Inc., New York; Pantheon Books Inc., New York. p. 134, Pls. 54, 55, 57 & 58.

*Figure 242. A small percentage of the faience fragments being sorted by feature.*

# CHAPTER TEN
# GLASS

Given the fragility and brittle nature of the material, it can be no surprise that very little glass has survived on the WB1 site. It is nonetheless striking that with the exception of fragments from a single bottle, all the glass recovered has been in the form of inlays.

Some of these inlays have survived in remarkably good condition and this is probably due to their being fugitive pieces which dropped out when the coffins and mummy masks were being moved or when they were being dismantled.

Other glass inlays, including the largest and thickest pieces, have not fared well. Thanks to the intense heat of the fires they have warped out of recognizable form. In many cases the glass fragments have bubbled, indicating temperatures in the region of 1,600°C[1].

The distribution of glass fragments was approximately as follows:

| Shaft Two | 26% |
| Shaft Three | 9% |
| Shaft Four | 38% |
| Shaft Five | 19% |
| Surface and spoil-heaps | 8% |

The higher quantity of fragments recorded in the fill of Shaft Four, Chamber B, a fill which contained a high proportion of charcoal and was noticeably dark in colour, originally suggested that a high proportion of the burial dismantling activity took place on the spoil-heaps to the south of that shaft.

However, recent re-clearance of the floors of Shaft Four has revealed glass inlays embedded in an unidentified, dark brown to black brittle substance (*Figures 243 and 244*). This may be melted unguents or black bitumen from furniture. The inlays recovered from just inside the doorway on the eastern side of Chamber Ba in Shaft Four suggest that a small coffin was burned *in situ* near this spot. An eye inlay of very small size and a gilded fragment of what appears to be cartonnage were recovered next to a vertically-striated glass coffin inlay.

As discussed above (Chapter Four) it now seems highly likely that major fires took place within the southern chambers (B, Ba, Bb and possibly Bc) of Shaft Four and in the three chambers of Shaft Three. The arrangement of the chambers and shafts may have had the effect of concentrating these fires in what was in effect a furnace. It is difficult to account for how these objects, if they were all melted in the shafts, came to be moved to the surface. Fires in the tomb chambers do not, of course, rule out additional burning on the surface.

---

1. Glass liquifies at temperatures between 1,400 °C and 1,600°C. Bubbles start to appear between 1,600°C and 1,700°C. Nicholson and Henderson state that the temperatures in excess of 1,700°C needed to melt pure silica could not have been achieved in ancient times. Nicholson, P. and Henderson, J. 2000 "Glass" pp. 194-224 in Nicholson, P. and Shaw, I. ed. (2000) "*Ancient Egyptian Materials and Technology*", Cambridge University Press, Cambridge. See also Nicholson, P. (1993) "*Egyptian Faience and Glass*", Shire Publications.

*Figure 243. The floor of Shaft Four Chamber Ba. Small gilded coffin fragments (arrowed) have been glued to the floor by melted black resins.*

*Figure 244. In the centre of the photograph is a vertically-striated glass inlay also embedded in the floor of Shaft Four Chamber Ba.*

The glass finds were widely scattered as illustrated by the single glass vessel (*Figure 245*) which was reconstructed from fragments in Shaft Three Chambers A and Ab and from Shaft Four Chamber B.

This is a core-formed vessel of *krateriskoi* form with marvered decoration, typical of the XVIIIth dynasty royal glass industry[2] and of the reign of Amenhotep III[3]. It is of a type and colouring found particularly at Malqata, on the West Bank at Thebes and later at Akhetaten. Similar decorative techniques were found in XVIIIth dynasty royal tombs and in the tomb of Kha and Merit.

Apart from this vessel, the remainder of the glass recovered consisted of decorative fragments belonging to larger objects. These glass fragments provide strong evidence of the nature of those larger objects.

*Figure 245. The only glass vessel found. Reconstructed from pieces retrieved in Shafts Three and Four.*

The corpus of reference material for these smaller glass elements ranges from the coffins and funerary masks in Yuya and Tuyu's tomb (KV46)[5] to the coffin in tomb KV55 and the coffins in Tutankhamun's tomb (KV62). Another burial which contains similar inlays is that of Aper-el in Saqqara[6].

The glass inlays indicative of the great wealth of the burials originally interred in the WB1 shafts are the glass *rishi*-work chevrons. This design is known to have been the prerogative of royal individuals. Examples of earlier coffins which display this design (and have lost their inlays) are the huge outer coffins of Ahmose-Nefertari and Meryetamun[7].

---

2. Nicholson, P. (1993) op. cit..
3. Kozloff, A. and Bryan B., (1992) "*Egypt's Dazzling Sun: Amenhotep III and his World*", Cleveland Museum of Art. Plates 44 & 45.
4. Examples of which are noted by Hayes, W., (1959) "*The Scepter of Egypt: Part II*", Metropolitan Museum of Art, New York p. 194.
5. Davies, T. (1907) op. cit. Plates VIII, IX, XIII, XIV and XV.
6. Zivie, A., (1990) "*Decouverte a Saqqara: Le vizier oublie*", Editions du Seuil, Paris.
7. Ikram, S. and Dodson, A., (1998) "*The Mummy in Ancient Egypt*", Thames & Hudson, London pp. 207 and 208.

There are only two known burials which contain coffins inlaid with similar glass chevrons in place. The first is the coffin in the enigmatic burial in KV55. This coffin had been adapted for a king from a coffin originally made for Akhenaten's consort, Kiya. As it is the only other coffin known to have made for the consort of a king in the late XVIIIth dynasty it is naturally of relevance to the WB1 site.

*Figure 246. Detail of the coffin base from KV55 in the Egyptian Musuem in Cairo.*

The only other burial containing such a coffin[8] is the tomb of Tutankhamun (KV62). The second, inner wooden coffin is decorated with an extensive pattern of *rishi*-work chevrons.

Comparison of these two coffins (*Figure 247*) with the glass inlays found on the WB1 site shows that the KV55 coffin inlays are of poorer quality. The coffin in that tomb suffered badly from water damage and has been reconstructed. However, the inlays are flat and lack the convexity which is apparent in the WB1 examples and those on the second coffin of Tutankhamun.

*Figure 247. Comparison between the rishi-work inlays on the second coffin of Tutankhamun (left) and on the KV55 coffin (right)[9].*

---

8. The KV62 coffins could also, of course, have been made originally for a female. See Reeves, N. and Wilkinson, R. (1996) "*The Complete Valley of the Kings*", Thames & Hudson, London p. 43 and p. 126.
9. See also Kemp, B. (2012) "*The City of Akhenaten and Nefertiti: Amarna and its People*", Thames & Hudson, London. Pl. XLVII.

*Figure 248. A composite of some of the rishi-work inlays recovered from the WB1 shafts. Both the top chevrons and the middle fragment below retain traces of gilding.*

The *rishi*-work chevron inlays from the WB1 shafts vary in quality. Several have snapped in half. Some are blackened by fire, some have turned white from moisture. Several (see *Figure 248*) retain traces of gilding confirming that they were originally inserted in wooden coffins which were gilded.

Of the other types of inlays the best preserved are a collection of figurative inlays forming parts of hieroglyphic inscriptions. They come from Shaft Five. A group of three blue pieces was recovered from Chambers B and Bb. All are similar in style and were affected by chemical changes which have created white dots in the glass. A fourth piece, a *hr* face, of similar colour and workmanship was recovered from Shaft Four.

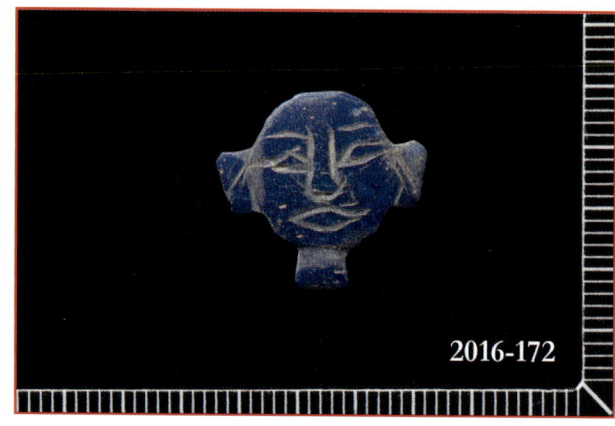

*Figure 249.*
*A blue glass hr face inlay from Shaft Four.*

*Figure 250.*
*Blue glass duck inlays from Shaft Four.*

*Figure 251. Fire-damaged figurative inlays recovered from Feature 1001 - the surface.*

*Figure 252. A blue glass head inlay from Shaft Five.*

*Figure 253. A blue glass head inlay from Shaft Five.*

*Figure 254. A blue glass quail chick inlay from Shaft Five.*

Other fragments recovered in considerable numbers from the shaft fill and from the surface are the elements which would have created the necklace decoration on coffins and funerary masks. Very few of these survive in good condition. Again, most are broken and many are burned.

These inlays are identical to those found in the gilded gesso and wood coffins and funerary masks of Yuya and Tuyu.

*Figure 255. The decorative detail from the funerary mask of Tuyu.*

*Figure 256 detail of the outer coffin of Tuyu (both from KV 46 and now in the Egyptian Museum in Cairo).*

*Figure 257. A selection of inlays from WB1 similar to those on the outer coffin of Tuyu.*

*Figure 258. A further selection of mainly "fingernail" inlays from the WB1 shafts.*

Amongst the most frequent of the shaped inlays were vertically-striated fragments (*Figure 259*) in a variety of colours. These were used in many different types of decorative patterns and were found in large numbers in the tomb of Aper-el[10]. They are also to be seen on the coffins from KV46 (*Figure 260*).

---

10. Zivie, A. (2007) *"The Lost Tombs of Saqqara"*, cara.cara.edition, Toulouse. p37.

*Figure 259. Vertically-striated inlay fragments from the WB1 shafts.*

*Figure 260. The second coffin of Yuya from KV46 now in the Egyptian Museum in Cairo.*

The largest inlays, in some cases up to a centimetre thick, are the ones in the poorest condition. Some of these clearly came from outer coffins, and one surviving wooden coffin fragment suggests where these might have been used (*Figure 261*). A number of these have bubbles on the surface and distortions in their shape. These indicate the very high temperatures to which they have been subjected.

*Figure 261. A thick glass inlay from the WB1 shafts inserted into a wooden fragment also from the WB1 shafts and thought to come from a coffin.*

*Figure 262. Fire-damaged glass inlays from the WB1 shafts.*

Large quantities of spirally-incised glass tubes were also found in the shafts and in the spoil-heaps. Almost all of these fragile tubes were broken but some have survived intact and have been shaped to be attached to a flat surface. As all these glass spirals were found individually it was difficult to envisage what their function may have been.

Three spirals were found in Shaft Four in a plaster matrix *(Figure 263)*. This suggests that they were parts of a decorative element covering a wider surface. It is now thought that these are the spirals which formed the wigs on inner coffins. Large numbers of similar wooden spirals (see below *Figure 301*), some retaining traces of gilding, performed the same function on outer coffins, on coffins of lesser quality or on statuettes.

*Figure 263. Glass spirals held together in a plaster matrix.*

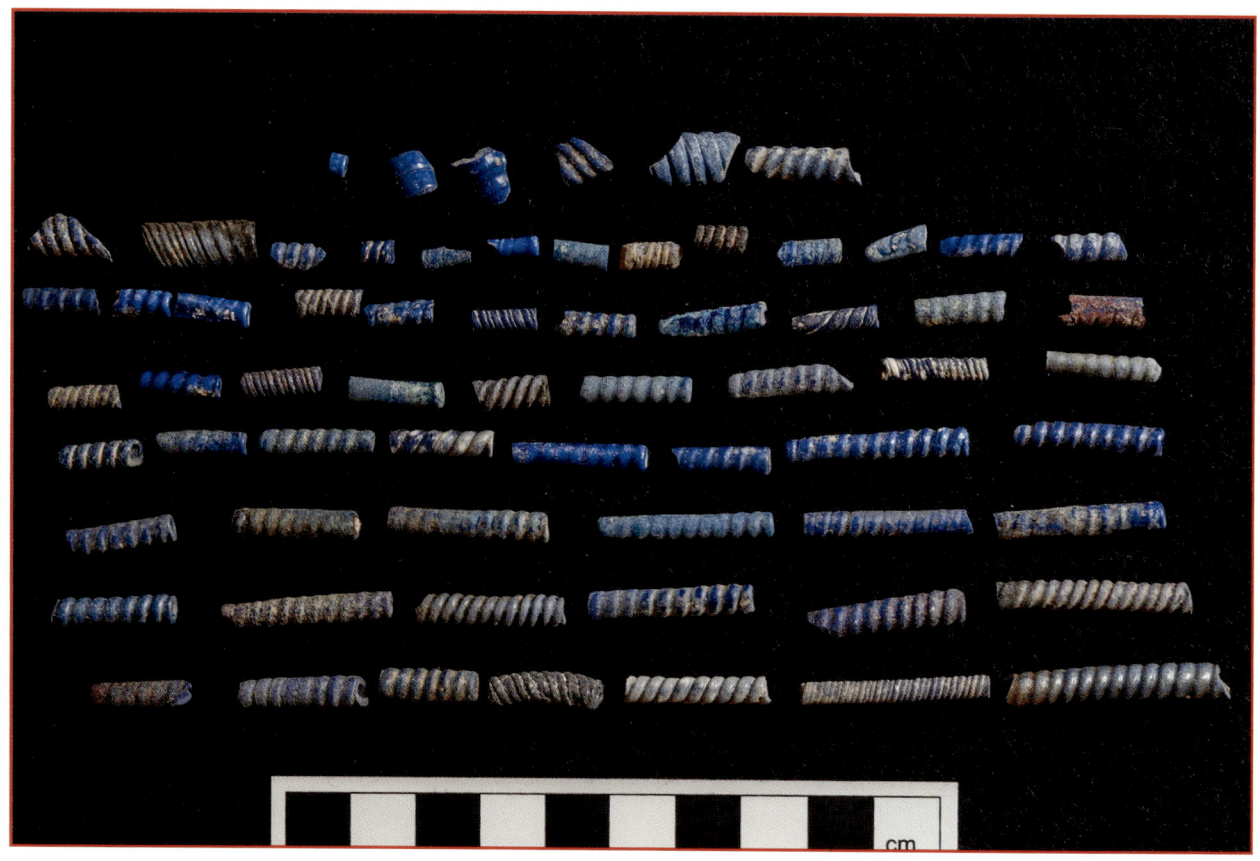

*Figure 264. Some of the glass spirals and fragments recovered in large numbers from the WB1 shafts.*

We also recovered a quantity of blue glass inlays which were clearly the eyebrow-inlays from coffins. Less easy to understand were flat inlays which it transpired were the deeply-inset inlays from coffin eyes. Some of these were badly damaged and distorted by fire. Enough survived for it to be possible to determine that before their destruction there were coffins in a variety of sizes.

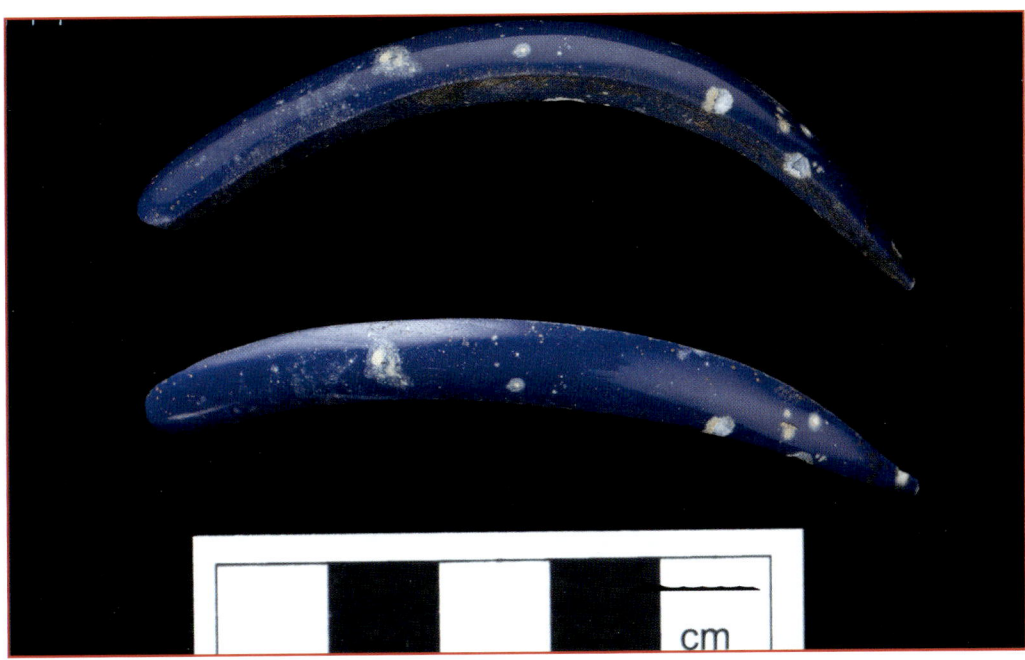

*Figure 265. Two views of the same eyebrow inlay from Shaft Two.*

*Figure 266. Two views of the same eye inlay rconstructed from three fragments from (Shaft Five).*

Other eye components were discovered, including obsidian eye pupils and white stone *sclera* eye surrounds (two with pink-painted caruncles) (*Figures 267 and 268*).

*Figure 267. Obsidian eye pupil from Shaft Four (scale in millimetres).*

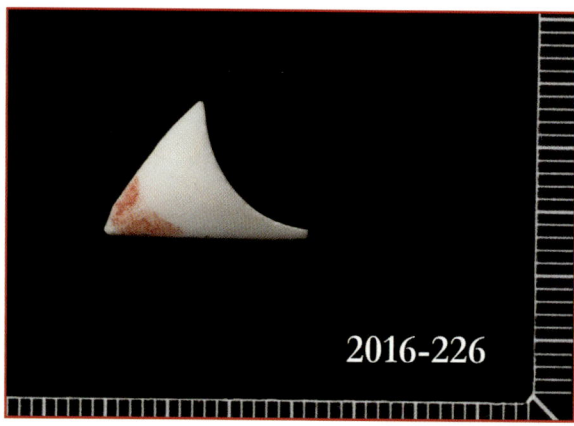

*Figure 268. White stone sclera with pink painted caruncle (scale in millimetres).*

We would have expected to find many more glass beads from necklaces broken during the destruction of the burials. Small pieces like these would all too easily have fallen or rolled into crevices, particularly on the chamber floors. However, all the beads except one were recovered from the surface. A single bead was recovered from the fill of Shaft Four.

*Figure 269. All the beads recovered from the WB1 shafts.*
*The bead third from the left on the bottom row is faience. All the others are glass.*

A single finger or thumb inlay of turquoise glass was recovered on the surface, at the mouth of Shaft Four (*Figure 270*). Although it is just 2cms in length the detail of the fingernail is clearly visible. This object seems to belong stylistically to the Amarna period - in other words the very end of the reign of Amenhotep III and beginning of the reign of Amenhotep IV/Akhenaten[11]. If this is correct, then this provides further evidence for these tombs being used over an extended period spanning almost all of the reign of Amenhotep III.

*Figure 270. The glass finger or thumb inlay found at the mouth of Shaft Four (scale in millimetres).*

---

11. The author of this work accepts the probability that Amenhotep III and his son shared a co-regency.

# CHAPTER ELEVEN
# WOOD: INCLUDING DOCKETS, DUCK SPOONS, FURNITURE, COFFINS, SHABTIS

Wood is clearly not a material which survives as well as inorganic stone, faience, glass and metal. The wooden objects from the WB1 site suffered from a number of factors over the millennia since the burials took place.

First, the objects made of wood (which included coffins, sarcophagi, statues, furniture and articles of daily use) were very clearly dismantled and subjected to an attempt to destroy them, their constituent parts broken and cut into small pieces. There is a sufficient collection of small fragments cut on both sides and of larger fragments also bearing cut-marks for this to be beyond doubt (*Figures 272 and 273*).

Second, many of the wooden obects were burned. This may have been to collect gold foil, but equally this simply may have been part of the deliberate destruction of the burials.

Third, much of what remained was then attacked by termites which were active as long as the site was sufficiently moist to sustain them (*Figures 290, 291 and 298*). At some stage the weather changed and the site dried out. There was no sign of termite activity in the shafts when we cleared them.

The wood, thoroughly dessicated, was retrieved in many, many hundreds of fragments. *Figure 271* gives some idea of the quantity and range of these fragments as they were presented for sorting and study.

*Figure 271. Wooden fragments prior to sorting.*

*Figure 272. Wooden fragments showing clear cut-marks.*

*Figure 273. A larger wooden fragment showing a deep gouge from a sharp instrument.*

*Figure 274. A small, partially-burned wooden fragment with surviving traces of gilding.*

The process of sorting through the wood is still in progress. To date it has produced the following categories of objects:

- furniture;

- coffins and sarcophagi fragments and components;

- dockets;

- fans;

- mirrors;

- shabtis;

- statues;

- Anubis fetish components;

- other objects of daily use.

### a) Furniture

Only fragments of the furniture buried in the WB1 shafts survive. In some cases we have the whole of an individual furniture member. In rarer cases two members have been left joined together. Most of the wood, however, is in the form of splinters of various sizes which are unrecognisable. Many of these are also badly charred.

Several pieces have survived with partial inscriptions visible. It has not been possible to determine from the few signs which survive on these pieces what their function was. Shape has generally been the best guide to function.

*Figure 275. A slightly convex panel with part of the inscription surviving.*

*Figure 276. Shaped furniture components. The two pieces at the top right are possibly from statues.*

*Figure 277. Further furniture parts, some with dowels still in place.*

*Figure 278. Fragments painted in black and white probably from storage boxes[1].*

---

1. Killen, G. (2017B) "*Ancient Egyptian Furniture: Volume II: Boxes, Chests and Footstools*" Second Edition, Oxbow Books, Oxford. pp. 37-62.

*Figure 279. Chair fragments from Shaft Five[2].*

*Figure 280. White-painted leg and stretcher probably from a stool[3].*

---

2. Killen, G. (2017A) "*Ancient Egyptian Furniture: Volume I: 4000-1300 BC*" Second Edition, Oxbow Books, Oxford. Plates 89-92.
3. Killen, G. (2017A) op. cit. Plates 75 and 76.

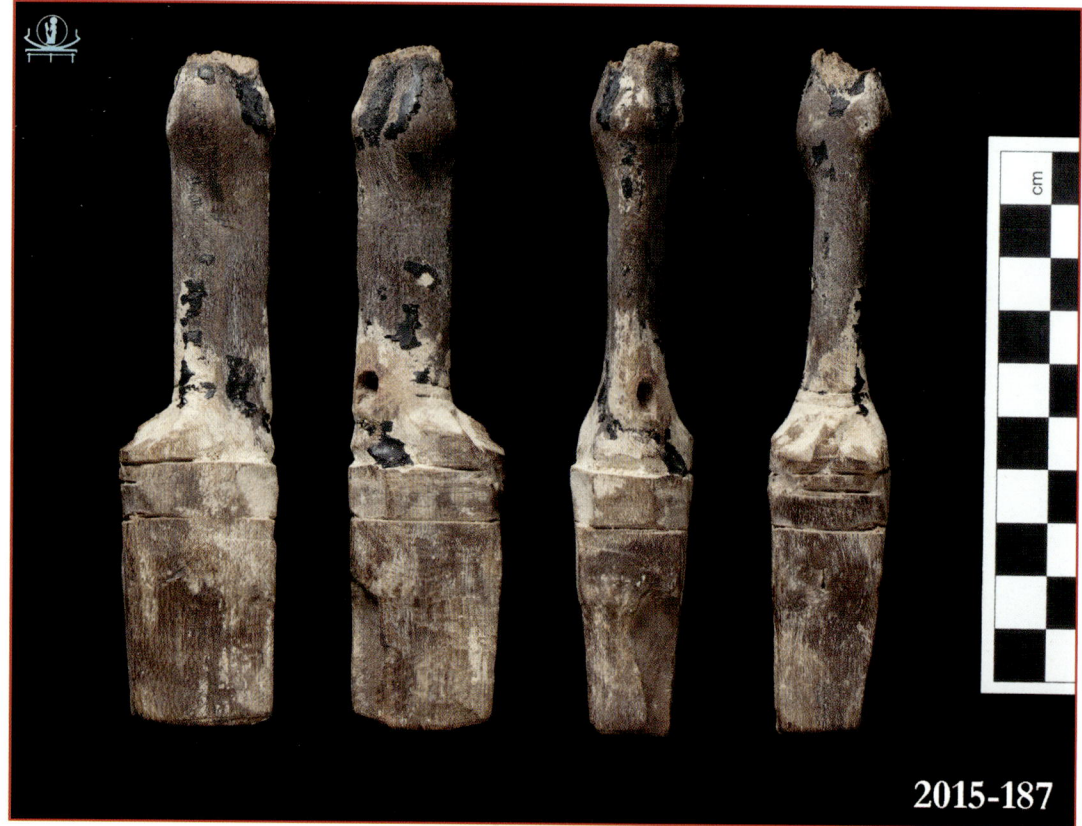

*Figure 281. Composite of a single furniture leg from Shaft Two Chamber Bc*

A single leg from Chamber Bc in Shaft Two (*Figure 281* 2015-187) is from a small item of furniture. The "foot" of the leg is likely to be a lion's paw but the condition of the piece does not make this clear. In its present state the leg looks crudely carved.

## Duck stools

*Figure 282. The head of a stool member shaped like a duck's head from the shaft-fill of Shaft Four.*

One of the pieces recovered is a broken ebony fragment carved into the shape of a duck's head (*Figure 282*). The end of the piece which constitutes the beak of the duck has a smooth groove running transversely across the beak. This makes it highly likely that this piece is from a duck stool[4]. Close examination of this piece reveals traces of gilding (*Figure 283*).

*Figure 283. A composite of the traces of gilding visible on the 2015-356 duck-stool fragment (the scale is in millimetres).*

These traces of giding could have been transferred from other gilded objects which melted when burnt. There are other ebony fragments which may be parts of this piece of furniture. They retain insufficient evidence of working for it to be possible to decide on their original placement on the stools. Most of the pieces are badly damaged by fire.

## Furniture knobs

 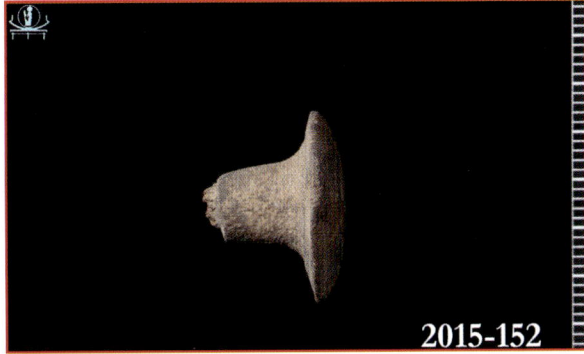

*Figure 284. A furniture knob from Shaft Four Chamber Ba (left).*

*Figure 285. A furniture knob from Shaft Two Chamber Bc (right).*

---

4. Killen, G. (2017A) op. cit. Plates 57 to 64.

*Figure 286 (above) and Figure 287 (below).*
*Two furniture knobs found together in Shaft Four Chamber Bb.*

A variety of furniture knobs was recovered of differing profiles and woods. None was attached to any identifiable piece of furniture.

*Figure 288. A single furniture knob from Shaft Four Chamber A.*

## b) Coffins and sarcophagi fragments and components

There are very few coffin fragments which can be identified with any confidence. The most striking is part of a simple, black-painted coffin where the curved silhouette and the dowel hole and its corresponding pin-hole for closing the coffin are also visible. The piece has been badly-eaten by termites and the outside colour of the coffin is not discernible. It is interesting that the coffin is painted black on the inside.

*Figure 289. Two views of coffin fragment (2015-138) from Shaft Five Chamber Ba.*

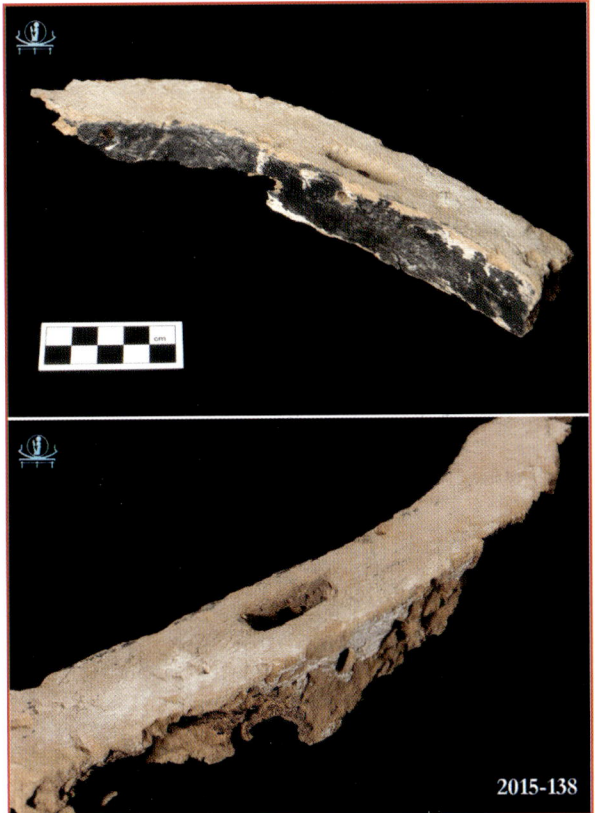

*Figure 290. Details of the same coffin fragment (2015-138) taken from different angles. Both clearly show the dowel and pin-holes for closing the coffin. The lower view shows the damage caused by termites.*

Some of the surviving coffin fragments are inscribed or inlaid with partial texts. In the majority of cases the inlays unfortunately do not survive but the plaster which held these in place is still there in several instances.

*Figure 291. Two views of the same inscribed, concave coffin fragment (2014-369 from Shaft Five Chamber Bb). This is inscribed on the inner surface; the outer surface (which has been badly eaten by termites) is painted black.*

*Figure 292. Another view of coffin fragments 2014-369 showing its convex profile.*

*Figure 293. A further inscribed coffin fragment (2014-348B from Shaft Five Chamber B). The inscription is on the outer surface.*

**2014-348B**

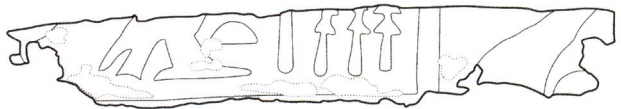

*Figure 294. Facsimile of the text of 2014-348B.*

*Figure 295. A further inscribed coffin fragment (2014-358C from Shaft Five, Chamber B). The inscription is on the outer surface.*

**2014-348C**

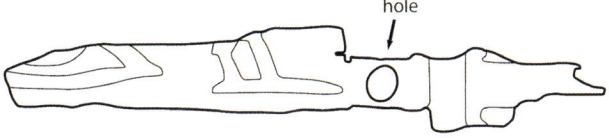

*Figure 296. Facsimile of the text of 2014-348C.*

*Figure 297. Inlaid coffin fragment with what may be a fragment of faience - on the right (Shaft Two Chamber A).*

*Figure 298. An inlaid coffin fragment, with traces of what may have been faience inlays. This may be the wrist from the crossed arms on a coffin. (Shaft Two Chamber Bc).*

There are other inlaid fragments without inscriptions. Some of these appear to be related to heavily-inlaid outer coffins (see above *Figure 261*) and others to finer inner coffins. The condition of these pieces, however, makes interpretation extremely difficult.

*Figure 299. A further inlaid fragment from a point at which the decorative scheme changes (Shaft Four Chamber Bb).*

*Figure 300. Composite back and front view of a possible coffin fragment with traces of gilding where the 'fingernail' inlays would have been (see Figure 258). The piece is made of a dense, dark wood, possibly ebony (Shaft Four).*

Amongst the other objects which may be associated with coffins are spirally-engraved wooden tubes found in great numbers in every shaft and scattered across the spoil-heaps (*Figure 301*). These are mostly broken and therefore vary in length. They are all of roughly the same diameter (approximately 6mm). The few intact examples have ends shaped to be inserted into some other object. Others are shaped at angles to be attached to some flat surface.

Close examination of these reveals that many retain traces of gilding (*Figure 303*). It is suggested, therefore, that these played the same decorative role as the glass spirals, which they resemble in shape, as parts of the wig decoration on coffins or statuettes.

*Figure 301. A small selection of wooden spirals from various features similar to those in Figure 24.*

*Figure 302. A damaged wooden spiral on the left and a complete one on the right. Both found together in Shaft Two Chamber Bb. The one on the right shows traces of gilding.*

*Figure 303. A detail of a wooden spiral showing traces of gilding. This square-profile example was found in Shaft Two Chamber Bc.*

Other elements apparently of wig decorations survive in different forms. Some of these have a simple zigzag "water" decoration (*Figure 304*) and may indeed be from pallets or spoons.

*Figure 304. A possible wig or spoon fragment.*

*Figure 305. Ebony wig fragments from Shaft Four Chamber Ba.*

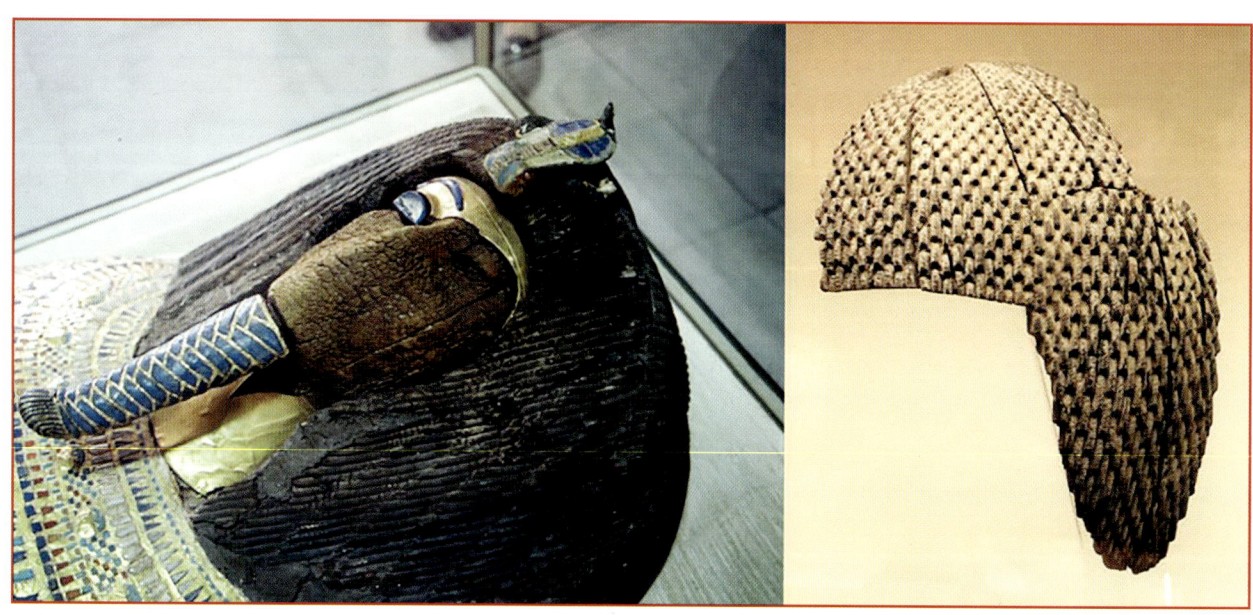

*Figure 306. Wig details: on the left is the head of the KV55 coffin in the Egyptian Museum, Cairo; on the right is the top of an XVIIIth dynasty statue or coffin fragment (Inv. BSAe 1307) in the Antikenmuseum Basel und Sammlung Ludwig.*

*Figure 307. Possible wig or "winged" figure elements of ebony from the fill of Shaft Five.*

*Figure 308. An ebony wing probably from a coffin. From Shaft Four Chamber Bb.*

# Sledge runners

A number of sledge runners were found in the shafts. These vary in size from very small pieces, probably from shrines, to much larger pieces which probably come from either canopic chests or sarcophagi.

*Figure 309. A complete small sledge runner from Shaft Four Chamber A.*

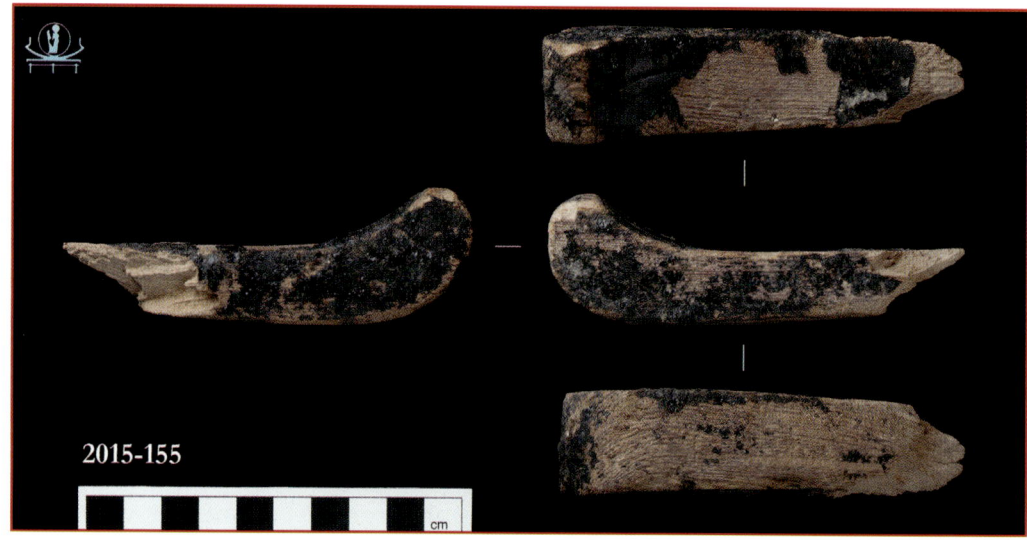

*Figure 310. A composite of a sledge fragment from Shaft Two Chamber A.*

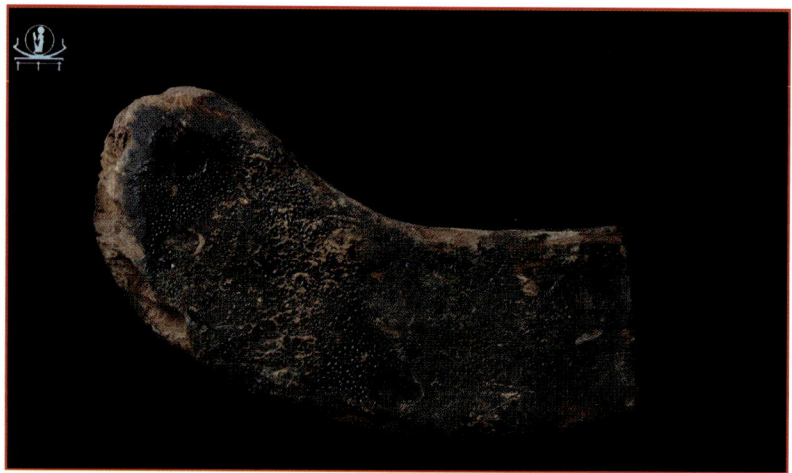

*Figure 311. A large sledge fragment from Shaft Two Chamber A.*

## c) Fans

The first fan fragment to appear came from Shaft Two Chamber A. It was the only one to survive with an inscription. It also brought to light the first royal name in these shaft tombs.

Figure 312. *Wooden fan fragment bearing the name and title of the King's Ornament, the King's Wife, Henut.*

The name and titles are unusual. The title "Ornament of the King" (ẖkr.t n(y)-sw.t) is outside the cartouche but the additional title and name are within the cartouche: "the King's Wife Henut" (ḥm.t n(y)-sw.t Ḥnw.t). These fragments were originally identified with reference to the notebooks of Bernard Bruyère and a surviving fan with handle in the Boston Museum[6].

Further fragments of fans all came from Shaft Two and from both northern and southern chambers.

---

5. Available on-line: http://www.ifao.egnet.net/bases/archives/bruyere/?&os=301
6. Accession number 49.1918.

*Figure 313. Four of the fan fragments from Shaft Two.*

*Figure 314. Further fan fragment from Shaft Two Chamber Bc.*

*Figure 315. Probable fan handle terminus found on the surface.*

## e) Shabtis

Shabtis would have been present in very large numbers in these burials. Even if there were only four buried with each person there should be in excess of a hundred of these objects. Many of these would have been wooden. The pieces of wooden shabti we have recovered are badly burned and with the exception of one long, partial profile (*Figure 316*) (also badly burned) are small in size. Most of the fragments are feet.

*Figure 316. A composite of the inverse and obverse of the badly burned remains of he rear part of a shabti figure from Shaft Two Chamber A.*

An enigmatic inscribed "stick" (*Figure 317*) could be a rudimentary shabti or part of some quite different object. The inscription is partially preserved and crudely cut, although once inlaid.

*Figure 317. Inscribed wooden object which may be part of a shabti.*

*Figure 318. Two shabti foot fragments from Shaft Two Chamber Aa.*

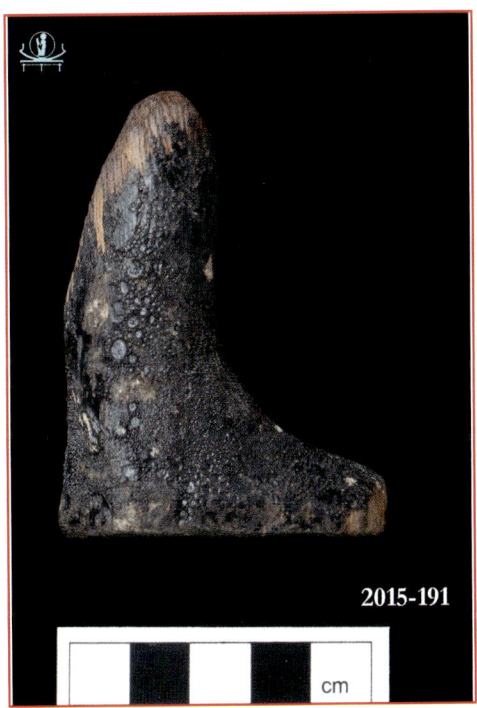

*Figure 319. The burned foot of a shabti from Shaft Two Chamber A.*

*Figure 320. The front of the foot of a shabti from Shaft Four.*

*Figure 321. The foot of a wooden shabti from Shaft Two.*

*Figure 322. Composite front and back views of an object for funerary use - possibly a shabti or part of a shabti sarcophagus - belonging to a royal female (from Shaft Two Chamber Bc).*

We also recovered the feet from two stone shabtis (Chapter Six: *Figures 184 and 185*), neither of which preserves the name of the owner.

## f) Statues

Amongst the wooden fragments were several pieces which seem to come from statues. Two hands (*Figures 323 and 324*) could possibly be from coffins. However, as they are coated with black resin on both sides this would argue for their being part of free-standing objects.

*Figure 323. The first of two hands. From Shaft Two Chamber A.*

The first of these hands was found in Shaft Two, the second in Shaft Three. They are of different sizes, the Shaft Three hand (2014-288) being smaller. They therefore appear to be from different objects and this in turn suggests there was more than one black-painted statue accompanying these burials.

*Figure 324. The second hand. From Shaft Three, Chamber A.*

From Shaft Four Chamber Bb came a badly damaged foot. This was clearly attached to a leg at the ankle but apart from the fact that it was coloured black its condition precludes any other conclusions. There is no obvious sign of attachment to a plinth on the underside of the foot.

*Figure 325. Statue foot from Shaft Four Chamber Bb.*

Slightly more enigmatic is a badly-burned fragment (2014-229) with traces of linen, plaster and black colouring. It has been hollowed out by fire on the inside but appears originally to have been oval in plan and flat-topped (*Figure 326*).

*Figure 326. Composite of the possible statue fragment (from Shaft Two Chamber Aa). Above is a view of what is apparently the top. The middle view is of the burned inside and the bottom photograph shows the outside.*

*Figure 327. A detail of the chair of Sitamun found in KV46 and now in the Egyptian Museum in Cairo (© Getty Images).*

This fragment may have been part of a flat-topped piece of headgear from a statue similar in form to the head found on the chair of Sitamun in KV46. It has none of the peripheral decoration common in flat-topped headgear of this sort in the XVIIIth dynasty. It is possible that this decoration has fallen away.

## g) Anubis fetish components

In addition to the limestone bases of the Anubis fetishes dealt with above (see *Figure 181*), two wooden fragments from these objects were also found in the WB1 shafts.

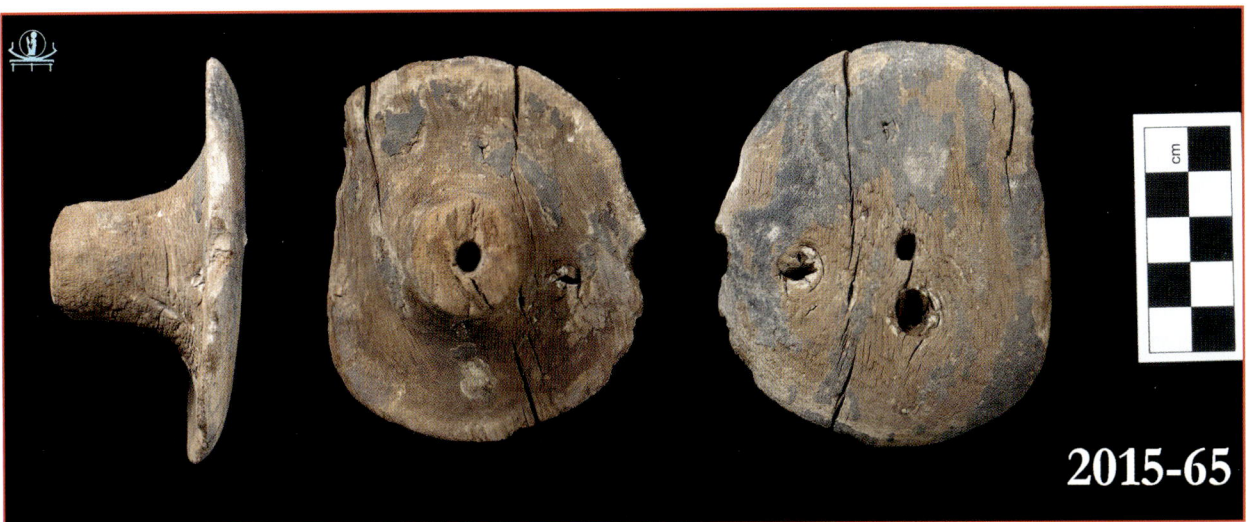

*Figure 328. Flower-head terminus from an Anubis fetish standard found in the shaft-fill of Shaft Four.*

Initially the object recorded as 2015-65 was thought to be a furniture knob. It is large for such an object, however and the dowel hole is very small. This suggests this knob was not designed to withstand pulling or pushing but was ornamental.

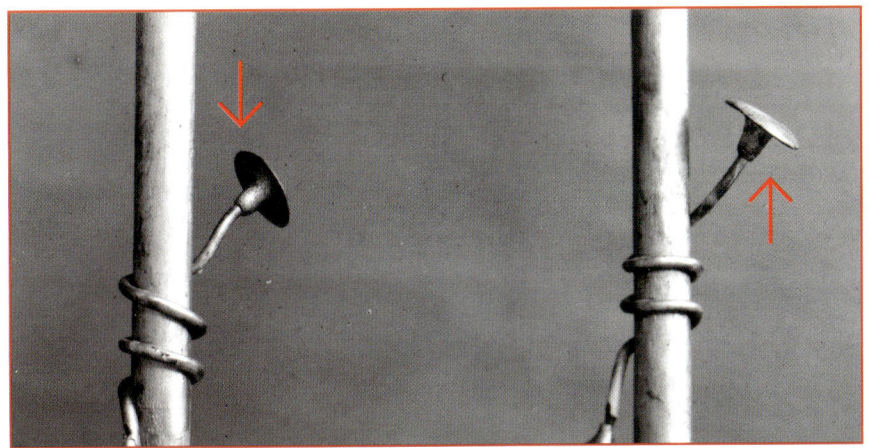

*Figure 329. Detail of Figure 181 of Anubis fetishes from Tutankhamun's tomb (KV62) with the flower head termini arrowed.[7].*

---

7. Reproduced with permission of the Griffith Institute, University of Oxford.

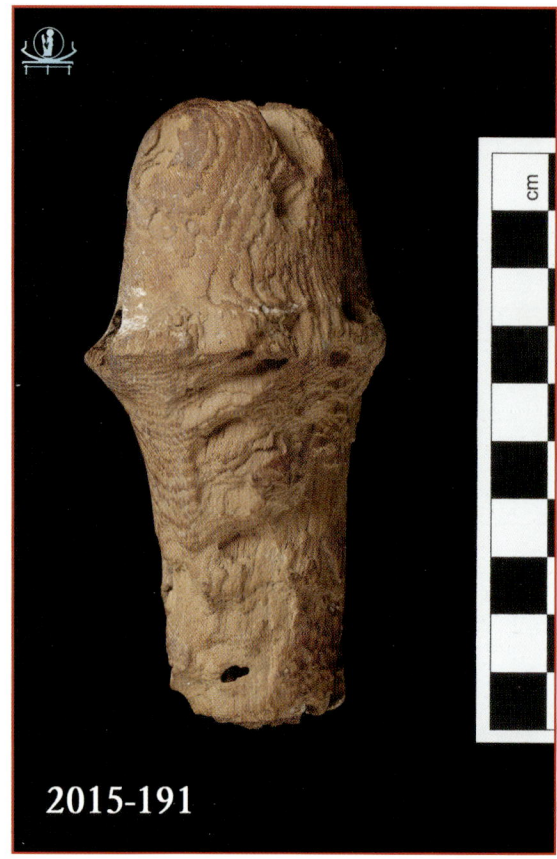

*Figure 330. The end of a staff from an Anubis fetish. Found in Shaft Four Chamber Bb.*

The wooden end of the staff found in Chamber Bb of Shaft Four matches exactly in profile the top of Anubis fetish poles as portrayed in temples and tombs of the period (see *Figure 331*). The diameter of the shaft of the staff head also fits the holes in the limestone bases.

*Figure 331. An Anubis fetish in the Temple of Seti I at Abydos. The top of the pole has the same profile as 2015-191 in Figure 330.*

## h) Other objects of daily use

### Mirrors

*Figure 332. A composite of two views of the mirror component recovered from Shaft Two Chamber Bc*

The metal parts of mirrors would of course all have been removed from the site for re-cycling or re-use. It is therefore not very surprising that the only part of such an item which has been recovered from the WB1 shafts should be of wood. The wood appears to be ebony and to have once been coated with plaster and probably gilded. This fragment was found in Shaft 2 Chamber Bc.

### Combs

 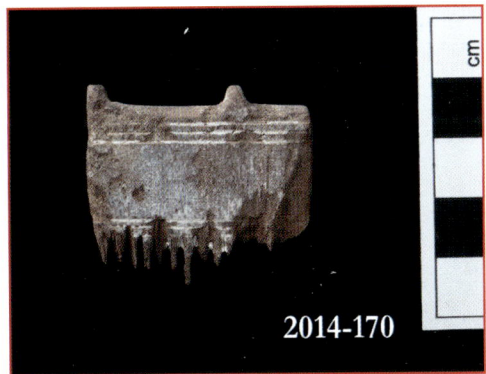

*Figure 333. Wooden comb fragment from Shaft Four Chamber Ba.*    *Figure 334. Wooden comb fragment from Shaft Two Chamber A.*

*Figure 335. Wooden comb fragment from Shaft Two Chamber A.*

# Hairpins

*Figure 336. Hair-pins or kohl applicators from Shaft Two Chamber B.*

*Figure 337. Fragment of a hair-pin or kohl applicator from Shaft Two Chamber B.*

# Lamp stands

*Figure 338. The base of a lamp-stand from Shaft Two Chamber Bc.*

# Duck 'cosmetic' spoons

*Figure 339. Part of the body of a ritual spoon in the shape of a duck fund in Shaft Two Chamber A.*

Several fragments of ritual spoons in the shape of duck bodies were found in the burial debris. Also found were pieces of the wing coverings and the necks of the ducks.

*Figure 340. Various fragments from a cosmetic spoon.*

*Figure 341. A composite of a painted duck wing from a cosmetic spoon. Found in Shaft Two Chamber Bc.*

*Figure 342. The painted body of a cosmetic duck spoon with holes for attachment of the neck on top. A hole underneath may be to attach the swimming figure of a girl as in Figure 333. Found in Shaft Three Chamber Ab.*

*Figure 343. Cosmetic duck spoon in the Louvre Museum (© Getty Images).*

# Dockets

*Figure 344. A docket bearing a partial inscription. Found in Shaft Two Chamber A.*

"Itesresu of the House of the King's Wife life [prosperity, health]"

*Figure 345. A hieroglyphic transliteration and translation of the 2015-171 docket[8].*

---

8. I am grateful to Jacobus van Dijk for this reading

*Figure 346. A second broken docket bearing a partial inscription. Found in Shaft Two Chamber A.*

Mutu[y from (?)] the mansion of the [Dazzling]-Aten (?), the Great-one [...]]

*Figure 347. A hieroglyphic transliteration and translation[9] of 2014-188.*

Only two inscribed wooden dockets were recovered from the burials. These are of interest in that they suggest that these dockets were created at the time of the original burials rather than when bodies were moved and re-buried as might be thought. This is of interest in connection with the similar dockets found in the Rhind Tomb[10] attached

---

9. I am grateful to Mark Gabolde for this reading.
10. Rhind, A. (1862) *"Thebes: Its Tombs and Their Tenants"*, Longman, London; also Dodson A. and Janssen, J. (1989) *"A Theban Tomb and Its Tenants"*, JEA volume 75 pp. 125-138.
11. Černý, J. (1965)."*Hieratic Inscriptions from the Tomb of Tutankhamun*", Griffith Institute, Oxford University Press, Oxford. pp. 15-17.

to what appear to be re-buried bodies. Similar dockets were found in the tomb of Tutankhamun[11] and they too date to the original burials.

Several other wooden dockets were found (*Figure 348*) but sadly without any trace of an inscription surviving.

*Figure 348. A small complete label which on which no trace of an inscription remains. Found in the fill of Shaft Four.*

*Figure 349. A possible dowel, either from a coffin or a piece of large furniture, inscribed with the nefer sign. From Shaft Two Chamber Ab*

Some shaped wooden pieces with inscriptions (and many more without) have survived but most of them are broken (*Figure 349*). These would seem to be dowels from coffins or from the joints of large pieces of furniture which required pinning together. The shrine panels in KV55 had similar dowels or tenons but made of copper.[12]

---

12. Davis, T. (1910) "*The Tomb of Queen Tiyi*", Constable & Co. Ltd, London plate XXIII.

# CHAPTER TWELVE
# OTHER FINDS

## Cartonnage

Figure 350. Cartonnage fragments from Shaft Two Chamber B.

Figure 351. Cartonnage fragments from Shaft Two Chamber A.

The cartonnage (decorated plasterwork reinforced with glue and linen) fragments are all badly damaged and it is not clear to what parts of the coffins or funerary masks they belong. There are simpler painted examples which include parts of head-dresses, wigs and faces. There are also pieces of thin, gilded plaster with incised decoration and thicker fragments with more complex decorative traces. Enough survives to indicate variety but not enough to to determine whether that variety existed within single or multiple sets of burial equipment. Most of the cartonnage was found in Shaft Two.

Figure 352. Further cartonnage fragments from Shaft Two Chamber A.

*Figure 353. Cartonnage fragments from Shaft Two Chamber Aa.*

*Figure 354. A cartonnage nose from Shaft Two (the scale is in millimetres).*

*Figure 355. Further fragments of cartonnage from Shaft Two Chamber A.*

*Figure 356. Moulded plaster fragments from Shaft Four from which the surface colour or gilding has been lost.*

*Figure 357. Gilded and coloured plaster fragment from Shaft Four (the scale is in millimetres).*

Thicker pieces of plaster were recovered from Shaft Four. Some of these had lost their colour completely possibly as a result of water damage. Others retained gilding and, in the case of 2015-201 (*Figure 357*), traces of colour.

Further gilded examples were recovered from the spoil-heaps. Some of these were gilded plasterwork and cartonnage in the process of disassembly (*Figures 358 and 359*).

*Figure 358. Fragments of plaster and gold leaf recovered from the spoil-heaps.*

*Figure 359. Gilded cartonnage fragment rcovered from the spoil-heaps (the scale is in millimetres).*

The gilded fragment in Figure 360 possibly shows most of the *st* (Q1) sign moulded in relief. This sort of relief is found on a number of coffins such as the inner and outer coffins of Tuyu and the second and outer coffins of Yuya (all from Tomb KV46 in the Valley of the Kings) and the coffins of Kha (*Figure 361*) in the TT8 tomb of Kha and Merit at Deir el-Medina[2].

1. Davis, T. (1907) "*The Tomb of Iouiya and Touiyou*", Archibald Constable & Co. Ltd, London. Plates VII, VIII, IX, XIII and XIV.
2. Schiaparelli, E. (1927) "*La tomba intatta dell'architetto Cha nella necropoli di Tebe*", R. Ministero della pubblica istruzione, Direzione Generale delle Antichita e Belle Arti, Museo di Antichita, Torino. Figures 22-24, 28 & 29.

*Figure 360. A gilded plaster fragment probably from a coffin similar to Figure 361. Recovered from the spoil-heaps (the scale is in millimetres).*

*Figure 361. Detail of the coffin of Kha from the tomb of Kha and Merit (TT8 in Deir el-Medina) now in the Egyptian Museum in Turin (Photo by Nicola Dell'Aquila and Federico Taverni / Museo Egizio.)*

*Figure 362. A plaster fragment recovered from the spoil-heaps and originally thought to be stone. It may be part of the feathers at the end of a wing.*

Further fragments recovered from Shaft Four included one piece initially thought to be limestone (*Figure 362*). It is of a plaster so hard that it appears to be stone. One surface bears decoration which perhaps can be interpreted as the ends of feathers such as appear at the ends of wings spread protectively over the bodies of coffins. Two other similar fragments (*Figures 363 and 364*) likewise have striations and retain patches of gilding.

*Figure 363. A plaster fragment from the spoil-heaps similar to 2018-73 but retaining some gilding (the scale is in millimetres).*

*Figure 364. A partially burned plaster fragment from the spoil-heaps. It retains some gilding and has the same shallow striations as 2018-73 (Figure 362) and 2015-37 (Figure 363) (the scale is in millimetres).*

*Figure 365. A piece of striated and gilded plaster probably from Shaft Two but recovered from the spoil-heaps (the scale is in millimetres).*

*Figure 366. A gilded plaster fragment recovered from the spoil-heaps.*

Similar striated decoration appears on a piece of gilded plaster still attached to a wooden fragment (*Figure 365*) of the object it originally decorated.

Other gilded fragments of plaster attached to wood were recovered from the spoil-heaps but in such small sizes that it is impossible to identify the objects to which they belong.

*Figure 367. One of several wooden fragments from the spoil-heaps covered with gilded plaster (the scale is in millimetres).*

At the edge of the northern spoil-heaps under fine debris which had fallen down the sides, we found traces of gold foil, already badly fragmented. Some of the gold foil was adhering to plaster fragments. These two elements lay alongside what initially appeared to be a solidified discolouration in the debris. This proved to be the wood from a badly decayed object which had once been plastered and gilded (*Figures 368 and 369*).

*Figure 368. Decayed wood, plaster fragments and gilding from an object found in fragments at the edge of the spoil-heaps.*

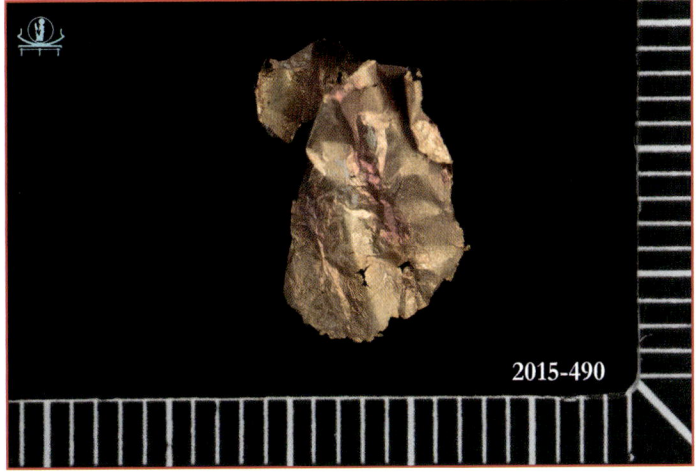

*Figure 369. One of the fragments of gold-foil originally attached to the decayed object in Figure 358 (the scale is in millimetres).*

# Amulets

*Figure 370. A tyet amulet (front and back views) made of an identified material (the scale is in millimetres).*

Apart from the two faience amulets or necklace components (Chapter Nine, *Figures 231 and 232*) only two further definite pieces were found and both these came from the spoil-heaps. One is a nearly complete *tyet* amulet (*Figure 360*) and the other is part of a stone amulet, pierced for suspension. This could be an ankh figure but is more likely to be another *tyet* amulet[3].

*Figure 371. A fragment of a stone amulet, the top pierced for suspension (the scale is in millimetres).*

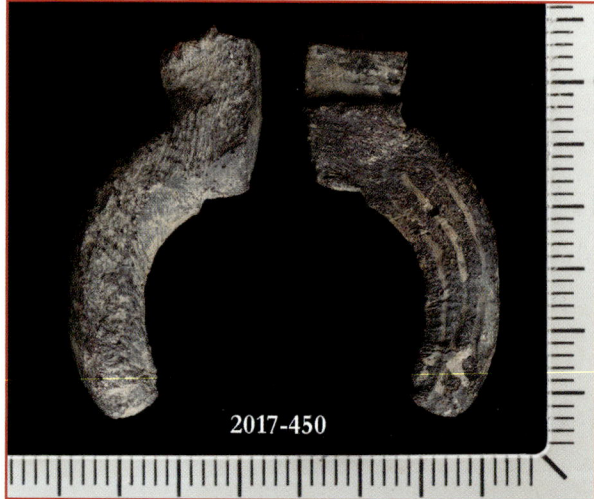

*Figure 372. A composite of a badly-melted glass fragment which is either an inlay or part of an amulet (the scale is in millimetres).*

*Figure 372* shows two views of a fire-damaged glass fragment which could also be part of an amulet but could be an inlay with an entirely different function.

---

3. Andrews, C. (1990) "*Ancient Egyptian Jewellery*", British Museum Press, London Figure 32k.

## Sealings

There were several types of sealings and seal impressions found on the WB1 site. The first were mud seals similar to those recovered intact in KV62 and used to seal objects. These were similar to the Type L seals bearing the jackal and nine captives of the necropolis found in the tomb of Tutankhamun[4]. The WB1 seals were found principally in the shafts. A large number came from Shaft Four.

*Figure 373. Seal impression of the necropolis found in Shaft Two (the scale is in millimetres).*

*Figure 374. A seal impression of the necropolis found in Shaft Four (the scale is in millimetres).*

The example in *Figure 374* has been scorched by fire. The back of the seal retains the mark left by the cord by which it was attached it to some object. Traces of gilding also survive.

---

4.  El-Khouli, A. et al. (1993) "*Stone Vessels, Pottery and Sealings from the Tomb of Tut'ankhamūn*", Griffith Institute, Oxford. p. 157.

Perhaps the single most important sealing (*Figures 376 and 377*, 2016-204) was discovered in material from Shaft Four. It consists of two identical impressions divided down the middle by the removal of the linen strip to which the mud sealing was attached. A clear impression of this linen strip remains.

*Figure 375. Two impressions of the seal of the necropolis.*

This object is of paramount important because the top and bottom halves combine to give the inscription "Nebmaatre, King of Upper and Lower Egypt" providing clear inscribed evidence of the date of some of the activity in the tombs. The absence of the king's *nomen* (Amenhotep) may indicate that this seal dates from late in the reign of this king.

*Figure 376. Seal bearing the name Nebmaatre (the scale is in millimetres).*

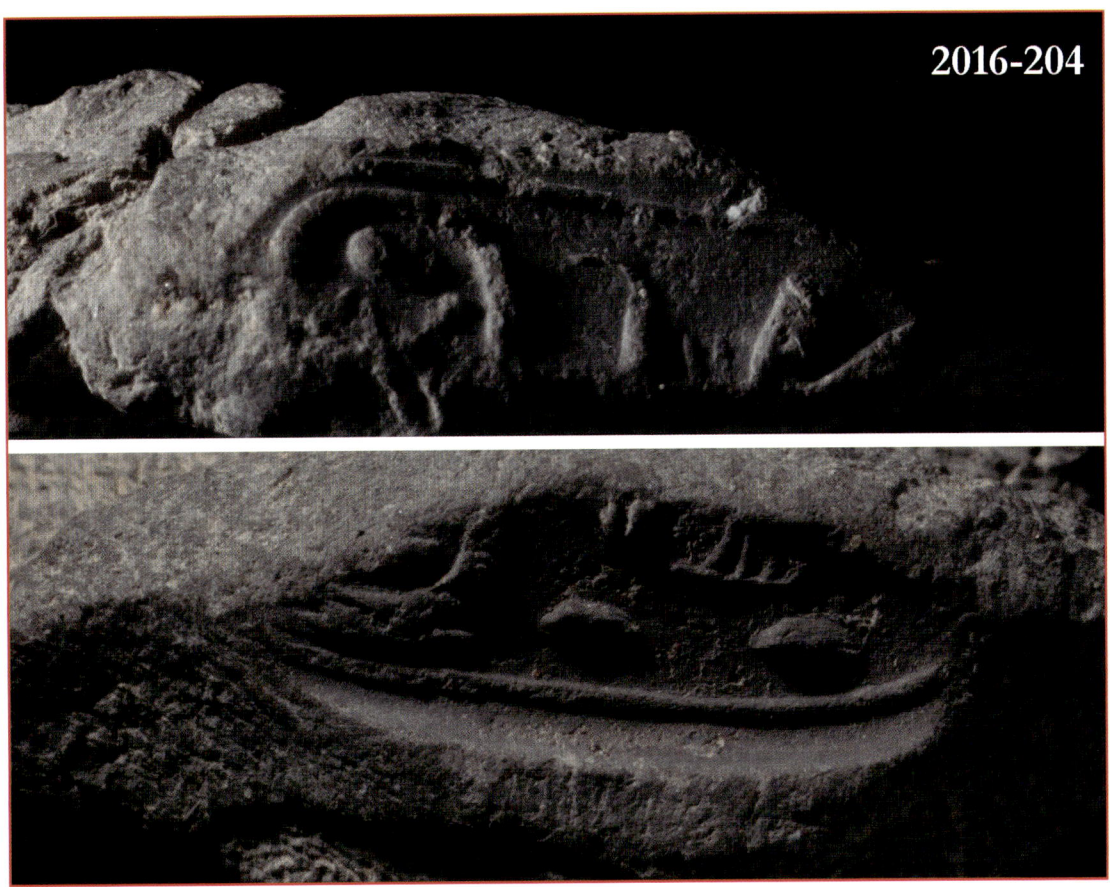

*Figure 377. Composite enlargment of 2016-204.*

This suggestion receives some support from a second category of sealings. These are jar sealings. Only one of these (*Figure 378*, 2015-109) survived more or less intact. The sealing on the top is badly abraded and the inscription as a whole remains obscure. Visible in the upper part of the two cartouches are a "*rʿ*" sign and a "*ṯḥn*" sign, both components in the name of the Dazzling Aten and similar to type HH (*Figure 379*) sealings recovered in longer form from Malqata[5]. Amenhotep III only began to call himself by this name towards the end of his reign.

*Figure 378. Double seals from a jar.*

---

5. Hayes, W. (1951) "*Inscriptions from the Palace of Amenhotep III*", Journal of Near Eastern Studies Vol. 10, No. 1. pp. 35-56.

Mud sealings were in place on some of the remaining blockings in the tombs but for the most part these had been made with very rough Nilotic mud mixed with straw. The straw had mostly decayed leaving lacunae in the sealings which made them impossible to read. A large part of the sealing to Shaft Five, Chamber A, has been consolidated by us and left *in situ*. So far it has proved impossible to interpret any of the seal impressions. Fragments of this sealing are shown in *Figures 380 and 381*. Individual signs are clear but the inscriptions as a whole remain obscure.

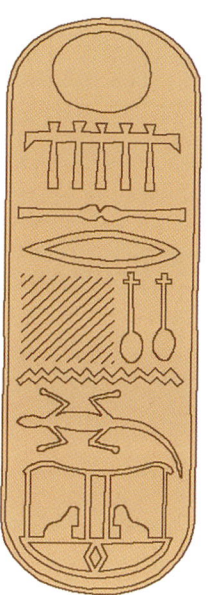

*Figure 379. A copy of a type HH seal from Malqata with the same two initial signs as 2015-109 (adapted from Hayes, W. 1951).*

*Figure 380. A fragment of the sealing from Shaft Five Chamber A.*

*Figure 381. A fragment of the sealing from Shaft Five Chamber A showing a wen sign.*

## Mud for sealing

An inconspicuous object retrieved from the spoil-heap material is a ball of mud (*Figure 382, 2015-619*) bearing the clear impression of having been contained within a linen bag.

*Figure 382. Sealing mud once contained in a linen bag.*

This object is of importance in suggesting the presence on the site of one or more embalming caches. The mud once contained in the now decayed linen bag is the mud used to form the necropolis seals. As part of the funerary material which had touched the deceased and their burial goods it would have been buried along with any surviving embalming material once the tomb was been sealed. This may explain the purpose of Shafts One, Six and Seven.

Similar mud remnants from sealing activity were found in KV54, the embalming cache of Tutankhamun[6]. Interestingly these bear finger-prints which it might at some date be possible to compare with other similar material.

---

6. www.metmuseum.org/art/collection/search/550177.

# Metal

Very few metal objects were recovered from the shafts and the best of them came from just under the surface of the spoil-heaps. The workmen's tools will be covered in the chapter on the clearance of the spoil-heaps (Chapter Fourteen). This leaves just one object made of metal: the yoke and two baskets which would have accompanied a shabti (*Figure 383*). This assembly was found at the south-west corner of the spoil-heaps where it had in all likelihood slid down from the top. Similar shabti tools (*Figure 385*) were found in the tomb of Yuya and Tuyu (KV46 in the Valley of the Kings)[7].

*Figure 383. The shabti baskets and yoke found just under the surface of the spoil-heaps.*

*Figure 384. Another view of the 2015-358 shabti equipment.*

---

7. Davis, T. (1907) op. cit. Plate XXI.

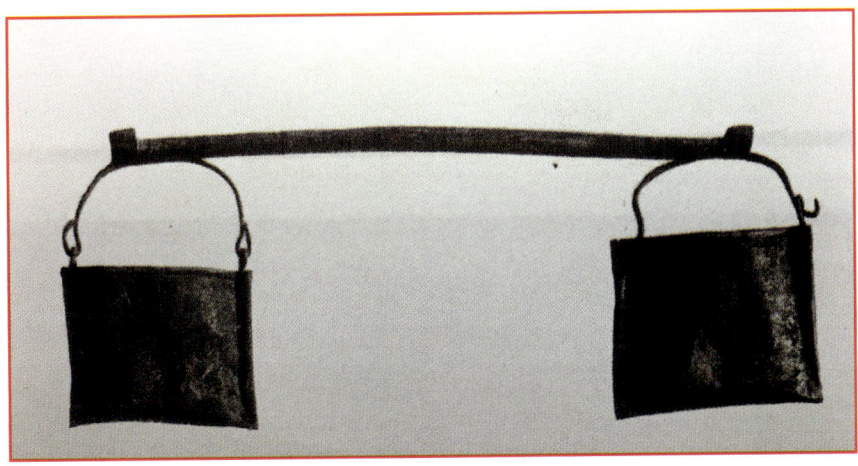

*Figure 385. Similar shabti equipment found in KV 46, the tomb of Yuya and Tuyu (photograph from Davis, T. 1907).*

## Linen

In keeping with the other finds the linen found in the shafts consisted in the main of very small fragments, in some cases mere strands. Only one largely intact linen object was found and this was a belt or fringe, possibly of Coptic date (Chapter Three, *Figure 23* above) found early in the clearance of Shaft Two.

*Figure 386. Charred and singed linen from Shaft Four prior to sorting.*

Other linen recovered from the shafts included charred material from Shaft Four, much of it reduced to charcoal but held together by charred unguents. Some of this material seems to have come from canopic jars, judging by its shape.

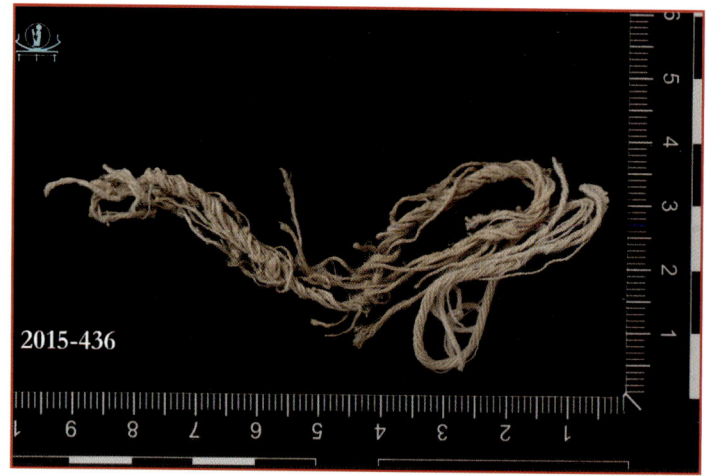

*Figure 387. Linen cord or string from the spoil-heaps.*

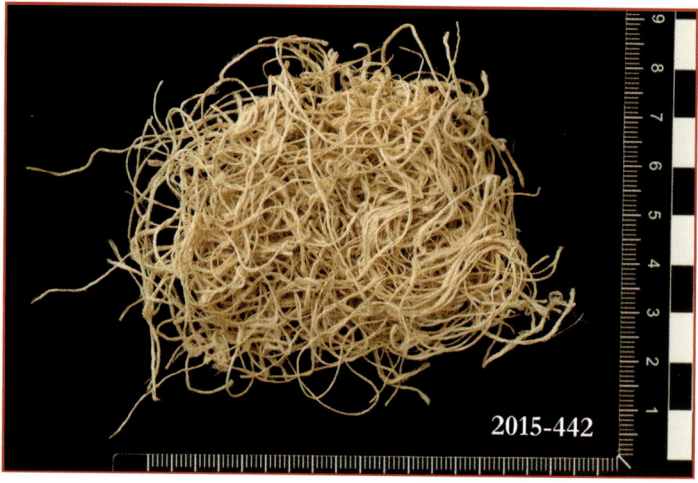

*Figure 388. Many hundreds of strands like these were recovered from the top layers of all the spoil-heaps and had in many cases fallen through into the layers below.*

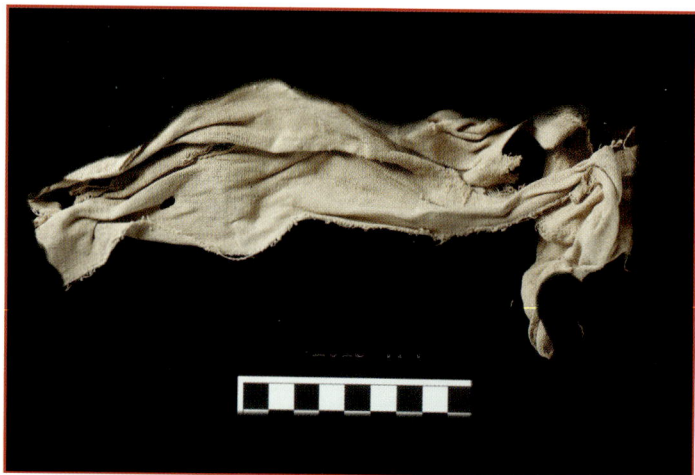

*Figure 389. The largest single piece of linen recovered from the spoil-heaps. Parts of it were impregnated with white gypsum or plaster.*

This material is still being sorted and will be given specialist coverage in the catalogue volume of finds. The samples below consist of fragments which appeared in the spoil-heaps.

*Figure 390. A detail of the weave of 2015-474 (the scale is in millimetres).*

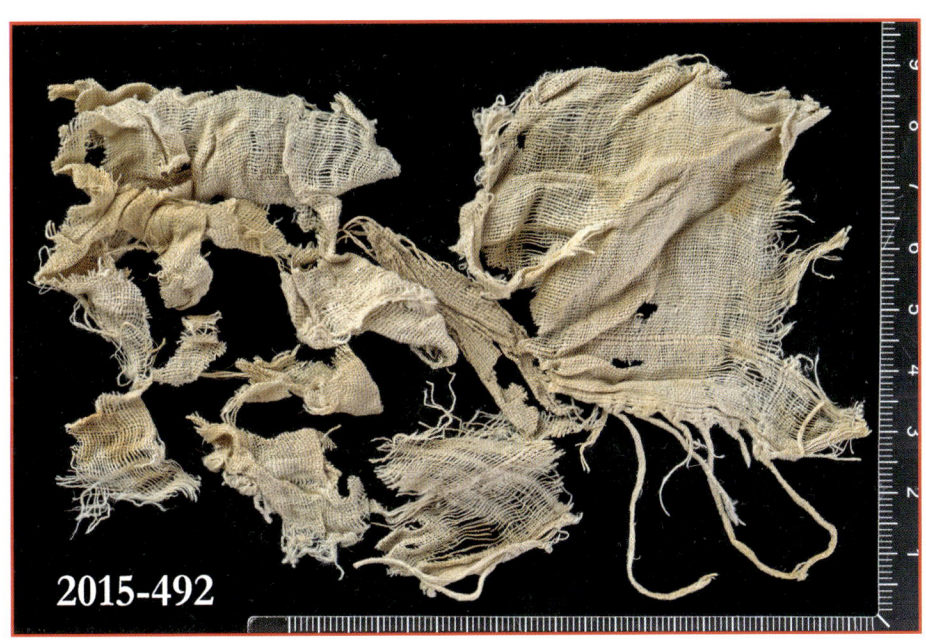

*Figure 391. Fragments of a fringed garment recovered from the spoil-heaps.*

*Figure 392. Detail of the sewn edge of a linen fragment from the spoil-heaps (the scale is in millimetres).*

# Leather

All the leather objects from the WB1 site were found in the spoil-heaps and many of them in the top layers. Again, like the linen these have not yet been subject to specialist study and will be covered in the catalogue volume. Any conclusions about their identification are therefore tentative.

*Figure 393. Leather sandals of unknown date.*

*Figure 394. Sole of a leather sandal.*

*Figure 395. Leather basket handles.*

*Figure 396. A large piece of leather of unknown purpose.*

# Rope & basketry

All the fibrous rope and coiled basket fragments were recovered from the spoil-heaps and the majority of those were found in the upper layers.

*Figure 397. Centre fragment from a coiled basket.*

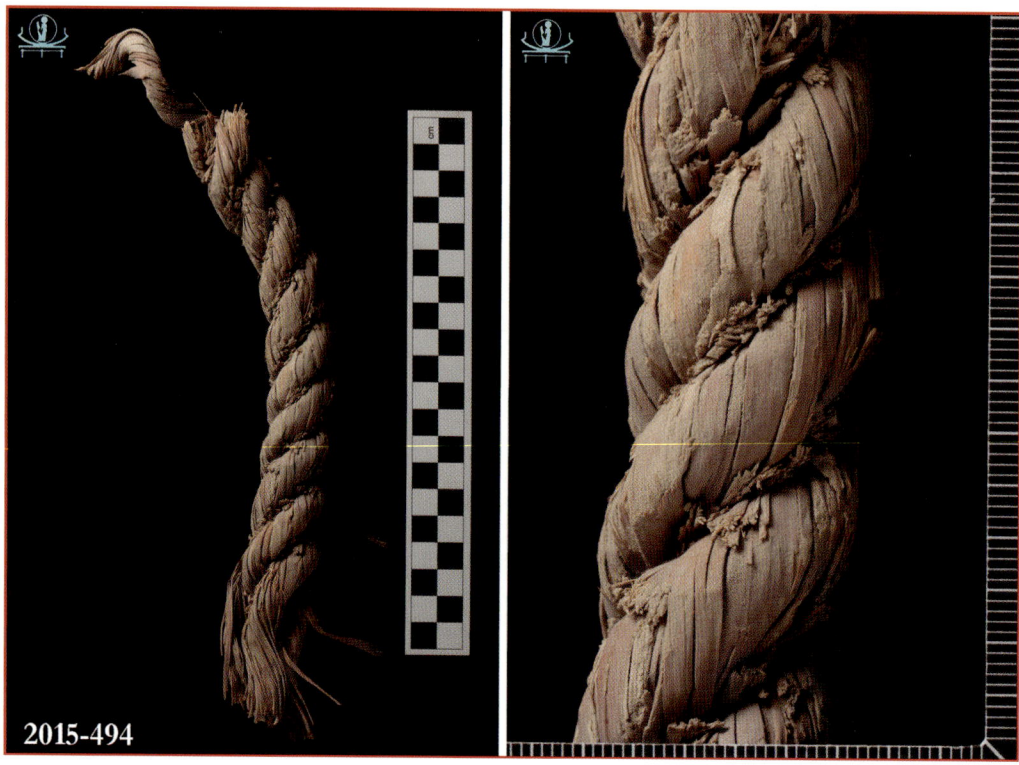

*Figure 398. Thick fibre rope (the scale on the right is in millimetres).*

*Figure 399. Medium fibre rope (the scale on the right is in millimetres).*

*Figure 400. Fine fibre rope.*

# Flora

Many of the smaller finds are still the subject of expert study and will be covered in detail in a later catalogue volume. The descriptions and images here form a small selection of the material uncovered. Most of the floral material was uncovered in the spoil-heaps although some dom-palm nuts came from the shafts. The survival of individual leaves under the many tons of rock debris is remarkable.

*Figure 401. A leaf from the disarticulated frond found under the upper spoil-heap debris (the scale is in millimetres).*

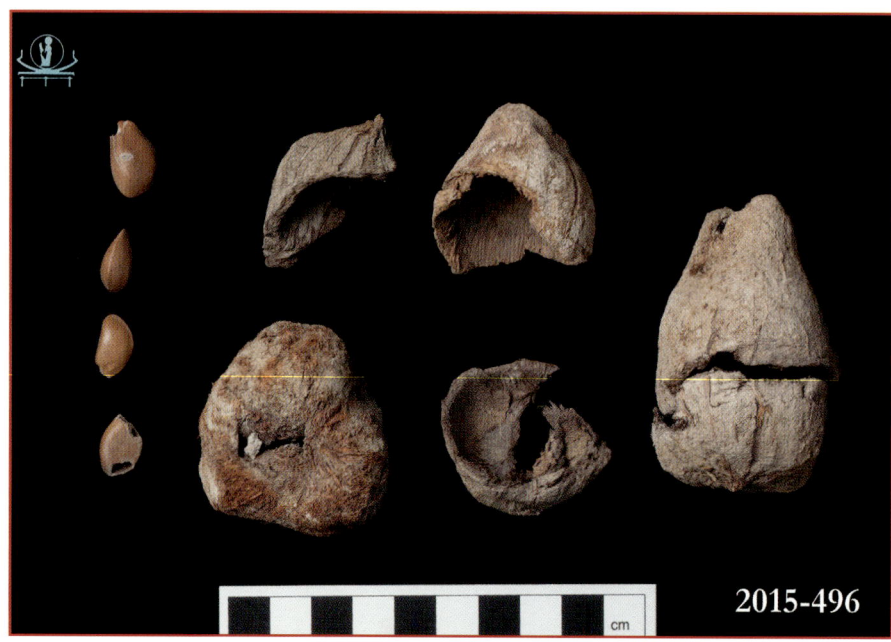

*Figure 402. A selection of persea nuts (left) and dom-palm nuts (right) found in the upper spoil-heaps.*

*Figure 403. A fig from the spoil-heaps.*

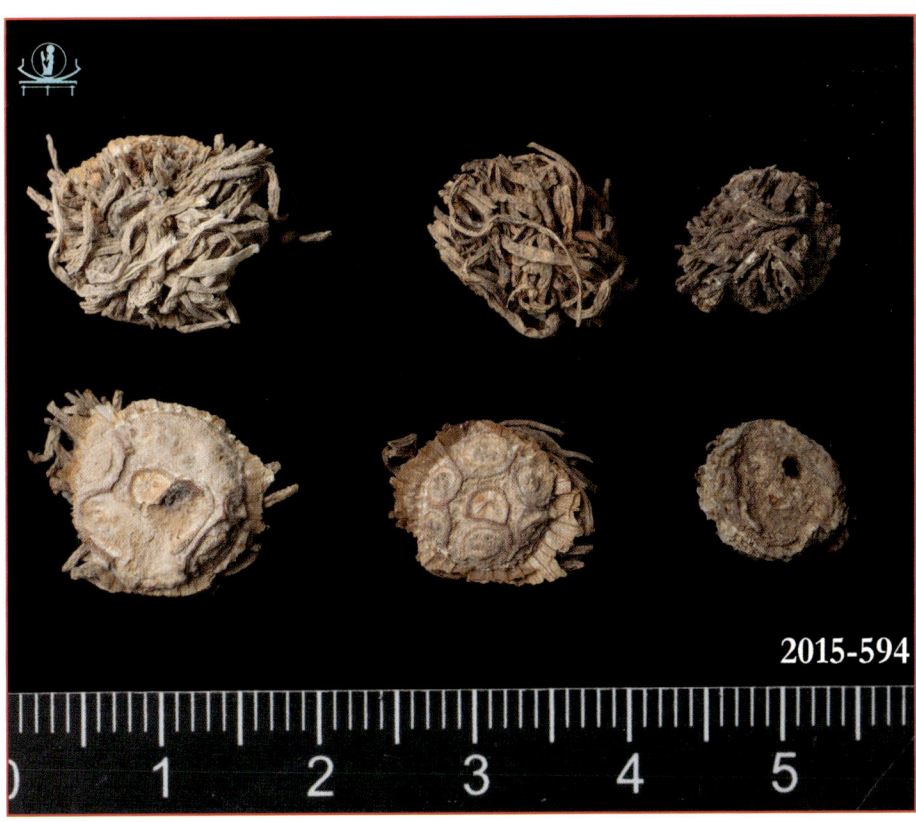

*Figure 404. Composite front and back views of the remains of onions found in the spoil-heaps.*

# CHAPTER THIRTEEN
# ANIMAL BONES

(Salima Ikram contributed the analysis and evaluation of the animal bones)

A brief archaeozoological investigation of the bones at the site of WB1 was carried out in February 2017, by Salima Ikram and further bird-related photographic material was studied by Megan Spitzer. A fuller account of their findings will be published in a later volume in this series. What follows here is a summary of the main observations.

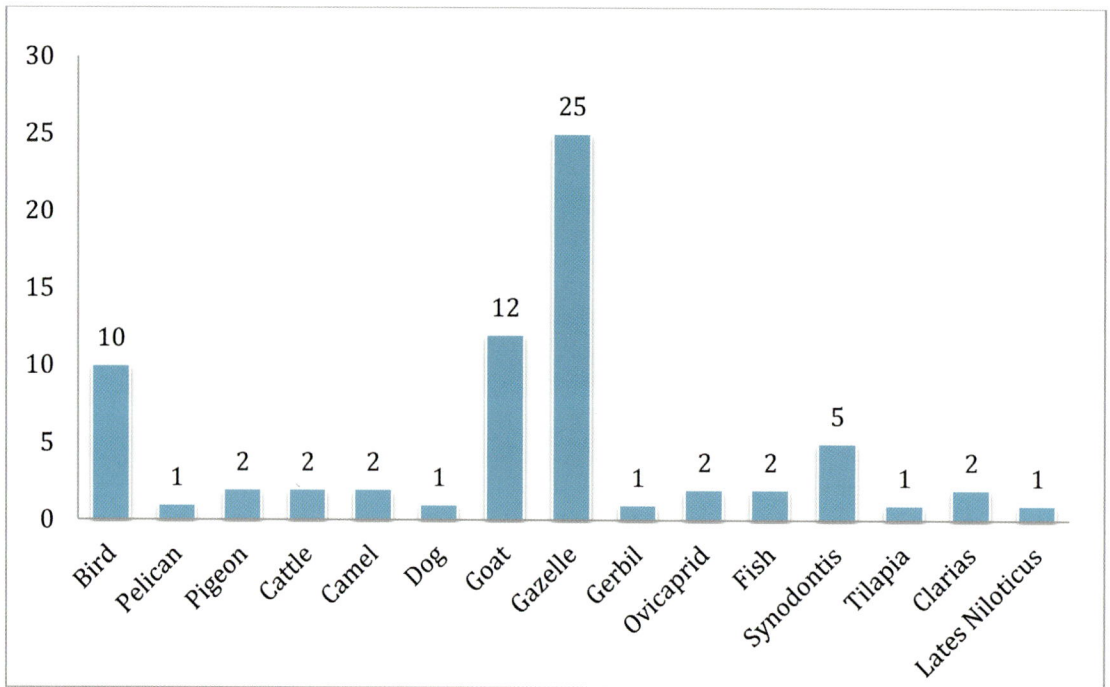

Table 1. Distribution of identified species

Identification of 106 bones was carried out on-site using published material from other sites and images of particular bones. In some instances, when bone fragments were too small (limb bones, ribs, and vertebrae) to be reliably identified as to species, they have been ascribed to Mammal Large, Medium-Large, Medium, or Small, and counted as such. Thus, those designated as Large Mammals (ML) are cow, horse, or donkey size; Medium to Large Mammals (MML) are young cattle, antelope, and young equid size; Medium Mammals (MMD) are sheep, goat, gazelle, and dog size. It should be noted that the fragments from Large Mammals are probably all from cattle, while those from Medium Mammals are almost certainly from ovicaprids, while the Medium to Large Mammals fragments are probably derived from young cattle.

## Findings

Out of the 106 bones identified, 13 belong to birds, 82 to mammals of different types, and 11 to fish (Table 1, Chart 1). Thus far, F1001 (the surface) yielded the greatest number of bones with the greatest range of species (41), and F1090 the least (2); see Table 1.

| Taxon | F1001 | F1011 | F1022 | F1023 | F1026 | F1080 | F1090 | F1158 | Grand Total |
|---|---|---|---|---|---|---|---|---|---|
| Bird | 4 | 1 |  | 3 | 1 | 1 |  |  | 10 |
| Pelican Pelecanus onocrotalus |  |  |  |  |  |  | 1 |  | 1 |
| Pigeon Columba sp. |  |  |  |  |  |  | 1 |  | 2 |
| Cattle Bos taurus | 1 | 1 |  |  |  |  |  |  | 2 |
| Camel Camelus dromedarius | 2 |  |  |  |  |  |  |  | 2 |
| Goat Capra aegagrus f. hircus |  |  | 6 | 6 |  |  |  |  | 12 |
| Ovicaprid | 1 |  |  | 1 |  |  |  |  | 2 |
| Gazelle Gazella sp. |  |  |  |  | 25 |  |  |  | 25 |
| Gerbil | 1 ind. |  |  |  |  |  |  |  | 1 |
| Dog Canis familiaris | 1 |  |  |  |  |  |  |  | 1 |
| Mammal | 1 |  |  |  |  |  |  |  | 1 |
| Mammal Large | 5 |  |  |  |  |  |  |  | 5 |
| Mammal Medium | 19 |  |  | 3 | 2 | 1 |  | 2 | 27 |
| Mammal Med-Lrg | 4 |  |  |  |  |  |  |  | 4 |
| Fish | 1 |  |  |  |  |  |  | 1 | 2 |
| Catfish Synodontis sp. |  |  |  |  |  | 4 |  | 1 | 6 |
| Bulti/Nile Tilapia Oreochromis niloticus/Tilapia nilotica | 1 |  |  |  |  |  |  |  | 1 |
| Catfish Clarias sp. |  |  |  |  |  |  |  | 2 |  |
| Nile Perch Lates Niloticus |  |  |  |  |  |  |  |  | 1 |
| Grand Total | 41 | 3 | 6 | 13 | 28 | 7 | 2 | 6 | 106 |

*Table 2 Number of Identified Specimens Indicating Range of Species by feature.*

## Birds

Out of the nine species identified by Spitzer and Ikram, the most interesting are the Great White Pelican, the Demoiselle Crane and the Common Moorhen as one would expect these species to stay close to the Nile. Instead they were found on the WB1 site 7.5 to 10km away from that abundant water source. The other birds (doves/pigeons, crows, raptors) are all still seen in the area.

In modern times there is nothing to attract water birds to the WB1 area. It is possible that a rainstorm might create a wet area or a temporary pond, which could attract birds that were in flight. The existence of such a recurring temporary water source is a possibility for different times in Egyptian history. Historically, pelicans were very common in Egypt and Shelley reports a sighting of several thousand of them flying through Upper Egypt in 1870[1]. They continue to be common migrants[2]. Moorhen remain abundant most of the year. Demoiselle Cranes tend to be most common during the autumn[3]. Although historically common, particularly as migrants[4] until the start of the 20th century, they have since become increasingly rare. It is possible that the pelican and crane from our site died while migrating in October/November. It should be noted that there is some pictorial evidence to suggest that the Egyptians kept pelicans for their eggs[5] This might argue against an autumn death date for the birds, if they had been tamed and had escaped from captivity. There are also Old Kingdom images of cranes being force-fed in the 6th Dynasty tomb of Mereruka, which shows that they were tamed and kept in the same way as the pelicans.

*Figure 405. Demoiselle Crane.*

The following birds were identified from photographs by Megan Spitzer:

1. Demoiselle Crane (Anthropoides virgo);

2. Hooded Crow (Corvus cornix) or Brown-necked Raven (C. ruficollis);

3. Pharaoh Eagle-Owl (Bubo ascalaphus);

4. dove (Streptopelia sp.), possibly Eurasian Collared-Dove (Streptopelia cf. decaocto) or, less likely, Stock Pigeon (Columba oenas);

---

1. Shelley, G. (1872) "*A handbook to the birds of Egypt*", John van Voorst, London. pp. 293-4.
2. Goodman, S. and Meininger, P. ed. (1989) "*The Birds of Egypt*", Oxford University Press, Oxford pp. 125-127.
3. Miles, J. (1998) "*Pharaohs' Birds*", Miles and Miles of Countryside, Cairo p. 41.
4. Houlihan, P. 1988. "*The Birds of Ancient Egypt*", American University in Cairo, Cairo and Goodman, S. M. and Meininger, P. ed. (1989) op. cit. p. 227.5.
5. Houlihan, P. (1988) op. cit.

5. Long-eared Owl (Asio otus); 6. sandgrouse?? (cf. Pterocles sp.) or dove?? (cf. Streptopelia sp.);

7. Great White Pelican (Pelecanus onocrotalus);

8. Common Moorhen (Gallinula chloropus);

9. possibly Laughing Dove (Streptopelia cf. senegalensis);

10. pigeon (Columba sp.), Stock Pigeon (C. oenas) or Common Wood-Pigeon (C. palumbus).

*Figure 406. Pharaoh Eagle-owl, Demoiselle Crane, Brown-necked Raven and possibly Sandgrouse or Dove.*

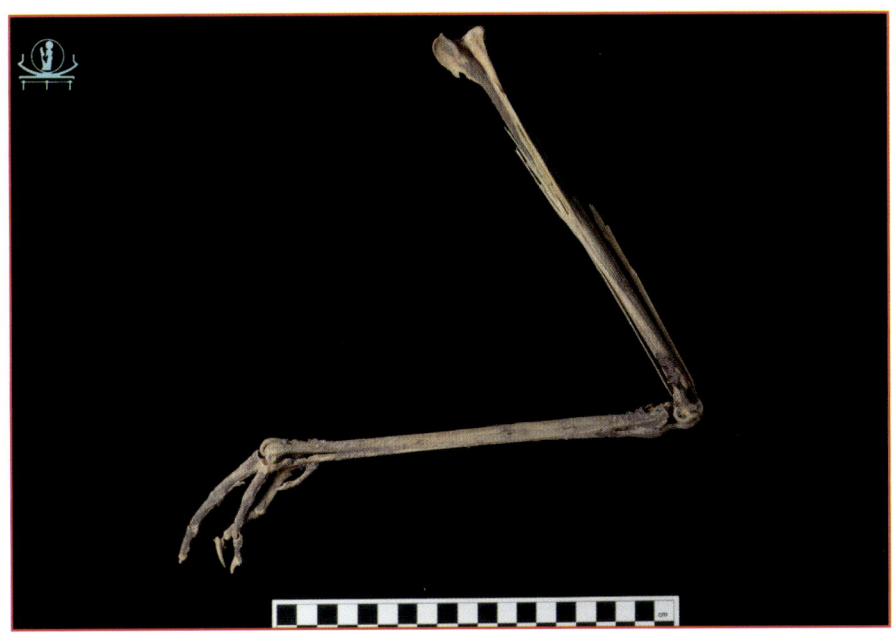

*Figure 407. Demoiselle Crane.*

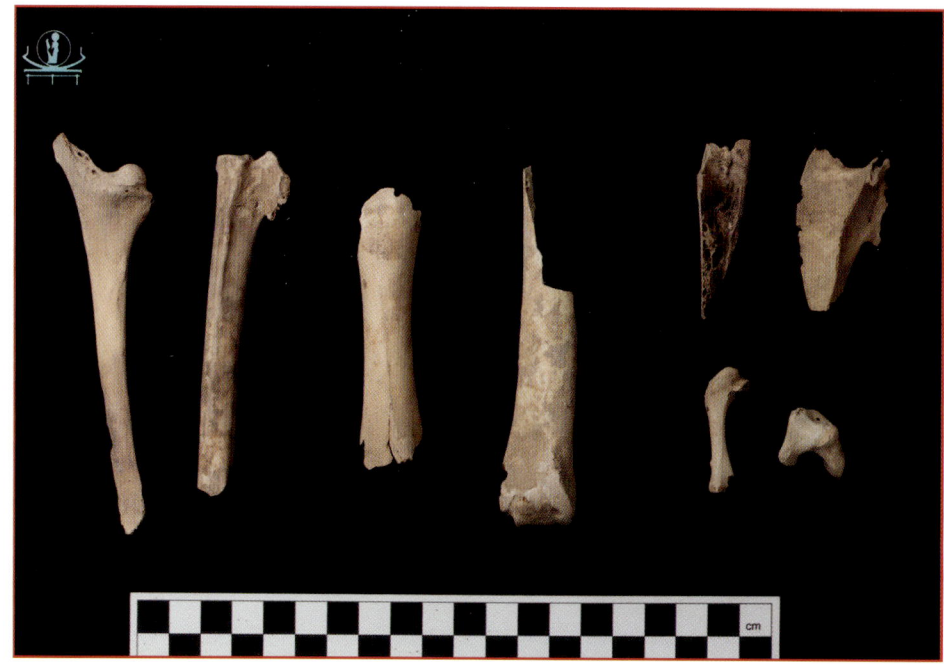

*Figure 408. Great White Pelican and possibly Eurasian Collared-Dove.*

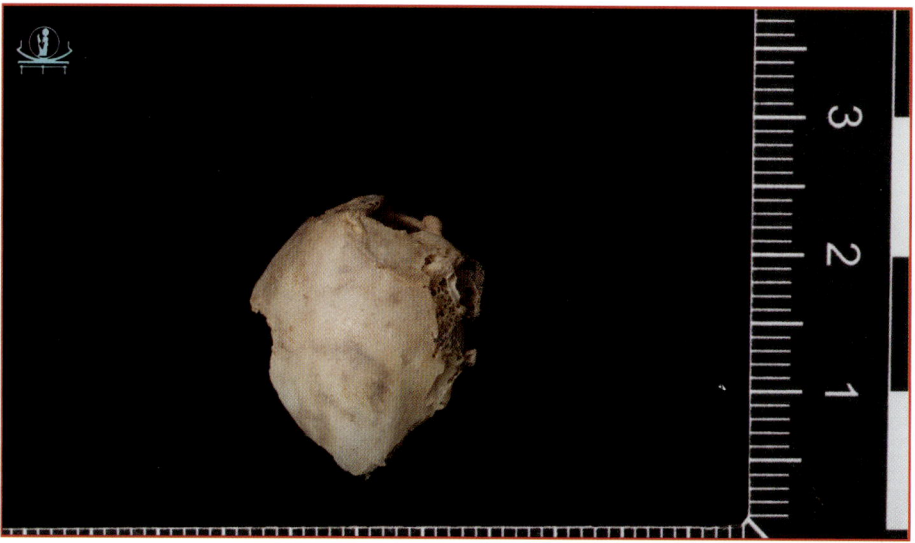

*Figure 409. Common Moorhen.*

## Fish

The presence of fish is somewhat surprising at this site. Synodontis and the Clarias, both forms of catfish, do not feature among funerary food offerings. Indeed, the bones from the latter fish indicate a large individual—between 60-80cm in length at least. Even though catfish can travel short distances overland and hibernate in mud there is no reason to believe that catfish were present in this area—particularly given the height of the WB1 site. It is possible that the fish were deposited here by human action or were brought by the pelican - although catfish are not a favoured meal due to their hard, boney heads.

## Mammals

The majority of bones derived from mammals consist mainly of medium-sized animals - ovicaprids, gazelle, and dogs, most probably. The number of gazelle bones gives a slightly incorrect picture as 16 bones are definitely from the same individual, and possibly nine others also belong to the same creature. This suggests that only one gazelle was found. As the gerbil was articulated and still had its skin covering it, the individual bones were not identified.

Fragments of a camel - clearly dating to post Persian times, and most probably relatively recent - is an indication of relatively modern activity at this site. The only animals found here that might relate to the original tomb contents are the cattle and ovicaprids. Although ovicaprid offerings[6] are not usual, given the prominence of cattle as food offerings, they are not unknown, and might have been given as offerings to less prominent members of the royal family or to elite individuals in lieu of offerings of cattle.

## Conclusion

It is difficult to establish incontrovertibly whether the bones originally came from the tombs or are later deposits. Certainly, some species might have been placed in the tombs as food offerings (pigeon, dove, goat, cattle, gazelle) or as pets (gazelle), as has been found in other contexts[7]. However, the majority of identified animal remains appear to have been deposited here by natural forces (see Table 1 and the list provided by Spitzer, above), and are an environmental rather than cultural indicator. Brown-backed Ravens nest in the Wadi El-Agaala two kilometres to the west of the WB1 site to this day.

---

6. Ikram, S. (1995) "*Choice Cuts: Meat Production in Ancient Egypt*", Peeters, Leuven.
7. Ikram, S. and Iskander, N. (2002) "*Catalogue General of Egyptian Museum: Non-human Mummies*", Supreme Council of Antiquities Press, Cairo and Ikram, S. (1995) op. cit..

# CHAPTER FOURTEEN
# INVESTIGATION AND CLEARANCE OF THE SPOIL-HEAPS

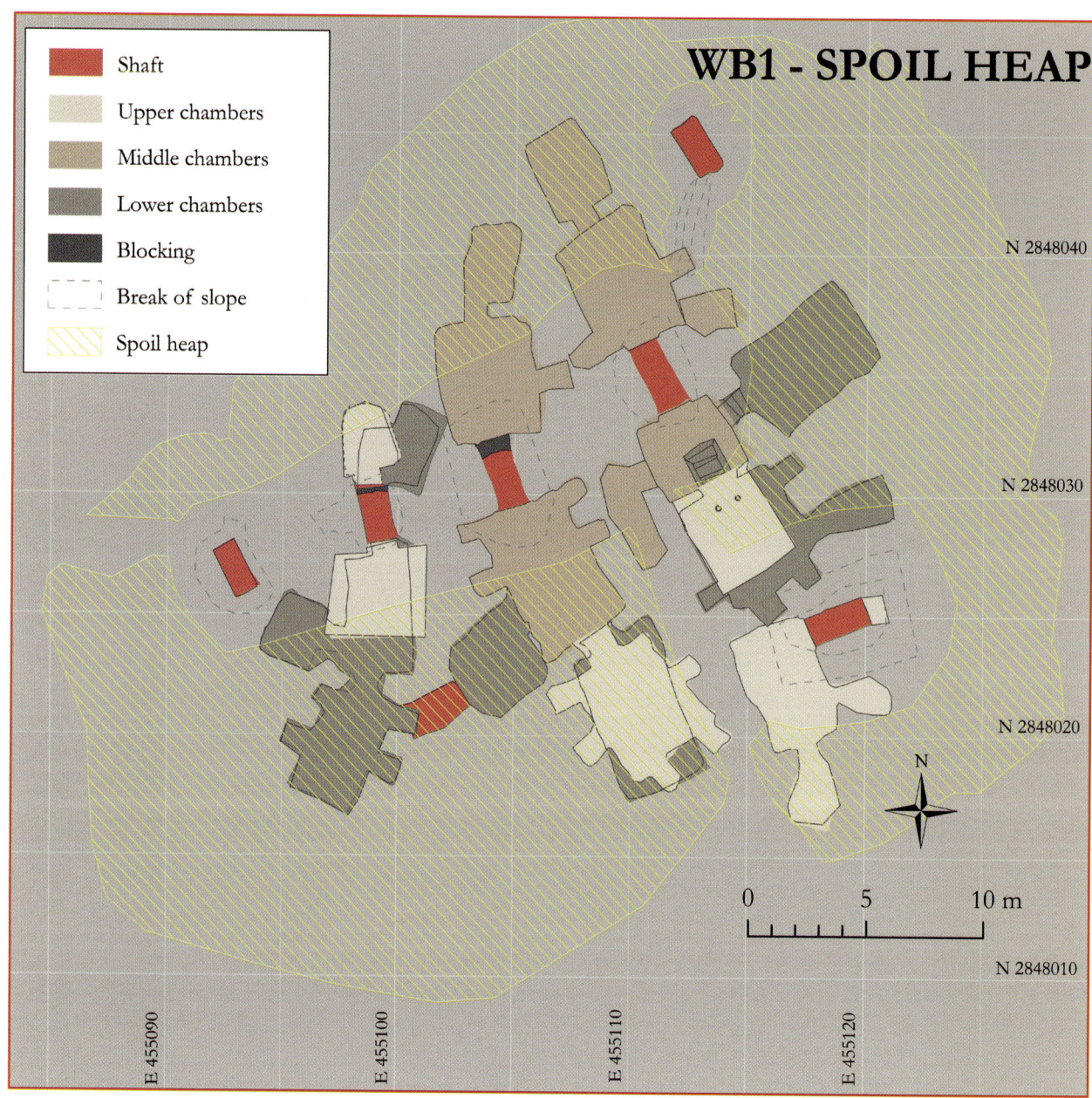

*Figure 410. The extent of the spoil-heaps as they related to the shafts and tombs below.*

*Figure 411. The spoil-heaps before clearance, looking east.*

*Figure 412. The initial removal of the top 15cms of loose material across the spoil-heaps.*

*Figure 413. A fragment of basket in situ in the spoil-heaps.*

## Clearance and finds

Work clearing the spoil-heaps began in October, 2015. We were hoping to discover:

- at what dates the spoil-heaps were created;
- how much of the debris related to construction and how much to the subsequent emptying of shaft fill during robberies;
- whether there was any trace of buildings;
- if there were any further shafts hidden by the debris;
- evidence concerning the construction of the tombs.

Some of these objectives proved elusive.

The spoil-heaps were not consistent in height or composition. Along the southern border they stood over 3.0m high and consisted of a mixture of large stone blocks, smaller stone fragments, coarse gravels and desert marl. Thanks to the natural slope of the ground, on the north side they were less than a metre deep and consisted mainly of coarse gravels and desert marl with smaller rocks interspersed.

In view of the large numbers of fragments (of faience, glass, ceramics, linen and wood) visible on the tops and sides of the spoil-heaps, the first step was to remove the top 15cms right across the southern spoil-heaps (*Figure 412*). This work was conducted from west to east and was followed by the removal of the outermost layer of the sides of the spoil-heaps created by smaller fragments of desert marl sliding down the sides. In the process these took with them many object fragments. Amongst the objects found in this top layer were the copper shabti baskets (*Figure 383*). All through the top layer many hundreds of strands of fine linen thread 10-15cms in length were found widely scattered

(*Figure 388*). In some cases the linen strands were found in hanks. Many fragments of basket and palm fibre were also found in this layer (*Figure 413*).

As the edges of the spoil-heaps receded areas filled with very fine powdered dirt mixed in parts with a white powdered substance began to appear. These were roughly 30-40cms in depth but as they extended under the spoil-heaps it was initially difficult to understand what these were.

They turned out later to be the remains of the sealing of the shafts (*Figure 418*). The shafts were apparently sealed with a mixture of fine aggregate and gypsum which then formed the bottom layer of the spoil-heaps, being the first material extracted after any landscaping cover was removed.

A decision was eventually taken to clear the eastern end of the spoil-heap south of Shaft Six. Here a large pile of large stones (F1080 in *Figure 425*) spread south from a shallow ditch (F1081 in *Figure 425*) which ran roughly east-west along the top of Shaft Six before

*Figure 414. Looking north. Feature 1080 running south down the centre of the photograph from just to the left of the buried opening to Shaft Six (below the drystone retaining wall).*

turning south some ten metres to the west. Very nearly parallel to the line of the ditch running south stones were piled in a more or less straight line. It became apparent that the shallow ditch (F1081 in *Figure 425*) was the outline of a planned shaft due west of Shaft Six. This shaft was never started. The stones which lay in the line proceeding south (F1080 in *Figure 425*) seem to have been part of the corridor fill of the shafts and may therefore constitute the original position of the architectural debris from the tombs.

Further in towards the shafts we found very large stones covered in layers of white gypsum plaster and aggregate, the former being the sealing of the shaft tops. As work proceeded round the tops of the shaft the stratification became clearer thanks to a section cut though the spoil-heap from south to north between Shafts Five and Four (*Figure 417*).

The composition of the bottom 2.5m of the spoil-heaps in the area to the south of, and between, Shafts Four and Two was made up almost entirely of larger stones (*Figures 416 and 417*).

To the north of Shafts Two, Four, Five and Six the northern (uphill) spoil-heaps consisted in great part of smaller fragments. Mixed in amongst these were a number of objects. Fragments of gold came to light at the eastern end of the southern spoil-heap north of Shaft Three. These proved to be decayed gilded cartonnage, a detail of which is shown in Chapter Twelve *Figures 358 and 359*. Another find, from the northern edge of these uphill spoil-heaps, was a decayed wooden object (the wood fragmented into formless and crumbling pieces) which had once been partly covered in black lacquer and at least partly gilded (Chapter Twelve *Figure 368*). Also found in this area were leaves, possibly from a bouquet (*Figures 401 and 420*), dom-palm nuts and persea nuts (*Figure 402*), figs (*Figure 403*) and the remains of onions (*Figure 404*).

Under the northern spoil-heaps Feature 1079 (*Figure 425*) contained pottery sherds later identified as Third Intermediate Period (Chapter Seven *Figures 196 and 197*) which, as noted, confirm some activity on the site during that period.

Towards the end of October a section was cut through the southern spoil-heaps south of Shaft Five in order to understand better the composition. This revealed two things.

The first was a section showing tipping lines of debris emptied to the south (*Figures 417 and 419*). These appear to be related to the initial destructive intervention on the site as the lower strata consist of the white gypsum and aggregate mixture which was used to seal the shaft openings.

*Figure 415. Looking south-west. Below the metre scale is the eastern end of Feature 1081 which runs off the photograph to the right. The northern end of F1080 is visible in the upper right of the photograph.*

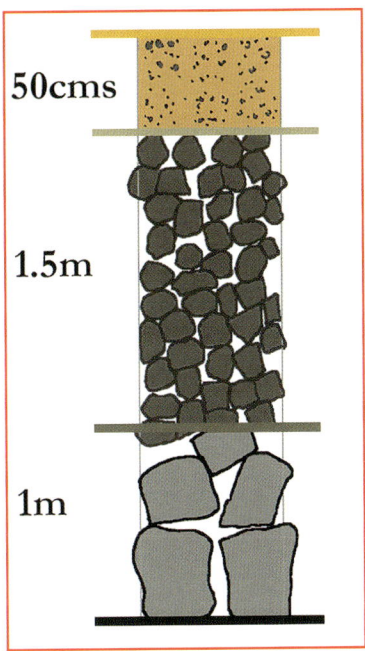

*Figure 416. A schematic sketch of the section of the central part of the spoil-heaps.*

*Figure 417. Photograph of the section through the main southern spoil-heaps between Shaft Four and Five during clearance. The top layer of fine debris has been removed.*

The second revelation was what looked initially like the opening to a previously untouched shaft (Shaft Seven) (*Figure 421*).

We had a suspicion that there might be further shafts under the spoil-heaps. This was based on the plans of the tombs (*Figure 422*). As previously noted, Shaft Two has a straight axis.

By contrast, Shaft Four, immediately to the west, has an eccentric axis. The northern chambers bend markedly eastwards. The southern chambers do the same, giving the overall design a distinct curve.

Shaft Five also displays a less than straight axis. The lower northern room of Shaft Five bends away to the east. It then stops with the north-west corner of the incomplete Chamber A (where it nearly collides with Shaft Four Chamber A). The upper northern room, Chamber A1, is also truncated. So there was a suspicion that something underground to the north of Shaft Five's Chamber A1 accounted for this.

*Figure 418. The remains of the edge of the sealing of Shaft Six can be seen arcing from the right hand top of the photograph down towards the centre foreground.*

*Figure 419. Tipping lines in the spoil-heaps south of Shaft Six.*

*Figure 420. Floral remains from the northern spoil-heaps.*

Additionally, Shaft Five's Chamber Ba and Shaft Four's Chamber Ba are moving away from each other as though avoiding some other hidden underground obstacle. On this basis we were alert to the possibility that there might be further chambers hidden under the spoil-heaps in these locations.

These speculations proved baseless except in the area between Shaft Five's and Shaft Four's southern chambers. It was here, some seven metres vertically above Niche 1 in Shaft Five Chamber Ba, we uncovered what looked like the opening to a small shaft previously concealed under the spoil-heaps (*Figure 421 and 423*) and oriented east-west like Shaft Three. Although this discovery naturally raised the hope of another tomb, and one possibly untouched since ancient times, it was always clear from its position that there could not be a deep shaft here as this would have collided with Shaft Five below.

This shaft proved to be only a metre deep. The opening had at some stage been sealed with the same aggregate mixed with gypsum which sealed the entrances to the other shafts.

It is possible, therefore that this was a foundation deposit although the complete absence of cultural material inside it is a puzzle. Mud used for creating object seals and once stored in a bag (Chapter Twelve *Figure 382*) had been retained on site and this would almost certainly have been buried in an embalming cache[1]. Shafts One, Six and Seven are all candidates for consideration as embalming caches but they could also have been used for perfunctory burials - of children perhaps.

Before moving on to the XVIIIth dynasty surface revealed under the spoil-heaps, it is important to emphasise that the composition of the spoil-heaps, with fine, white aggregate and gypsum sealing material at the bottom (with clear tipping lines rising to the south of the shaft mouths) and what was probably shaft fill on top of that (mixed

---

1.  Material identical to this was found in the KV54 embalming cache of Tutankhamun in the Valley of the Kings. see Chapter Twelve p. 239 above.

*Figure 421. Shaft Seven when uncovered.*

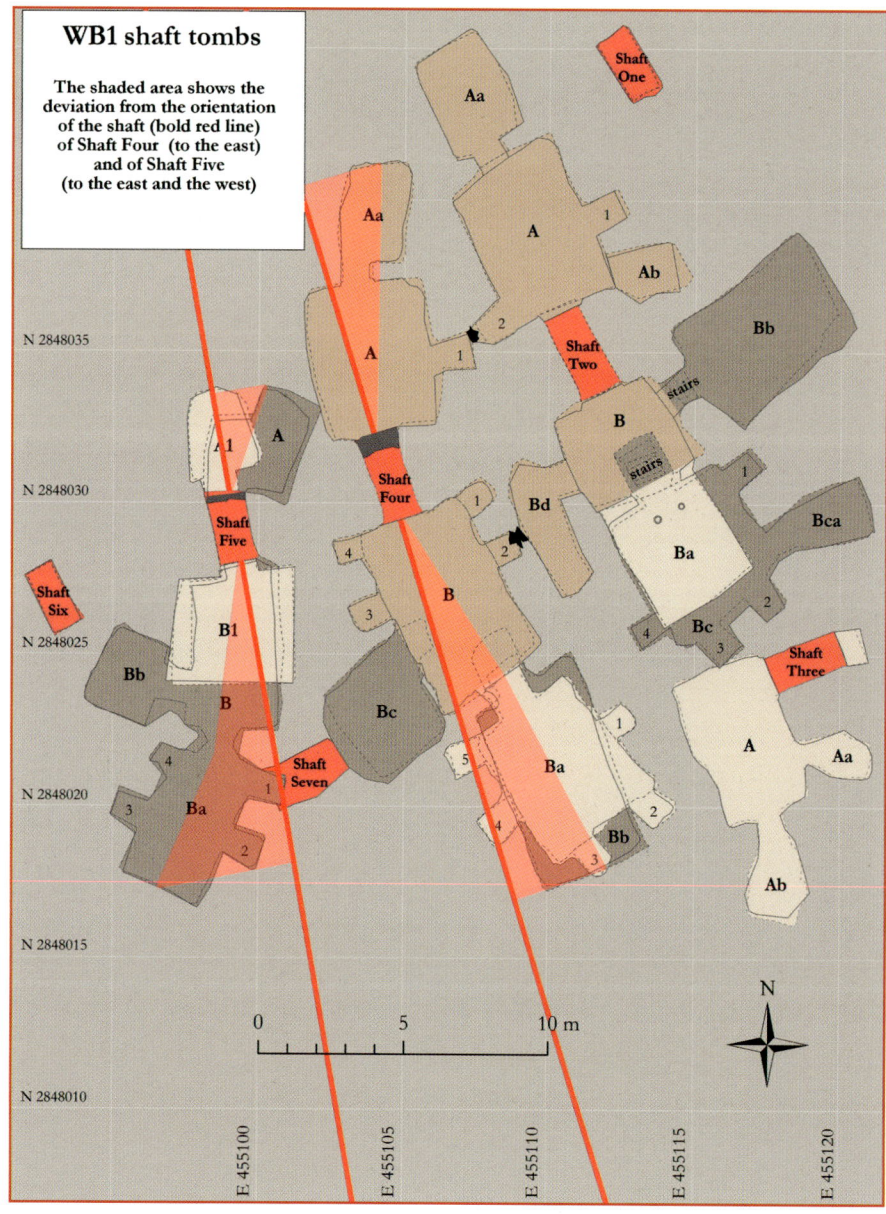

*Figure 422. Once the survey data was available it looked as though Shaft Five and Shaft Four both bent away from something between them, Shaft Five Chamber Ba turning west and Shaft Four Chamber Ba turning east. Similarly, Chamber A of Shaft Five and Chambers A and Aa of Shaft Four appeared to bend westwards.*

in at the lower levels with construction debris from the original creation of the shafts), the whole then covered with accumulations of wind-blown desert marl, supports the view that the tombs were completely emptied at some stage in antiquity in what may have been a single destructive event. The tomb chambers would have been empty - as indeed Shaft Four's Chamber Ba and the lower chambers (A, B, Ba and Bb) of Shaft Five remained - until material from the surface of the spoil-heaps was washed and blown

*Figure 423. Shaft Seven post-clearance looking south-east. At the right-hand end of the feature a grey line of the hard gypsum and aggregate which sealed the top in ancient times is visible.*

*Figure 424. A detail of the remains of gypsum and aggregate sealing at the eastern end of Shaft Seven.*

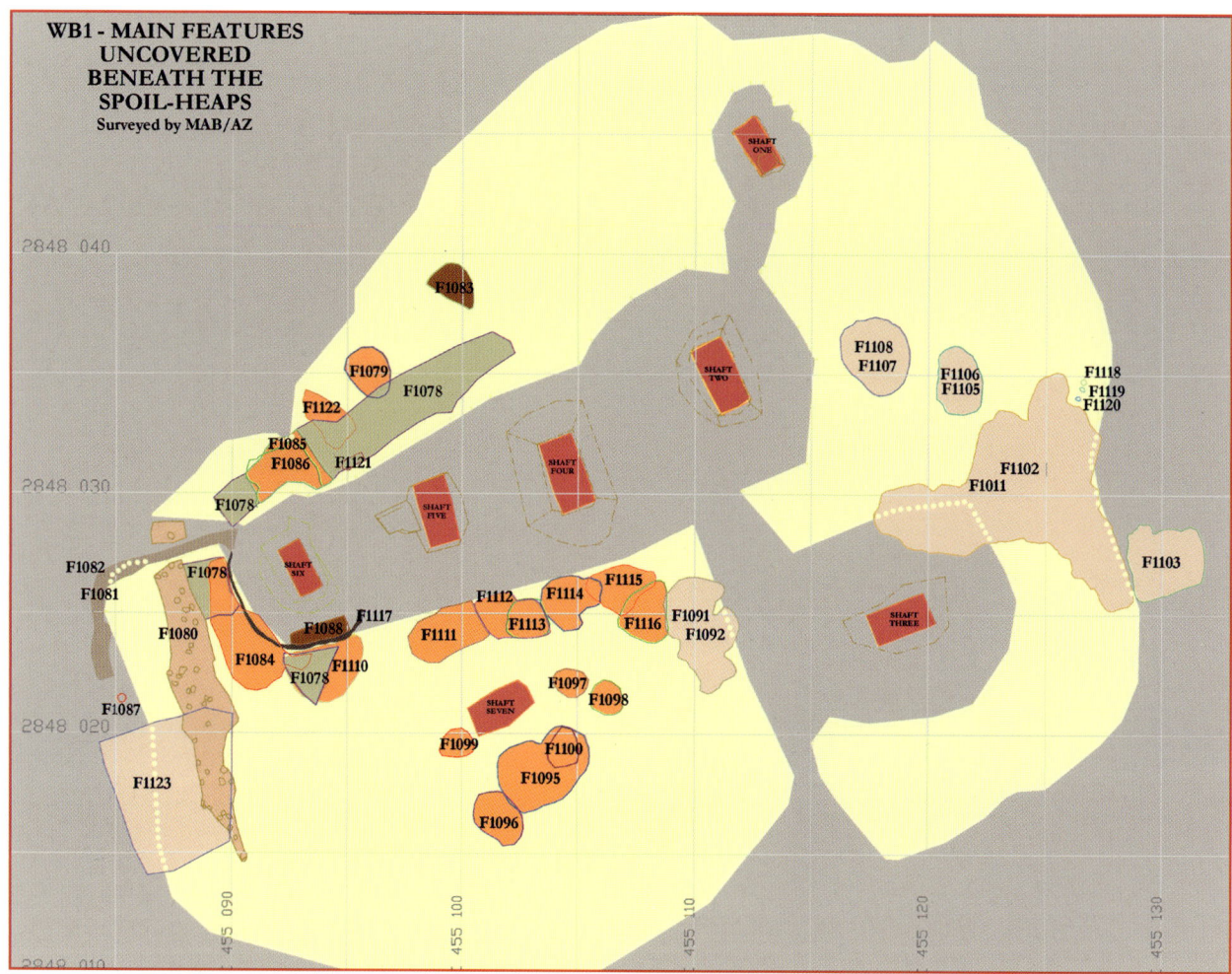

*Figure 425. A summary of the features found under the spoil-heaps and referred to in the text. The pale yellow outline shows the original extent of the spoil-heaps immediately after the shafts had been cleared.*

back into the shafts. Of course it is possible that particular chambers were emptied (or re-emptied) in later periods. Chamber Ba in Shaft Four, for instance, could well have been cleared for use as a Coptic shelter.

## Dating of the spoil-heaps

The spoil-heaps contributed little to the dating of the emptying of the tombs although ceramics confirmed the presence of visitors to the site in the Third Intermediate Period. Later Roman and modern ceramics contributed to a picture of constant intervention on the site from the time of the original destruction of the burials through to the present.

## The nature of the debris

It was difficult to separate the building or construction material from the fill which had been removed from the shafts as the two categories were intermingled. What had formerly been construction debris had been used in ancient times to fill the shafts. This had in turn been removed completely and scattered across the surface with the balance of the construction debris.

It was clear that construction debris had always been evident on the surface and that little or no attempt was made to conceal the location of the tombs. It would have been easy to tip the construction debris over the cliffs on the northern side of the plateau into which the tombs were sunk. Recent flash floods have eroded the base of the cliffs but clearance of this area has revealed no evidence of tomb debris.

A rough calculation of the volume of the debris removed from the surface during our clearance of the spoil-heaps compared with the volume of the tombs suggested a large discrepancy in favour of the spoil-heaps. This briefly supported the view that there might be further undiscovered shafts. However, a more likely explanation now seems to be that some form of landscaping using locally-sourced material took place to cover the tomb entrances.

## Structures

Apart from Feature 1080 (*Figures 414 and 415*) there was no trace of any structure or building under the spoil-heaps. The irregular shape of Feature 1080 suggests it was simply an initial dumping line of extracted stone fragments.

## Surface features

The first of the features (Feature 1091 in *Figure 425*) indicative of an original XVIIIth dynasty level emerged at the eastern end of the main southern spoil-heap just south-east of Shaft Four. A depression in the surface of irregular outline but longer north-south than east-west proved to be a bowl or pit where mud plaster was mixed. The feature contained clear finger and knee impressions and two deeper impressions which may have been caused by donkey hooves. The relatively hard consistency of the surface was created when fine mud powder was mixed with powdered gypsum and water in this depression to create a plaster for the tomb walls.

Shortly after this another area of mud plaster was found north-east of Shaft Three (F1101 in *Figure 425*). This was an extensive feature with some characteristics of a floor, being flatter and larger (10m N-S and 10m E-W at its biggest). Embedded in the mud plaster were strands of linen of the same sort as those found in great numbers in the spoil-heaps. Fragments of plaster recovered from Shaft Two also contained traces of linen threads (*Figure 433*).

One of the more remarkable discoveries was found in F1102 which is the fill of F1101 (see *Figure 425*). After the area had been brushed down ready for photography early the next morning, a strong wind blew through the site overnight and stripped away a further thin layer of dust left in place by the brushing. The removal of this additional layer of dust revealed an almost perfect human footprint (*Figure 431*) of one of the workmen who constructed the tombs.

It was just north of Feature 1101 (in *Figure 425*) that we founded the largest piece of linen discovered on the WB1 site. It has not been possible yet to determine what sort of garment this is or indeed to what period it relates. Ceramics found mixed in with the upper layers of the spoil-heaps included late Byzantine wares and a copper nail which seems to be of Roman date (*Figure 432*).

In addition to the food traces (the figs, nuts and onions which may have been part of the stocking of the tomb) there were also many finds at the lowest levels of the spoil-heaps which related to the workmen who constructed the tombs.

*Figure 426. Feature 1091, the mud-mixing pit to the south-east of Shaft Four. The possible donkey hoof marks are visible just below and to the right of the photographer's right foot.*

*Figure 427. Partial hand-print in Feature 1091.*

These included leather sandals (*Figure 393*) and leather basket handles (*Figure 395*) which are still the subject of expert study. Large pieces of leather may be parts of water-skins (*Figure 396*).

Amongst the workmen's tools recovered was a broken chisel-tip (*Figure 434*) and a whetstone bearing traces of copper from the sharpening of chisels (*Figure 435*).

*Figure 428. Aerial view of (left to right and top to bottom) features 1107, 1105 and 1101.*

*Figure 429. Feature 1108 from the north.*

*Figure 430. Feature 1105 from the north. The upturned basketful of plaster is clearly visible above the right-hand end of the metre scale.*

Two types of flint pounders were recovered. One type consisted of spherical pounders easily held in the hand (*Figure 436*) and of a type found across the Theban hills in great numbers. The other type was more easily held in two hands[2] (*Figure 437*) and bear percussion marks where they have been brought down with force to fracture rock for extraction.

Other stone objects included a stone pestle (*Figure 438*) and a large variety of flint blades (*Figures 439*) which either date to earlier periods and were collected for re-use or were made for use during the XVIIIth dynasty. Many of these were found concentrated round the surface above Shaft Two.

A large quantity of broken wooden pestle heads (*Figure 441*) were recovered along with their handles (*Figure 440*). Inspection of the flat surfaces of the heads reveals pitting consistent with their having been used to crush relatively soft material. From the colouration this would appear to have been gypsum.

A pair of badly termite-damaged mallets were recovered from the last portion of the debris cleared just to the south of Shaft One (*Figure 442*). These were strangely heavy because termites had replaced most of the interior wood with mud.

The condition of these mallets and of some of the wood found in the shafts is indicative of levels of moisture higher than those which pertain today. Termites need moisture in quantities not present today to survive. We were to find further compelling evidence of high levels of moisture when the spoil-heaps were finally and completely cleared.

---

2. Carnarvon & Carter, H. (1912) *"Five Years' Exploration at Thebes"*, Oxford University Press, Oxford Figure 8, p. 10.

*Figure 431. Human footprint in the F1102 mud-fill of F1101.*

*Figure 432. A copper nail from the spoil-heaps.*

*Figure 433. A plaster fragment from Shaft Two with the same threads as were visible in the floor of Feature 1101.*

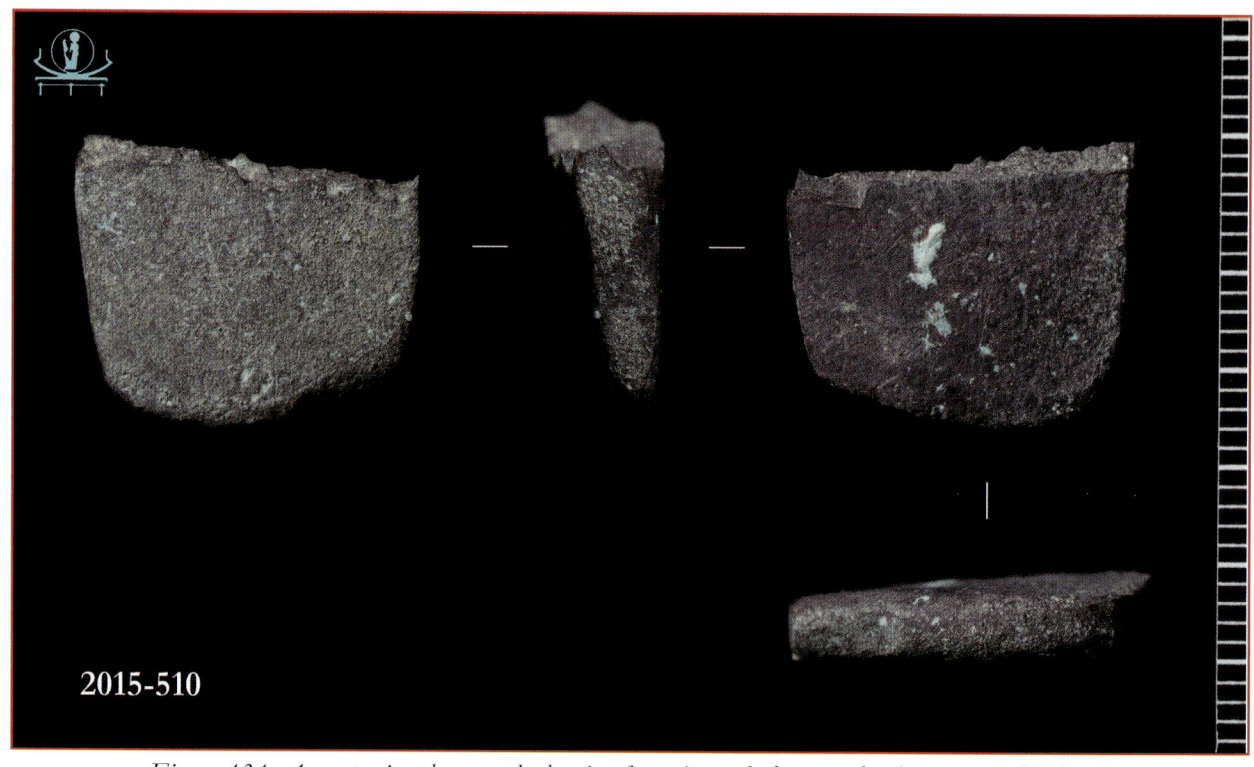

*Figure 434. A composite photograph showing four views of the same broken copper chisel-end.*

*Figure 435. A whetstone: composite photograph showing all sides and an enlargement of copper traces on the stone (detail bottom left).*

When the spoil-heap debris had been removed the remains of the gypsum and aggregate sealing around Shaft Six became obvious in a ridge looping round the entire southern side of the central line of shafts (*Figure 443*).

Similarly, once the debris had been completely removed and the XVIIIth surface was revealed it became apparent that quantities of water had been used on site to create the mud for plastering. This water could, of course, have been brought to the site in jars.

*Figure 436. A flint pounder showing the hand-fit.*

*Figure 437. A two-handed flint pounder or hammer-stone with percussion marks.*

*Figure 438. A flint pestle.*

However, it was not just the surface of the mud-mixing pits (Features 1092, 1108, 1106, 1103 and 1102 in *Figure 425*) which bore traces of water. It was already clear that water had run down the northern side of the upper spoil-heaps and into Shafts Six and Five. Initially we had assumed this to be the effects of the sporadic storms which occur every decade or so in the Theban hills. However, the entire surface of the site had been soaked in water leaving a mud-cracked surface (*Figure 445*).

*Figure 439. Flint blades from the XVIIIth dynasty surface.*

*Figure 440. The handles of wooden pestles the broken heads of which are shown in Figure 441.*

*Figure 441. The broken heads of pestles many of them bearing traces of gypsum powder and of percussions marks on the flat surfaces.*

*Figure 442. Two wooden mallets, badly eaten by termites, found at the eastern extreme of the spoil-heaps.*

The XVIIIth dynasty surface of the slope above the upper spoil-heaps shows sign of two phenomena: first, water erosion (*Figure 444*); second, sub-surface bio-turbation. Given the height of the site above the wadi floor, this erosion cannot have been caused by water coursing down the Wadi Bairiya. It must have fallen in the form of rain.

*Figure 443. The remains of the gypsum and aggregate sealing (arrowed in red) surrounding the top of the shafts looking due east. The dry-stone walls are modern and are part of the protection of the shaft tops. The shafts have been re-buried in this photograph.*

Inspection of the surface of the site south of the shafts (*Figure 445*) produces a similar picture, consistent with rain having fallen across this area and of the soil having subsequently dried out (and cracked).

Further to the west of the site. along the edges of the Farchout Road which crosses the WB1 site, we examined three apparent wells (Chapter Fifteen). These consisted of two large piles of stones surrounded by broken ceramics and a hole of indeterminate date. Clearance of these is covered below but the surfaces round these features once cleared showed similar signs of mud-cracking across a wide area.

*Figure 444. The slope north of the upper spoli-heaps showing the water-eroded XVIIIth dynasty surface.*

*Figure 445. Looking north towards the line of shafts running east-west across the upper part of the photograph with the slope behind. In the foreground the cracked surface of the once wet XVIIIth dynasty surface is clearly visible. The leaf trowel in the middle of the photograph is 25cms long.*

This mud-cracking therefore appears to be consistent at an XVIIIth dynasty level across the site and has implications for the state of the climate during the early New Kingdom. The bio-turbation under the surface is consistent with there being plant and insect life (see *Figures 446 and 447*) on the site at that time.

*Figure 446. Plant roots in the soil just below the XVIIIth dynasty surface in Feature 1091.*

*Figure 447. Further examples of very fine plant roots under the XVIIIth dynasty surface in Feature 1091.*

# CHAPTER FIFTEEN
# INVESTIGATION AND CLEARANCE OF THE HUTS AND WELLS

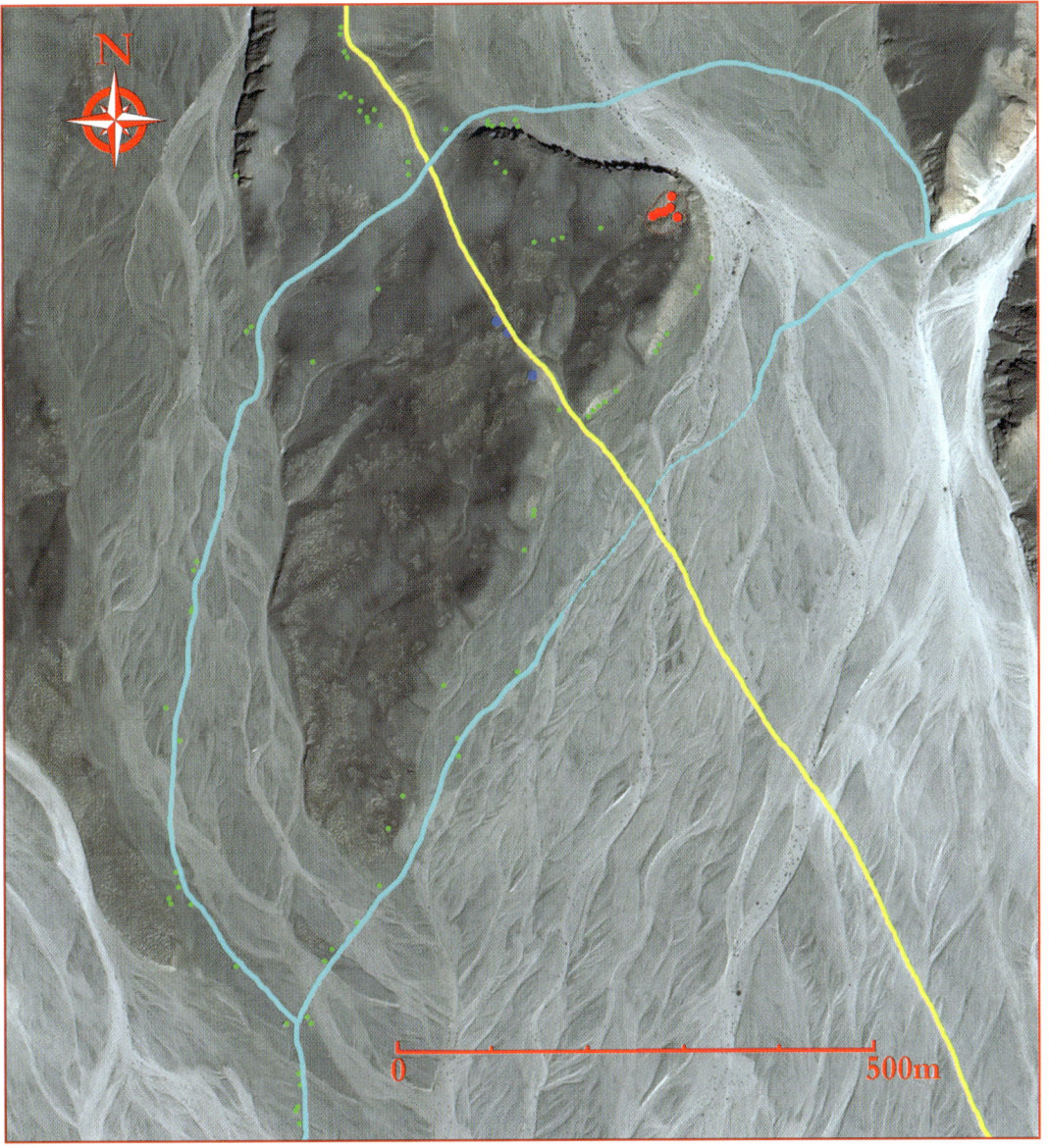

*Figure 448. A summary of the huts (green) and wells (dark blue). The light blue line is the prepared road. The dots mark its conjectural routes. The yellow road is the Farchout Road. The red dots mark the location of the WB1 shaft tombs. Other visible tracks are modern. The 0.5km scale is approximate.*

## Huts

The presence of huts was noted when we first examined the WB1 site in 2013. Carter says of the site: "*Higher up on the rising ground there are many stone huts of the type adapted to workmen.*[1]" However, it was not until we had surveyed the wider site that it became apparent just how many huts there are. In the immediate vicinity of the WB1 shaft tombs, the area covered by *Figure 448*, there are 86 huts.

These are of three types, one (Type 1) is typical of the workmen's emplacements found across the Theban hills and especially in and above the Valley of the Kings. The second, (Type 2) is more complex and consists in some cases of several rooms. The third type

---

1. Carter, H. (1917) op. cit. see Chapter One p. 2.

(Type 3) is more rudimentary and consists in most cases of no more than a small rectangle of stone possibly for supporting and storing amphorae. No examples of this type were found in the immediate vicinity of the site but there are many examples along the margins of the roads.

Our initial examination of the WB1 site and its immediate surroundings revealed huts down the eastern margin of the site, across the plateau and on the high ground to the north-west of the site. Huts have subsequently been discovered all along the prepared

*Figure 449. Huts along the eastern margin of the site, looking north when first found.*

road leading in the direction of Kom el-Abd and lining either side of the Farchout Road after it crosses the WB1 site and heads north-west towards the high desert. These huts will be dealt in the subsequent chapter on the broader landscape (Chapter Seventeen). They appear to be part of a system of official management of these roads.

This volume will merely give examples of the various types of huts, differentiating those which appear to be associated with the construction of the tombs from those which relate to the two different types of road connected to the site.

One group of huts in particular deserves to be looked at in more detail in future. This is the group at the western end of the cliffs which form the northern margin of the tomb-site. They sit tucked-in under the cliffs just to the east of the point where the prepared road crosses the Farchout Road. The site is in the shade for most of the day and protected from the wind. It therefore offers ideal shelter.

The huts were numbered from north to south down the eastern side of the WB1 site and then from south to north up the western side.

There are thirteen huts along the eastern margin of the site from Hut 1 just below the path now used to access the site to Hut 13 which is just south of the point where the Farchout Road starts to rise and cross the site.

*Figure 450. Hut 2 just south of the modern path up to the site.*

Hut 2 is a typical Type 1 hut. It is rectangular and seems to have one access point to the south.

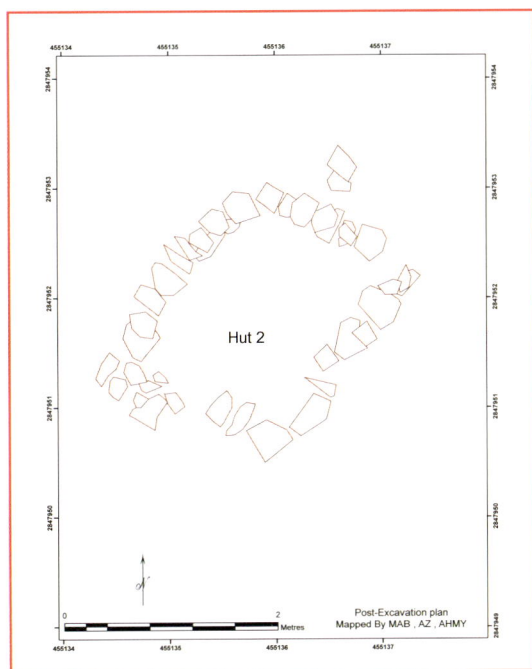

*Figure 451. Plan of Hut 2.*

Hut 2 contained a variety of sherds, mostly too small to identify with certainty but including New Kingdom and Roman sherds. It also contained animal bones and a fragment of a canopic jar.

*Figure 452. Hut 5.*

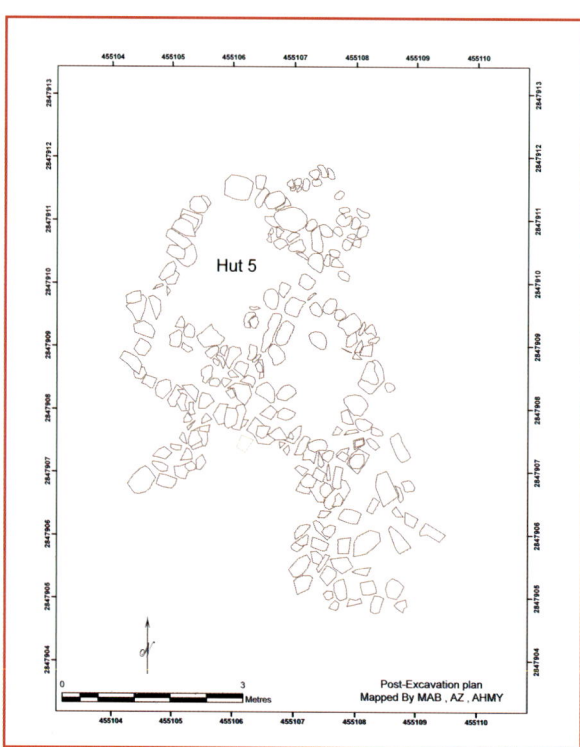

*Figure 453. Plan of Hut 5.*

Hut 5 is typical of the Type 2 huts with several chambers, Hut 5 has at least four separate "rooms" but the stones have been moved about in modern times and it is not possible to reconstruct fully the original layout of the hut. It contained sherds of the usual mixture, bone fragments from small animals and traces of charcoal.

*Figure 454. On the left a typical Type 3 hut made to accommodate an amphora.*

*Figure 455. On the right its modern equivalent made by our workmen to support a water jar.*

*Figure 456. Hut 11 on the edge of the Farchout Road.*

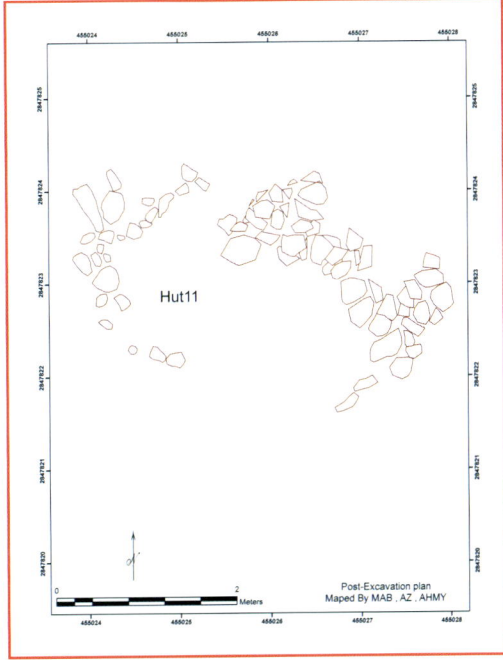

*Figure 457. Plan of Hut 11.*

Hut 11 was the most interesting of the huts along this margin. It contained XVIIIth dynasty, Third Intermediate Period, Byzantine (Late Roman), Ottoman and modern ceramics. Several beads were also recovered from the floor as well as chicken bones and feathers which may relate to attempts by modern robbers to "open the way" to hidden treasure using magic.

## Wells

As mentioned, the prepared road is lined with huts which appear at roughly 50-metre intervals. Along this prepared road there is also a previously unrecorded well, now dry, which is surrounded by sherds dating from the early through to the late Roman periods.

This well is further evidence of a difference in climate during ancient times which will be summarised in the final chapter of this volume. At this stage it is worth observing that evidence uncovered on the WB1 site and on the Wadi Bairiya floodplain supports the view that there were periods of unusual rainfall in this region (and most likely elsewhere in the Nile Valley) during the early New Kingdom and Late Roman periods.

Further support for this suggestion comes from three "wells" positioned along the Farchout Road approximately 200m to the south-west of the WB1 shafts. These were numbered from north to south. They are marked in dark blue in Figure 400 above.

### Well 1 (W1)

The northernmost (W1) consisted of a circular pit fringed with extracted material and wind-blown sand mixed in with sherds.

*Figure 458. Well 1 before clearance looking south. The tracks of a modern bulldozer can be seen following the course of Farchout Road to the left.*

A modern bulldozer had passed by this feature in 2012[2] and its tracks can be clearly seen in *Figure 458*. The creation of the pit in this feature pre-dates the activities of this bulldozer and was there prior to 2007.

Clearance of the debris ringing the top of the opening revealed many sherds and, underneath the stones a surface which had been soaked with water. There was no sign of where this water might have come from. Mud in the bottom of the pit underneath the fine sand filling which had blown in could have formed from occasional rainstorms over many hundreds of years.

*Figure 459. Well 1 after clearance.dozer can be seen following the course of Farchout Road to the left.*

*Figure 460. Detail of the section through the northern rim of Well 1. This section contained New Kingdom and Byzantine sherds.*

---

2. This bulldozer travelled 2.4km up the Farchout Road to the foot of the steep escarpment rising to the high desert. It appears to have stopped along the way and scooped out bucketfuls of terrain everywhere there were dumps of pottery and huts. The scooped out earth piles and resultant holes are clearly visible on satellite photographs.

*Figure 461. The interior of Well 1 before clearance looking south.*

*Figure 462. The interior of Well 1 post-clearance looking north-west.*

## Well 2 (W2)

The central well (W2) was some five metres south of W1 in a similar position at the western edge of the Farchout Road. It consisted of a roughly circular pile of stones 50 cms high and approximately 4m in diameter. It also contained ceramic sherds and fine, wind-blown sand.

*Figure 463. The second well, W2, as found looking south. The excavation just above and to the right of the metre rod is mirrored by another on the opposite side to the south.*

*Figure 464. A section through W2 which was filled with sand. The mix of ceramics was approximately the same as W1 (90% Byzantine, 10% New Kingdom).*

*Figure 465. Clearance of the southern half of the stone pile revealed a surface once saturated with water surrounding a circular feature with a scooped out edge just to the right of the metre rod.*

*Figure 466. W2 once the entire surface had been cleared of stones.*

*Figure 467. Looking north. The scooped out feature post clearance. The mud surface is clearly visible forming a ring round some central feature.*

*Figure 468. Looking south. Well 2 after it had been completely cleared. The central bar of soil was left in place to preserve the section. However, it looks as though there was some form of natural basin here fed by a pipe which emptied through fine gravel just above the metre rod.*

## Well 3 (W3)

The third well (W3) was similar to W2 but 50m to the south-east almost on the edge of the raised ground. This was cleared to the level of the presumed XVIIIth dynasty level which, in keeping with the area surrounding the other wells and the large area swept clean south of the main shafts on the WB1 site, had been saturated with water.

*Figure 469. W3 was similar to W2 in form but sat right at the edge of the rising ground.*

*Figure 470. Section through W3. This was also filled with wind-blown sand and sherds of New Kingdom and Byzantine date.*

*Figure 471. Once cleared the surface revealed formerly saturated soil which extended far beyond the pile of stones which formed W2.*

These three wells all had similar concentrations of ceramics (New Kingdom pottery 10% of the total, Roman and Byzantine pottery 90% of the total). And although Well 2 provided clear evidence of water collection in the scooped out lip to the south, the evidence for water collecting in actual formal wells was not convincing. It looks as though these three areas were more in the form of springs. Well 2 contains a visible "pipe" formed by water flowing underground from higher levels. This water seems to have collected in a bowl subsequently filled in with loose debris and then covered with stones to mark the location. Well 1 may have been excavated in ancient times to catch rainwater or, indeed, larger quantities of spring water. However it is also possible that the excavation of the round hole here was made in relatively recent times.

The presence of these water features nevertheless confirms the wetter weather patterns in two periods, on the one hand, and the shorter usage of the WB1 site in the XVIIIth dynasty and a longer period of usage of the Farchout Road during the Roman and Coptic periods.

We have discovered further water features and accumulations of ceramic sherds further north at the edge of the Wadi Bairiya and investigation of the ceramics there will tell us much more about the periods of usage of this branch of the Farchout Road.

# CHAPTER SIXTEEN
## WADI EL-AGAALA AND WADI BAIRIYA

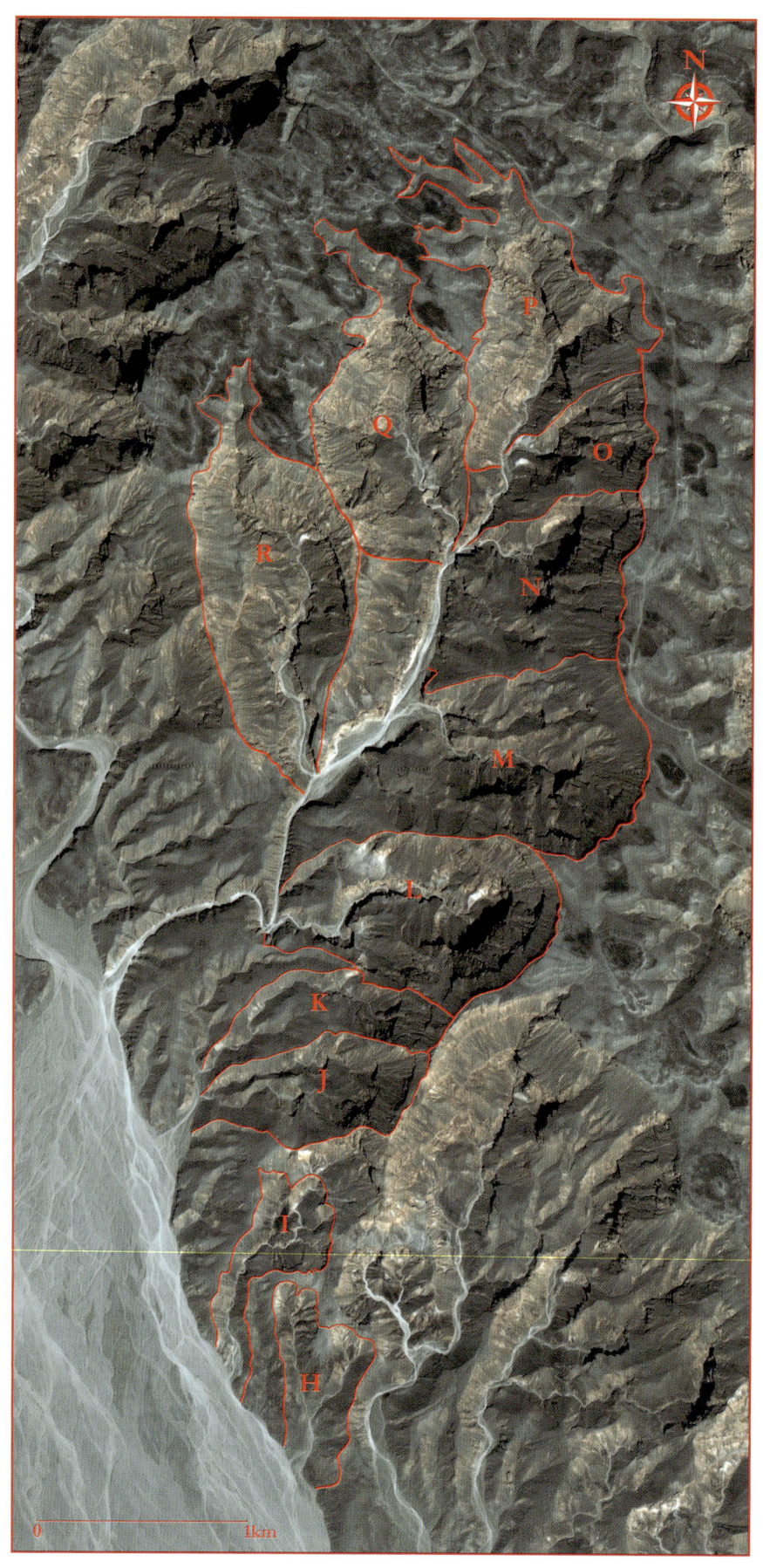

*Figure 472. The naming of the wadis in the Wadi El-Agaala.*

Exploration of the two large wadis within our concession was conducted on foot. All accessible paths were followed and recorded and, based on previous experience in Wadis A-G (as described by Howard Carter[1]) we have tried to inspect all the surfaces on which graffiti were likely to have been inscribed. In Appendix 3 there is a map showing the coverage by the team. Some cliffs which look accessible from satellite photographs and Google Earth turn out not to be so and many of the tracks which show up on those images prove to have been made by animals - in particular jackals.

Where graffiti were found they were recorded epigraphically and by camera and they have been numbered in our files. We have taken great care to leave no trace of our activities behind.

Graffiti throughout the Theban mountain have suffered very badly from modern copyists writing record numbers and using chalk. Many people in modern times have thought it appropriate to add their own names to the wadi walls. In several cases they have scratched over and nearly obliterated ancient graffiti. In some cases spurious graffiti have been added. In Wadi F there is a large figure scratched high up on the eastern side of the wadi which is obviously modern. The HC which has been added to give 'authenticity' is back-to-front. In other cases ancient graffiti have been scratched out altogether. Howard Carter's initials have been crossed out several times in Wadi F. Original graffiti have also been crossed out by someone who has decided they are not worth recording. The result of all these annotations and additions is a lamentable loss of clarity when it comes to trying to understand the reasons why graffiti were added in the positions they are.

Fortunately not all graffiti are accessible and many new ones have been uncovered by our mission. We have been making sure that these fragile indications of ancient human activity are properly recorded.

We have also recorded the positions of all the ceramics and flint-working sites as well as all other human activity including those places where tufla and mud have been extracted.

## The Wadi el-Agaala

The Wadi el-Agaala consists of seven principal constituent wadis (Figure 472). We have continued Carter's lettering from the Western Wadis, proceeding up the eastern side of the Wadi Bairiya flood-plain with letters H-K. The seven wadis within the Wadi el-Agaala therefore have the letters L-R.

The overall wadi has the shape of an inverted "T". The stem of the "T" extends just over 3km from the junction in a northerly direction. At its widest the Wadi el-Agaala is approximately 2.4km from cliff-top to cliff-top, measured east-west.

The inverted bar of the "T" is formed by the narrow entrance, 20-30m wide, off the Wadi Bairiya to the west and by Wadi L to the east. The name given to this overall wadi is taken from Carter's 1916 survey. He attributes the name to the Arabic word for "wheel" given to it because of the circular roads in the centre of the wadi to the west of Wadi M[2].

---
1. Carter, H. (1917) op. cit..
2. Carter, H. (1917) op. cit..

## Wadi L

Wadi L is approached via a narrow opening 350m to the west of the WB1 site leading off the Wadi Bairiya and bounded by cliffs some 30m in height. At this entrance point the prepared road which encircles the WB1 site is visible entering the Wadi el-Agaala. The narrowness of the wadi here has meant that flash floods will have emptied into the Wadi Bairiya flood-plain with great force The cliffs bear signs of under-cutting by such floods and so it is not surprising that only slight traces of the prepared road survive.

After a kilometre the Wadi el-Agaala reaches a T-junction and the main wadi turns to the north (left). Wadi L begins here and continues straight ahead to the east for just over 1.1km, widening and then curving north to resume its eastern progress to a large bay of two levels of cliffs which reach the high desert level at a height of 500m.

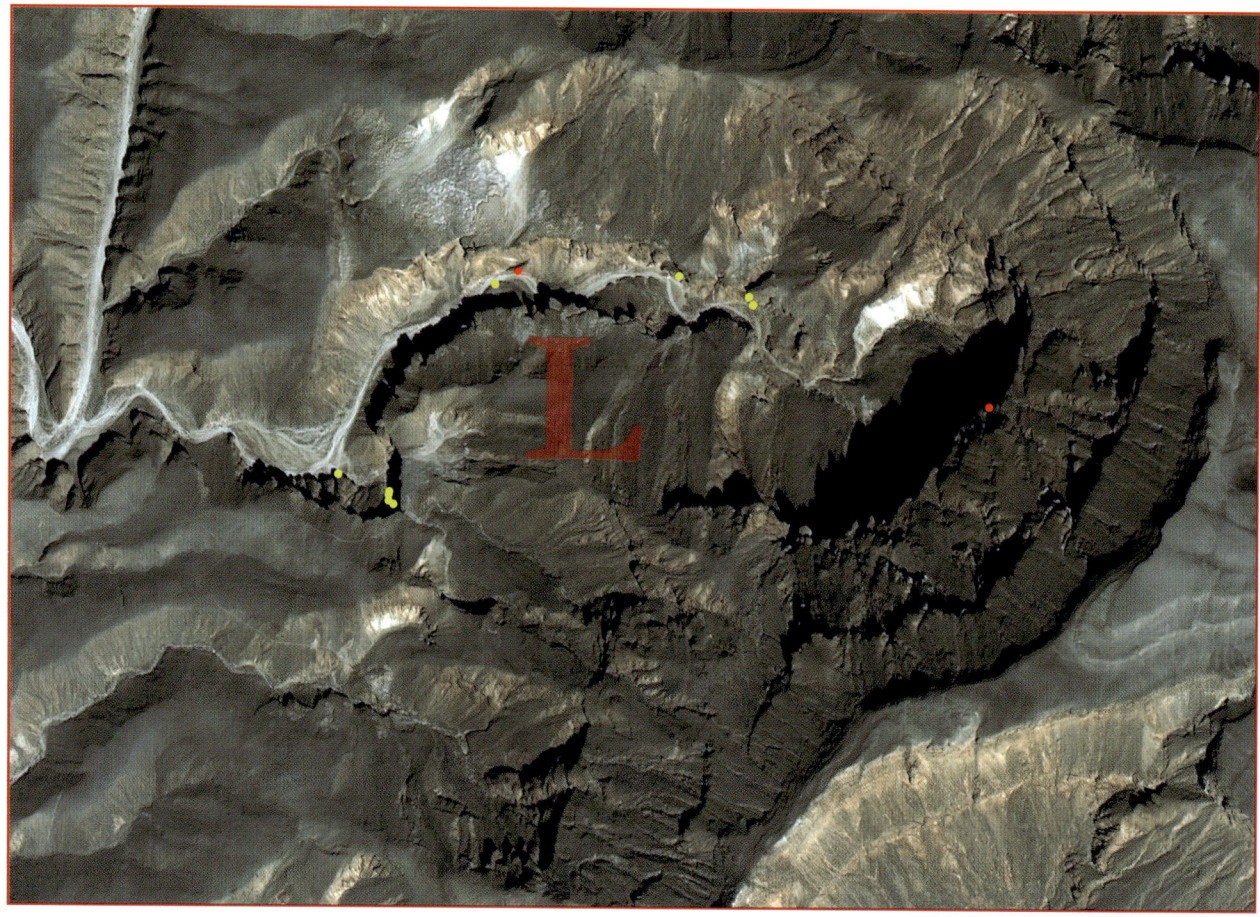

*Figure 473. Wadi L (all the photographs of wadis are oriented to the north). Red dots show previously recorded graffiti. Yellow dots show new graffiti. The photograph is oriented north-south.*

This wadi marks the limit of previously recorded exploration eastwards of the Wadi el-Agaala. Černy recorded two groups of graffiti here as marked on *Figure 473* in red. He did not find the graffiti now recorded and marked in yellow in *Figure 473*.

The newly discovered graffiti are still the subject of study but those in this wadi all appear to be of pharaonic date. The most complex group consists of two sets of "tomb" graffiti and an inscription apparently recording the visit of a workman possibly

---

3. I am grateful to Fredrik Hagen for his work on this inscription large parts of which are extremely difficult to read.

called Nebnedjem, an un-named scribe and a "wab-priest of Amun-Re king of the gods and chief of workmen Nebnefer[3]" (*see Figure 475*).

*Figure 474. Looking west down Wadi L towards the WB1 site.*

*Figure 475. A copy of the text recording the visit of Nebnedjem and Nebnefer. The text has been computer-enhanced in white.*

The easternmost and highest graffito is Cerny's 3876 (*Figure 476*) which may record the name of Herihor or, since it lacks a determinative, a priestly title relating to the cult of Horus in the sky.

*Figure 476. The graffito in the eastern cliffs of Wadi L given Cerny's number 3876.*

*Figure 477. The eastern end of Wadi L. The red dot shows the location of Cerny's 3876 graffito.*

Apart from these graffiti there are no other convincing signs of ancient human activity in this wadi. A single flint pounder and scattered late Roman sherds washed down close to the wadi mouth are the only artefacts found to date. Above the first layer of cliffs to the north there is evidence of extensive tufla extraction (visible as the white areas in *Figure 473*) but this is impossible to date.

## Wadi M

This side wadi breaks to the east of the main northern bed of the Wadi el-Agaala just to the north of the point where the main wadi opens up into a vast natural amphitheatre roughly 450m long and 200m wide. It is round this amphitheatre (now eroded down the centre) that the ancient "prepared road" used to run (see *Figure 479*).

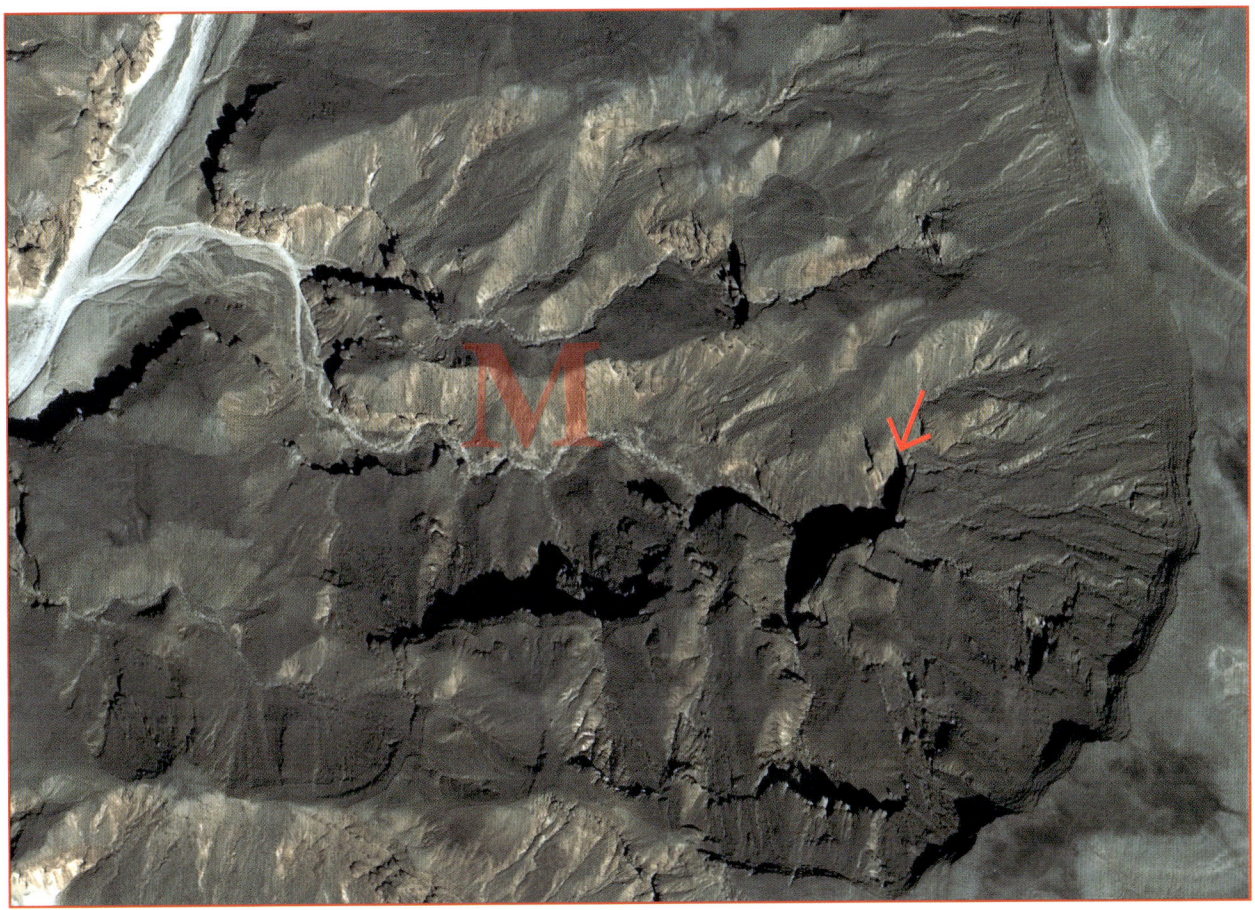

*Figure 478. Wadi M. At the northern end of the oblique patch of shadow on the right of the photograph there is an excellent location for a tomb (arrowed - see Figure 482). The photograph is oriented north-south.*

*Figure 479. Looking west from Wadi M to the central "amphitheatre" of the Wadi el-Agaala.*

The main southern wadi bed of Wadi M meets a line of impassable cliffs just to the west of the easternmost bay of cliffs. Access to the base of these cliffs is only possible via the ridge which runs between the two tributary beds of the wadi. The descent to the base of the cliffs is very steep and only just possible without ropes. There is no trace of any graffiti on the cliffs in this easternmost bay. At the entrance to the wadi there are some modern Arabic graffiti.

*Figure 480. The waterfall blocking further progress along the wadi floor in Wadi M.*

*Figure 481. Looking west down Wadi M from the cliffs at its eastern end. Access to the cliffs at the eastern end of the wadi is impossible through the central gulley.*

At the north-eastern corner of the easternmost bay of cliffs there is an ideal location for a tomb. It is in a fissure in the rock (*Figure 482*) and is beautifully concealed. However, given the difficulty in reaching these cliffs it is an impractical location. A tomb could easily have been concealed here but transporting grave goods to this location would have been extremely difficult. On the ridge above here there were a few sherds of Late Roman date but no other cultural material was found in this wadi.

*Figure 482. The north-east corner of the eastern cliffs in Wadi M (arrowed in Figure 478). The fissure in the corner provides an ideal place for a tomb. However this part of the wadi is all but inaccessible.*

## Wadi N

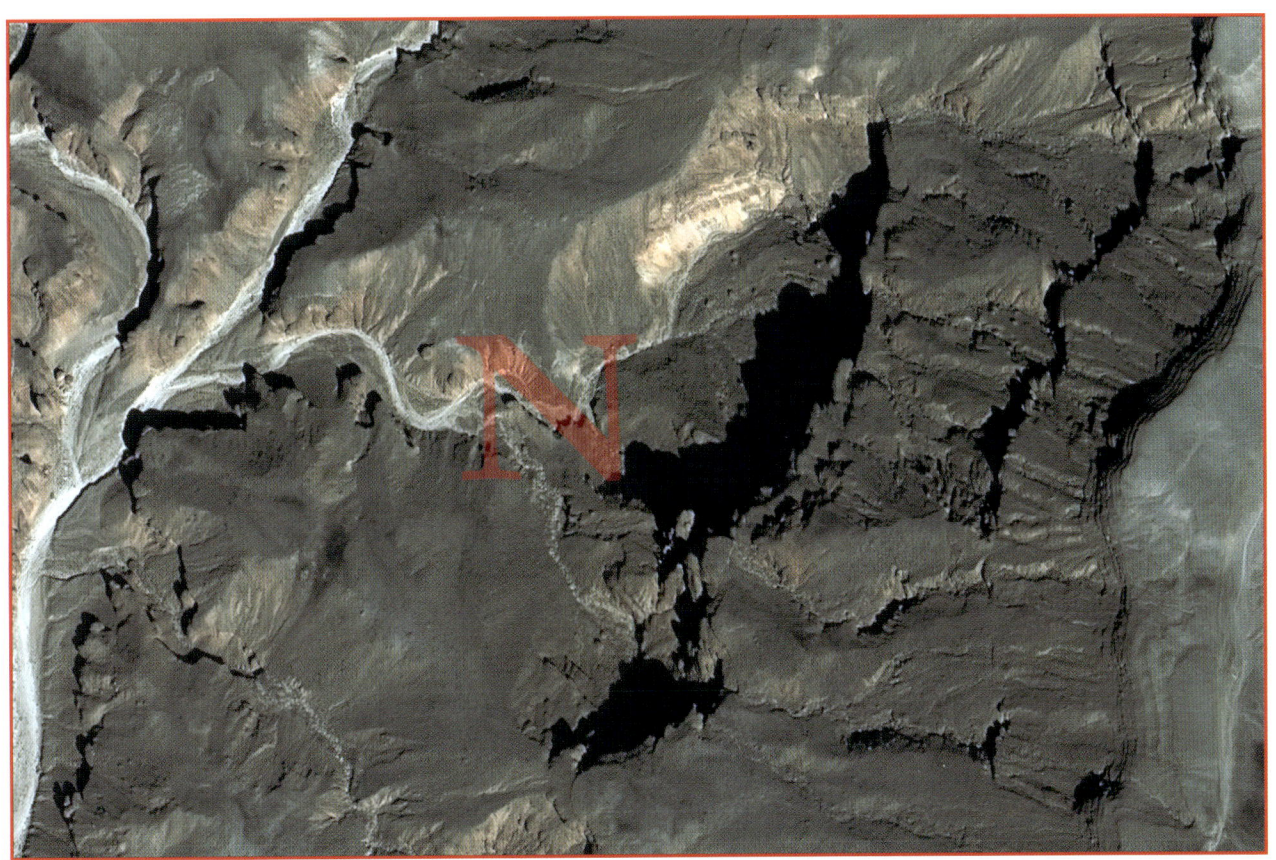

*Figure 483. Wadi N, opening to the east of the main Wadi el-Agaala. The photograph is oriented north-south.*

Wadi N opens off the main Wadi el-Agaala approximately 750m to the north of Wadi M. After heading east for 200m it divides into two branches. The southern branch descends steeply from cliffs to the south. It is divided by a buttress from the main north-south arc of cliffs to the north.

*Figure 484. The southern branch of Wadi N.*

*Figure 485. The northern bay of cliff in Wadi N, only accessible via a steeply-stepped ravine.*

No evidence of human activity was found in this wadi.

# Wadi O

*Figure 486. Wadi O which opens off the main Wadi el-Agaala to the east. The yellow dots mark the approximate position of the graffiti low in the main wadi bed. The photograph is oriented north-south.*

The branch off the main wadi to Wadi O is situated 400m north of Wadi N. Both the small bay off the Wadi el-Agaala just to the south of the entrance and the northern side of the entrance to Wadi O both show evidence of extensive extraction of tufla (the white areas in *Figure 486*).

The main arm of Wadi O curves to the north and narrows into a ravine which is 3-4m deep. This ends in a cliff face, or dry waterfall, which prevents further access to the cliffs from the wadi floor.

No trace of additional human activity was found in Wadi O. Just to the south of its entrance a large body of graffiti was found low down on the walls to the east of the main Wadi el-Agaala floor. These graffiti will be covered in detail in the final volume in this series. Some of them are undoubtedly of pharaonic date and include signs used by the Deir el-Medina workmen. Others, which include portrayals of animals which may be a hare, a bull, a dog (with rounded ears, a barred coat and hair at the throat) like an African Wild Dog (*Figure 491*) and a donkey, are more difficult to date.

*Figure 487. Wadi O looking east from the main Wadi el-Agaala.*

*Figure 488. The main northern branch of Wadi O.*

*Figure 489. The dry waterfall preventing further progress up the main northern arm of Wadi O.*

*Figure 490. Copies of part of the large group of graffiti discovered just south of the entrance to Wadi O. This photograph has been computer-enhanced in white.*

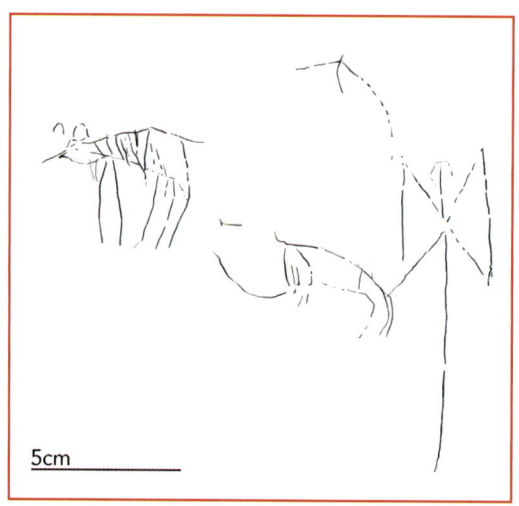

*Figure 491. Copies of further graffiti from the same location as Figure 490. The graffito on the left bears some resemblance to an African Wild Dog (Lycaon pictus). The sign on the right composed of two triangles and a long vertical stroke is a sign believed to be used by workmen from Deir el-Medina.*

## Wadi P

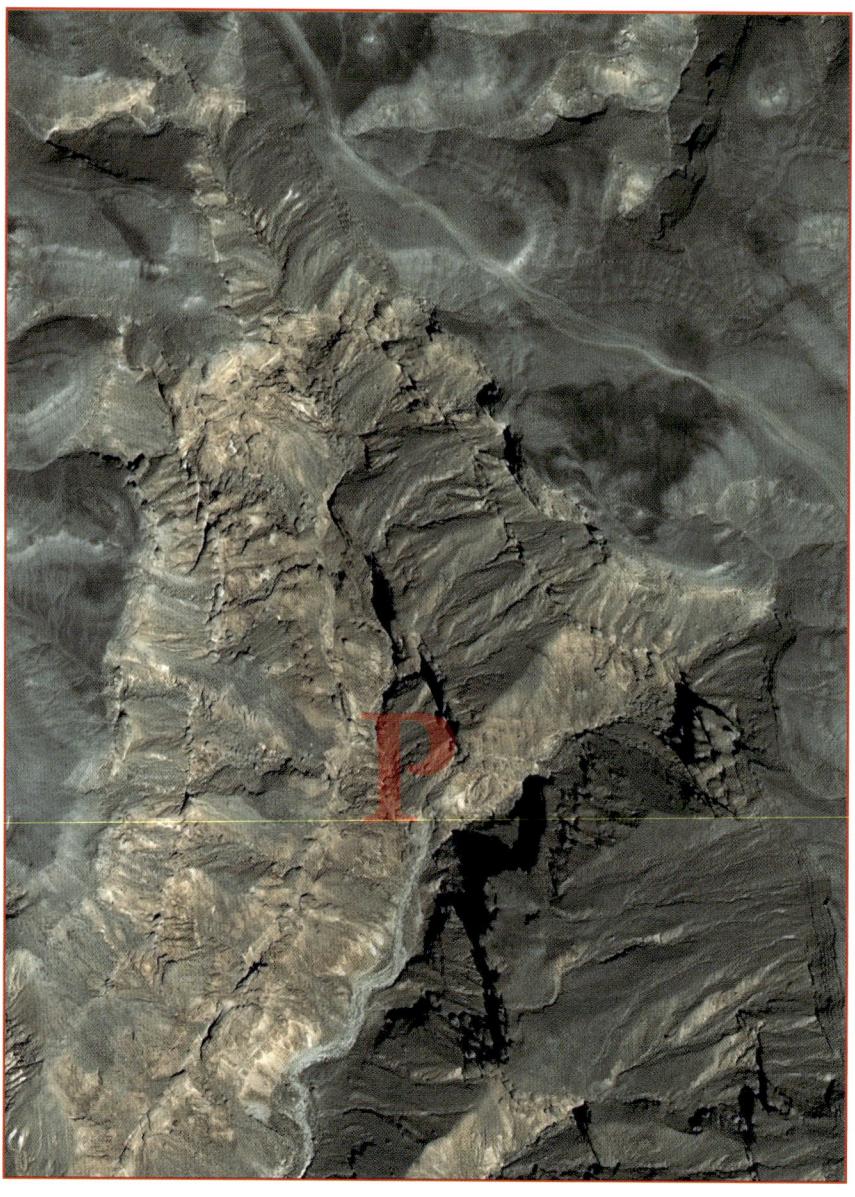

*Figure 492. Wadi P which forms the northern terminus of the main branch of the Wadi el-Agaala. Note the Eastern Farchout Road running parallel to the north-eastern cliffs on the high desert. The photograph is oriented north-south.*

Wadi P is fairly open until the wadi floor bends slightly to the west and the floor climbs in steps gaining complexity as the sides of the wadi steepen. The floor is strewn with very large boulders and ends in a bay of cliffs over 100m in height. Water has clearly flowed down these cliffs with great force. The floor below these cliffs contains large water-polished boulders and dried mud from extensive water pooling.

*Figure 493. The point at which the gradient in the Wadi P floor starts to climb rapidly.*

*Figure 494. The great shelf in Wadi P which cuts off access along the wadi floor.*

*Figure 495. The cliffs at the terminus of Wadi P.*

*Figure 496. Looking south from the base of the cliffs forming the terminus of Wadi P. These cliffs are over 90m high.*

No graffiti were found in this wadi but the wadi floor contained items washed down from the cliffs above including unidentified animal bones, plastic bags and paper. The Eastern Farchout Road passes close to the cliff-tops (see Figure 492) but there is no possible pedestrian route down from there into Wadi P.

# Wadi Q

*Figure 497. Wadi Q which branches to the west off the main Wadi el-Agaala opposite the entrance to Wadi N. The photograph is oriented north-south.*

The entrance to Wadi Q is marked by some large blocks lying in the western part of the wadi floor which were extensively inscribed with modern graffiti dated to the 1970s. These pertain to several visits to this spot by the same apparently German-speaking family.

*Figure 498. The Byzantine amphorae fragments just south of the entrance to Wadi Q.*

Near these rocks the remains of several late Byzantine amphorae were gathered in one spot, with further pieces in a recess in the wadi wall.

The Wadi Q floor twists and turns as it heads north and west and on top of one of the bends formed by these changes in direction there is evidence that tufla has been collected.

*Figure 499. Tufla collecting on the southern side of the entrance to Wadi Q.*

The shoulders running along the side of the deep watercourse marking the centre of Wadi Q are host to several flint-working sites, small areas where flint cores have been knapped. Given their position and the undisturbed nature of the workings in places where chronic rainfall would have shifted objects these do not seem to be prehistoric.

*Figure 500. One of several flint-working sites in Wadi Q.*

*Figure 501. The cliffs marking the terminus of Wadi Q. These are the first in several steps rising to the high desert.*

*Figure 502. The western cliffs of Wadi Q.*

# Wadi R

*Figure 503. Wadi R which opens to the west of the main Wadi el-Agaala just before it opens into the natural "amphitheatre". The yellowdots mark the approximate locations of the groups of graffiti. The photograph is oriented north-south.*

The opening to Wadi R is 1.2km south of the entrance to Wadi Q. Its overall orientation is north-south but its bed meanders as it climbs and narrows towards its terminus veering west for the last 300m.

The lower part of Wadi R contains a number of coptic and pharaonic graffiti grouped either in shelters well above the wadi floor or near places where water would have pooled in ancient times.

*Figure 504. The broad entrance to Wadi R. Many of the graffiti in this wadi were concentrated around the point where the wadi narrows in the centre of this photograph.*

*Figure 505. Coptic text from Wadi R. The text has been computer-enhanced in red.*

On the high ground which forms the western side of Wadi R there are several flint-working sites and areas where tufla has been extracted. An additional flint-working site sits under a high rock overhang which overlooks Wadi R 280m south of its terminus (see *Figure 508*).

*Figure 506. Wadi R looking north-east - seen from the clifftops to the south.*

*Figure 507. Graffiti in Wadi R from the cliffs on the right-hand side of Figure 506. The graffiti have been computer-enhanced in white.*

*Figure 508. Flint-working under a rock shelf high up on the south-western side of Wadi R.*

*Figure 509. The terminus of Wadi R.*

# The central portion of the Wadi el-Agaala

*Figure 510. Part of the "prepared road" running down the western side of the central "amphitheatre of Wadi el-Agaala. Just to the right of the photograph up against the cliffs are two graffiti showing a lion and a gazelle with young.*

The central portion of the Wadi el-Agaala merits a separate mention because, as noted, the prepared roads which surround the WB1 site cross the Wadi Bairiya, enter the Wadi el-Agaala and run around the natural amphitheatre which runs from Wadi R up to the entrance to Wadi N.

At Akhetaten roads of this type appear to have been used to patrol boundaries, running, for instance, round the Workman's Village there and also around the Stone Village[4]. The roads round the WB1 site are not inconsistent with this interpretation. The site is contained within a road loop which then runs down in the direction of Kom el-Abd where Barry Kemp raised the possibility of chariot activity[5].

The central portion of the Wadi el-Agaala contains no surviving settlement or structures to merit being guarded. So it is a puzzle why chariots were being driven along the narrow chasm of the Wadi el-Agaala entrance and into this broad arena. The wetter climate would have seen animals here in far larger numbers than now exist in the arid condition which prevail in the twenty-first century.

4. Stevens A. (2012) op. cit. Vol I pp. 69-80 & II pp. 199-200.
5. Kemp, B. (1977) op. cit..

The graffiti collected from this central part of the Wadi el-Agaala include a lion and gazelles. Together with the graffiti near the entrance to Wadi O, they give strong support to the idea that these wadis were once home to a variety of animals not now seen there. A sketchy portrayal next to the bull in Figure 490 may be an individual firing a bow. Whilst there is no further evidence to support the suggestion that this amphitheatre might have been a place where the king came on his chariot to shoot animals, it is worthy of consideration. The narrow exits and entrances to the central part of the wadi are easy to block and animals driven in here could, as a result, be easily coralled and herded.

*Figure 511. The central portion of the Wadi el-Agaala looking south. In the foreground the complex intersection of prepared roads is visible. The main avenue seems to terminate at the foot of the cliffs, the tops of which are just visible at the bottom of the photograph.*

*Figure 512. A lion graffito from the central "amphitheatre". of Wadi el-Agaala. The outline has been computer-enhanced in red.*

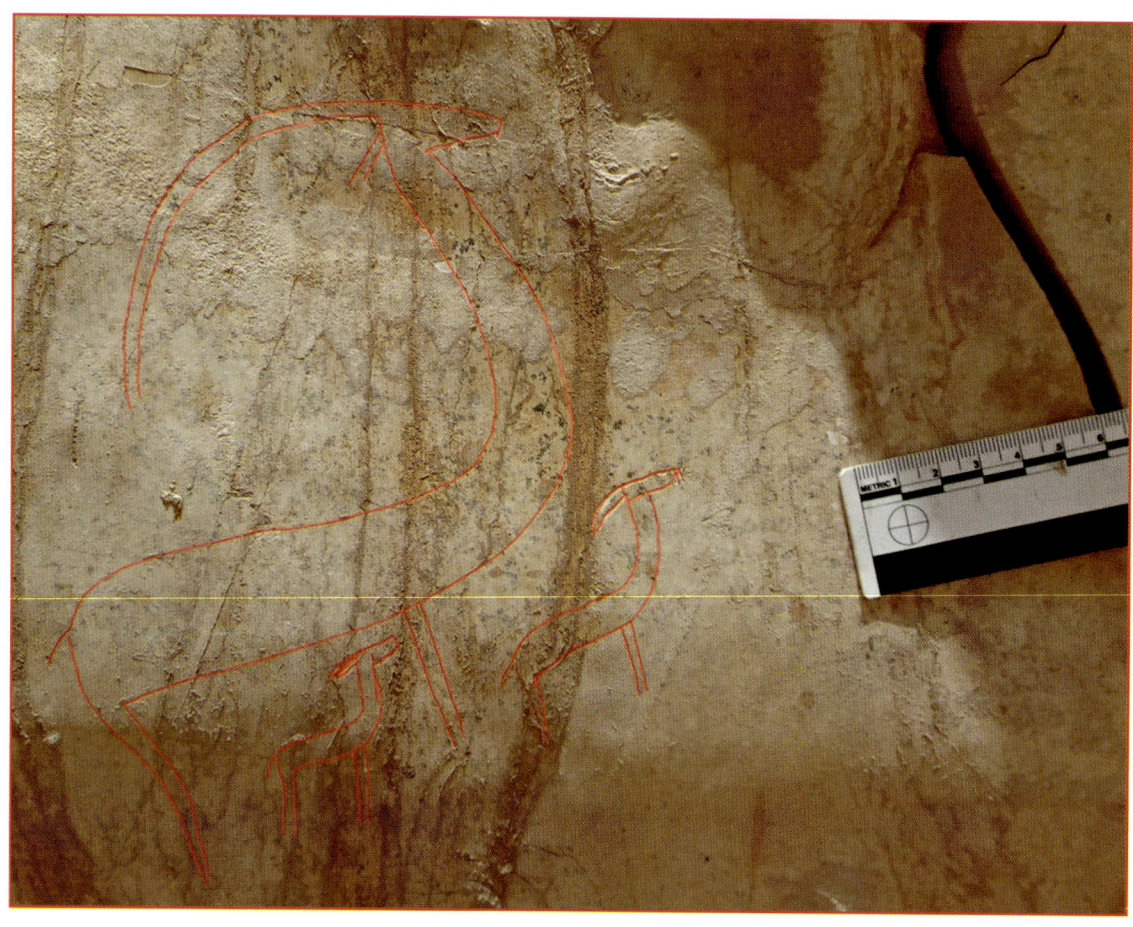

*Figure 513. Three gazelles near the Figure 512 lion in the central portion of the amphitheatre of Wadi el-Agaala. The figures have been computer-enhanced in red.*

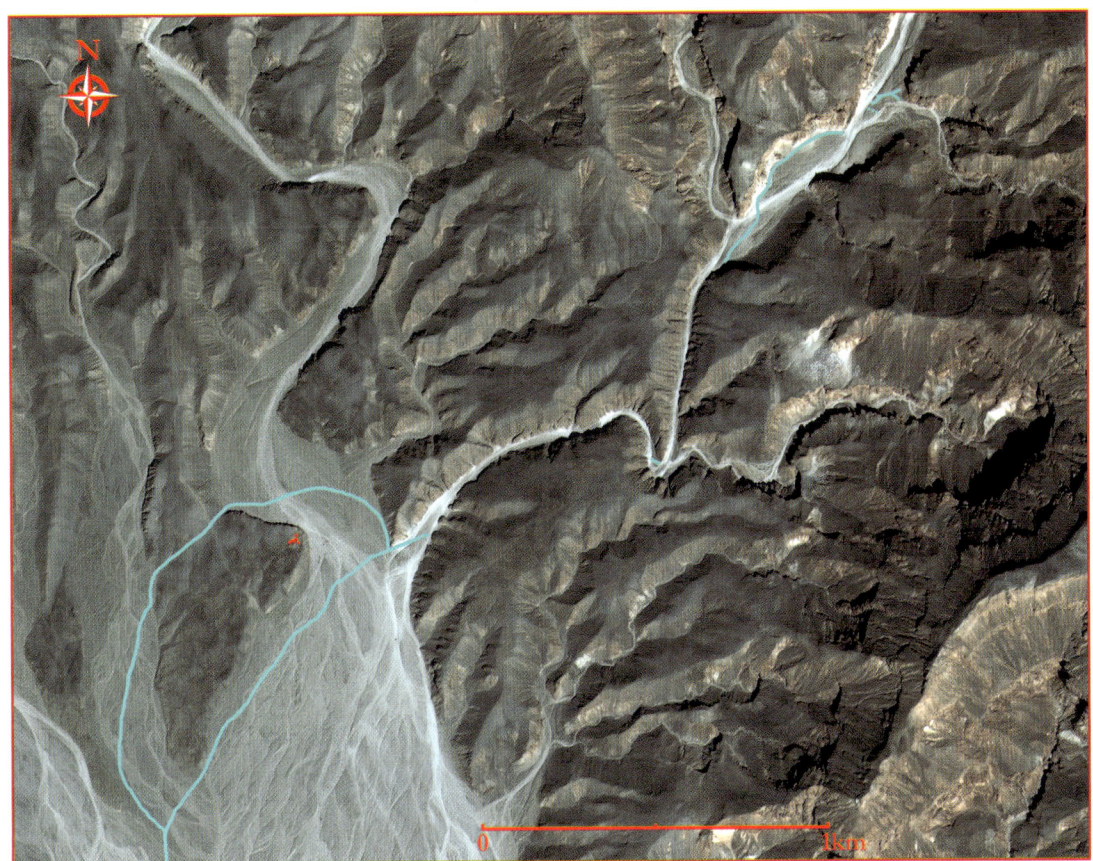

*Figure 514. The prepared roads which enter the Wadi el-Agaala from the Wadi Bairiya and penetrate the central "amphitheatre".*

*Figure 515. A detail of Figure 469 showing details in blue of the route of the prepared roads in the central "amphitheatre" of the Wadi el-Agaala.*

# The Wadi Bairiya

*Figure 516. The nomenclature given to the sub-wadis of the Wadi Bairiya.*

The Wadi Bairiya shares many similarities with the Wadi el-Agaala on its eastern side. It is a vast collecting bowl for water falling on the high desert which empties through a twisting, narrow gorge at its southern end. It is considerably bigger than the Wadi el-Agaala, measuring nearly six kilometres from north to south and 3.25km east-west. It contains no pharaonic graffiti that we have been able to discover. However, the Western Farchout Road comes up from the direction of Malqata, crosses its floodplain and heads up the western side of the wadi, climbing onto the high desert where, five kilometres further on, it joins the Eastern Farchout Road.

The only evidence of human activity consists of:

    a) widespread flint-working;

    b) tufla collection;

    c) Coptic settlements.

There are six definite Coptic sites (WB2, WB5, WB6, WB7, WB8 and WB9) marked by ceramics of the late Byzantine period. In addition there are three aditional sites (WB3, WB4 and WB10) which may have been used in Coptic times. WB8 is at the very north of the Wadi Bairiya (Wadi Z), where the Eastern Farchout Road skirts the edge of the cliffs. It is undoubtedly a major watering site with a cistern and a vast collection of discarded sherds mainly of New Kingdom date but including Late Roman ceramics. Next to the cistern is a shelter with shelves similar to other Coptic shelters (e.g. WB5, WB6 and WB7).

Remarkably, the only graffito which has been found in this extensive area is an Arabic graffito written high up on the southern side of Wadi Gamma which, judging from its height and barring very heavy erosion of the wadi floor, was possibly written by someone on horseback. It seems to be several centuries old. The text is not complete but it appears to be a form of farewell prayer or lament.

# Wadis S, T and U

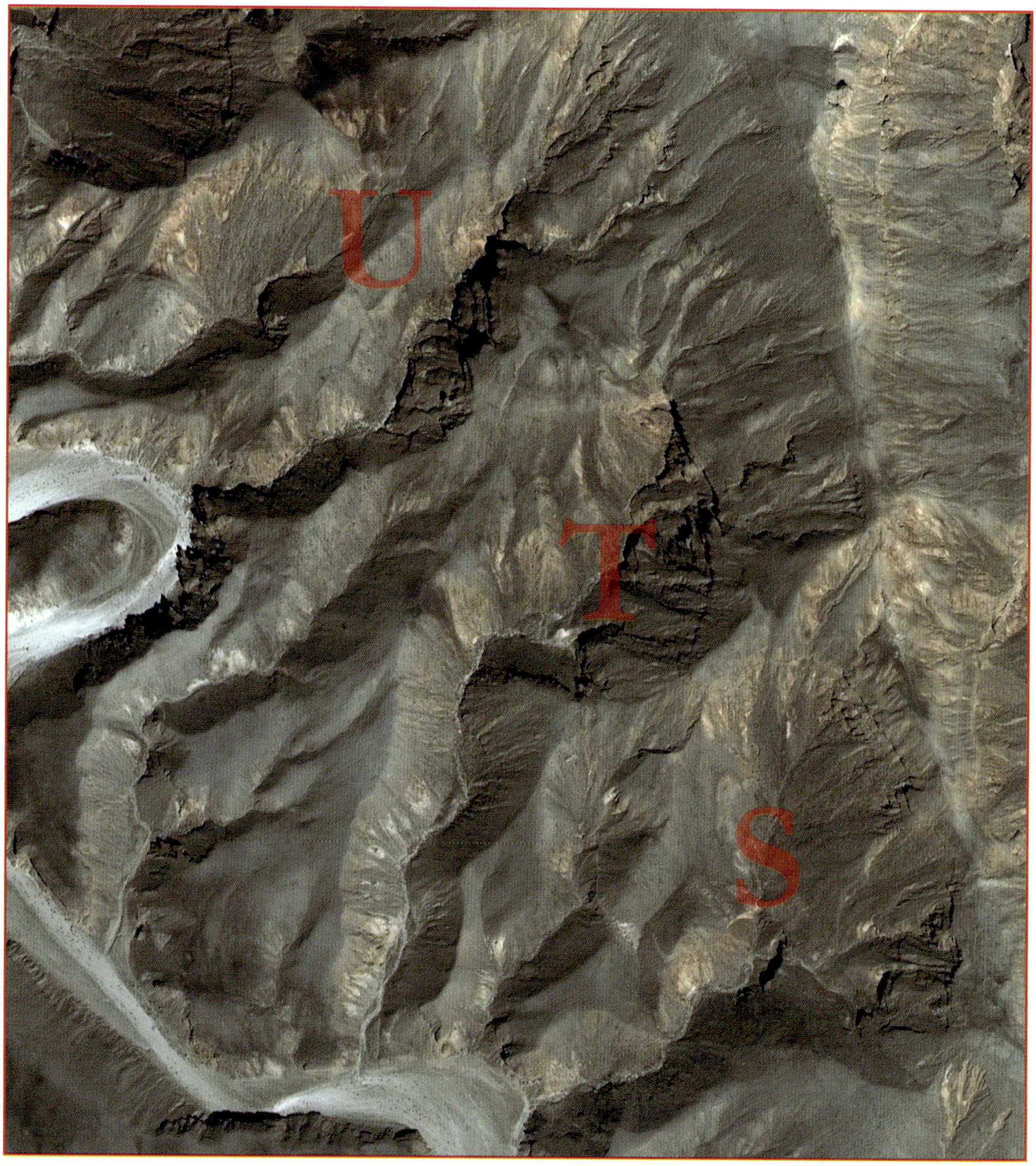

*Figure 517. Wadis S, T and U.*

*Figure 518. The ridge leading north and forming the eastern side of Wadi S. To its left is Wadi T and over the high ridge running down from the high desert to the left of that is Wadi U.*

These three small wadis form the southernmost part of the ridge dividing the Wadi Bairiya from Wadi R in the Wadi el-Agaala to the east.

Wadis S and T are simple, gradual run-offs from the higher ground descending over very low cliffs of protruding limestone on which there is no sign of graffiti.

*Figure 519. The bay of low cliffs in Wadi S.*

Wadi U is more complex than either of these smaller wadis and along its eastern side a path ascends from the first Coptic site in the floor of the Wadi Bairiya (designated WB2) and climbs onto a small plateau littered with flints before ascending to the high desert. At the point at which it meets the high desert late Byzantine amphora sherds were found.

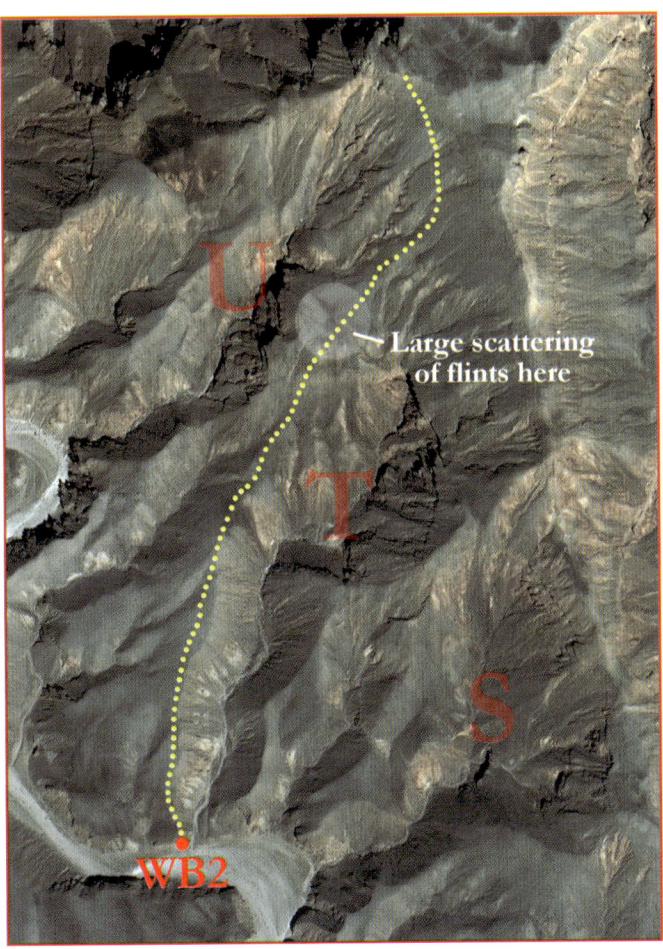

*Figure 520. The path (yellow) which rises to the high desert between Wadis T and U from the Coptic site WB2.*

*Figure 521. The WB2 Coptic site. The path to the high desert ascends to the right.*

*Figure 522. The scatter of flints on the plateau leading up to the high desert.*

*Figure 523. Late Byzantine amphora sherds on the high desert above Wadi U.*

# Wadi V

*Figure 524. Wadi V which opens to the east of the Wadi Bairiya.*

*Figure 525. The entrance to Wadi V looking due east.*

*Figure 526. The narrow entrance to the uppermost accessible level of cliffs.*

*Figure 527. The upper cliffs of Wadi V looking south.
The figure to the left of centre at the bottom of the photograph gives an idea of scale.*

Wadi V is a wadi which narrows as it climbs towards the eastern cliffs, then broadens out below fan-shaped cliffs typical of so many of the wadis in the Theban area. Access to these cliffs is via a narrow central gorge. The cliffs have been eroded into complex contours with many buttresses and potential places of concealment. No traces of human activity were found in the accessible parts of the cliffs

# Wadi W

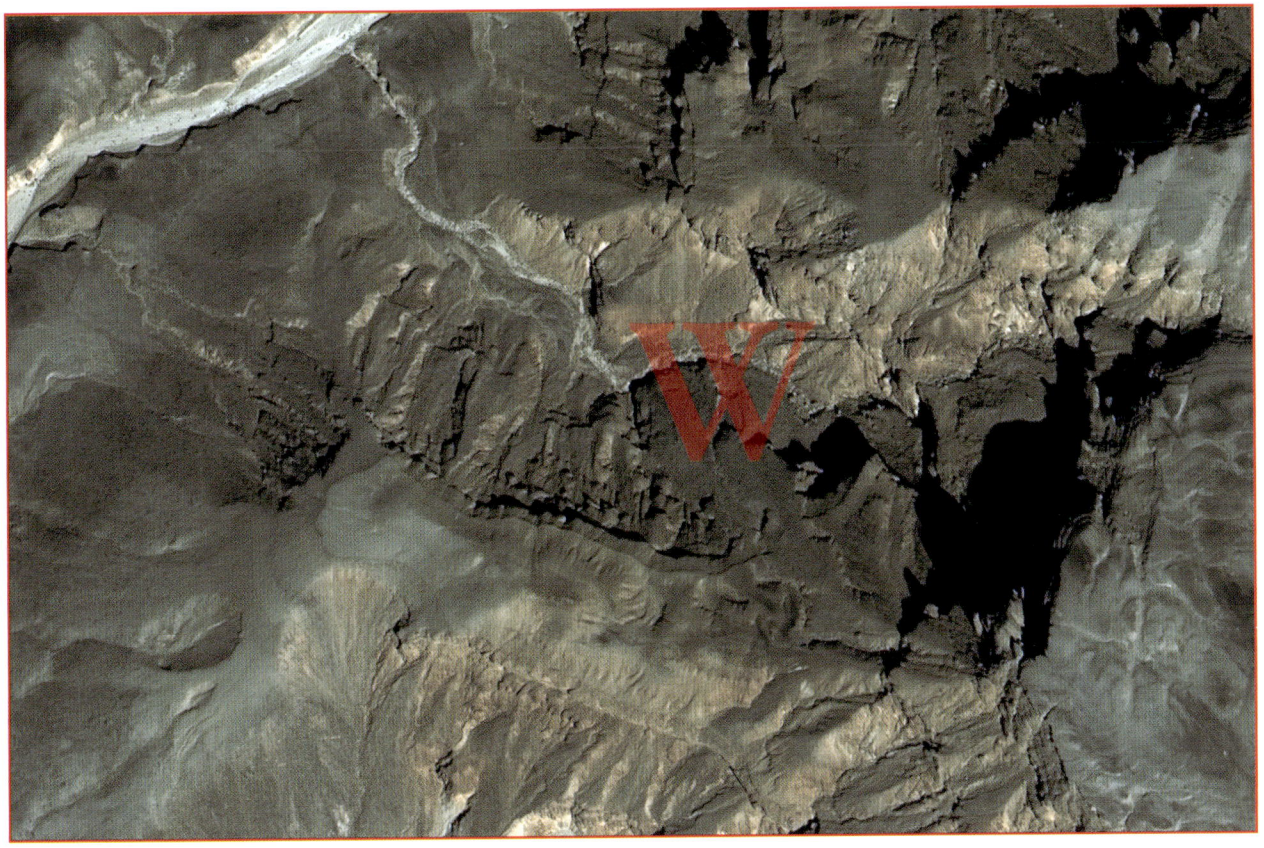

*Figure 528. Wadi W which opens south-east off the eastern branch of Wadi Bairiya.*

*Figure 529. The lower level of cliffs in Wadi W.*

Wadi W opens off the eastern main branch in the Wadi Bairiya. It is relatively narrow, being 225m wide at its widest, and extends 700m from its opening off the Wadi Bairiya to the eastern cliffs of the high desert.

*Figure 530. Flint-working low down inside the entrance to Wadi W.*

Wadi W has two distinct layers of cliffs below the steep rise to the high desert. In one of the niches in the second layer there was evidence of flint working. A small number of flints was also found low down near the wadi entrance.

*Figure 531. Looking west along the northern bay of cliffs in Wadi W.*

Along the ridge dividing the southern side of Wadi W from Wadi V there are several areas of flint-working on the shoulders of the ridge as it descends. The largest is 25-30m across.

*Figure 532. One of the large scatters of flint-working on the ridge between Wadis V and W (looking due west).*

*Figure 533. Close-up of the worked flints on the ridge between Wadis V and W.*

# Wadi X

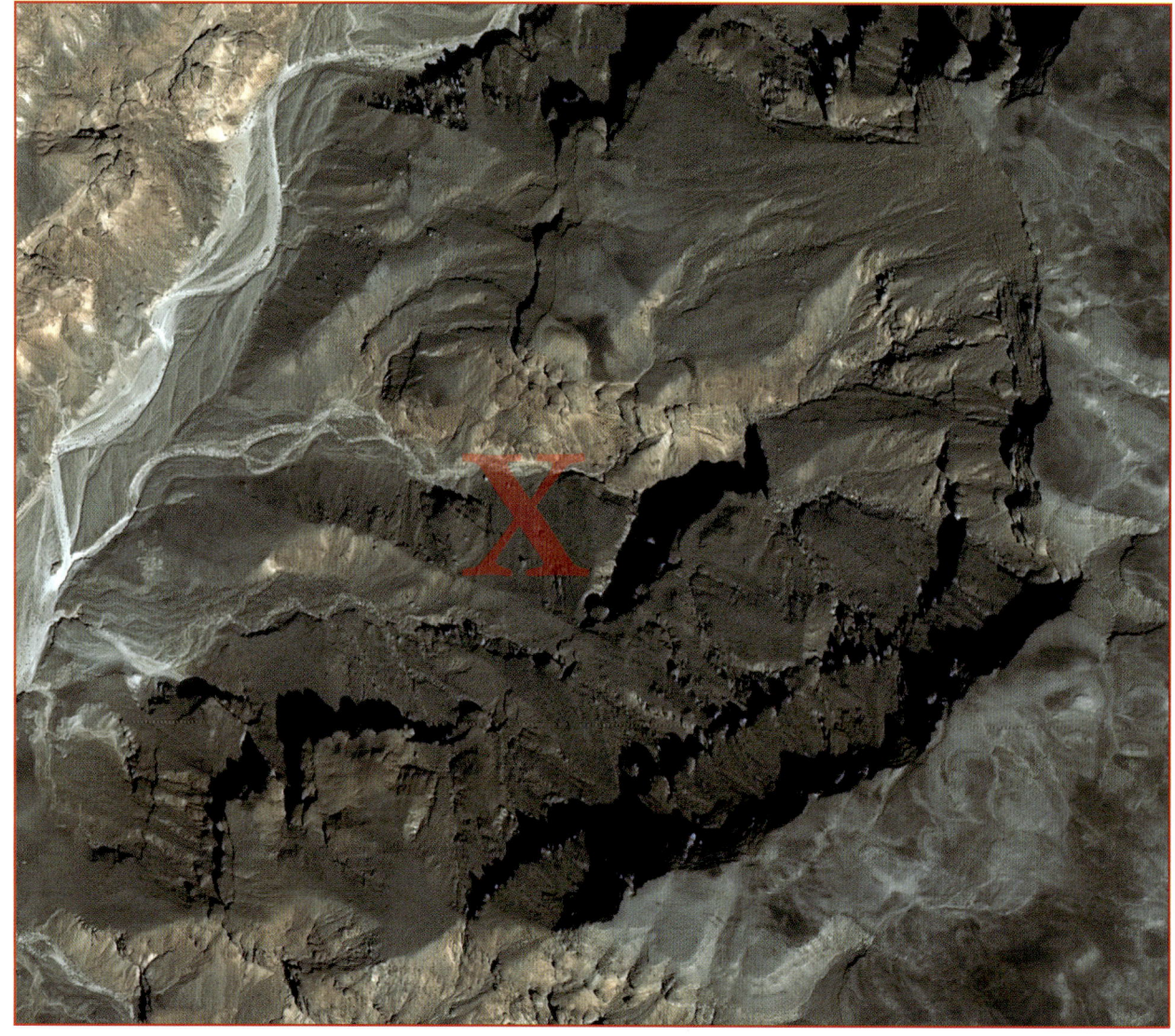

*Figure 534. Wadi X which extends east off the eastern branch of the Wadi Bairiya.*

Wadi X has a simple structure, extending 430m east from its opening off the eastern branch of the Wadi Bairiya to a first line of impassable cliffs. From the top of these cliffs the ground slopes upwards towards a second tier of cliffs which in turn lead up to a third line of cliffs immediately abutting the high desert. From the entrance to the high desert cliffs is 840m. At its widest Wadi X is 350m wide. This includes the small subsidiary wadi to the south.

There were worked flints in the wadi floor of Wadi X but no trace of graffiti or other human activity was detected.

*Figure 535. The entrance to Wadi X looking east.*

*Figure 536. Worked flints in the wadi floor of Wadi X.*

# Wadi Y

Figure 537. Wadi Y at the terminus of the eastern branch of the Wadi Bairiya.

Figure 538. The approach to Wadi Y.

Wadi Y is, appropriately, the Y-shaped terminus of the eastern branch of the Wadi Bairiya. The main wadi forms a rough triangle 275m across the north-eastern side from wadi-end to wadi-end, by 275m from the northern terminus to the wadi entrance, and by 325m from the wadi entrance to the southern terminus.

The cliffs at the end of the wadis are sheer and form a ninety-metre drop from the shelf above which rises steeply to the foot of the cliffs immediately below the high desert.

*Figure 539. Looking into the northern fork of Wadi Y.*

*Figure 540. The terminus of the southern fork of Wadi Y.*

*Figure 541. The cliffs marking the terminus of Wadi Y's southern arm.*

These high cliffs have seen massive and chronic rainfall. At their base the remains of a circular pond or basin, now dry and filled with dessicated plants, has been hollowed out by the waterfall from above. No traces of any human activity were found in these wadis.

# Wadi Z

*Figure 542. Wadi Z which forms the large and northernmost terminus on the eastern side of the central branch of the Wadi Bairiya.*

Unlike Wadi Y, which it resembles in being positioned at the end of a main branch of the Wadi Bairiya, Wadi Z has only one major fork and that is to the north. The southern part of Wadi Z is formed by two rounded bays of cliffs of friable rock which have seen recent collapses.

*Figure 543. The approach to Wadi Z.*

*Figure 544. The southern bay of cliffs in Wadi Z. The white patch in the middle is the result of a recent rockfall.*

In early 2015 it was noticed that small rounded, water-worn sherds were deposited in the floor of the Wadi Bairiya. These were found as far down as the WB1 site. They were tracked up the central branch of Wadi Bairiya to Wadi Z. At the time we expected to find the source of these sherds in Wadi Z.

*Figure 545. One of the larger water-worn sherds in Wadi Z.*

However, although there were sherds in the wadi floor, there was no trace of any settlement or deposit of jars to account for their presence here, or to account for the sherds washed down the entire length of the Wadi Bairiya for a distance of over six kilometres.

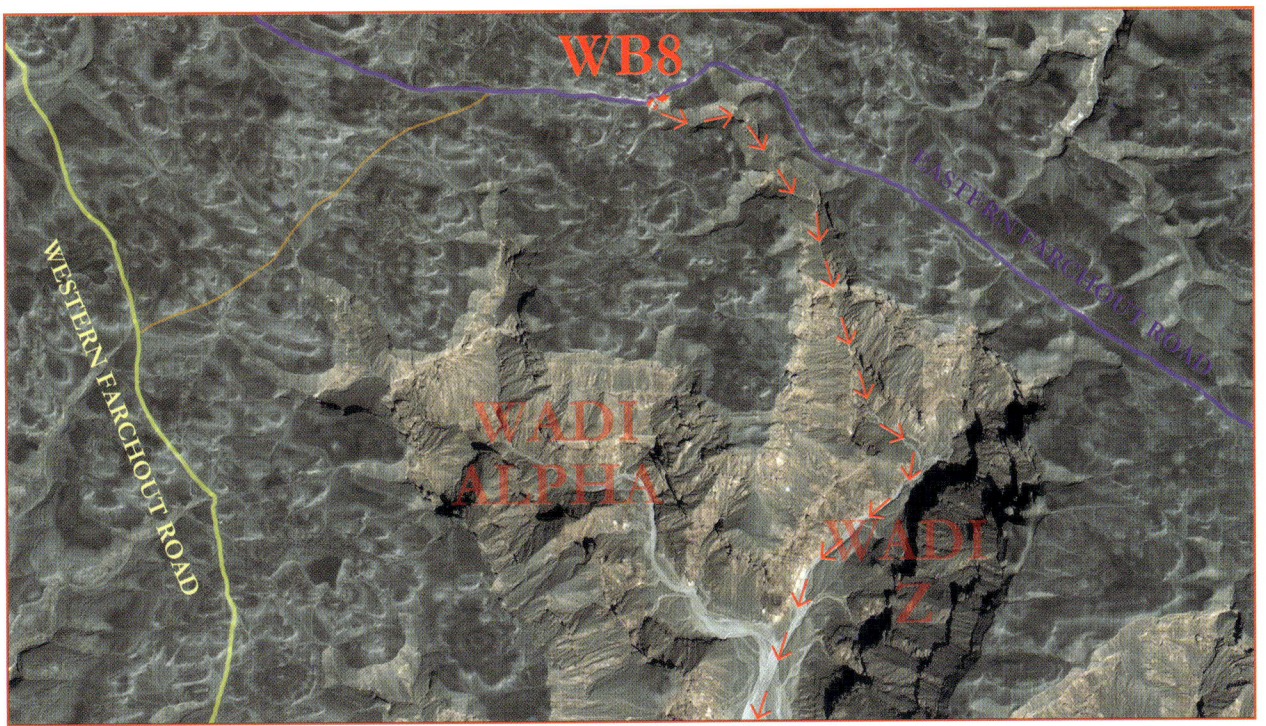

*Figure 546. The WB8 site at the nothern end of Wadi Z. The red arrows show the direction in which sherds were carried by water into the Wadi Bairiya and over 6km down past the WB1 shaft tombs.*

We therefore looked at the very top of Wadi Z, at the point where the highest cliffs meet the Eastern Farchout Road. There we discovered a natural cistern under the cliffs surrounded by pottery sherds which cover an area approximately 60m by 50m. These had been washed down by persistent rainfall over the Wadi Z cliffs and then carried down the length of the Wadi Bairiya (see *Figure 546*).

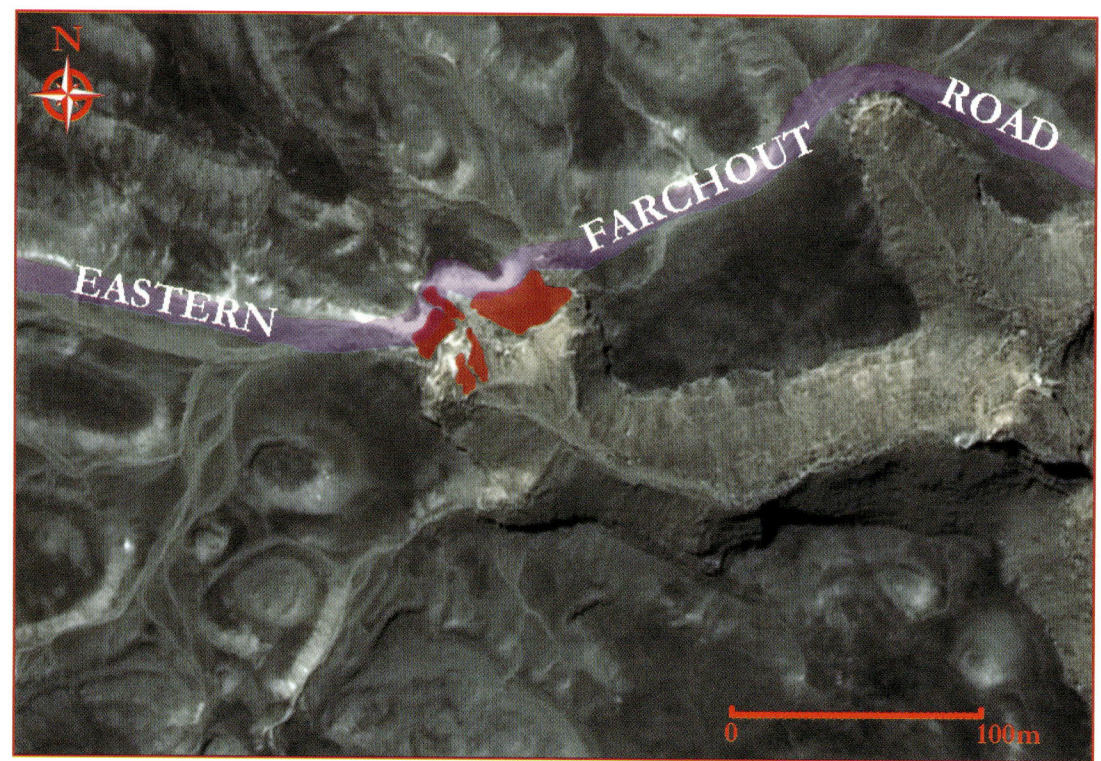

*Figure 547. Detail of the WB8 site with the pottery scatter shaded red.*

*Figure 548. The depth of the sherds covering the surface of the Western Farchout Road on the WB8 site. The scale is 60cms long.*

*Figure 549. The terminus of the northern arm of Wadi Z with stepped and undercut cliffs.*

# Wadi Alpha

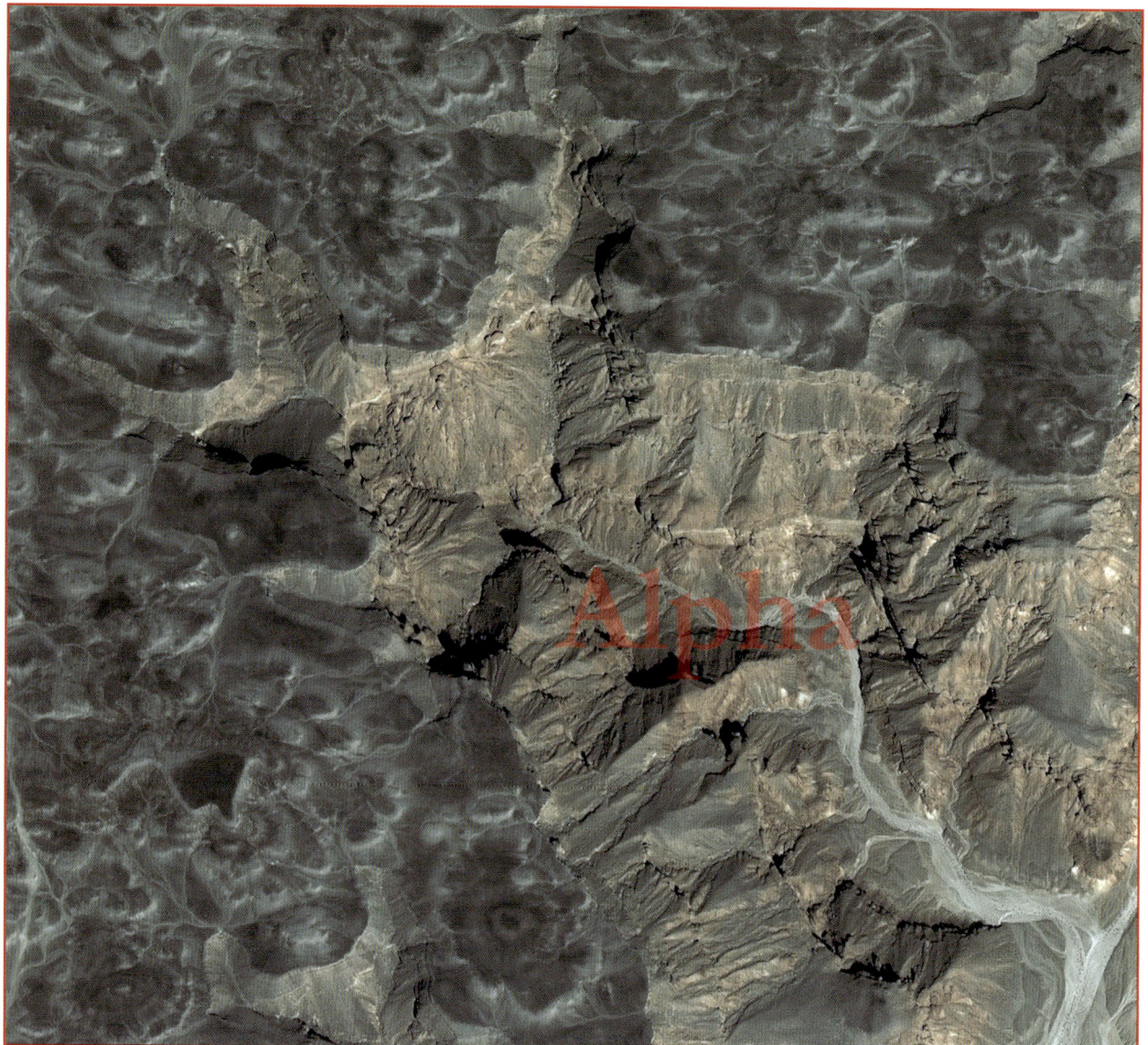

*Figure 550. Wadi Alpha.*

Wadi Alpha marks the northern end of the central portion of the Wadi Bairiya on the western side. It consists of a long, fairly straight floor which extends 940m from the main wadi to the cliffs which form its northern end. The lower cliffs form a corridor 350m wide at their greatest extent. The wadi floor climbs gradually towards the cliffs at the northern end of the wadi. In the floor of the wadi below the cliffs there is a dried pool with the remains of dessicated bushes. These have been fed from above by water coming through a very narrow crack from three higher arms of the wadi to the north, north-west and south of the wadi terminus.

At the mouth of the wadi, near the main floor of the Wadi Bairiya there is a small shelter made of dry stones piled round a larger rock (*Figure 552*). To the south of this in the main wadi floor there is extensive evidence of flint-working and of the gathering of large flint nodules (*Figures 553* and *554*).

*Figure 551. The cliffs at the terminus of Wadi Alpha.*

*Figure 552. The shelter in the main wadi floor just to the south of the entrance to Wadi Alpha.*

*Figure 553. Flint-working by a large boulder just to the south of the entrance to Wadi Alpha.*

*Figure 554. Flint nodules gathered just south-west of the entrance to Wadi Alpha.*

# Wadi Beta

*Figure 555. Wadi Beta which opens to the north-west off the western arm of the Wado Bairiya.*

Wadi Beta ascends very gradually from the Wadi Bairiya and then steepens in a series of steps which climb through a narrowing gorge. This divides into two final arms which finish in cliffs 90m in height.

There were no graffiti found in this wadi and no traces of other human activity other than black plastic bags washed or blown down from the high desert.

*Figure 556. The lower end of Wadi Beta as it start to ascend gradually from the Wadi Bairiya floor.*

*Figure 557. The narrow gorge of the upper reaches of Wadi Beta.*

*Figure 558. Looking east back down the Wadi Beta from the high point beneath the cliffs.*

# Wadi Gamma

Figure 559. Wadi Gamma opening off to the west of the western arm of the Wadi Bairiya.
The yellow dot shows the location of the only graffito found in the Wadi Bairiya.

Figure 560. The southern side of the lower part of Wadi Gamma. The Arabic graffito was found in the lower patch of shadow right of centre.

*Figure 561. The location of the Arabic graffito in Wadi Gamma.*

*Figure 562. Detail of the Arabic graffito. The text is poorly-written and the bottom half of it has broken off.*

The main element of Wadi Gamma extends west from a point just below the entrance to Wadi Beta. Several small branches break south off the main Wadi Gamma bed but it is in the lowest cliffs on the southern side of the main branch that the only graffito found in the Wadi Bairiya is located. The lower portion of this graffito has broken off and is lost. The inscription is in an antique form of Arabic and difficult to read clearly. It appears to be a form of lament or prayer.

*Figure 563. The point at which Wadi Gamma ascends in a series of shelves.*

Some two hundred metres to the west of this graffito there is a high step in the wadi floor (*Figure 563*) which gives onto a water-worn gorge. This twists and turns for over a hundred metres before the wadi climbs further through large rocks to high cliffs bearing signs of heavy water-flows.

No further evidence of human activity was found in this wadi but on the flatter terraces to the south of the entrances to Wadi Gamma and Wadi Beta there were several locations where flints had been worked.

*Figure 564. The water-worn gorge in Wadi Gamma.*

*Figure 565. The final cliffs in Wadi Gamma.*

# Wadi Delta

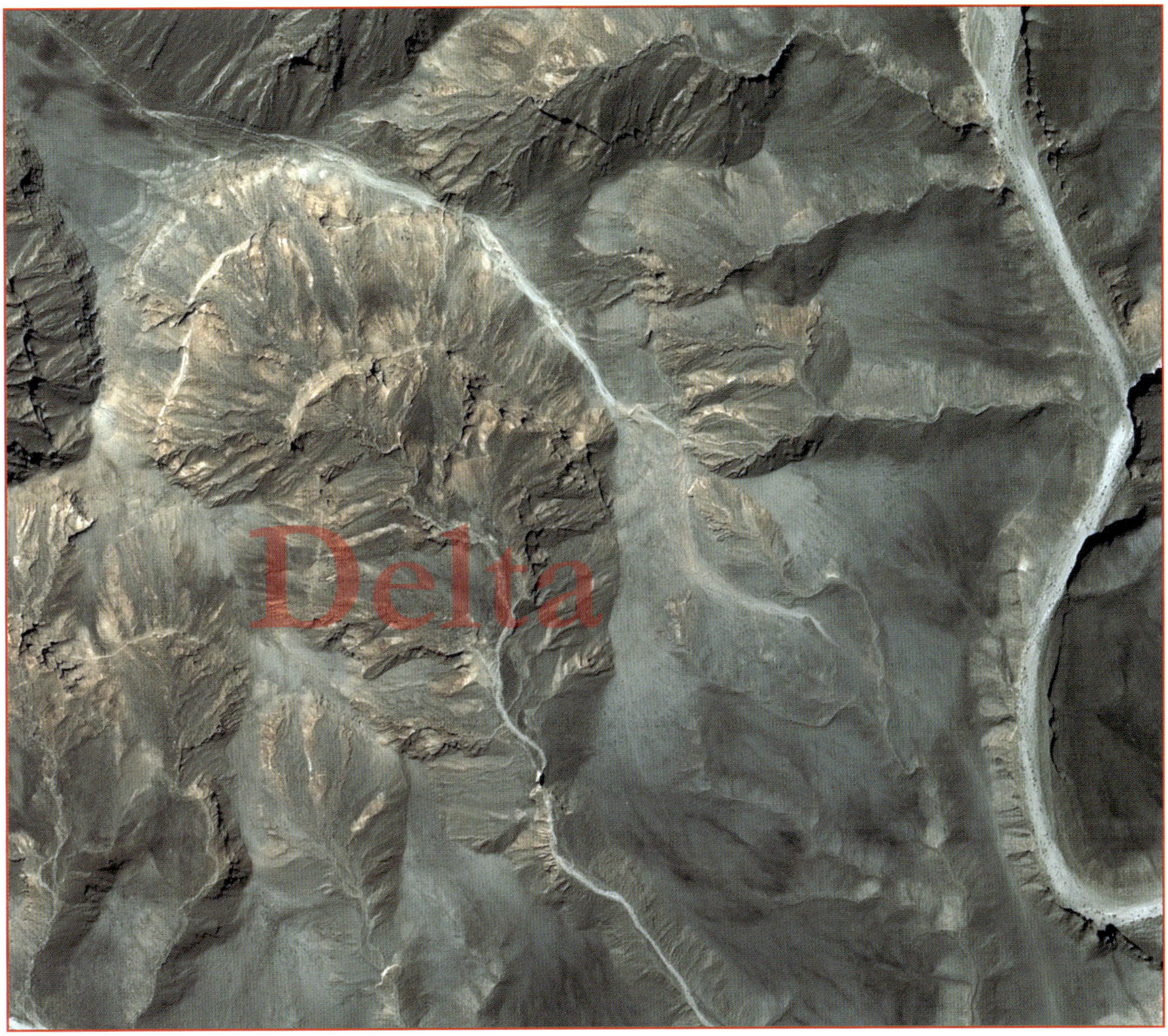

*Figure 566. Wadi Delta which is immediately south of Wadi Gamma on the western side of the Wadi Bairiya. The Western Farchout Road runs up and and around its north-eastern side.*

*Figure 567. The distinctive crescent shape of Wadi Delta (on the right) viewed from a distance of 2km. in the early morning. The much wider Wadi Epsilon is on the left.*

When looking north-west from the WB1 site the crescent-shaped bay of of cliffs in Wadi Delta forms a striking backdrop with the Western Farchout Road climbing up its eastern arm. It is accessed by following the route of the Western Farchout Road to the point where it begins its ascent, then turning left (west) along a path which leads stright to the centre of the wadi. Despite its proximity to the Western Farchout Road the only signs of human activity were the path which leads into the wadi and a single flint-working site (*Figure 571*).

*Figure 568. Looking north-west into Wadi Delta.*

*Figure 569. The western cliffs of Wadi Delta.*

*Figure 570. Looking due south towards the Nile from the foot of the cliffs in Wadi Delta.*

*Figure 571. Flint working in the very centre of Wadi Delta just above the point where the wadi bed divides below the high cliffs.*

**Wadi Epsilon**

*Figure 572. Wadi Epsilon on the western side of the Wadi Bairiya, due west of Wadi Delta.*

The centre of Wadi Epsilon is a mere 800m from the centre of Wadi Delta. However, access to it is through a narrow, wadi floor entered 1.4km west of the WB1 site. This winds north for approximately 2km before dividing at a fork. The western fork peters out in a series of low, complex steps and ridges. The eastern branch is bounded to the east by high cliffs with many flat surfaces and fissures offering potential shelter. No graffiti were found here and there was no sign of human activity along the base of these higher cliffs. There were four flint-working sites (*Figure 578*) on the terraces just above the wadi floor and one on a shelf high under the cliffs at the very north of the wadi.

The eastern branch of the wadi terminates in high, water-worn cliffs (*Figure 577*).

*Figure 573. Wadi Epsilon from a distance of approximately 3km where the end of the wadi debouches into the Wadi Bairiya.*

*Figure 574. The approach to the north-eastern side of Wadi Epsilon.*

*Figure 575. The western side of Wadi Epsilon.*

*Figure 576. The north-eastern cliffs of Wadi Epsilon.*

*Figure 577. The north-eastern terminus of Wadi Epsilon.*

*Figure 578. Flint-working in Wadi Epsilon.*

# Coptic and other sites in the Wadi Bairiya[1]

## 1. WB2

*Figure 579. The interior of the shelter looking north.*

WB2 (*Figure 579*) is just over 1km in a straight line to the north of WB1. It consists in an archway cut into the cliffs above the wadi floor. This has been enlarged to provide standing room (*Figure 533*). The archway was once plastered with mud plaster and contains niches. The remains of a wall a metre from the rock face and running roughly east-west are visible. This wall seems to have been joined to the rock face and to have created a small shelter. There are abundant pottery sherds of Byzantine form in amongst the rocks to the south of the site. To the west of the arch is a small opening high in the wadi wall (and now inaccessible) which may once have provided additional shelter.

---

1. For a map showing the location of all the Coptic sites see Chapter Seventeen Figure 597.

*Figure 580. 240m south-east of WB2 in the main Wadi Bairiya bed is this place where water would naturally have pooled in ancient times and where it clearly continues to collect in times of occasional flooding. Similar dried pools are to be found near WB4, WB5, WB6 and WB7.*

## 2. WB3

WB3 is located just under 1.5km north-west of WB2 under the cliff edge which marks the eastern side of the Farchout Road. At this point the road climbs steeply from the sloping plateau level of the WB1 tombs to the high desert following the ridge above. Modern excavations in this shelter have created a shaft three metres deep. It is not clear whether this was made in search of alabaster seams or by treasure-hunters. The spoil heap is unweathered and therefore looks recent. A speculative interpretation is that WB3 was originally a simple shelter created by enlarging the naturally eroded overhang below the road. It commands a good view of the Farchout Road below and of the Wadi Bairiya access to WB4, WB5, WB6 and WB7. Most Coptic shelters are near water supplies and there was no pottery in the vicinity of WB3 which could be associated with this feature.

*Figure 581. WB3 is below the red arrow. The photograph was taken from the Western Farchout Road which passes just above the WB3 opening.*

*Figure 582. The location of WB3 under the lip of the Farchout Road which climbs round the rim of the cliffs from the left. The red piles were created after the revolution in 2012 when a tracked excavating machine scooped out soil wherever there were huts and pushed other huts to one side (bottom right).*

*Figure 583. The WB3 shaft.*

## 3. WB4

*Figure 584. The site of WB4 in the dark shadow in the centre of the photograph. The site is just off the edge of the central bed of the Wadi Bairiya.*

The WB4 site is a very small hole in the limestone just over 400m north-east of WB3. It lies in a natural buttress forming a corner where a small side wadi enters the main Wadi Biriya floor. The hole is just big enough to accommodate an adult lying down and there are signs of the ground round its entrance having been artifically flattened. The only pottery associated with this site (of Byzantine date) was found in the main Wadi Bairiya floor 15m below and consisted in a few sherds which may well have been washed down from higher up the Wadi Bairiya. The hole may therefore be a shelter used by jackals.

## 3. WB5

*Figure 585. The WB5 site on the eastern side of the Wadi Bairiya.*

*Figure 586. The WB5 shelter which is just large enough for a person to stand in.*

The WB5 site consists of an enlarged natural fissure in the rock which is 2m high internally and extends approximately 2.5m into the rock. It is located in the main Wadi Bairiya floor 340m north of WB4. The shelter has many small niches cut in its sides and there is a wide scatter of Byzantine pottery lying below its entrance in the wadi floor.

*Figure 587. Byzantine amphora fragments below the WB5 shelter.*

## 5. WB6

*Figure 588. The WB6 site. The higher opening is just large enough for an adult to lie down in and is two metres above the wadi floor. The lower niche would barely accommodate a sitting adult.*

The WB6 site is situated 215m north-west of WB5 just inside, and on the northern face, of the western branch of the Wadi Bairiya. Access to the higher shelter is only possible with a ladder. It contained a small piece of carpet-like material and many animal bones. On the surfcae of the wadi floor there were sherds of Byzantine date. Less than two hundred metres away in the central branch of the Wadi Bairiya, to the north of, and opposite WB5 is a dried pool where water continues to accumulate when it rains.

# 6. WB7

*Figure 589. The WB7 shelter which is just large enough to accommodate an adult lying down.*

WB7 is 400m north of WB6 in the central branch of the Wadi Bairiya with a dry pool just to the south and another 150m to the north. WB7 is similar to WB5 but slightly smaller. The interior has the same shelves cut out of the rock and the whole is again enlarged from a natural fissure in the rock. There were no sherds around the mouth of the shelter but waterflows in this part of the wadi will have swept the material away.

# 7. WB8

The WB8 site is entirely different to the preceding sites. It is located at the very edge and northern extreme of the Wadi Bairiya in a lip over the top of which the Eastern Farchout Road runs over a vast dump of ceramic fragments. These ceramic fragments date from many periods but are predominantly from the New Kingdom. There are some Late Roman and Ottoman ceramics The natural cistern which forms part of the shelter has clearly been used over many centuries. To the right (east) of this is a shelter shaped like the other Coptic shelters and provided with small niches. It is therefore plausible that subsequent to its primary use as a watering station serving the Eastern Farchout Road this site was also used during the Coptic period.

*Figure 590. The WB8 shelter under the Farchout Road. This is formed of two parts: to the left is a natural cistern roughly two metres deep and a metre across by a metre and a half wide. To the right is a space sufficient to accommodate a prostrate adult.*

## 8. WB9

*Figure 591. The site of the WB9 shelters. All along the western margin of this side wadi of the Wadi Bairiya floodplain there are sherds of Late Roman date. These appear to relate to shelters under the cliffs.*

The WB9 site is on the eastern side of the Wadi Bairiya floodplain 875m south-east of the WB1 shaft tombs. It is located 300m inside the side wadi created by Wadis J and K emptying into the Wadi Bairiya. The rock shelves along the northern side of this side wadi have in many cases collapsed but they still offer shelter in particular places. There is a considerable quantity of Byzantine amphorae sherds in this area.

*Figure 592. Byzantine ceramics by the WB9 shelters in the lower Wadi Bairiya.*

## 9. WB10.

*Figure 593. The small side-wadi in Wadi U concealing the WB10 site.*

WB10 is situated in a side-wadi in the lower reaches of Wadi U. It is very difficult to distinguish between the natural mud coatings which occur frequently on the limestone walls in these wadis as a result of rainfall and the man-made mud wall-plaster which is characteristic of Coptic sites. An initial examination of this site seemed to indicate the presence of several mud-plastered walls. Late Roman sherds also found here appear to confirm that these are indeed the remains of a Coptic settlement composed of several shelters. However, this site will be re-examined in later seasons.

*Figure 594. The walls behind the standing figure bear traces of mud plastering which extends into the niches behind the figure.*

*Figure 595. A further plastered wall of the wadi with Late Roman pottery.*

*Figure 596. The lighter patch on the vertical wadi wall bears traces of mud plaster and there are Late Roman sherds on what appears to be the remains of artifical floor.*

# CHAPTER SEVENTEEN
# LANDSCAPE AND CLIMATE

*Figure 597. A satellite photograph showing the major flint-working sites (red), tufla-extraction sites (orange), pottery sherds (purple) and graffiti (yellow). Also marked are the locations of sites WB1 to WB10.*

## Raw materials

Analysis of the landscape and climate are inextricable. Perceptions that a landscape is arid and inhospitable inevitably affect thinking about the potential of that landscape and possible activity within it.

In his 1917 article, when considering the possibility of burial activity in the Wadi el-Agaala, Howard Carter states, *"The remoteness of the valley, however, makes the question of water for the workmen one of some difficulty."*[1]

---

1. Carter, H. (1917) op. cit..

The first impression of the WB1 site was certainly of a remote and exposed burial site in an arid part of the desert devoid of life. As Howard Carter demonstrated, there is inevitably an initial temptation to regard current conditions as unchanged since ancient times. Indeed, there is a widespread assumption amongst Egyptologists that there was a permanent change in climate in the fourth millennium B.C. which created the Nile Valley landscape visible today.[2]

As *Figure 597* demonstrates, the landscape around the WB1 site was certainly frequented and was being visited regularly in ancient times by people involved a number of different activities associated with extracting natural resources. These included:

- the collection and processing of flint;

- the collection of fine mud for plastering (and possibly pottery);

- the collection of "tufla" for plastering;

- extraction on the high desert of "alabaster".

Some of these activities have continued into modern times and many of the sites are difficult to date. However, judging by the terraces on which they appear, not all the flint-working sites are pre-historic. The sequence of terraces that follow the incision of the wadis suggests that there have been at least three different episodes of flint-working since the beginning of the Holocene.

## Flint

Flint continued to be used throughout the pharaonic period. The flint sites identified in this landscape are of two types. The first, most of which are high up above the wadi floors on the shoulders of the ridges which descend from the high desert, are broad scatters of flint cores and worked flakes which are up to to forty metres in extent. These appear to be places where flints have been gathered to be worked on on a large scale.

*Figure 598. Many of the larger flint-working sites were positioned high up on the shoulders of ridges.*

---

2. Almost any history of Ancient Egypt produces this assumption. See for example Wilkinson, T. (2010) "*The Rise and Fall of Ancient Egypt*", Bloomsbury, London p. 24: "Egypt was set on a course towards statehood. The final drying out of the deserts around 3600 must have injected further momentum into this process."

*Figure 599. Another flint-working site positioned high on the shoulder of a ridge.*

*Figure 600. One of the larger flint-working sites low down just north of the point at which the Wadi Bairiya forks to the east towards Wadi Y. It extends for roughly 40m away from the camera and is roughly 20m wide.*

It is impossible to date these "workshops" but if they are prehistoric then they suggest a considerable demand for flints and thus either a very large prehistoric population or usage over an extended period.

The other flint sites, which occur on lower terraces, are small collections of flints, in some cases no more than two or three cores which have been worked on. Many of these are located next to Coptic sites which, in turn, are located near places where water collected in the wadi floors. The patina on the exposed surface of some flints indicates weathering during wetter periods in the Holocene.

The different heights of the terraces suggest that at least some of the flint-working activity in these smaller groupings of flakes and cores dates to pharaonic times. Work on these sites and on the flints recovered on the WB1 site is continuing.

*Figure 601. A detail of the large flint-working site in Figure 600.*

*Figure 602. Prehistoric flints recovered from Wadi G.*

## Mud

It is certain from the plastering of the WB1 tombs that mud was sourced in the vicinity in pharaonic times. Further work needs to be done on comparing plaster from extant structures. It would be interesting, should it ever prove possible, to compare the plaster which has survived at Malqata and Kom el-Samak, for instance, with that on the WB1 site and the mud-pits shown in *Figure 606*.

Some of the mud extraction in the Wadi Bairiya is undoubtedly modern, judging by the lack of erosion in the pits. In other places the erosion which has taken place at the margins of the mud-extraction and tufla-extraction pits and the weathering of the flints points to sourcing activity in this landscape over many thousands of years.

The sheer number of pits from which mud was extracted points to work over both an extended period and work to meet major demand. The mud-pits are too numerous to record effectively on a map of very large scale but *Figure 606* shows the extent of this activity in the immediate vicinity of WB1. The pits tend to be along the tops of the plateaus which represent the first shelf above the major wadi floodplains. They are to be found all around the surface of the WB1 site and they consistently relate to a layer of fine, brown soil roughly 30cms deep which we refer to as the "Abdul Ghany layer" (*Figure 603*) after our inspector who first drew attention to this feature. In all cases the stones within the pits have been sieved and thrown into piles which are one of the identifiers of the process of extraction (see *Figure 605*). The pits are no more than four metres across and appear in groups suggesting episodic activity to meet repeated small demand such as might come from the plastering of individual rooms or buildings.

*Figure 603. The Abdul Ghany layer of fine soil.*

Evidence of usage of this mud for plaster is to be found on the walls of the tombs at WB1 and in the mud- and gypsum-mixing pits we have uncovered on the XVIIIth dynasty surface around the tomb shafts. In these pits the mud and gypsum has been ground into powder ready for mixing with water. Experiments we have conducted show that this mixture produces a smooth plaster which adheres well to vertical surfaces.

*Figure 604. Typical mud-extraction pits on the plateau south of the entrance to the Wadi el-Agaala.*

*Figure 605. Detail of a typical mud-sourcing pit showing the way in which the stones have been sorted, sieved and thrown into piles (either side of the north arrow).*

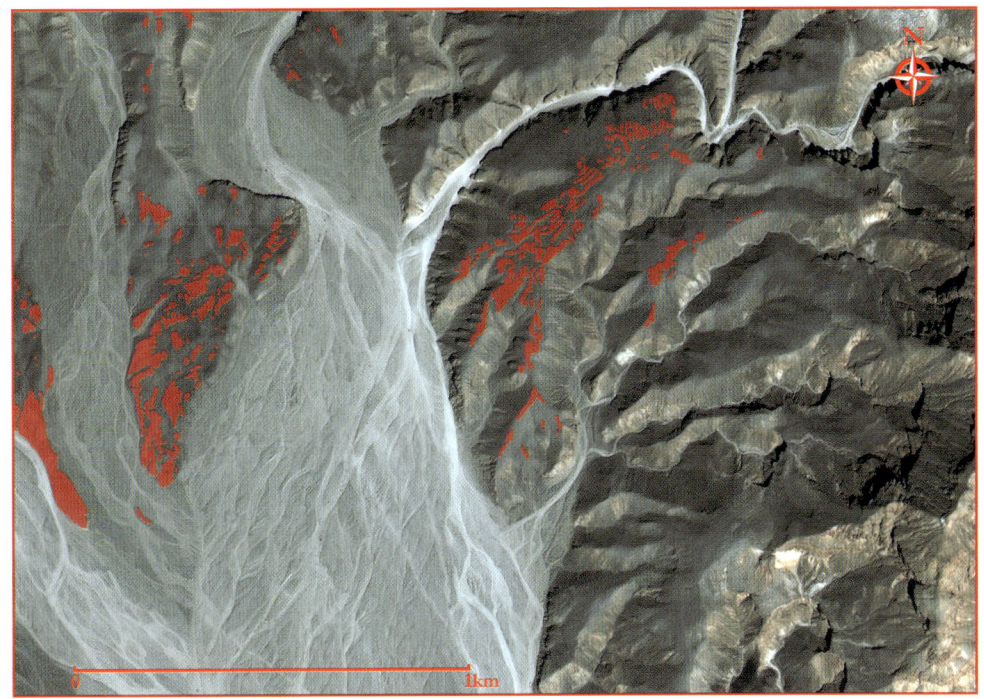

*Figure 606. The areas shaded red show the extent of mud-sourcing in the immediate vicinity of the WB1 site.*

## Tufla

The fine grey to white flakes of limestone which appear in particular locations all over this landscape, and which are generally referred to as tufla, are clearly highly-valued. People continue to travel long distances to collect this material. The basket-load of tufla in *Figure 607* (which looks as though it has fallen from a donkey and is at the top of a steep, narrow footpath) is over eight and a half kilometres from the nearest village. The pile shows very few signs of weathering so is likely to be relatively recent.

*Figure 607. Just to the left of this path in the Wadi Bairiya is a basket-load of grey tufla whch has been dropped here in recent times, presumably when it fell off a donkey.*

*Figure 608. A typical tufla extraction site. This one is in the Wadi Bairiya south-east of Wadi Beta.*

Tufla extraction sites vary in size from ten metres across to much larger sites - visible on satellite maps - such as those along the northern margin of Wadi L. One of these is 150m by 75m. As with the mud-mixing pits, the paths leading to these sites are in all cases devoid of any signs of mechanised transport.

## Alabaster[3]

On the high desert there are seams of a form of alabaster which is mined either laterally, where the seams are exposed, or vertically. Two sites where these two different types of activity have been recorded. One (*Figure 609*) is just to the east of the WB8 site at the northern end of the Wadi Bairiya. The other (*Figure 610*) is north-east of Wadi F at the head of the Wadi el-Gharby.

*Figure 609. Extraction of alabaster near the WB8 site. This natural cave is just below the Farchout Road. The thin seams of alabaster can be seen at the bottom of the area where the red conglomerate has been cut back.*

---

3. The material being extracted is a low-grade, heavily-fractured, crystalline rock or schist found in seams running through limestone. For want of a better recognisable term this is referred to here as alabaster.

*Figure 610. A shaft just over a metre and a half square on the high desert to the north-east of Wadi F. The seam is just over two metres down and small light brown fragments can be seen on the left.*

*Figure 611. A seam of alabaster running underneath the two large rocks with fragments lying in the foreground. Chunks from the seam can be seen scattered in the lower half of the photograph.*

This was, therefore, a landscape which, far from being empty and unused, was being visited for the extraction of raw materials. Some of this activity took place in prehistoric times (judging by the type of worked flints) and some (judging by the modern rope and sieves found by some mud-pits) is modern. Some can be dated with precision to the time of the WB1 shaft tombs. This activity therefore ranges over an extended period. Further work on the lithics in particular should refine the timing of some of this activity.

# Roads

## 1. The Farchout Road

The WB1 landscape looked initially to be remote and isolated. The nearest known monument was in the Western Wadis where the burial of the Three Foreign Wives of Thutmose III had taken place in Wadi D 2.8km to the south-east of WB1 sixty or more years prior to the estimated date of the WB1 burials. Carter and Černy had recorded graffiti in Wadi L 1.8km to the east but they did no more than confirm single visits to that wadi in the Third Intermediate Period.

Our access route to the WB1 site today takes us up the eastern margin of the Wadi Bairiya and then cuts across the wadi floor to reach the foot of the plateau. The central part of the Wadi Bairiya floodplain is littered with stones and scree washed down over the millennia and there is no obvious road running diagonally from the direction of Malqata (south-east) to the WB1 site (north-west). However, this is because the road which exists is a typical caravan road of many single strands all heading in the same direction (*Figure 612*). It is diffuse and only visible when on foot and facing in the right direction.

*Figure 612. The Western Farchout Road cutting across the Wadi Bairiya floodplain and heading straight towards the WB1 site which on the first piece of rising ground in the middle distance.*

Along the line of this road there are low piles of stones positioned in such a way as to come into a pedestrian's view at intervals so pointing out the route ahead. This road can be traced from the Birket Habu spoil heaps, up the Wadi Bairiya floodplain, across the WB1 site and then up onto the high desert to the point where it joins the Eastern Farchout Road 6.5km north of WB1. Along the lower (southern) parts of this road there are occasional sherds but most have been washed away. Once the road climbs onto higher ground there are regular "huts" all along its length and these contain sherds which are predominantly of XVIIIth dynasty and Late Roman date. Mixed in with them there are Ottoman and modern sherds but the gaps in the pharaonic record are striking.

*Figure 613. A Google Earth photograph showing the Eastern Farchout Road in purple, the Western Farchout Road in blue and the combined road in red (Map data: Google, DigitalGlobe).*

The Eastern Farchout Road starts just north-east of the Valley of the Kings and north of Dra Abu el-Naga. It therefore originates in an area which the concentration of funerary monuments tells us was heavily-used in the XVIIth and early XVIIIth dynasties. The Western Farchout Road starts just north of the south-western spoil-heaps of Birket Habu, an area where the surviving monuments date almost exclusively from the reign of Amenhotep III (*Figure 613*).

Travellers, messengers, soldiers and merchants cutting across the great Qena Bend via the high desert from Malqata to Farchout on the Western Farchout Road would have passed within 200m of the WB1 tomb shafts.

Judging by the amounts of pottery left on these roads they were in constant use. The provision of water along these routes is well-organised and attested by several possible wells and at least two enlarged cisterns surrounded by dumps of pottery (of which one is the WB8 site).

On a high shoulder above the point at which the Western Farchout Road passes above the WB3 site to the east and Wadi Delta to the west there is a narrow passage through rocks on either side. This would preclude camels taking this route but donkeys and small horses could have passed through without difficulty.

The regularity of the "huts" along the higher reaches of this road and the shelters erected at obvious break-points (such as at the top of the road where it meets the high desert having climbed 340m) confirm organisation and supervision. Some of the larger piles of stones along the Farchout Road are unlikely to have been created without organised labour. Together with the sheer scale of the pottery debris at the WB8 site they support the view that this was an official route.

*Figure 614. Looking south-east over the Wadi Bairiya from the high desert edge with the route of the Western Farchout Road from Birket Habu across the WB1 site and up towards the high desert shown in red.*

*Figure 615. The Western Farchout Road just below the high desert with the Wadi Bairiya to the left.*

*Figure 616. Huts on the edge of Western Farchout Road at the point where it meets the high desert. The area around this hut is covered in ceramic fragments.*

*Figure 617. One of the features along the route of the Western Farchout Road. Stones are piled in a circular formation redolent of the wells investigated on the WB1 site. In amongst the stones are large numbers of ceramic fragments.*

*Figure 618. One of the larger stone piles, with mixed in ceramic fragments along the Eastern Farchout Road on the high desert.*

## 2. The prepared roads

It very quickly became apparent that there were traces of other roads in the wadi floor. In his 1917 article Howard Carter says, "*A large, wide road crosses the plain below these remains* [the shaft tombs] *and, at a sharp bend, enters the valley* [Wadi el-Agaala], *where it continues up the great northern arm, but how far I have not yet been able to ascertain. I have traced it as far as the first lateral valley on the east; here it divides into two for a short distance, and further on possibly ends in a loop; or else it may form a loop and proceed further. It is from this road that the valley derives its name* ['agala' means a wheel] *and the question arises to what does it lead?* "[4].

The striking thing about these roads is that they cut across the wadi in places rather than following the easy low ground smoothed by the water. The roads were prepared by moving all the larger stones and small rocks to one side leaving a uniform and smooth surface which varies between 3.5m and 4m in width.

The roads are best seen in raking light (*Figures 619 and 620*) when their margins of pushed-aside stone throw a shadow either side of the smoothed central way. Rather than going from point to point in as straight a line as possible, the roads meander. In places their tracks have been eroded but enough survives for it to be clear that they run up the western side of the Wadi Bairiya floodplain to a fork 900m south-west of the WB1 tombs. The road divides and one arm travels north up the western side of the WB1 tongue of rising ground while the other travels up the eastern side. On the eastern side much of the track is lost but it re-appears further north and crosses the Wadi Bairiya floodplain heading for the entrance to the Wadi el-Agaala. On the western side of the

---

4. Carter, H. 1917 op. cit..

WB1 tongue of rising ground the road veers to the east, crossing over the rising ground and descending into the floodplain 230m to the west of the tombs. From there is arcs across the floodplain and joins the other arm just before the entrance to the Wadi el-Agaala (*Figure 619*).

*Figure 619. The path of the prepared road crossing the Wadi Bairiya is highlighted here by the arrows. It descends from the neck of rising ground on the right (where there are the remains of deflated mud ramp) and arcs across the floodplain to the entrance of the Wadi el-Agaala.*

*Figure 620. Part of the prepared road east of the WB1 site.*

*Figure 621. The prepared road entering the "amphitheatre" in Wadi el-Agaala on the right of the photograph and moving towards the centre.*

Much of the road has been washed away by the huge floods which will have been directed through the narrow opening of the Wadi el-Agaala but enough survives for its route up into the main wadi at the T-junction which leads east to Wadi L to be visible. Just south of the "amphitheatre" it is visible again (*Figure 621*) and appears to make a circuit of the western side of the widening wadi before turning by the entrance to Wadi M and, possibly, returning south. On the eastern side of the "amphitheatre" no convincing traces of the road survive.

From the fork south of the WB1 tongue of rising ground the prepared road heads south down the western side of the Wadi Bairiya floodplain. This road has unfortunately been used by modern traffic but its definition is clear enough from the stones pushed to one said along its route. All along this road there are piles of stones which may in some cases merely be the larger stones removed from the road. However, many of these are formed into huts (*Figure 624*) and in and around these huts sherds dating from the XVIIIth dynasty mixed with larger amounts of Late Roman ceramics are scattered.

The prepared road disappears from view in a modern sand quarry 3.4km south of the WB1 shaft tombs. The only known monument in the direction in which the prepared is heading when it disappears from view is Kom el-Abd. That site is 3km further south of the sand quarry. Early (2005) Google Earth photographs indicate a possible route of the prepared road to the south of the quarry stopping 450m north-west of Kom el-Abd. However, it has not been possible to check this route on foot and the area is currently inaccessible. The University of Heidleburg mission which found the stela of Nebamun referred to above in Chapter Five (page 124) was able to drive up the prepared road from a point just to the east of Kola el-Hamra in 1980[5].

---

5. Personal communication with Dr Dina Faltings who discovered the stela.

The function of the Farchout Roads seems to be to allow traffic to cut across the Qena Bend. The distance is approximately 70km from the South Village at Malqata to the modern location of Farchout. This is a journey which could be made on foot in two days although it would have taken longer with donkeys carrying heavy loads.

*Figure 622. The path of the prepared road through the central amphitheatre of Wadi el-Agaala seen from above looking north-east.*

*Figure 623. The path of the same piece of prepared road in the central amphitheatre of Wadi el-Agaala as in Figure 567 at eye-level and looking in the opposite direction south-west.*

The function of the prepared roads is less clear. They are certainly not utilitarian in design and their route from the direction of Kom el-Abd, round the WB1 site and then deep into the Wadi el-Agaala is not helpful in explaining what they were used for.

*Figure 624. The prepared road (on the right) on the floodplain south-west of the site (the white tents of which can just be seen beneath the distant high desert). Along its length at regular intervals there are huts like these containing ceramic sherds.*

Looking at the other evidence which is available may provide an explanation for the form and function of these roads.

Roads which accommodate human or animal traffic, like the Farchout Road, do not need to be smoothed. The surviving prepared roads cover a distance of over 8km and it would have required a large workforce to prepare such a route. They have intentionally been created to meander across the landscape and both this impractical routing and the amount of labour required suggests they were created by powerful people. Their existence in a landscape close to Malqata and Kom el-Abd and their route round the burials of court women suggests royal involvement. The roads vary in width between 3.5m and 4m and this size and their smoothed surface makes them ideal for chariots. Similar roads exist at Akhetaten and there they are called patrol roads[6]. In the case of the Wadi Bairiya and Wadi el-Agaala roads the idea of patrolling might well explain the road round the WB1 shaft tomb site. On the other hand the route taken by the road which circumnavigates the site does not seem to have been chosen for its ability to monitor closely the tomb site. Puzzlingly, it steers away from the site at various points.

---

6. Kemp, B. (2012) op. cit. p. 104 plate XI.

## Chariots and climate

Barry Kemp thought that Kom el-Abd might be rest house for people involved in chariotry[7]. Sandstone blocks of XVIIIth dynasty appearance which were re-used at, and recovered from, Phoebammon during excavations in the 1950s, show chariots[8]. Phoebammon is 4km south-west of WB1 at the top of the enigmatic strip of desert cleared durign the reign of Amenhotep III and which runs from there down to Kola el-Hamra. This too is thought by some to have been connected with chariot racing[9].

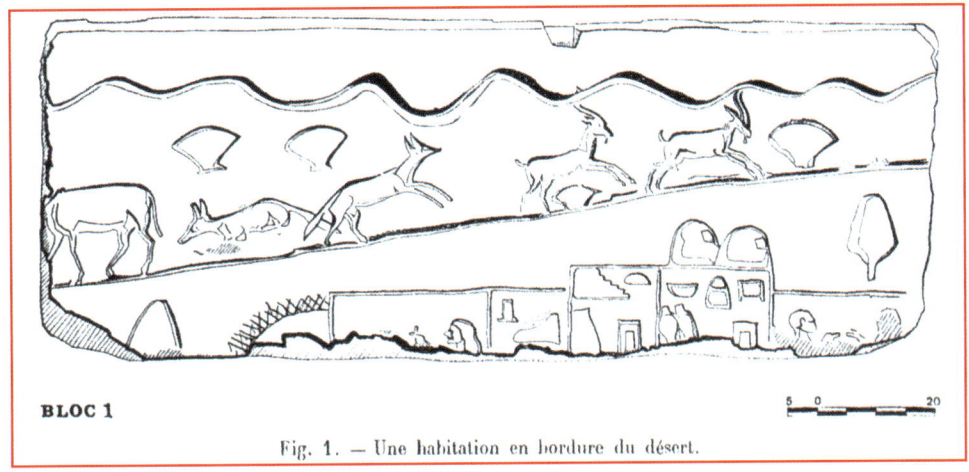

*Figure 625. A bloc published by Pierre Anus in 1971 and showing jackals and wild goats in a hilly landscape with bushes and trees close to habitation (© Ifao).*

Blocks re-used at Karnak but originally from the memorial temple of Amenhotep III at Kom el-Hettan were published by Pierre Anus in 1971[10]. These include portrayals of a landscape which shows hills with scattered trees and bushes and wild animals (*Figure 625*). One of the blocks from this group shows a palace with grapes and trees growing

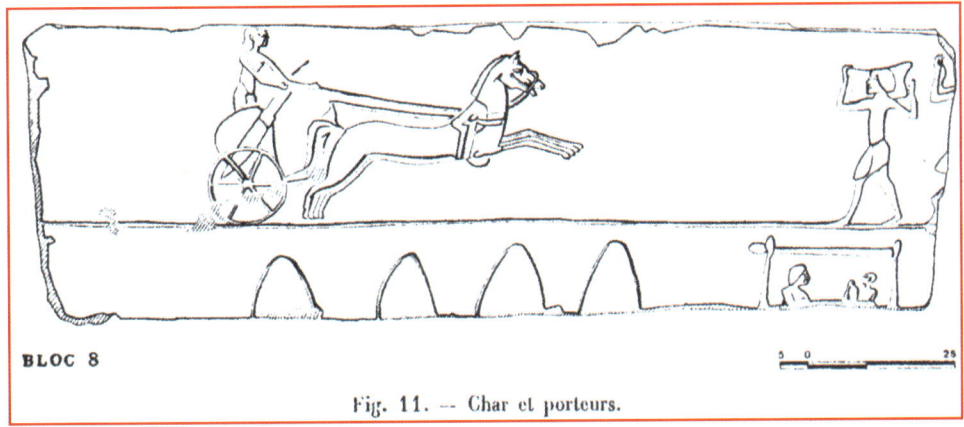

*Figure 626. Another of the blocks published by Pierre Anus in 1971 showing a chariot equipped for archery and what may be copper archery targets being carried on the right (© Ifao).*

---

7. Kemp, B. (1977) op. cit.
8. Bachtaly, C. et al (1961) "*Le Monastère de Phoebammon dans la Thébaïde*", Société d'archéologie copte, Le Caire.
9. Kemp, B. (1977) op. cit..
10. Anus, P. (1971) "*Un domaine thébain d'époque <amarnienne>. Sur quelques blocs de remploi trouvé à Karnak*", BIFAO 69, pp. 69-88

next to it and with livestock and what appear to be caged lions (*Figure 627*). Aude Gräzer Ohara[11] has suggested that the right-hand margin of this block shows the spoil-heap mounds of Birket Habu and that the building portrayed is therefore part of the palace complex at Malqata. It is likely, therefore, that this set of blocks as a whole portrays scenes of the area round Malqata. A further block published by Pierre Anus shows a chariot and men carrying copper ingots which may be targets for archery (*Figure 626*).

*Figure 627. This block was also originally published by Pierre Anus in 1971. Aude Gräzer Ohara has identified the shapes on the right-hand end of the block as the mounds of Birket Habu. The block shows a palace with a window of appearance, gardens and livestock in a verdant landscape.*

The evidence for chariots is fragmentary but the various strands give credibility to the suggestion that the prepared roads were used for chariotry. Considered together the blocks from Kom el-Hettan produce a picture of a landscape which far from being arid is actually verdant and fruitful. If Aude Gräzer Ohara's identification is correct then this greenery was once in a place which is now very definitely arid.

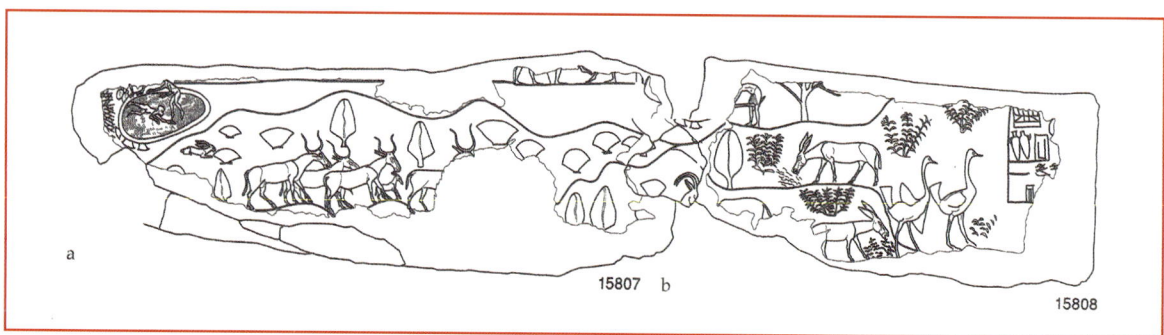

*Figure 628. Block from Kome el-Hettan published by Hourig Sourouzian(© Memnon/Amenhotep III Project). The block shows ostriches, wilds asses, a hare and antelope in a landscape with bushes and trees close by a building (on the right). In the top left-hand corner there is a pool of water with plants and two figures possibly swimming or merely leaning over the water.*

---

11. Gräzer Ohara, A. (2012) "*Le palais des monts sur un bloc de remploi de Karnak : marou d'Amon et/ou complexe jubilaire d'Amenhotep III à Malqata ?*" BIFAO 112, Le Caire pp. 191-214.

Further blocks found in situ at Kom el-Hettan and published by Hourig Sourouzian[12] show a hare, ostriches, wild asses and antelope and, in addition, a pool of water with small figures around it (*Figure 628*). The landscape portrayed here is hilly and accords well with the landscape north and west of Malqata. The representations may be in the form of conventions aimed at portraying a particular type of landscape. The pool suggests it was not just a little wetter but that water accumulated well away from the Nile for sufficient periods and in sufficient quantities for plant growth.

Our own understanding of what is conveyed by the word "desert" and the understanding of ancient Egyptians of their word which we now translate as desert may be some way apart.

*Figure 629. Evidence of bio-turbation just below the XVIIIth dynasty surface at WB1.*

*Figure 630. The fact that the lowest level of stones in these huts below the WB1 site are buried provides further evidence of rainfall coming down the slope behind.*

Taken together with the evidence from the WB1 site, there seems to be a very high probability that the landscape in the XVIIIth dynasty was much wetter than it is today and that the monsoon rain-bands did not simply disappear in the fourth millenium BC.

On the WB1 site we have a surface which has been eroded by water flows and which has cracked as it later dried out. We have found evidence of bio-turbation (caused by insects - *Figure 629*) and plant roots (*Figures 446 and 447*). We have the three "wells" or water collection points on the site which were used during the XVIIIth dynasty (and Late Roman Period).

---

12. Sourouzian, H. (2015) "*L'Art proto-amarnien au temple d'Amenhotep III a Thebes*", Memnonia XXVI pp. 157-177 reproduced with permission © Memnon/Amenhotep III Project.

From the shafts we have recovered a variety of faunal remains the most telling of which are the bones of fish, pelicans and a moorhen. The other animal bones can be explained in terms of accidental visitors. The gazelles could have fallen into the shafts when they were left open. The owls and the vulture could also have fallen in here. The fish might have been a meal for a human or a bird. However the telling point about the pelican and the moorhen is that neither travels very far from water. This suggests that at some stage there was water very much closer than there is today - unless, of course, pelicans and moorhens were pets or offerings.

Singly many of the pieces of evidence can be excused and explained away. However, taken as a body, with the Kom el-Hettan blocks and the rainfall on the WB1 site they provide a case which is less easy to dismiss.

Even very small levels of increased moisture in the wadi floors will re-green them bringing in insects and birds. This also attracts gazelles and gazelles in turn attract larger animals.

Perhaps, therefore, one of the explanations for the entry into the Wadi el-Agaala of the prepared roads is that they were used for organised hunting. As has been observed, the central part of the Wadi el-Agaala, entered through a narrow gorge, provides a natural amphitheatre. On the walls of this wide open area there are graffiti which seem to

*Figure 631. Possible hare graffito from Wadi el-Agaala. A small stone imperfection has been used by the draughtsman for the eye. The edges of the inscription have been enhanced by computer in white.*

suggest that certain animals not now found near these wadis were once thought about here. There being thought about does not prove they were here but the graffiti create an association readily explained by hunting. The lion and gazelle graffiti (*Figures 512 and 513*) in the amphitheatre may be prehistoric but they differ from the undoubtedly prehistoric graffiti in Wadi G.

Further up the wadi are graffiti which may portray a hare (*Figure 631*), a wild bull and what might be a schematic man shooting a bow (*Figure 490*). *Figure 491* shows what may be an African Wild Dog.

It seems entirely possible that the prepared roads were put in place to allow the sort of orchestrated hunting which saw the young Amenhotep III shoot 96 bulls and over a 100 lions[13]. With higher levels of moisture and the sort of trees and bushes portrayed on the Kom el-Hettan blocks there would certainly have been a variety of game to shoot in these wadis as the graffiti found there seem to suggest.

*Figure 632. The root and, right, the trunk, of an as yet unidentified tree in Wadi G.*

*Figure 633. Some of the leaves from the tree found in Wadi G.*

---

13. Berman, L. (1998) "*Overview of Amenhotep III and His Reign*" in ed. O'Connor, D. and Cline, E. (1998) "*Amenhotep III: Perspectives on His Reign*", The Universty of Michigan Press, Ann Arbor pp. 111-115.

At the very end of the last season we discovered during clearance work in Wadi G in the Wadi el-Gharby the remains of a tree (*Figure 632*). This tree had been crushed by a rockfall which had preserved the trunk (though it has been damaged by termites), roots and several hundred leaves (*Figure 633*). Nearby are clear layers of soil - made up of plant and animal material. The tree and one of these layers of soil containing the dung of what are either gazelles or goats is (judging by the height of graffiti in the area) at XVIIIth dynasty level. Beside the tree is a well-preserved wasp-nest. All these items are the subject of ongoing study and details will be published at a later date. However, they provide strong support for the view that the climate was very different in the XVIIIth dynasty to what we see today.

In Wadi F, further north in the Wadi el-Gharby than Wadi G, we have begun to analyse the very great numbers of graffiti. One of the striking things about this body of written records is the number of birds which are portrayed. These are predominantly falcons but they include a number of portrayals of duck on their own, duck in what seem to be reeds and duck apparently being netted. These are very odd images to find in what are today dry wadi beds. However, inspection of the sections in these wadis has revealed that for long periods the area referred to as 'the ravine' in Wadi F held standing water for long enough for sediments and clear edges to the resultant pools to form.

**Further climate considerations**

There are other reasons to suspect that the climate was very different at this time. Temperature records retrieved from the Greenland Ice Cores (*Figure 634*) give a very generalised picture of global weather patterns at various times. Whilst these are not easy to apply with precision they nonetheless give an overall picture of rainfall (which rises with temperature). If this picture were to disagree with the evidence we have been uncovering then this would clearly be a problem. However, the evidence we have found on the WB1 site and in the surrounding wadis tallies with the global weather pattern.

This Greenland Ice Core data suggests that rainfall in the so-called "Minoan warming" period rose to a level it had not reached for four thousand years. It was a level not to be matched again in the period covered. The only period in which rainfall rose sharply again was during the late Roman Period. However, it did not rise to the same levels as in the early New Kingdom. If the Greenland Ice Core data has any validity for early New Kingdom Egypt then we should expect to see a spike in agricultural activity both then and in Late Roman Egypt.

This is very much what we do see. The ceramic record on the WB1 site and in the huts along the Farchout Road - and indeed the prepared road from the direction of Kom el-Abd - contain an abundance of both early New Kingdom pottery and Late Roman pottery. What is peculiar is the absence of other New Kingdom ceramics and Late Period ceramics in anywhere near the same quantities. There is a distinct gap between the early New Kingdom and the late Roman Period. Put another way, there is a distinct peak in the ceramic record which matches closely the global rainfall peaks suggested by the Greenland Ice Core data.

With the late Roman Period there is a full suite of evidence which we have uncovered which points to a wetter climate during that time. There are, in addition, at least seven Coptic sites in the Wadi Bairiya dated by similar ceramics. This evidence is further corroborated by written records dating from the late Roman Period which record a wetter Eastern Mediterranean[14].

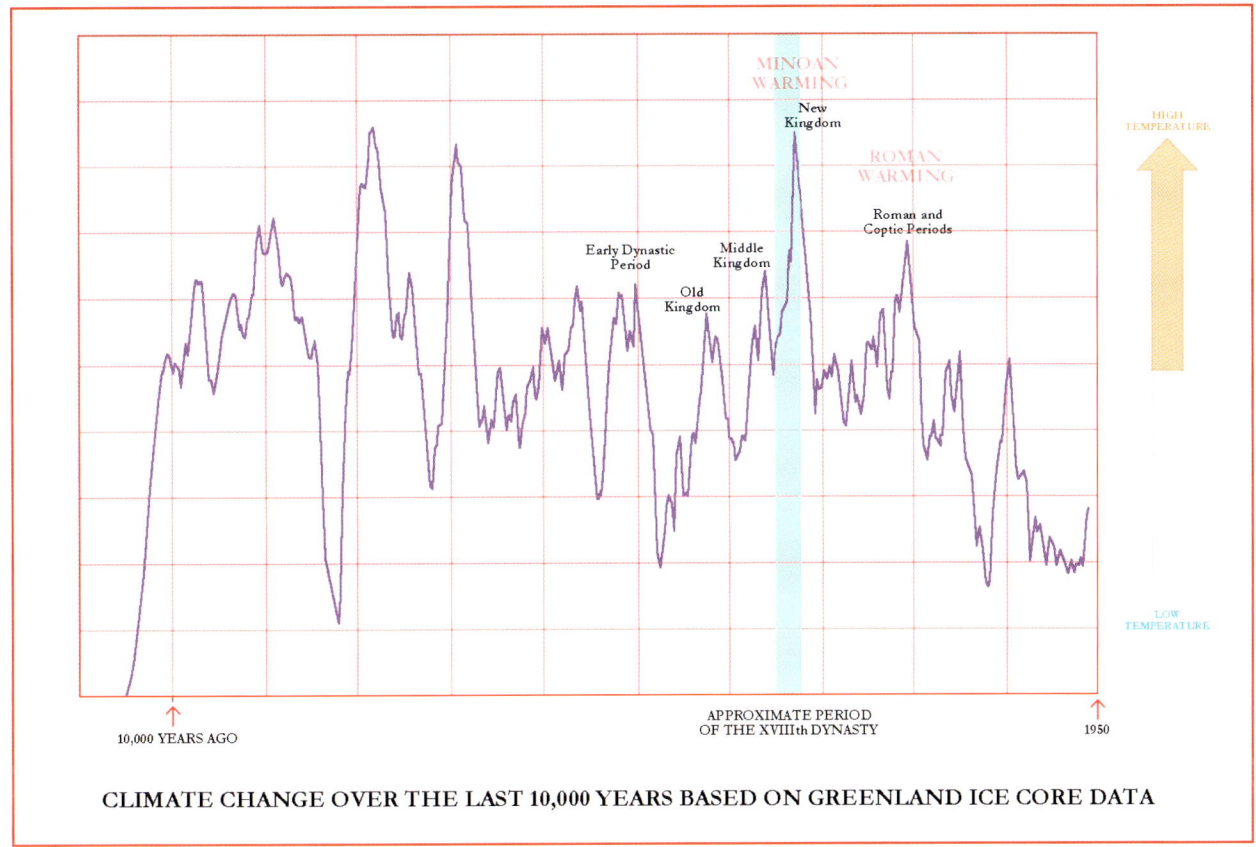

Figure 634. *A chart employing data from the Greenland ice cores showing temperature change (high temperature correlates with high rainfall).*

2.7km south of the WB1 site and 700m north of the point at which the prepared road disappears in the modern sand quarry there is a previously unrecorded well. Scattered across a bank immediately to the west of the prepared road (which at this point has been repeatedly used by modern traffic) are sherds which date from the Early Roman through to the Byzantine period. It has not been possible to see whether there are earlier sherds beneath these Roman remains (*Figures 635 and 636*).

Cut down into the bank is a well, U-shaped and lined with a drystone wall of uncertain date (*Figure 637*). The opening is to the south-east. Scattered about this well are modern tin cans and pieces of flattened metal sheet such as may have been used for covering the well. The present floor of the well is composed entirely of dried mud. Excavation of this site would certainly add further valuable information. As it stands it is further confirmation of the existence of water here on the Wadi Bairiya plain in Roman times in a place where none exists today.

14. McCormick, M., Büntgen, U., Cane, M., Cook, E., Harper, K., , Huybers, P., Litt, T., Manning, S., Mayewski, P., More, A., Nicolussi, K., Tegel, W. (2012) "*Climate Change during and after the Roman Empire: Reconstructing the Past from Scientific and Historical Evidence*", Journal of Interdisciplinary History, xliii:2, pp. 169–220.

*Figure 635. The site of the Roman well just to the west of the prepared road 2.7km south-west of the WB1 shaft tombs. The redder brown colouring is scattered pottery sherds.*

*Figure 636. The pottery sherds accumulated on the bank of the Roman well.*

*Figure 637. The Roman well. It is approximately 1.5m in diameter.*

The ceramic evidence for the XVIIIth dynasty parallels that of the late Roman Period. There would seems to be no written records other than the Tempest Stela of Ahmose which record higher levels of flooding or of rainfall. However, the blocks which originated from Kom el-Hettan published by Pierre Anus, Aude Gräzer Ohara and Hourig Sourouzian provide inscriptional support for climate patterns in ancient Egypt suggested by the global Greenland Ice Core data.

It is interesting that the Greenland Ice Core chart suggests spikes in rainfall consistent with the beginnings of the Old Kingdom and Middle Kingdom as well as the New Kingdom. Although weather patterns at local levels are very complex and there is always a possibility that the Theban weather was for extended periods quite distinct from that 2,500 km further south, the very sharp rise in rainfall indicated at the beginning of the New Kingdom would most likely have been accompanied by high Niles due to higher rainfall in Uganda and Ethiopia. These in turn would have driven an increase in agricultural production which accords with the economic strength which saw Egypt transformed into an imperial power in the New Kingdom and the dominant power in the Eastern Mediterranean.

This rainfall drops off very dramatically at some stage in the later XVIIIth dynasty. It is not possible to pinpoint the date of this decline this with any precision but it looks as though it happens towards the end of the reign of Amenhotep III. Recent work by

Angus Graham, Willhelm Toonen and their team endorses the idea that there was a drying out in the New Kingdom but the work is unable to date this more precisely[15].

Although the initial stage of this purported decline would have resulted in some contraction in marginal land, levels of rainfall remained at higher levels than the average during the Old and Middle Kingdoms. Changes at the margin can have severe effects and it is certainly worth considering whether or not the change in direction from increasing to decreasing rainfall contributed in any way to the political stresses of the late XVIIIth dynasty.

If the approximate calibration in the chart is correct, by the end of the New Kingdom rainfall would have been nearing the low level which matches the First Intermediate Period. At the end of the New Kingdom, in the reign of Ramesses III complaints by workmen at Deir el-Medina about the failure of grain deliveries are indicative of grain shortages (also recorded in the Turin Strike Papyrus)[16]. Two decades later, in the reign of Ramesses VII, grain shortages are again evident from the sharp increases in prices[17].

These more speculative considerations aside, it is clear that the climate in the XVIIIth dynasty was very different to the climate today. It was wetter. The area around the Malqata palace was fertile and filled with vines and trees. These could, of course, have been sustained by irrigation, but the trees and bushes and pools shown in the various blocks ultimately sourced from Kom el-Hettan would not have been artificially sustained.

The WB1 tombs were, therefore, situated in a frequented landscape which might even be described as busy. Soldiers, messengers and traders would have passed along the Western Farchout Road within sight of the tombs. Workmen sent out to retrieve flints, tufla and mud would have been travelling with donkeys into the wadis. Later Roman period occupation of the wadis, which would have taken place at lower levels of rainfall than the XVIIIth dynasty enjoyed, has produced an abundance of ceramic evidence and eight definite Coptic shelters. It seems fair to assume that higher levels of rainfall would have resulted in higher levels of activity in the XVIIIth dynasty.

The presence in these wadis of the prepared roads, which link the tombs to something in the direction of Kom el-Abd, suggest the repeated presence of those elite enough to have the use of chariots - so members of the court, certainly, and members of the royal family most likely. The people buried in the WB1 shaft tombs were attached to various court entities which, despite the peripatetic nature of the court, may have been located in particular places. "The House of the Dazzling Aten" has been associated closely with Amenhotep III's apartments at Malqata. "The House of the King's Wife", if it refers to Tiye rather than Nebetnehet, would probably have been near the King's residence. "The House of the Heirs of the King" could have been anywhere but a secure location and

---

15. Graham, A., Strutt, K., Hunter, M., Pennington, B.,. Toonen, W. and Barker, D. (2014) "*Theban Harbours and Waterscapes Survey, 2014*" Journal of Egyptian Archaeology 100 pp. 35-47 and Toonen, W., Graham, A., Pennington, B., Hunter, M., Strutt, K., Barker, D., Masson-Berghoff, A. and Emery, V. (2017) "*Holocene fluvial history of the Nile's west bank at ancient Thebes, Luxor, Egypt, and its relation with cultural dynamics and basin-wide hydroclimatic variability*", Geoarchaeology. 2017; 1–18.
16. Wente, E. (1961) "*A letter of complaint to the Vizier To*", Journal of Near Eastern Studies 20:4 pp. 252-257 and Edgerton, W. 1951 "*The Strikes in Ramses III's Twenty-Ninth Year*", Journal of Near Eastern Studies. 10.3 pp. 137-145.
17. Van Dijk, J. (2000) "*The Amarna Period and the Later New Kingdom*" p. 308 in Shaw, I. ed., "*The Oxford History of Ancient Egypt*", Oxford University Press, Oxford.

one near the court women seems likely. It is also possible that the word *pr* refers to some non-geographical entity.

I have suggested that what brought members of the royal family up into the area of the WB1 shaft tombs was hunting activity. The graffiti in the Wadi el-Agaala supports the view that game was present in that wadi in ancient times. An enduring question is just why this exposed spot was chosen as a burial site. In this connection it is certainly noteworthy that the entire prepared road circuit round the WB1 tongue of raised ground can been seen only from a point just above the location of the shaft tombs. If chariot driving was to be witnessed this was a place for an audience to stand.

A much more complex and active XVIIIth dynasty landscape to the west of Medinet Habu emerges from these suggestions. When the known XVIIIth dynasty sites of the cleared strip and Kola el-Hamra are brought into the picture alongside activity at Deir el-Shelwit, the entire axis of activity in the reign of Amenhotep III shifts westwards. Whatever may have existed on lower ground between Kola el-Hamra and Kom el-Abd, and between Kom el-Abd and the south-western corner of the Birket Habu body of water will have been washed away by powerful effects of later occasional flooding from the Wadi Bairiya and Wadi Haybah. A more complete picture of the occupation of this landscape in the XVIIIth dynasty may no longer be recoverable.

The cleared strip was never completed. The WB1 tombs seem to have been left incomplete. Shaft Five is incomplete and both the lower and upper chambers have notably low ceilings. A shaft was clearly planned to the west of Shaft Six but never started. Shaft Six itself, if it was not prepared as an embalming cache, was never completed. Work to deepen the shaft of Shaft Three and extend it to the east was abandoned.

The explanation for these events, as indeed, for the abandonment of Malqata, might lie in the creation of Akhetaten. The question which has always lain open is why it was necessary for that new city to be created for "my father the Aten". It is just possible that a contributing factor may have been climate change.

The buildings at Malqata survive predominantly in the form of the buildings used and decorated for the final jubilee of Amenhotep III. It may appear therefore that the Malqata site was used only for the celebration of the jubilees. There is no question, judging by the labels recorded by William Hayes[18], that activity at Malqata peaked during these periods. However, whilst the peripatetic lifestyle[19] of a king of Egypt surely makes anachronistic our idea of a "capital" of Egypt, there are good reasons to believe that there was a more or less permanent residence in the area known as Malqata during the reign of Amenhotep III.

The first of these reasons is the portrayal on the block in *Figure 627* of a palace in the vicinity of the Birket Habu mounds. It is not at all clear where exactly this palace was but it is not absolutely certain that a jubilee palace is portrayed. In any event, it suggests

---

18. Hayes, W. (1951) op. cit..
19. Hagen, F. (2016) "*On Some Movements of the Royal Court in New Kingdom Egypt*" in Van Dijk, J. ed. (2016) "*Another Mouthful of Dust*", Orientalia Lovaniensa Analecta 246, Peeters, Leiden.

the presence of a palace of a fairly permanent nature with lions, cattle and vines all in the vicinity.

Second is the presence of burials in this locality. Nine hundred metres to the north of Malqata is a small valley called the Wadi 300 by Howard Carter[20]. It contains at least forty-nine small shaft tombs excavated by Lortet and dated by him to the reign of Amenhotep III[21]. It has not been investigated since Daressy and Lortet but it may be the original burial site of some of the XVIIIth dynasty re-burials in the Valley of the Kings. Burials suggest nearby occupation of some sort. No burials, be they in Memphis or Elephantine, are totally removed from some form of permanent settlement. The WB1 shaft tombs are a further 4.5km away but they too indicate some form of permanent belonging in the area.

A Great Wife of the King would not have been buried in a place where no visitation was possible. The relationship between the WB1 tombs and the TT90 tomb of Nebamun in turn points to the origins of the people buried in the WB1 tombs being local. They belonged here. Although the court moved constantly, people were buried in particular locations. Some royal women were buried at Saqqara, some at Gurob, some at Soleb and some on the west bank at Waset: all in the vicinity of settlements or entities to which they belonged.

The third piece of evidence is the roads and the Western Farchout Road in particular. This gave access to the "remote" WB1 site but the very existence of these roads, acting as a short-cut across the Qena Bend and substitute for the Eastern Farchout Road, together with the ceramic evidence of continual usage during the early New Kingdom suggest that whatever settlement lay at the beginning of the road was not created just for a decade of jubilees. The prepared roads also suggests something marginally more permanent than the jubilees, the more especially as they are connected to something - most likely Kom el-Abd and other conjectural buildings - way to the west of the jubilee palace.

---

20. Thomas, E. (1966) op. cit..
21. Thomas, E. 1966 op. cit. p.189

*Figure 638. A summary overview of the landscape around the WB1 site (Map data: Google, DigitalGlobe).*

# CHAPTER EIGHTEEN
# CONCLUSIONS

Early in this volume the following questions were raised:

- How many shafts were there in total and were these part of a larger burial ground?
- Were these separate tombs connected by robbers' holes or components in a single piece of architecture intentionally connected underground?
- Why were two of the shafts made so large (1.5m by x 3m)?
- Why were the spoil-heaps so immense?
- Why were the tombs not better hidden and was the there always visible surface debris around the shaft tops?
- Why was this remote site chosen?
- Why are the tombs situated on such open, exposed ground detached from the main Theban massif?
- Who were the people buried here?

Whilst the details are still being worked on and will be the subject of study for some years to come, the answers to most of these questions are now known. The answers to the first five questions can be given with some confidence.

There are seven shafts on the site but only four of these were developed into tombs. They are not part of a larger burial ground and there are no other burials in the vicinity of these closely-grouped shafts.

Three of the tombs show a combination unique in Egyptian funerary architecture of shafts, multiple chambers off the shafts in opposing directions and chambers on different levels. The architectural complexity of the tombs seems to derive principally from their being repeatedly enlarged to accommodate new burials. The two largest tombs (Shafts Two and Four) most likely received the burials of the most senior people and would have seen the introduction not only of large sarcophagi but also, possibly of shrine panels. This would account for the size of the shafts.

There are probably two factors behind the size of the spoil-heaps. First the sheer volume of the tombs and, second, given that the architectural debris was never moved away from the site, it seems likely - though this is conjecture - that material was brought in to landscape the site and cover the shafts once they had been sealed with the gypsum and aggregate closure which has survived in places around the tops of the shafts (*Figure 443*).

---

1. cf WV24 1.63m by 2.7m; KV40 2m by 2.24m; KV56 1.6m by 2.42m; KV58 1.49m by 1.98m. Only KV27 has similarly large dimensions being 1.48m by 3.2m.
2. It is worth bearing mind that, windborne debris aside, the spoil-heaps would originally have been bigger by the volume of material equal to that which had fallen back into the tomb chambers.

The choice of such an exposed site is less easily accounted for. It is exposed to the sun, unlike the known burial sites in the Western Wadis, as has been observed above. As the theology of Amenhotep III's reign developed and he became more and more closely identified with the sun-disc it may have been increasingly important for members of his family and court to express their own identification with this solarisation. We have also noted that the site chosen is one from which it is possible to see the prepared road which circumnavigates the raised ground of the WB1 plateau. It is an eminence from which it is possible to see most of the vast floodplain of the Wadi Bairiya stretching south-east towards the modern cultivation. The line of the cultivation may well have been much further north in the XVIIIth dynasty given both the much wetter climate (with frequent light precipitation) and the very different path of the Nile's branches as they passed through the area encompassed by the modern name Luxor.

The site was connected to the vicinity of Malqata by the Western Farchout Road. In the 1980s the prepared road route heading south from the WB1 site down the western side of the Wadi Bairiya floodplain penetrated much further south beyond the area currently obscured by sand extraction from the surface and from quarries. It went much further in the direction of Kom el-Abd[3]. As stated, the main wash from the Wadi Haybah, to the west of the Wadi Bairiya, and the second of two main channels at the bottom of the Wadi Bairiya both drain towards the Nile in the region of Kom el-Abd (which has survived because it is on relatively high ground). The site was therefore most likely connected to Kom el-Abd but also possibly to something in the region of Kom el-Abd which has been washed away. Roads move between destinations and there must have been something at the southern end of the prepared road.

The site was not, therefore, isolated. Its remoteness has to be seen in the context of an environment which was then more habitable. Even if this region was described in the XVIIIth dynasty as 'desert' it was not the wasteland we see today but the landscape portrayed in the blocks ultimately from Kom el-Hettan and referred to in Chapter Seventeen. These show ponds, canals, shrubs, trees, hares, goats, ostriches, jackals (or wolves) and chariots. If our analysis of both the climate and the use of the landscape for sourcing raw materials is correct then this was a busy and much-frequented area.

The Theban Necropolis appears to have spread steadily west and then north during the XVIIIth dynasty as described in our first publication[4]. A few burials of members of the royal family were located in what is today called the Valley of the Queens. The Wadi 300, just to the west, contains a further forty-nine burials (at least). Another eight hundred metres to the west a small wadi contains seven characteristically XVIIIth dynasty shaft tombs. A further five hundred metres north-east of that small wadi is Wadi A where the main tombs are the cliff tomb prepared for Hatshepsut and the Baraize tomb. 800m from Hatshepsut's unused tomb is the tomb probably prepared for her daughter, Nefrure, with two incomplete shafts nearby. Just under 300m further north is the cleft in Wadi D with the concealed tomb of the three Syrian wives of Thutmose III.

---

3. Personal correspondence with Dina Faltings.
4. Litherland, P. (2014) op. cit.

There is then a gap to the WB1 site. In distance this is 2.8km. In time this covers the reigns of Amenhotep II and Thutmose IV. In Wadi F, which is between WB1 and Wadi D, graffiti which are unquestionably of pharaonic date, name both Thutmose III (who is portrayed smiting a captive) and Amenhotep II whose two cartouches are clearly portrayed. However, there is no sign of burial activity so far apparent in that wadi[5].

The WB1 site therefore represents the furthest point to which the Theban necropolis expanded to the north and west. For the rest of the New Kingdom the direction in royal burials is centripetal, with a contraction towards the known residential areas. At the end of the New Kingdom and beginning of the Third Intermediate Period this contraction becomes more pronounced with burials which were initially located elsewhere re-buried in single tombs, bodies often being moved several times[6] into caches some of which were located in the Valley of Kings.

The reduction in the extent of the burial ground seems to have taken place for security reasons. If that is correct then the positioning of the WB1 shaft tombs would appear to represent the zenith of a period of confidence and security. This suggestion fits well with a reign in which the agricultural economy was performing well enough for massive building programmes under Amenhotep III to be undertaken. The excavation of Birket Habu and the creation of Akhetaten, which Akhenaten states clearly was undertaken on the instructions of his father the Aten (i.e. Amenhotep III), were hugely expensive and indicative of a thriving agricultural economy.

Such confidence, and the fact that this region was frequented during the reign of Amenhotep III - the cleared strip in the Wadi Haybah indicating further unrealised plans even further west - explains the location and lack of concealment of the WB1 shaft tombs. The stela of Nebamun found by the University of Heidelburg suggests that this site was visited and there may indeed have been some mud-brick superstructure which was destroyed when the burials were attacked and which has now disappeared. The progressive dismantling of the burials is confirmed by the fact that the Nebamun stela fragments were found eight hundred metres away.

Of the people buried here virtually nothing is known which is not derived from the WB1 site itself. The only exception to this is the connection with the TT90 tomb of Nebamun. The abandonment of his Sheik Abd el-Qurna tomb and Nebamun's burial in one of the WB1 shafts (suggested by the canopic fragments in the Egyptian Museum in Cairo and the stela of his found by the University of Heidleberg eight hundred metres from the WB1 site) indicates a change of plan. It seems possible that Nebamun's family was related in some way to the other court women whose burials were in these shaft tombs.

By great good fortune, we have identified from the hieratic inscription on top of her head (*Figure 639*), a canopic jar stopper belonging to a person with the name Iuy

---

5. The total number of burials in these various locations of known and probable XVIIIth dynasty date is over 150. This puts into perspective the question of just how many are still missing.
6. Reeves, C. (1990) "*Valley of the Kings: The Decline of a Royal Necropolis*", Studies in Egyptology, Kegan Paul International, London.

(SV105). Of the few pieces in the Egyptian Museum in Cairo purchased by Legrain in 1903 which we have been able to relocate three belong to people with the same names as daughters of Nebamun: Iuy, Mutnofret and Tawosret. The style of the inscriptions on these jars is similar enough for it to be highly likely that they are not only contemporary with each other but come from the same workshop (*Figure 640*).

Nothing else is known of the Great Wife Nebetnehet or of the Wife of the King and

*Figure 639. The top of the SV105 canopic head. Just visible in the centre are the remains of the black hieratic giving the name "Iuy".*

*Figure 640. Three canopic jar inscriptions from the WB1 site and now in the Egyptian Museum in Cairo. All are have similar inlays and hieroglyphic styles.*

Ornament of the King Henut. These women appear on no temple scenes and in no other tombs. A single faience jar naming a Henut is known from the dispersion of the Michaelides collection in Cairo but we have been unable to trace this. Its location is currently unknown. Nothing is known of the Son of the King Menkheperre. Judging by the style of the one surviving head from his canopic suite, he was born towards the end of the reign of Amenhotep III. The size of his canopic jars suggests he was a child but it is not possible to know how young. If Nebetnehet was his mother (which is likely from the juxtaposition of their surviving grave goods in Shaft Four) her being of child-bearing age towards the end of the reign of Amenhotep III would position her as a younger wife of the king. Amenhotep III's death soon after the period during which she flourished may help explain why she appears on no surviving monuments of the king[7].

One of the other royal women buried in the WB1 shaft tombs, and fragments of whose canopic jars were recovered from Shaft Three, was a Daughter of the King, Tiaa. Another fragment of her canopic jar is in the Petrie Museum at University College London[8].

A wooden docket recovered from the first of the two Rhind Tombs and now in Edinburgh describes a Tiaa who is the daughter of a king and identifies that king as Thutmose IV[9]. One of the other dockets in this Rhind Tomb refers to an XVIIIth dynasty mummy of Nebetia (a grand-daughter of the king and re-buried at the same time as Tiaa). The docket makes reference to a year 27. This would most likely be year 27 of Amenhotep III[10]. A daughter of Thutmose IV (and thus sister or half-sister of Amenhotep III) who died around Year 27 would fit the range of usage of the WB1 tombs. The absence of any mention of canopic equipment in the Rhind Tomb also suggests re-burial."

There is a remote possibility that these Tiaas could be the same person. However, such an identification is problematic insofar as it suggests the burials at the WB1 site were re-organised during the reign of Amenhotep III. This is just possible. On the other hand, Tiaa is a relatively common name and it is more likely that there was more than one Tiaa at the court bridging the reigns of Thutmose IV and Amenhotep III.

The assumption that these tombs were created for a group of people who were related is suggested by two factors: one, the way in which the tombs nest together in a fairly small, distinctive location; two, from the fact that the vast majority of humerus bones recovered from the tombs have the same genetic variation in the form of a septal aperture of the coranoid fossa. As noted, this is a trait shared by several royal mummies but its occurrence in a very high percentage of the people identified in these tombs suggests a marked degree of consanguinity.

✳✳✳

These initial questions do not cover the entire scope of what has been revealed by our

---

7. It is equally possible that some of the figures of king's wives currently attributed to Tiye (and which bear little resemblance to her other potraits) may be of Nebetnehet.
8. UCL15809
9. Dodson, A. and Janssen, J. (1989) op. cit. pp. 125-138.
10. Aidan Dodson (personal correspondence) now believes these dockets to have been written in the XVIIIth dynasty. Similar dockets found at WB1 support the view that these dockets relate not to re-burials but to the original burials and this in turn supports and XVIIIth dynasty date.

work. Perhaps the most puzzling questions which follow on from those we asked initially are why these tombs were deliberately destroyed and when this destruction took place.

The canopic jars could have been damaged during robberies. However, chisels were used to break these vessels into many pieces. A great deal of time and effort is required to break over 200 stone vessels into ten times that number of fragments. The archaeological evidence suggests that the tombs were completely emptied of their contents at some stage and this too is not consistent with mere robbery. The lower chambers in Shaft Five, untouched by modern robbers, contained disarticulated human remains, stripped of all coverings, a few storage jars containing embalming refuse and nothing else of value. Notably, there were no canopic jars in these chambers.

No evidence has survived within the tombs to indicate when this clearance of the tombs might have happened. There are a few Third Intermediate Period sherds amongst the ceramics recovered from the spoil-heaps and these confirm that there were visitors to the site during that period. The discovery of the names of the Aten might be suggested as a reason for the destruction. However, there are many canopic jars which bear no references to the Aten and many valuable objects which could easily have been re-used during a period in which we know that Butehamun was clearing burials to re-cycle their contents. They were all broken up instead.

The Ramesside kings are said to have harboured particular antipathy towards Akhenaten[11] but there is nothing to associate these women with Akhenaten. Their sole connection seems to have been with the court of Amenhotep III. The only king mentioned on the site is "Nebmaatre", although he is often referred to merely as "The Dazzling Aten".

Possible explanations must include the perpetration of some ancient crime against the king, possibly a court vendetta of some sort. Akhenaten himself is known for his destructive tendencies. In his reign Kiya disappears from view, albeit leaving more evidence than survives for Nebetnehet and Henut. One can speculate about rivalries between court women and between Tiye, in particular, and any challengers to her unusually powerful position in the reigns of both Amenhotep III and Akhenaten. There is no evidence to support such speculation.

For the moment the issue of why and when an entire family group of royal women at the court of Amenhotep III, headed by a Great Wife of the King, Nebetnehet, was destroyed and very successfully erased from history must remain one of the enduring mysteries from these tombs.

The epithets of these court women provide new insights into the structure of the court of Amenhotep III and work on the transliteration and translation of the texts will be presented in the volume in this series covering the Stone Vessels. Our current understanding of these epithets is that they refer to religious offices rather than to anything more salacious[12].

---

11. See for instance Murnane, W. (1999) "*The Return to Orthodoxy*" in ed. Freed, R., Markowitz, Y. and D'Auria, S. (1999) "Pharaohs of the Sun", Museum of Fine Arts, Boston, Bullfinch Press/Little, Brown & Co., Boston p. 185.
12. contra the suggestions of Millet, N. 1988 op. cit..

The ceramics confirm a date range for these tombs from early in the reign of Amenhotep III to the end of his reign or beginning of the reign of Akhenaten. The names of the Dazzling Aten in the canopic jar inscriptions and the seals recovered all support this dating and provide specific references to Amenhotep III.

The other fragments of grave goods which have survived provide a range both temporally and in status as would be expected in a hierarchical society and, specifically, in a group of women with differing and carefully-recorded ranks. At the highest levels there is evidence to confirm (from the glass and faience fragments in particular) burials of a standard comparable to that in the KV46 tomb of Yuya and Tuyu. The coffin inlays suggest there were coffins here of a standard better than the KV55 coffin prepared originally for Kiya in the reign of Akhenaten.

The human remains endorse the picture of deliberate destruction of these burials and the number of individuals recovered accords well with the number of canopic jars which have survived. The animal remains are rather more difficult to interpret as it is impossible to distinguish between those animals which may have been interred with the original burials (pet gazelles, for instance) and animals which may have been brought to the site by predators like jackals. The fish bones (which were more or less intact) could have been an offering but they could have been inside the pelican. The moorhen could have been brought by a jackal from the riverbank. On the other hand, it is less easy to explain the presence of a vulture as the result of accidental intrusion.

The preservation under the spoil-heaps of the XVIIIth dynasty surface with its mud-mixing pits, human hand- and foot-prints and many of the tools used in the construction of the tombs has shed new light on how local materials were sourced. However, the most striking result of the clearance of this surface and of the neighbouring huts has been the information which has come to light about the climate.

The evidence for rainfall is impossible to ignore. The entire surface of the WB1 plateau retains the same saturated surface beneath the more recent layers of cracked rock and desert marl. The "wells" where water accumulated and where there is evidence of springs, the erosion at the bottom of the cliffs and, most importantly of all, the plant roots and clear signs of bio-turbation speak of not just occasional rainfall but a sustained level. This was different to the catastrophic occasional rainfall seen every decade or so in modern times. Evidence in the neighbouring wadis supports the view that during the XVIIIth dynasty the soil was held together by plant life and eroded less easily than it did subsequently when the rainfall became less frequent and, consequently, more damaging.

The implications of higher rainfall in the XVIIIth dynasty for understanding better the landscape of the West Bank cannot be overstated. Debate will rage about just when major changes in weather took place but there can be no doubt that agricultural production must have been strong in the two periods in which there is a plethora of ceramic evidence: the early New Kingdom and the Roman Period. The global weather patterns recorded in the Greenland Ice Core data support this pattern.

Inscriptional and written evidence for the New Kingdom effects of the Minoan Warming come in the form of the blocks from Kom el-Hettan portraying the desert in the region of Malqata as full of life, life which we have found in the form of tree and plant roots and animal dung. There is then evidence of a change in weather patterns in the weakening of government in the later New Kingdom with rising grain prices and failures to deliver grain.

The recovery in rainfall suggested by the Greenland Ice Core data in the Roman period is supported not only by the ceramics we have found scattered across the landscape but by the presence of Coptic shelters near water pools and by written evidence recording the wetter weather in the Eastern Mediterranean.

Whether or not climate change could have been a contributing factor to some of the Amarna period upheavals is impossible to prove especially as the dating of changes in weather patterns remains imprecise. However, the apparent abandonment of the huge investment which had taken place on the West and East Banks under Amenhotep III is not easily dismissed as a mere whim of pharaoh. There must have been a powerful trigger for something which seems to have been quite sudden. The unfinished tombs at WB1 and the rudimentary state of the work on whatever the cleared strip was intended to be also suggest haste.

***

When we began work on clearing these shaft tombs and extending our survey of the landscape around them we believed that we were dealing with some remote tombs deliberately placed in the desert, possibly for safety.

However, we now know first of all that they were not built in the desert. This region was not desert at the time (as we understand the meaning of that word). It was a region filled with shrubs, bushes, and small trees. The wadi floors would have held gazelles, hares, wild cattle and possibly even lions.

Second, it was not remote. There was a main arterial road crossing the site from Malqata to Farchout which was used frequently and which was officially managed with water supplied in wells and cisterns. There were also prepared roads, leading from Kom el-Abd to the WB1 site and reaching deep into the Wadi el-Agaala. These can only have been prepared for the king. Their width and the carefully prepared flat surface indicate that they were not used for people on foot but for chariots. Our hypothesis is that these were chariot roads possibly prepared for the king to hunt game.

Other work in the wadis has shown that people have been visiting these wadis to collect a mud rich in natural gypsum for use as plaster, to collect tufla for plaster and to collect flints which were used extensively throughout the pharaonic period.

Graffiti in the Wadi el-Gharby and our study of the geology there suggests a much kinder landscape in which certain wadis would have held water for extended periods. This water would have attracted all manner of wildlife, including duck and other wildfowl. These in turn would have attracted hunters. In the WB1 shaft tombs we have found the bones of pelicans and moorhens. The bones of pelicans and moorhens in the WB1 shaft tombs can be explained in a number of ways but however this is done they speak of an environment different to that of today.

An overall picture emerges of a much-used landscape very different from today's emptiness. Within that landscape members of a family closely connected with the king were buried in tombs exposed to the sun. Judging by the inscriptions on their canopic jars, these very senior members of the court were closely engaged in the cult of "the Dazzling Aten" - in other words of the deified Amenhotep III himself.

We very much hope to continue our work and in particular to try to establish an explanation for the destruction of the burials of intimate members of the family of Amenhotep III. The next volume in this series will cover the Stone Vessels and further volumes are planned to provide a fuller catalogue of the finds. We will also be publishing our continuing work in the Western Wadis concentrating in particular on the graffiti and climate.

These tombs have brought to light a group of people never recognised before. Despite the deliberate destruction of the burials and robberies which must have taken place throughout the three thousand three hundred years since the shaft tombs were closed it is surprising what has survived. As discussed, the re-assembled canopic jars from this site represent the largest collection of canopic jars ever found in Egypt. Despite this wealth of material the resultant information has raised as many new questions as it has answered. The central mystery of the fate of the royal women buried here and the destruction of their tombs may remain unresolved for many decades.

# APPENDIX ONE - DIMENSIONS OF THE TOMBS

| | TOMB DIMENSIONS | | | |
|---|---|---|---|---|
| | Height | Width (E-W) | Length (N-S) | Height off the ground |
| **Shaft One** | 1.40 m | 1.15 m | 2.30 m | |
| **Shaft Two** | | | | |
| Shaft | 7.80m - 8.08m | 1.50m | 3.00m | |
| Chamber A | 2.73 | 3.6 | 5.62 | |
| *Chamber A1* | 1.50m | 0.96m | 1.10m deep | |
| *Chamber A2* | 1.90m | 1.10m | 1.20m | |
| Chamber Aa | 1.60m | 2.87m | 3.62m | |
| Chamber Ab | 1.45m | 2.25m | 1.80m | |
| Chamber B | 3.16 | 3.8 | 3.4 | |
| Chamber Ba | 1.1 | 3.6 | 4.25 | |
| Chamber Bb | 1.95m - 1.70m | 5.70m | 4.05m | |
| Chamber Bc | 2.3 - 2.6 | 4.55 | 4.2 | |
| Chamber Bca | 1.60m | 2.70m | 1.10m | The floor level is higher, by about 0.81m, than the floor level of chamber Bc |
| *Chamber Bc1* | 0.95 | 1.35 | 0.95 | 0.85 |
| *Chamber Bc2* | 0.85 | 1.2 | 1.1 | 0.85 |
| *Chamber Bc3* | 1.1 | 1.2 | 1.1 | 0.85 |
| *Chamber Bc4* | 1.8 | 1.2 | 1.1 | |
| Chamber Bd | 1.80m | 4.65m | 1.35m | |
| **Shaft Three** | | | | |
| Shaft | 7.95 m | 2.62 m | 1.40m | |
| Chamber A | 1.70m | 3.40m | 5.80m | |
| Chamber Aa | 0.90m high | 1.95m | 1.60m | The floor is higher than the floor level of Chamber A by about 0.65m |
| Chamber Ab | 0.95m - 1.45m | 2.05m | 2.90m | |
| **Shaft Four** | | | | |
| Shaft | 7.60m deep | 1.45m | 3m | |
| Chamber A | 2.60m | 4.20m | 5.20m | |
| Chamber A1 | 1.20m high | 1.00m | 1.15m depth | |
| Chamber Aa | 1.57m | 2.45m | 3.20m | |
| Chamber B | 2.46m | 4.00 m | 3.20 : 6.50 m | |
| *Chamber B1* | | 1m wide | 1m depth | The floor level of niche 1 is higher, by about 0.67m, than the level of chamber B floor. |
| *Chamber B2* | | 1m wide | 1m depth | |
| *Chamber B3* | | 0.90m wide | 1.16m deep | |
| *Chamber B4* | | 0.80m | 0.98m deep | |
| Chamber Ba | 1.90m | 4.25 m | 6.15 m | |
| Chamber Ba1 | 1.30m | 1m | 0.88m deep | The floor level higher by 0.60m than chamber floor level |
| Chamber Ba2 | 1.17m | 1.10m | 1.10m deep | The floor level is higher, by 0.70m, than the floor level of chamber Ba |
| Chamber Ba3 | 1.08m | 0.95m | 1.08m deep | The floor level is higher, about 0.80m, than the floor level of chamber Ba |
| Chamber Ba4 | 1.25m | 1.05m | 1.17m deep | Its floor level is higher, about 0.85m, than the level floor of chamber Ba |
| Chamber Ba5 | 1.16m | 1.07m | 1m deep | The floor level is higher, about 0.78m, than the floor level of chamber Ba |
| Chamber Bb | 2.15m | 3.90m | 6.90: 7.30m | |
| Chamber Bc | 1.60m | 3m | 3.60m | |
| **Shaft Five** | | | | |
| Shaft | 8.70 - 8.85 m | 1.30m | 2.80 m | |
| Chamber A1 | 0.80 :1.00m | 2.30m | 3.10m | |
| Chamber B1 | 0.90 : 1.20m | 4.45m | 3.75m | |
| Chamber A | 1.50m | 2.10m to 3.30m | 2.45 m to 3.50m | |
| Chamber B | 1.60m | 3.10m | 5.70m | |
| Chamber Ba | 1.20m | 2.90m | 5.05m | |
| *Chamber Ba1* | 1.40m | 1.20m | 1m | |
| *Chamber Ba2* | 1.30m | 1.10m | 1m | |
| *Chamber Ba3* | 1.15m | 1.10m | 1.10m | |
| *Chamber Ba4* | 1.30 m | 0.90m | 0.95m | |
| Chamber Bb | 1.15m | 2.30m | 3.00m | |
| **Shaft Six** | 4.18 - 4.25 m | 1.05 m | 2.25 m | |
| **Shaft Seven** | 1.10 m | 2.75 m | 1.25 m | |

# APPENDIX TWO - MASTER EXPLORATION TACKS

*The red lines show the coverage of the archaeological survey.*

# APPENDIX THREE - FAUNA

## Fauna found in the Wadi el-Agaala and Wadi Bairiya in the seasons 2014-2018

### 1. Egyptian wolf or jackal

There appears to be debate about whether or not the animals found along the desert margins are wolves or jackals. There are at least four pairs of these resident in the area between the Wadi Gabbanat el-Qurud and the Wadi Bairiya. They cover a wide territory stretching up onto the high desert. We have seen them returning from the cultivation in the early morning and have also seen them in the early morning along the high desert section of the Farchout Road.

*Prints of Egyptian wolves or jackals which have been following the footprints of members of the mission.*

### 2. Foxes

The wadis closer to the cultivation contain numbers of desert foxes. These appear to be Nile Red Foxes. A family of these inhabit the main entrance wadi to the Wadi el-Agaala.

## 3. Snakes

*Saharan Cliff-racer above Wadi G.*

We have seen three different types of snake: Saharan Cliff-racers, Horned Vipers and a small, thin snake of the Psammophis family.

## 4. Lizards and geckos

We have seen many geckos in the Wadi el-Agaala and Wadi Bairiya. These tend to scare easily and disappear before they can be photographed. Also resident around the WB1 site were several Agama lizards, very pale and well-camouflaged.

*An Agama lizard on the WB1 site.*

*A gecko in Wadi Bairiya.*

## 5. Birds

The WB1 site is home to a nesting pair of White-crowned Wheatears and attracts a large number of Trumpeter Finches. Brown-backed Ravens nest in the Wadi el-Agaala and Sand Grouse and Nile Valley Sunbirds are occasionally seen.

*White-crowned Wheatear perched on a water jar on the WB1 site.*

# SOURCES OF ILLUSTRATIONS

Unless otherwise stated all photographs, maps and drawings were created by the New Kingdom Research Foundation. Satellite images unless otherwise stated were purchased from Mapmart.

Figure 1      Map data: Google, DigitalGlobe.

Figure 76     Reproduced with the permission of University of Strasbourg.

Figure 77     Reproduced with the permission of University of Strasbourg.

Figure 91     Adapted from Leblanc, C. 1989 "Architecture et évolution chronologique des tombes de la Vallée des Reines", BIFAO 89, Le Caire pp. 227–47.

Figure 92     NKRF and adapted from Arnold, D. 2003 "An Encyclopaedia of Egyptian Architecture", I.B. Tauris & Co. Ltd, London and New York p161

Figure 165    NKRF: Egyptian Museum, Cairo.

Figure 178    Reproduced with the permission of University of Strasbourg.

Figure 181    Reproduced with permission of Griffith Institute, University of Oxford.

Figure 182    Photograph and permission purchased from British Museum.

Figure 238    Reproduced with the permission of Sandro Vannini.

Figure 240    From "The tomb of Queen Meryet-Amūn at Thebes by H.E. Winlock" published in 1932 by the Metropolitan Museum in Publications of the Metropolitan Museum of Art Egyptian Expedition, volume 6. Photograph by Harry Burton.

Figure 246    NKRF: Egyptian Museum, Cairo.

Figure 247    NKRF: Egyptian Museum, Cairo.

Figure 255    NKRF: Egyptian Museum, Cairo.

Figure 256    NKRF: Egyptian Museum, Cairo.

Figure 260    NKRF: Egyptian Museum, Cairo.

Figure 306    Egyptian Museum, Cairo/Antikenmuseum Basel und Sammlung Ludwig - Inv. BSAe 1307.

Figure 327    Getty Images. Copyright Getty Images.

Figure 329    Reproduced with permission of Griffith Institute, University of Oxford.

Figure 343    Getty Images. Copyright Getty Images.

Figure 361    Photo by Nicola Dell'Aquila and Federico Taverni /Museo Egizio, Turin.

Figure 379    Adapted from Hayes, W. 1951.

Figure 384    Davis, T. 1907 Plate XXI.

Figure 625    Anus, P. (1971). Reproduced with permission of the service des archives et collections de l'Ifao (© Ifao).

Figure 626    Anus, P. (1971). Reproduced with permission of the service des archives et collections de l'Ifao (© Ifao).

Figure 628    Reproduced with the permission of Dr Hourig Sourouzian.

Figure 638    Map data: Google, DigitalGlobe.

Figure 634    Adapted from Greenland Ice Core data.

Figure 640    Map data: Google, DigitalGlobe.

# SELECT BIBLIOGRAPHY

ALLEN, J. (2002) "The Heqanakht Papyri", Metropolitan Museum of Art, New York

ANDREWS, C. (1990) "Ancient Egyptian Jewellery", British Museum Press, London.

ANUS, P. (1971) "Un domaine thébain d'époque <amarnienne>. Sur quelques blocs de remploi trouvé à Karnak", BIFAO 69 pp69-88

ARNOLD, D. (1991) "Building in Ancient Egypt", Oxford University Press, Oxford.

ARNOLD, D. (2003) "The Encyclopaedia of Ancient Egyptian Architecture", I.B. Tauris & Co. Ltd, London and New York

AUBRY, M. et al. (2008) "Pharaonic Necrostratigraphy: A review of Geological and Archaeological Studies in the Theban Necropolis, Luxor, West Bank, Egypt" Terra Nova, 21 (4).

AYRTON, E. (1908) "Recent Discoveries in the Biban el Moluk", PSBA 30.

BACHTALY, C. et al (1961) "Le Monastère de Phoebammon dans la Thébaïde", Société d'archéologie copte, Le Caire

BAKER, B., DUPRAS, T. and TOSHERI, M. (2005) "The Osteology of Infants and Children", Texas A&M University Press, United States of America.

BASEL, University of: http://aegyptologie.unibas.ch/forschung/projekte/university-of-basel-kings-valley-project

BASS, W. (1987) "Human Osteology: A Laboratory and Field manual", Missouri Archaeological Society, Columbia, Missouri, United States of America.

BELL, M. (1990) "An Armchair Excavation of KV55", JARCE XXVII pp89-137.

BERMAN, L. (1998) "Overview of Amenhotep III and His Reign" in ed. O'Conner, D. and Cline, E. (1998) "Amenhotep III: Perspectives on His Reign", The Universty of Michigan Press, Ann Arbor, United States of America.

BREASTED, J., (1906) "Ancient Records of Egypt - Volume II", The University of Chicago Press, Chicago.

BROCK, L. (1995) "Theodore Davis and the Rediscovery of Tomb 55" in Wilkinson, R., ed. (1995), "Valley of the Sun Kings: New Expeditions in the Tombs of the Pharaohs", University of Arizona Egyptian Expedition, Tucson.

BROCK, L. (1997) "The Final Clearance of KV 55" in "Ancient Egypt, the Aegean, and the Near East, Studies in Honor of Martha Rhoads Bell", Van Siclen Publications, San Antonio. pp121-136.

BIERBRIER, M. (1989) "The Tomb Builders of the Pharaohs", American University in Cairo Press.

BRYAN B. (2001) "Temples of Millions of Years" in Kent R. Weeks ed. (2001) "The Treasures of the Valley of the Kings: Tombs and Temples of the Theban West Bank in Luxor", American University in Cairo Press, Cairo.

BRYAN, B. (2000) "The Eighteenth Dynasty before the Amarna Period" Chapter 9 in Shaw, I. ed. (2000) "Oxford History of Ancient Egypt", Oxford University Press, Oxford.

BUIKKSTRA, J. and UBELAKER, D. eds (1994) "Standards for data collection from human skeletal remains", Arkansas Archaeological Research Report Vol. 44, Fayettville, Arkansas, United States of America.

CARNARVON and CARTER, H. (1912) "Five Years' Exploration at Thebes", Oxford University Press, Oxford.

CARTER, H., (1917) "A Tomb Prepared for Queen Hatshepsuit and Other Recent Discoveries at Thebes", Journal of Egytian Archaeology, Volume 4 pp 107-118.

ČERNÝ, J. (1965) "Hieratic Inscriptions from the Tomb of Tutankhamun", Griffith Institute, Oxford University Press, Oxford.

ČERNÝ, J. (2001) "A Community of Workmen at Thebes in the Ramesside Period". Institut francais d'archéologie orientale, Le Caire.

ČERNÝ, J.C, and SADEK, A. (1971) "Graffiti de la montagne thébaine", Institut francais d'archéologie orientale, Le Caire.

CLINE, E. and O'CONNOR, D., ed. (2006) "Thutmose III", The University of Michigan Press, Ann Arbor.

COQUE, R. et al (1972) "Graffiti de la Montagne Thebaine I,3 Complements aux secteurs A et C, Frange du Sahara Thebain", CEDAE, Le Caire.

DABBS, G. & DAVIS, H. (2013) http://www.amarnaproject.com/documents/pdf/STC-2013-bioarchaeology.pdf

DAVIES, N. (1923) "The Tombs of Two Officials of Tuthmosis the Fourth", The Egypt Exploration Society, London.

DAVIS, T. (1907) "The Tomb of Iouiya and Touiyou", Archibald Constable & Co. Ltd, London.

DAVIS, T. (1910) "The Tomb of Queen Tiyi", Constable & Co. Ltd, London.

DODSON, A. (2009) "Amarna Sunset", The American University in Cairo Press, Cairo.

DODSON, A. (2000) "The Burial of the Royal Family during the Eighteenth Dynasty" in Hawass, Z. ed. (2000) "Egyptology at the Dawn of the Twenty-First Century: Proceedings of the Eighth International Congress of Egyptologists", American University in Cairo Press Cairo.

DODSON, A. and HITTON, D. (2004) "The Complete Royal Families of Ancient Egypt", Thames & Hudson, London.

DODSON, A. and IKRAM, S. (1998) "The Mummy in Ancient Egypt", Thames & Hudson, London.

DODSON, A. and IKRAM, S. (2008) "The Tomb in Ancient Egypt", Thames & Hudson, London.

DODSON, A. and JANSSEN, J. (1989) "A Theban Tomb and Its Tenants", The Journal of Egyptian Archaeology, Vol. 75, pp. 125-138

DORFMAN, P. and BRYAN, B. (2007) "Sacred Space and Sacred Function in Ancient Thebes", Oriental Institute of the University of Chicago, Chicago.

DORN, A. (2016) "Choosing the Location for a Royal Tomb, the Workmen's Techniques and Tools, Units of Measurement, KV Huts and Workplaces" in ed. Wilkinson, R. and Weeks, K. (2016) "Oxford Handbook of the Valley of the Kings", OUP.

DUHIG, C., (2000) 'They are eating people here! Skeletal indicators of stress in the Egyptian First Intermediate Period.' Unpublished PhD thesis, University of Cambridge.

DZIOBEK, E., HOVELER-MILLER, M. and LOEBEN, C. ed. (2009) "The Mysterious Tomb 63: The latest discovery in the Valley of the Kings",Verlag Marie Leidorf GMBH, Rahden.

EDGERTON, W. (1951) "The Strikes in Ramses III's Twenty-Ninth Year", Journal of Near Eastern Studies. 10.3 pp. 137-145.

EID, Y. (1984) "A newly discovered Stela of Neb-Amon, Chief of the Western Desert Police", ASAE 70.

EL-KHOULI, A. et al (1993) "Stone Vessels, Pottery and Sealings from the Tomb of Tut'ankhamūn", Griffith Institute, Oxford.

FRIEDMANN, F. ed. (1998) "Gifts of the Nile: Ancient Egyptian Faience", Thames & Hudson, London

GABOLDE, L., et al., (1994) 'Le "Tombeau Suspendu" de la "Vallée de l'Aigle"', BIFAO 94 (1994), p. 173-259

GARDINER, A. and WEIGALL, A. (1913) "A Topographical Catalogue of the Private Tombs of Thebes", Bernard Quaritch, London.

GOODMAN, S. M. and P. MEININGER, P. (eds.) (1989) "The Birds of Egypt", Oxford University

Press, Oxford.

GRAEFE, E. and BELOVA, G. (2010) "The Royal Cache TT320", SCA Press, Cairo.

GRAHAM, A., STRUTT, K., HUNTER, M., PENNINGTON, B.,. TOONEN, W. and BARKER, D. (2014) "Theban Harbours and Waterscapes Survey, 2014", Journal of Egyptian Archaelogy 100 pp 35-47.

GRÄZER OHARA, A. (2012) "Le palais des monts sur un bloc de remploi de Karnak: marou d'Amon et/ou complexe jubilaire d'Amenhotep III à Malqata ?", BIFAO 112, Le Caire pp. 191-214.

HAGEN, F. (2016) "On Some Movements of the Royal Court in New Kingdom Egypt" in Van Dijk, J. ed. (2016) "Another Mouthful of Dust", Orientalia Lovaniensa Analecta 246, Peeters, Leiden.

HAENY, G. (1998) "New Kingdom 'Mortuary Temples' and 'Mansions of Millions of Years'" in Shafer, B. ed. 1998 "Temples of Ancient Egypt". I.B. Tauris, London.

HARRINGTON, N. (2013) "Living with the Dead", Oxbow Books, Oxford.

HART, G. (1986) "A Dictionary of Egyptian Gods and Goddesses", Routledge & Kegan Paul, London & New York.

HARRIS, J. and WENTE, E. (1980) ed. "An X-Ray Atlas of the Royal Mummies", University of Chicago Press, Chicago.

HAUSER, G. & de STEFANO, G. (1989) "Epigenetic Variants of the Human Skull", E. Schweizerbart'sche Verlagsbuchhandlung (Nägele u. Obermiller), Stuttgart, Germany.

HAWASS, Z. (2009) "The Lost Tombs of Thebes", Thames & Hudson. London.

HAYES, W. (1935) "Sarcophagi of the XVIIIth Dynasty", University Press, Princeton.

HAYES, W. (1951) "Inscriptions from the Palace of Amenhotep III", Journal of Near Eastern Studies Vol. 10, No. 1. pp. 35-56.

HAYES, W. (1959) "The Scepter of Egypt: Part II", Metropolitan Museum of Art, New York.

HILLIER, J., BUNBURY, J. and GRAHAM, A. (2007) "Monuments on a migrating Nile", Journal of Archaeological Science, 34 (7).

HOULIHAN, P. (1988) "The Birds of Ancient Egypt", American University in Cairo, Cairo.

HORNUNG E. (1982) "Tal der Könige", Artemis Verlag, Zurich and Munich.

HORNUNG, E. (1982) (trans. Baines, J.) "Conceptions of God in Ancient Egypt", Cornel University Press, New York.

HORNUNG, E. (2001A) "Funerary Literature in the Tombs of Valley of the Kings" in Kent R. Weeks ed. (2001) "The Treasures of the Valley of the Kings: Tombs and Temples of the Theban West Bank in Luxor" American University in Cairo Press, Cairo.

IKRAM, S. (1995) "Choice Cuts: Meat Production in Ancient Egypt", Peeters, Leuven.

IKRAM, S. and DODSON, A., (1998) "The Mummy in Ancient Egypt", Thames & Hudson, London.

IKRAM, S. and ISKANDER, N. (2002) "Catalogue General of Egyptian Museum: Non-human Mummies", Supreme Council of Antiquities Press, Cairo.

JAMES, T. (2001) "The Tomb of Horemheb" in Weeks, K. ed. (2001) "The Treasures of the Valley of the Kings: Tombs and Temples of the Theban West Bank in Luxor", American University in Cairo Press, Cairo.

JANOT, F. (2008) "The Royal Mummies", American University in Cairo Press, Cairo.

KEMP, B. (1977) "A Building of Amenophis III at Kôm el-'Abd", The Journal of Egyptian Archaeology, Vol. 63, pp. 71-82.

KEMP, B. (2012) "The City of Akhenaten and Nefertiti: Amarna and its People", Thames & Hudson, London.

KILLEN, G. (2017A) "Ancient Egyptian Furniture: Volume I: 4000-1300 BC" Second Edition,

Oxbow Books, Oxford.

KILLEN, G. (2017B) "Ancient Egyptian Furniture: Volume II: Boxes, Chests and Footstools" Second Edition, Oxbow Books, Oxford.

KLEIN, R. and CRUZ-URIBE, K. (1984) "The Analysis of Animal Bones from Archaeological Sites" The University of Chicago Press, Chicago, United States of America.

KONDO, J. (2013) "A Preliminary Report on the Re-clearance of the Tomb of Amenophis III (WV 22)" in Reeves, C.N. ed. (1992) "After Tutankhamun: Research and Excavation in the Royal Necropolis at Thebes", KPI, London.

KONDO, J. (1995) "The Re-clearance of Tombs WV 22 and WV A in the Western Valley of the Kings" in Wilkinson, R. ed. (1995), "Valley of the Sun Kings: New Expeditions in the Tombs of the Pharaohs", University of Arizona Egyptian Expedition, Tucson.

KOZLOFF, A., (2012) "Amenhotep III: Egypt's Radiant Pharaoh", Cambridge University Press, Cambridge.

KOZLOFF, A. and BRYAN, B. (1992) "Egypt's Dazzling Sun: Amenhotep III and His World", Cleveland Museum of Art, Cleveland, United States of America.

KLEMM, R. and KLEMM, D. (2008) "Stones and Quarries In Ancient Egypt", British Musuem Press, London.

LEBLANC, C. (1989) "Architecture et évolution chronologique des tombes de la Vallée des Reines", BIFAO 89, Le Caire pp. 227–47.

LEGRAIN, G. (1903) "Fragments de Canopes", ASAE Vol 4, Le Caire pp. 138-149.

LEGRAIN, G. (1904) "Seconde Note sur des Fragements de Canopes", ASAE Vol 5, Le Caire pp, 139-141.

LILYQUIST, C. (2003) "The Tomb of the Three Foreign Wives of Tutmose III", Metropolitan Museum of Art, New York.

LITHERLAND, P. (2013) "The Western Wadis of the Theban Necropolis", New Kingdom Research Foundation, London.

LITHERLAND, P. (2016A) "Skaktgravene i Wadi Bairiya - Den Gliterende Atens hustruer og hofdamer og deres familiegrave", Papyrus 36/2.

LITHERLAND, P. (2016) "The Archaeological Future of the Valley of the Kings" in Van Dijk, J. ed. (2016) "Another Mouthful of Dust", Orientalia Lovaniensa Analecta 246, Peeters, Leiden.

MAITLAND, M. (2017) "One Theban tomb, 1000 years of burial". Egyptian Archaeology (50); pp. 44-46.

MANNICHE, L. (2011) "I slutningen af 18 dynasti", Papyrus 31/1.

MARTIN, G. (1989) "The Royal Tomb at El-Amarna" Volumes I & II, EES, London

McDOWELL, A. (1999) "Village Life in Ancient Egypt", OUP, Oxford.

McCORMICK, M., BÜNTGEN, U., CANE, M., COOK, E., HARPER, K., , HUYBERS, P., LITT, T., MANNING, S., MAYEWSKI, P., MORE, A., NICOLUSSI, K., TEGEL, W. (2012) "Climate Change during and after the Roman Empire: Reconstructing the Past from Scientific and Historical Evidence", Journal of Interdisciplinary History, xliii:2, pp.169–220.

MILES, J. (1998) "Pharaohs' Birds", Miles and Miles of Countryside, Cairo.

MILLET, N. (1988) "Some Canopic Fragments of the Reign of Amenhotep III", GM 104 pp. 91-93.

MURNANE, W. (1999) "The Return to Orthodoxy" in ed. Freed, R., Markowitz, Y. and D'Auria, S. (1999) "Pharaohs of the Sun", Museum of Fine Arts, Boston, Bullfinch Press/Little, Brown & Co., Boston.

MURRAY, H. & NUTTALL, M. (1963) "A Handlist to Howard Carter's Catalogue of Objects in Tut'ankhamūn's Tomb", Griffith Insitute, OUP.

NAVILLE, E. (1907) "The XIth Dynasty Temple at Deir el-Bahari: Volume I", Egypt Exploration Fund, London.

NAVILLE, E. (1910) "The XIth Dynasty Temple at Deir el-Bahari: Volume II", Egypt Exploration Fund, London.

NAVILLE, E. (1913) "The XIth Dynasty Temple at Deir el-Bahari: Volume III", Egypt Exploration Fund, London.

NICHOLSON, P. (1993) "Egyptian Faience and Glass", Shire Publications.

NICHOLSON, P. & HENDERSON, J. (2000) "Glass" pp194-224 in Nicholson, P. and Shaw, I. ed. (2000) "Ancient Egyptian Materials and Technology", Cambridge.

NICHOLSON, P. and SHAW, I. ed. (2000) "Ancient Egyptian Materials and Technology", Cambridge University Press, Cambridge.

ORTNER, D. & PUTSCHAR, W. (1985) "Identification of pathological conditions in human skeletal remains", Smithsonian Institution Press, Washington.

PEET, E. (1925) "Fresh Light on the Tomb Robberies of the Twentieth Dynasty at Thebes", Journal of Egyptian Archaeology, Volume 11 1/2 pp. 37-55.

PIACENTINI, P. & ORSENIGO, C. (2004) "La Valle Dei Re Riscoperta", Universita degli Studi di Milano, Milan.

PIANKOFF, A. (1955) "The Shrines of Tut-Ankh-Amon", Pantheon Books, New York.

POLZ, D. (1995) "The Location of the Tomb of Amenhotep I: A Reconsideration", in Ed. Wilkinson, R. (1995) "Valley of the Sun Kings", The University of Arizona Egyptian Expedition, Tucson.

PORTER, B. & MOSS, R. (1964) "Topographical Bibliography of Ancient Egyptian Hieroglyphic Texts, Reliefs, and Paintings I: The Theban Necropolis, Part 2, Royal Tombs and Smaller Cemeteries", Clarendon Press. Oxford.

QUIBELL, J. (1908) "The Tomb of Yuaa and Thuiu", Imprimiere de l'Institut Francais d'Archaeologie Orientale, Le Caire.

QUIRKE, S. (1991) "The Cult of Ra", Thames & Hudson, London.

QUIRKE, S. (1996) "Hieroglyphs and the Afterlife", British Museum Press, London.

QUIRKE, S. ed. (1997) "The Temple in Ancient Egypt", British Museum Press, London.

RAISMAN, V. & MARTIN, G. (1984) "Canopic Equipment in the Petrie Collection", Aris & Phillips, Warminster

RAXTER M. et al. (2008) "Stature estimation in ancient Egyptians: A new technique based on anatomical reconstruction of stature", American Journal of Physical Anthropology, 136(2), pp.147-55.

REEVES, N. (1990) "Valley of the Kings: The Decline of a Royal Necropolis", Studies in Egyptology, Kegan Paul International, London.

REEVES, N., ed. (1992) "After Tutankhamun: Research and Excavation in the Royal Necropolis at Thebes", KPI, London.

REEVES, N. & WILKINSON, R. (1996) "The Complete Valley of the Kings", Thames and Hudson, London.

RHIND, A., (1862) "Thebes: Its Tombs and Their Tenants", Longman, London.

RICHARDS, J. (1999) "Conceptual Landscapes in the Egyptian Nile Valley" in Ashmore, W. and Knapp, A., ed. (1999) "Archaeologies of Landscape", Blackwell, Oxford.

RITNER, R. & MOELLER, N., (2014) "The Ahmose Tempest Stela: An Ancient Egyptian Account of a Natural Catastrophe", ROSAPAT 11.

ROBINS, G. (1993) "Women in Ancient Egypt", British Musuem Press, London.

ROEHRIG, C. (2006) "The Building Activities of Thutmose III in the Valley of the Kings" in Cline, E.

and O'Connor, D., ed. (2006) "Thutmose III" The University of Michigan Press, Ann Arbor.

ROEHRIG, C. (2015) "Royal Tombs of the Eighteenth Dynasty" in ed. Wilkinson, R. and Weeks, K. (2016) "Oxford Handbook of the Valley of the Kings", OUP, Oxford.

ROSE, J. (2000) "Tomb KV39 in the Valley of the Kings", Western Academic & Specialist Press Limited, Bristol.

SAUNDERS, S. & RAINEY, D. (2007) "Nonmetric Trait Variation in the Skeleton: Abnormalities, Anomalies, and Atavisms" in eds Katzenberg, M. and S. R. Saunders, S. (2007) "Biological Anthropology of the Human Skeleton", doi:10.1002/9780470245842.ch17.

SCHAEFER, M., BLACK, S. & SCHEUR, L. (2009) "Juvenile Osteology: A Laboratory and Field Manual", Academic Press, London.

SCHIAPARELLI, E. (1927) "La Tomb Intatta dell'Architetto Kha nella Necropoli di Tebe", Museo di Antichita, Torino.

SCHIFF GIORGINI, M. (1971) "Soleb II. Les Nécropoles", Sansoni, Firenze.

SCHMIDT, H. and WILLEITNER, J. (1994) "Nefertari: Gemahlin Ramses II", Verlag Philipp von Zabern, Mainz am Rhein. pp 106-7.

SCHEUER, L. & S. BLACK, S. (2000) "Developmental Juvenile Osteology", Elsevier Publishing, San Diego and London.

SETHE, K., (1927) "Urkunden der 18. Dynastie, Volume I", Hinrichs, Leipzig

SHAFER, B. ed. (1998) "Temples of Ancient Egypt", I.B. Tauris, London.

SHAW, I. (2003) "Exploring Ancient Egypt", Oxford University Press, Oxford.

SHELLEY, G. (1872) "A handbook to the birds of Egypt", John van Voorst, London, pp293-4.

SOUROZIAN, H. (2015) "L'Art proto-amarnienne au temple d'Amenhotep III a Thebes", Memnonia XXVI pp. 157-177.

STEVENS A., (2012) "Akhenaten's Workers: The Amarna Stone Village Survey 2005-2009 Volumes I & II", Egypt Exploration Society, London

STOCKS, D. (2003) "Experiments in Egyptian Archaelogy", Routledge, London

STROUHAL, E. (2008) "The Memphite Tomb of Horemheb Commander-in-Chief of Tutankhamun IV: Human Skeletal Remains", Egypt Exploration Society, London.

STROUHAL, E. (1992) "Life in Ancient Egypt", Cambridge University Press, Cambridge.

STRUDWICK, N. & H. (1999) "Thebes in Egypt", British Museum Press, London.

STRUDWICK, N. & TAYLOR, J. (2003) "The Theban Necropolis", British Museum Press, London.

SULLIVAN, E. (2010) "Karnak: Development of the Temple of Amun-Ra", UCLA Encyclopaedia of Egyptology, Department of Near Eastern Languages and Cultures, UC Los Angeles.

TAYLOR, J., (2016) "The Egyptian Concept of a Royal Necropolis" in Wilkinson, R. and Weeks, K. ed. (2016) "Oxford Handbook of the Valley of the Kings", OUP.

THOMAS, E. (1966) "The Royal Necropoleis of Thebes", privately printed, Princeton.

TOONEN, W., GRAHAM, A., PENNINGTON, B., HUNTER, M., STRUTT, K., BARKER, D., MASSON-BERGHOFF, A. and EMERY, V. (2017) "Holocene fluvial history of the Nile's west bank at ancient Thebes, Luxor, Egypt, and its relation with cultural dynamics and basin-wide hydroclimatic variability", Geoarchaeology. 2017;1–18. https://doi.org/10.1002/gea.21631

TYLDESLEY, J. (1994) "Daughters of Isis", Viking/Penguin, London.

VAN DIJK, J. (2000) "The Amarna Period and the Later New Kingdom" p. 308 in Shaw, I. ed. (2000) "The Oxford History of Ancient Egypt", Oxford University Press, Oxford.

VANDERSLAYEN, C. (1995) "Who was the First King in the Valley of the Kings?" in Wilkinson, R. ed. (1995) "Valley of the Sun Kings: New Expeditions in the Tombs of the Pharaohs", University of Arizona Egyptian Expedition, Tucson, United States of America.

VERNUS, P. & YOYOTTE, J. (2005) "Bestiare des pharaons", Agnès Viénot Éditions, Paris.

WALDRON, T. (2009) "Palaeopathology", Cambridge University Press, Cambridge.

WALLIS BUDGE, E. (1893) "The Mummy: Chapters on Egyptian Funerary Archaeology", Cambridge University Press, Cambridge

WEEKS, K. ed. (2001) "Valley of the Kings: The tombs and the funerary temples of Thebes West", White Star, Vercelli.

WEEKS, K. (1998) "The Lost Tomb", William Morrow and Company, New York.

WEEKS, K., ed. (2005) "Atlas of the Valley of the Kings: Study Edition", Publications of the Theban Mapping Project, American University in Cairo Press, Cairo.

WENTE, E. (1961) "A letter of complaint to the Vizier To", Journal of Near Eastern Studies 20:4 pp. 252-257

WHITE, T. & FOLKENS, P. (2005) "The human bone manual", Elsevier Academic Press, Burlington, San Diego, London.

WILKINSON, R. (1994) "Symbolic Location and Alignment in New Kingdom Royal Tombs and Their Decoration", Journal of the American Research Center in Egypt 31.

WILKINSON, R. (2003) "The Complete Gods & Goddesses of Ancient Egypt", Thames & Hudson, London.

WILKINSON, R. (2000) "The Complete Temples of Ancient Egypt", Thames & Hudson, London.

WILKINSON, T. (2010) "The Rise and Fall of Ancient Egypt", Bloomsbury, London

WINLOCK, H. (1924) "The Tombs of the Kings of the Seventeenth Dynasty at Thebes", Journal of Egyptian Archaeology 10.

WINLOCK, H. (1932) "The tomb of Queen Meryet-Amūn at Thebes", Publications of the Metropolitan Museum of Art Egyptian Expedition, Volume 6, The Metropolitan Museum of Art, New York.

WINLOCK, H. (1942) "Excavations at Deir el-Bahri 1911-1931", Macmillan, New York.

WINLOCK, H. (2010) "Tutankhamun's Funeral", The Metropolitan Museum of Art, New York.

YOSHIMURA, S. ed. (2008) "Research in the Western Valley of the Kings Egypt – the Tomb of Amenophis III (KV22)", Institute of Egyptology, Waseda University, Tokyo.

ZIVIE, A., (1990) "Découverte à Saqqara: Le vizier oublie", Editions du Seuil, Paris.

ZIVIE, A., (2007) "The Lost Tombs of Saqqara", cara.cara.edition, To

# INDEX

Abdul Ghany layer 20, Figure 17, Figure 18, 108, 371

accessory tubercle 154, Figure 212

age-at-death 152, 161, 166, 167

Ahmose-Nefertari 178

Akhenaten 3, 142, 145, 147, 174, 179, 189, 401, 404, 405

Akhetaten 3, 4, 178, 314, 384, 395, 401

alabaster mining 374-375, Figures 609-611

alabaster vessels 134-136

Amenhotep III 2, 3, 4, 7, 17, 106, 120, 123, 124, 125, 128, 131, 142, 143, Figure 195, 145, 171, 173, 178, 189, 236, 237, 377, Figure 628, 389, 393, 394, 395, 396, 400, 401, 403, 404, 406, 407

Amenhotep III, bull and lion hunts 389

Amherst, Lord 115

amulets 234, Figures 370-372

animal bones in WB1 tombs 388

Anubis fetish 2014-180 Figure 36, 32, 137, Figure 180, Figure 181

Anubis fetish staff 2015-191 Figure 75, 58

Anus, Pierre 385, 386, Figure 625, Figure 626, 393

Aper-el 178, 183

Ay 123

Baraize tomb 400

beer jars (New Kingdom) 17, 146

bio-turbaton on WB1 site Figure 629

birds 250, 251

Birket Habu 3, 6, 401

British Museum 116

Brown-necked raven 253, Figure 406, 255

bull graffito 301, Figure 490

By, Ornament of the King 119

Byzantine sherds 144

camel 250, 251

canopic head SV102 Figure 28, 27

canopic head SV103 Figure 29, 27

canopic head SV104 Figure 31, 29

canopic head SV106 Figure 28, 25

canopic jar SV38 (By) Figure 37, 33

canopic jar SV46 (Mutnofret) Figure 84, 64

canopic jar SV5 (Sati) Figure 37, 33

canopic jar SV6 (Tawosret) Figure 37, 33

canopic jars 7, 115-129

canopic jars, alabaster 128

Carter, Howard 6, 279, 367, 368, 380, 396

cartonnage 226-233 Figures 350-369

cattle 250, 251, 255

ceramics: open forms 145; closed forms 145; stands 145

chariots 385, Figure 626,, 406

chisel marks Figure 159, 126

Clarias 250, 251, 254

clavicle 156

Common moorhen 251, 253, Figure 409

Common wood pigeon 253

copper chisel 272, Figure 434

copper nail 271, Figure 432

coptic belt Figure 23, 24

Coptic period 15, 24, 291, 362

cribra crani 152

cribra orbitalia 152, Figure 208, 161, Figure 217, Figure 218

damage, deliberate 125

Dazzling Aten 122, 123, 173, Figure 347, 237, 394, 404, 405, 407

Deir el-Shelwit 2, 395

Demoiselle crane 251, 252, 253, Figure 405, Figure 406, Figure 407

Description de l'Égypte 3

djed-tyet design 174

dog (African Wild Dog) graffito 301, Figure 491

dog 250, 251

dom-palm nuts 248, Figure 402

donkey graffito 301

donkey prints 268, Figure 426

Dra Abu el-Naga 1, 377

Duamutef 120

duck 406

duck in Wadi F 390

East Bank 1

Egyptian Museum, Cairo 115

El-Qurn 1

Elephantine 396

Eurasian collared-dove 252, 254

evidence of rainfall (WB1 surface) 277, Figure 445

faience 12

faience ankh loops 171

faience bead 170, Figure 232

faience Bes figure 170, Figure 230

faience distribution by weight 170

faience hair-ring 170, Figure 233

faience tiles retaining wood 171, Figure 235

faience tiles, shaped 171

faience wadjet eye 170, Figure 231

falcons in Wadi F 390

Farchout Road 9, 376-38-, Figures 612-618 280, 284

Farchout Road, Eastern 319

Farchout Road, Western 319, 396, 400

Feature 1001 17

Feature 1080 258, Figure 425, 267

Feature 1091 268

Feature 1091 268, Figure 426, Figure 427

Feature 1101 267

Feature 1101 269, Figure 428

Feature 1102 267, Figure 431

Feature 1105 269, Figure 430

Feature 1107 269, Figure 428

Feature 1108 269, Figure 429

femora 149, Figure 206, Figure 207, 158

figs 249, Figure 403

fire damage 128

fires in Shaft Four 176, Figure 243, Figure 244

fish 250, 251, 405

flint collection and working 368-370, Figures 598-602

flint-working sites Figure 597

flora 248-249, Figures 401-404, 263, Figure 420

foundation deposit material 145, Figure 198, Figure 199

Gabolde, Marc 123

gazelle 3, 250, 251, 255, 406

gazelle graffito 389

gerbil 250, 251

glass 12, 176-189, Figures 243-270

glass beads 188, Figure 269

glass bottle 178, Figure 245

glass chevron 2015-45 Figure 67, 54

glass distribution by weight 176

glass eye inlays 187, Figure 266, Figure 267, Figure 268

glass eyebrow inlays 186, Figure 265

glass finger 2015-1 Figure 64, 52, Figure 270

glass funerary mask inlays Figure 257, Figure 258

glass inlay, figurative burned 2016-157 Figure 69, 55

glass inlays Figure 70, 55

glass inlays, burned Figure 71, 56

glass inlays, figurative 180, 181, Figure 249, Figure 250, Figure 251, Figure 252, Figure 253, Figure 254

glass inlays, vertically-striated 184, Figure 259, Figure 260

glass rishi-work chevrons 178, 179, Figure 246, Figure 247, Figure 248, 180

glass wig spirals 185, Figure 263, Figure 264

goat 250, 251, 255

gold 18, 56, 190, Figure 358, 233, Figure 368, Figure 369, 260

gracility 154

graffiti locations Figure 597

graffiti, Arabic 12

Graham, Angus 394

Gräzer Ohara, Aude 386, 393

Great White pelican, 250, 251, 253, 254, Figure 408

Greenland Ice Core data 3, 390, 391, Figure 634, 405, 406

Gurob 147, 396

Hapy 120

hare graffito 301, Figure 631

hares 3, 406

Hat...., Ornament of the King 120

Hat...., Ornament of the King 120

Hathor vessel 147, Figure 201

Hatshepsut cliff-tomb 6, 400

Hedjti, Ornament of the King 119

Heidlberg, University of 382, 401

Henut, Ornament of the King and Wife of the King Figure 35, 32, 118, 121, 402, 404

Henuttaneb 119

Henuy 119

Hooded crow 252

houses 122, 123

human footprint 271, Figure 431

human remains 18, 24, 27, 29, Figure 57, 69, 70, 73, 96, 120, 128, 149-168, Figures 205-227, 404, 405

Hut 11 283, Figure 456, Figure 457

Hut 2 281, Figure 450, Figure 451

Hut 5 282, Figure 452, Figure 453

huts, Type 1 279

huts, Type 2 279

huts, Type 3 280, Figre 454, 455

ilia 149, 152, 167, Figure 225

Imsety 120

incisors, loss of 164, Figure 223

innomates 149, Figure 205, 152, Figure 216, 161

invaginated incisor 164, Figure 224

Isis 120

Itesresu, Ornament of the King 119, 223, Figure 345

Iuy, Ornament of the King 119, 401, 402, Figure 639, Figure 640

jar, beer 146

jar, red-slipped storage 146, Figure 200

jar, Thutmose III period 141, Figure 188, Figure 189

jar, white-painted storage 142, Figure 190, Figure 191, Figure 192, Figure 193, 145

jawbones 149

Kafi, Ornament of the King 119

Karnak 1

King's Son Figure 80, 62

Kiya 404

Kola el-Hamra 2, 6, 382, 385, 395

Kom el-Abd 2, 3, 6, 10, 280, 314, 382, 384, 385, 390, 394, 395, 396, 400, 406

Kom el-Hettan 3, 385, 386, Figure 628, 387, 388, 389, 393, 394, 400, 406

Kom el-Samak 2, 371

KV46 127, Figure 165

KV46 171

KV46 178

KV46 405

KV55 174

KV55 179

KV62 178

Lates niloticus 250, 251

Laughing dove 253, 255

leather 244-245, Figures 393-396

leather shoes 244, Figures 393-4

leaves 248, Figure 401

Legrain, Georges 59, 115, 118, 119, 120, Figure 157, 123, 124, 402

lids 132-136

linen 241-243, Figures 386-392

lion graffito 389

lions 3, 406

lithics 17, 274, Figure 439

long bones 156, 168, Figure 227
Long-eared owl 253
Luxor Figure 1, 4, 5, 115, 400
Malqata 2, 5, 9, 12, 147, 178, 237, Figure 379, 319, 371, 376, 377, 383, 384, 386, 387, 394, 395, 396, 400, 406
mandible 227
mandibular mental eminence 149
Marl-D amphorae 11, 17, 140, Figure 186, 143 , Figure 194, Figure 195, 145
Martin, Geoffrey 117
mastoid process 149
Medinet Habu 1
melted glass 176
Memphis 396
meningitis 152, Figure 209, Figure 210
Menkheperre 59, 96, 117, 118, 121, 125, 131, 403
Menkheperre canopic jars Figure 76, 59, Figure 77, 60, 117, 118
Meryetamun coffin 173, 178
metal shabti baskets 240, 241, Figures 383-385
molar, right mandibular 163
moorhen 388, 405, 406
mud-collection 371-373, Figures 603-606
Mut.... 120
Mutnofret, Ornament of the King 119, 402, Figure 640
Mutuy 119, 224 Figure 347
Nebamun 120, 121, 124-5, 401
Nebetia, grand-daughter of the King 403
Nebetnehet, Great Wife of the King Figure 79, 61, 62, 96, 118, 121, 122, 123, Figure 182, 138, 394, 402, 403, 404
Nebnedjem 295, Figure 475
Nefertari, tomb of 69, Figure 92
Nefrure cliff-tomb 400
Neith 120
Nebnefer 295, Figure 475
Nepthys 120
nicknames/epithets 123
Nile 1
onions 249, Figure 404
Ornament of the King 2, 117
ovicaprid 250, 251
parietal foramen 154, 159
pelican 388, 405, 406
pelvis 156
persea nuts 248, Figure 402
pestle 274, Figure 438
Petrie Museum, University College London 61, 115, 403
Pharaoh eagle-owl 252, Figure 406
pigeon 250, 251, 255
plant roots (WB1 surface) 278 Figure 446, Figure 447
plaster, gypsum 70, Shaft Four 93, Figure 123, Figure 124, Figure 125
plaster, mud 70
plaster (shaft) Shaft Five 86, Figure 114, Figure 115
polychrome vessels 147, Figure 202, Figure 203

Porter & Moss 177
pottery sherd locations Figure 597
pottery/ceramics 17
Qebesenuef 120
Qena Bend 3, 377, 383, 396
QV4 69
QV62 69
QV63 15
QV63 69
QV69 15, 69
rain 2, 6, 387, 393, 405
Ramesses III 1, 394
Rhind Tombs 403
rib 156
roads 376-384, Figures 612-624
roads, ancient 9
roads, caravan 3
roads, prepared 2, 3, 10, 380-384, Figures 619-624
rock quality 6
rock, condition of at WB1 71-72
Roman period 3, 15, 267, 284, 291, 362, 387, 390, 391, 393, 394, 405, 406
rope and basketry 246-247, Figures 397-400
Sand grouse Figure 406, 253
Sati, Ornament of the King 118
sciatic notch 149
seal, Amenhotep III (Nebmaatre) 236-238, Figures 376-379
sealing of shafts 276, Figure 443
sealing, mud used for 239, Figure 382
sealing, Shaft Five blocking 238, 239, Figure 380, Figure 381
sealings 235-239 Figures 373-382
seals, necropolis 235-236 Figures 373-375
septal apertures (of the coronoid fossa) 154, Figure 211, Figure 221, 164
Serket 120
serpentine 17, SV202 Figure 68, 54
serpentine vessels 133
shabtis 137, Figure 182, 138, Figure 183, 139, Figure 184 (see also wooden shabtis)
Shaft Five 12, 17, 19, 42-50
Shaft Five 69
Shaft Five architectural phases 86-92
  Shaft Five Chamber A 18
Shaft Five Chamber A 48-50
Shaft Five Chamber A1 45
  Shaft Five Chamber B 18
Shaft Five Chamber B 45-47
Shaft Five Chamber B1 44-45
Shaft Five Chamber Ba 47-48
Shaft Five Chamber Bb 47-48
Shaft Four 399
Shaft Four 7, 12, 15, 19, 51-66, 69
Shaft Four architectural phases 93-105
Shaft Four Chamber A 63-65
Shaft Four Chamber Aa 65-66

Shaft Four Chamber B 52-56
Shaft Four Chamber Ba 56-57
Shaft Four Chamber Bb 58-59
Shaft Four Chamber Bc 60-62
Shaft One 12, 19, 35-36
Shaft One architectural phases 106-7
Shaft Seven 19, 66-67
Shaft Seven 264, 265, Figure 421, Figure 423, Figure 424
Shaft Seven architectural phases 111-113
Shaft Seven sealing 265, Figure 424
Shaft Six 12, 19, 34-35
Shaft Six architectural phases 107-111
Shaft Three 12, 19, 37-41
Shaft Three architectural phases 72-76
Shaft Three Chamber A 39, 41
Shaft Three Chamber Aa 39
Shaft Three Chamber Ab 39
shaft tombs 2, 4
Shaft Two 12, 15, 19, 20-33
Shaft Two 399
Shaft Two architectural phases 77-86
Shaft Two Chamber A 30-33
Shaft Two Chamber Aa 33
Shaft Two Chamber Ab 34
   Shaft Two Chamber B 18
Shaft Two Chamber B 22, 23-25
  Shaft Two Chamber Ba 18
Shaft Two Chamber Ba 25-26
Shaft Two Chamber Bb 28-29
    Shaft Two Chamber Bb 82, Figure 107
Shaft Two Chamber Bc 26-28
Shaft Two Chamber Bca 26-28
Shaft Two Chamber Bd 29-30
Sheikh Abd el-Qurna 124, 401
sherds employed as tools 148, Figure 204
shrine panels 106, 174
skull fragments Figure 226
skulls 149, 152, 168
soil in wadi G 390
Soleb 396
Sourouzian, Hourig 387, Figure 628, 393
Spiegelberg, W.115
spoil-heaps Figure 410, Figure 411, Figure 412, Figure 413, Figure 416, Figure 417, Figure 419, Figure 425
spoil-heaps sections 261, Figure 416, Figure 417, Figure 419
spondylolysis 161, Figure 219, Figure 220
steps, Shaft Two Chamber Bc 79, Figure 104; Shaft Two Chamber Bb Figure 107, 79-82
Stock pigeon 252, 253
stone head 2014-355 Figure 62, 50
stone pounders 272, Figure 436, Figure 437
Strasbourg, University 60, 116
Surer 119, 121
surface features under spoil-heaps 266, Figure 425
SV102 130

SV104 130
SV104 402, Figure 639
SV105 130
SV106 130
SV108 131, Figure 170
SV111 129, Figure 164
SV159 131, Figure 168
SV16 127, Figure 161
SV160 131, Figure 169
SV175 121, Figure 156
SV3 126, Figure 160
SV38 127, Figure 162
SV46 121
SV5 126, Figure 160
SV58 127, Figure 162
SV6 127, Figure 161
SV75 Figure 158, 125
SV8 Figure 158, 125
SV85 130, Figure 167
Synodontis 250, 251, 254
Takhat A 118
Takhat B, Ornament of the King 119
Tawosret 402, Figure 640
Tawosret A, Ornament of the King 119
Tawosret B, Ornament of the King 119
teeth 149
Tentiunet 119
Tey 123
Third Intermediate Period 15, 144, Figure 196, Figure 197, 260, 266, 284, 376, 401, 404
Third Intermediate Period ceramics 144, Figure 196, Figure 197
Three Foreign Wives of Thutmose III 5, 6, 376 400
Thutmose III 5, 6, Figure 188, Figure 189, 376, 400, 401
Thutmose IV 124, 130, 147, 401,403
Tiaa, Daughter of the King 118, 403
Tilapia 250, 251
Tiye 174, 404
tjehen 173
tomb axis 112, Figure 149
Toonen, Willhelm 394
trees in Wadi G 390, Figures 632 and 633
TT90 401
tufla 373-374, Figures 607, 608
tufla-extraction sites Figure 597
Tuka, Ornament of the King 119
Turin Strike Papyrus 394
Tutankhamun 66, 107, 111, 132, Figure 181, 174, 178, 179, Figure 239, 225, 235, 239
Tuy, Ornament of the King 118
Tuyu funerary mask Figure 255, Figure 256
Valley of the Kings 5, 70
Valley of the Queens 15, 69, Figure 91, 400
vertebra 156, 161
Wadi 300 396, 400

Wadi A 7
Wadi Alpha 338-340, Figures 550-554
Wadi Alpha flint-working Figures 553-4
Wadi B 7
Wadi Bairiya 2, 3, 5, 318-366, 395, 400
Wadi Bairiya Copitc sites 319
Wadi Bairiya Coptic sites 354-366, Figures 579-596
Wadi Bairiya graffito 319
Wadi Beta 341-342, Figures 555-558
Wadi C 7
Wadi D 7
Wadi Delta 347-349, Figures 566-571
Wadi Delta flint-working Figure 571
Wadi E 7
Wadi el-Agaala "amphitheatre" 314, 315
Wadi el-Agaala "amphitheatre" gazelle graffito 316, Figure 513
Wadi el-Agaala "amphitheatre" lion graffito 316, Figure 512
Wadi el-Agaala 3, 6, 10, 293-317, 395, 406
Wadi el-Agaala Wadi el-Agaala prepared road 314-317, Figures 510, 511, 514, 515
Wadi el-Gharby 7, 406
Wadi Epsilon 350-353, Figures 572-578
Wadi Epsilon flint-working Figure 578
Wadi F 5, 7
Wadi G 7
Wadi Gamma 343-346, Figures 559-565
Wadi Gamma graffito 344, Figures 559, 561, 562
Wadi Haybah 395, 401
Wadi L 294-296, Figures 473-477
Wadi L graffiti 294, Figure 473, 295, Figures 475and 476
Wadi M 297-299, Figures 478-492
Wadi N 299-300, Figures 483-485
Wadi O 301-304, Figures 486-491
Wadi O graffiti 301
Wadi P 304-306, Figures 492-496
Wadi Q 307-309, Figures 497-502
Wadi Q ceramics 308, Figure 498
Wadi Q flint-working 309, Figure 500
Wadi Q tufla collection 308, Figure 499
Wadi R 310-313
Wadi R flint-working 313, Figure 508
Wadi R graffiti 311, 312, Figure 505, Figure 507
Wadi U ceramics Figure 523
Wadi V 323-324, Figures 524-527
Wadi W 325-327, Figure 528-533
Wadi W flint-working Figures 530, 532, 533
Wadi X 328-329, Figures 534-536
Wadi X flint-working Figure 536
Wadi Y 330-332, Figures 537-541
Wadi Z 333-337, Figures 542-549
Wadi Z sherds, 334, 335, Figures 545-548
Wadis S, T, U 320-322 Figures 517-523
Wadis U and T flint-working Figure 520, Figure 522
was-ankh-djed design 172, Figure 236, Figure 237, Figure 238
wasp-nest in Wadi G 390
water 2, 367
water erosion (WB1 surface) 277, Figure 444
water flows Shaft Six 109, Figure 145
WB1 2, 3, 4, 5, 406
WB1 cliffs 8
WB1 shafts, location 11
WB1, initial condition 8
WB10 364-366, Figures 593-596
WB2 354-355, Figures 579-580
WB2 Coptic site Figure 521
WB3 356-357, Figures 581-583
WB4 358, Figure 584
WB5 359-360, Figures 585-587
WB5 ceramics Figure 587
WB6 360, Figure 588
WB7 361, Figure 589
WB8 362, Figure 590
WB9 363, Figures 591-592
Well 1 284-6, Figures 458-462, 291
Well 2 286-289, Figures 463-468, 291
Well 3 290-291, Figures 469-471
well, Roman 391-393, Figures 635-637
wells 9, 387, 406, 406
West Bank 2, 5, 6
Western Wadis 2, 6, 7, 293, 376, 400, 407
whetstone 272, Figure 435
wild cattle/bulls 3, 406
Wilkinson, John Gardiner 3
wood, cut-marks 190, Figure 272, Figure 273
wood, gilded 192, Figure 274
wood, termite damage 190
wooden Anubis fetish components 217 Figures 328-331
wooden coffins 199-207 Figures 289-308
wooden cosmetic duck-spoons 221-222 Figures 339-343
wooden dockets 223-225 Figures 344-349
wooden duck-stools 197 Figure 282, Figure 283
wooden fan fragment 2014-186 Figure 35, 32
wooden fans 209-210 Figures 312-315
wooden fragments 17
wooden furniture 192-197 Figures 275-283
wooden furniture knobs 197-198 Figures 284-288
wooden mallets 275 Figure 442
wooden objects of daily use 219 Figures 332-338
wooden pestles 275, Figure 440, Figure 441
wooden shabtis 211-214 Figures 316-322
wooden sledge runners 208 Figures 309-311
wooden statues 215-216 Figures 323-327
wooden wig spirals Figure 24, 25
workmen's huts 9
Yuya 127, Figure 165
Yuya and Tuyu 171, 173, 178, 405
Yuya coffin inlays 184, Figure 260

# BIOGRAPHIES

**Piers Litherland** holds an M.A. from Oxford University and an M.Phil. in Egyptology from Cambridge University. He has been involved in the archaeology of the West Bank in Luxor since 1999 and founded the New Kingdom Research Foundation in 2010. He is currently an Honorary Research Associate of the McDonald Institute and a Director of Ancient Egypt Research Associates.

**Corinne Duhig** Ph.D., F.S.A., M.I.F.A., is a Senior Fellow of the McDonald Institute for Archaeological Research, College Research Associate and Director of Studies in Archaeology, Wolfson College Cambridge. She teaches and researches in archaeology and Egyptology and runs the osteoarchaeology and funerary-archaeology consultancy Gone to Earth.

**Salima Ikram** is Distinguished University Professor of Egyptology at The American University in Cairo. She received her M.Phil. in Museology and Egyptian Archaeology and Ph.D. in Egyptian archaeology from Cambridge University. She has participated in many archaeological missions throughout Egypt including the Animal Mummy Project, the North Kharga Darb Ain Amur Survey and the Valley of the Kings KV10/KV63 Mission, all of which she directed. She has lectured on her work internationally, and publishes in both scholarly and popular journals.